Therapeutic
FAMILY
MEDIATION

HOWARD H. IRVING • MICHAEL BENJAMIN

University of Toronto   *Private Practice*

Therapeutic FAMILY MEDIATION

Helping Families Resolve Conflict

SAGE Publications
International Educational and Professional Publisher
Thousand Oaks ■ London ■ New Delhi

For information:

Sage Publications, Inc.
2455 Teller Road
Thousand Oaks, California 91320
E-mail: order@sagepub.com

Sage Publications Ltd.
6 Bonhill Street
London EC2A 4PU
United Kingdom

Sage Publications India Pvt. Ltd.
M-32 Market
Greater Kailash I
New Delhi 110 048 India

Printed in the United States of America

Library of Congress Cataloging-in-Publication Data

Irving, Howard H.
  Therapeutic family mediation : helping families resolve conflict / by Howard H. Irving and Michael Benjamin.
      p. cm.
Includes bibliographical references and index.
  ISBN 0-7619-2313-6
  1. Family psychotherapy. 2. Family mediation. I. Benjamin, Michael. II. Title.
  RC488.5 .I785 2002
  616.89′156—dc21

                                        2002005570

This book is printed on acid-free paper.

02 03 04 05 10 9 8 7 6 5 4 3 2 1

Acquisitions Editor:	Nancy S. Hale
Editorial Assistants:	Alicia Carter and Vonessa Vondera
Production Editor:	Sanford Robinson
Copy Editor:	Gillian Dickens
Typesetter:	Siva Math Setters, Chennai, India
Indexer:	Teri Greenberg
Cover Designer:	Janet Foulger

Contents

Preface

Family mediation has become extremely popular in North America and in other industrialized countries around the world. This is so for pragmatic reasons. Divorce rates remain high and court dockets correspondingly clogged. Mediation provides an effective means of court diversion. Consequently, for the foreseeable future, litigation and family mediation will continue to go hand in hand.

That said, family mediation is not a static approach. Rather, it continues to evolve and change, grow and develop. One aspect of that development refers to its growing professionalism. Mediation is becoming steadily better organized and more explicit in its commitment to standards of professional and ethical conduct. There is also steady movement toward some form of certification.

Another aspect of that development concerns its steady proliferation. Once, labor-management negotiation was the only form of mediation available. In the 1980s, family mediation joined the roster. Now, in the new millennium, there is a long and growing list of fields in which there is a mediation component. Concomitantly, the number of professors, programs, and participants continues to expand.

Such ferment cannot but affect practitioners and model builders. As to the former, both novice and experienced, an expanding research and substantive literature has made it increasingly difficult to remain current. At the same time, there is increasing demand for more and better ways of effecting the objectives of mediation—that is, creative and innovative skills and techniques—and the means to convey them simply and clearly. The same is true of the growing list of available family mediation models.

As to the latter, among model builders, including ourselves, there is increasing pressure to convey available models in ways that make them accessible to an audience of practitioners and students that is decidedly heterogeneous. This is problematic in three senses. First, the heterogeneity of the audience is such as to define clarity and accessibility in different terms to different groups. Those with a mental health or social service background look to texts for particular information, whereas those with a legal background look to the same texts for different information. Either authors strive to meet both sets of needs by creating texts that are generic in character, or they speak to one audience while ignoring the other.

Second, the field of family mediation is unfinished. Various substantive issues remain controversial. In the absence of consensus, vigorous debate is ongoing. That debate is a healthy sign and is the standard marker of evolution in a field of endeavor. Even so, such debate creates a dilemma for authors in the field. A text may either address and explicate these issues, or its author may prefer a text that is confined to the description of mediation skills and methods.

Finally, models themselves do not remain static; they change and evolve with their authors. Thus, new texts are needed to introduce the models to students while apprising practitioners of recent changes and innovations. Similarly, the authors' perspectives on their own work may change. The prime movers of such change are the clients with whom they become involved. New clients constitute a new demand to adapt the model to their needs, with some clients being considerably more demanding than others. Contact with students and with colleagues is similarly demanding, as they repeatedly insist that authors be clear and specific in explicating the model they propose, thus changing the model in the process. Aging and personal change are also salient processes. Aging can bring into sharp focus processes in the lives of clients that were only dimly understood when the authors were themselves much younger. The same is true of personal experiences. Divorce means one thing when viewed from the smug confines of one's own happy marriage and quite another from the perspective of one's own unhappy divorce.

Such were our dilemmas in considering whether it was timely to prepare another text on the mediation model we propose, namely, *therapeutic family mediation* (TFM). Our first text was published in 1987 when both of us were relatively new practitioners. It had the further disadvantage of being available only in Canada. The next text, published in 1995, contained some explication of the model but was largely an issue-based text. Thus, we were left with a situation in which we had nowhere fully explicated the TFM practice model. Changes in the field were also relevant and, to us, troubling. Of the flood of new mediation texts, the vast majority were generic in character; only a handful of texts continue to espouse a clinical or therapeutic approach. New students, then, were apt to conclude that the generic approach was synonymous with mediation, with the family merely one among a host of groups amenable to this approach. We concluded that it was high time to add our voice to those advocating for the benefits of a clinical approach to mediation, with the family seen as a unique social form that required specialized skills and techniques.

Having decided to develop a new text, we then confronted the issues noted above. As both of us come to the field with a mental health background, that background will be quite apparent in how we define, approach, and discuss the various issues relevant to contemporary family mediation. However, this left us unclear as to how to speak to those colleagues who hail from a legal background. Given that their contribution to the field is substantial, we elected to speak to them in two ways, by addressing a range of legal issues and by trying to show that TFM can be as effective in court-based mediation as it can with private clients.

Next, we both agreed that it was important to review and discuss a range of substantive issues while describing the nuts and bolts of TFM in action. We realized at the outset that this could be problematic for some readers, including those asked to review our initial manuscript. But the nuts and bolts of any model are not created through an act of spontaneous creativity. Rather, they are created in response to issues in the field. Describing such structures out of any context would badly distort their presentation and might be seriously misleading for students new to the field who would have no reason to be aware of these ongoing debates. We believe such discussion enriches the final text, adding depth to what would otherwise be flat and spare. Even so, descriptive text has been presented such that it can stand on its own; readers irritated by our discussion of issues are free to skip these sections and move on.

Finally, those who take the time to compare this text with our first practice text from 1987 will not be surprised to find that the model has evolved quite considerably. These changes very much reflect our own professional growth, shaped in large part by the clients we have come to know over the years. If told this, the clients in question would probably be surprised, if not shocked, by the extent of their contribution. In their need, clients demand certainty and confidence on the part of their mediator. Typically, mediators are happy to oblige, in an effort to give support and build rapport. But inside, clients are perceived as an unceasing source of demand. Indeed, the most difficult and challenging clients are often the motive for innovation and change in clinical skills and techniques. In seeking to adapt TFM to meet their needs, changes were made that have become permanently incorporated in the model.

In the 15 years since our first practice text, at the very least we can claim to have learned a few things along the way. On one hand, we are now more temperate in our claims, for it has become abundantly clear that all clients are *not* amenable to mediation; the question as to whether this is a failing of theirs or ours has ceased to be relevant. Such experience demands renewed respect for the enormous challenge of divorce and the many simultaneous changes it necessarily brings. If some clients find themselves overwhelmed in the process, who are we to cast aspersions? Our obligation is to try to be helpful, if only to refer them to others for the help they need.

On the other hand, these same clients have demonstrated to us again and again that TFM works. It is an extremely powerful model that broadens the scope of clients to whom we can offer meaningful assistance in doing what is best for them and their children. Here, it is important to acknowledge that *not* all divorcing families are dysfunctional. Many are merely sad and confused and, with a little help, can do a fine job of mitigating the impact of divorce on their children while getting on with their individual lives. Of those who are dysfunctional in one way or another, these families range on a continuum, with only the most severely dysfunctional outside the reach of TFM.

Whatever the status of the client, TFM stretches the practitioner. Such practitioners, whatever their disciplinary origin, are expected to have and maintain a wide knowledge of matters relevant to mediation with divorcing couples. Further stretching necessarily occurs as they apply their knowledge and expertise to clients with a diverse range of problems and issues. We hope the interaction between the two brings out the best—in creativity, empathy, and collaborative problem solving—in both. We hope that that intention to instruct and expand is all too apparent in this text, and we welcome your comments, for only you can determine how successful we have been.

Howard H. Irving, Ph.D.
Michael Benjamin, Ph.D.
Toronto, Ontario
March 2002

Acknowledgments

We are most grateful to the many families whom we have worked with in mediation. They, along with our students and colleagues, were extremely helpful in giving their time, insights, and energy toward making this book a reality.

A special thanks to the students and staff at the University of Toronto Family Mediation Program. We are in debt to Tat Tsang, Virginia Hamara, Andrea Litwack, Melanie Kraft, Jennifer Shuber, and Linda Chodos.

Much is owed to the leaders and writers in the field of family mediation who have influenced and enhanced the ideas in this book. These include Joan B. Kelly, Hugh McIsaac, Isolina Ricci, Donald Saposnek, Robert Emery, and Mary Duryee, to mention only a few.

We thank the editors and staff at Sage Publications for their continuing support and guidance throughout the project, from proposal to publications. Thanks to Nancy Hale, Margaret Seawell, Vonessa Vondera, Alicia Carter, and Gillian Dickens.

On a more personal note, we are deeply thankful for the patience and understanding from our families. Thank you Fahla, Jay, Jonathan, Jennifer, Adam, Tamara, and Jessie.

Finally, this book is dedicated to the memory of the late Susan Adler, Sylvia and Samuel Irving.

PART 1

INTRODUCTION

1

Introduction

Conflict is a universal feature of human groups. This has been so throughout recorded history and is just as likely to be true in the future. Furthermore, this tendency toward conflict holds across all known groups, from family and religious or cultural groups to business and state or government systems. Such universality suggests that conflict is rooted in differences (Moore, 1996, pp. 26-27). Differences in feelings and relationships. Differences in values and principles. Differences in information and misinformation. Differences in interests and present or future goals. Differences in power, authority, competitive urges, and psychological states. In coming together in groups, participants carry their differences into their relationships and, in so doing, ensure the inevitability of conflict (Rubin, Pruitt, & Kim, 1984).

The fact that social conflict is widespread should be a source neither of surprise nor of distress. Rather, what is far more important is how such conflict is managed (Gulliver, 1979). Following Deutsch (1973) and others (MacFarlane, 1999; Pruitt & Carnevale, 1993), such management efforts distribute on a continuum, from those that are useful and constructive to those that are dysfunctional and destructive. In family systems, for example, conflict can serve a variety of positive functions: by identifying and highlighting difficult issues, by allowing members to air their grievances, and by engaging members in joint problem solving. These various efforts serve to repair breaches in relationship by ensuring that members feel heard and by addressing grievances in ways that allow for an orderly process of change. Alternately, conflict management efforts may reflect various degrees of family dysfunction (Burton, 1987; Donohue, 1991). Mathis (1998), for example, characterized interaction among "undifferentiated" spouses as involving "endless and repetitive arguments that deal with surface rather than core issues" (p. 44). Other variations on dysfunctional conflict include pouting, sulking, crying, acting angry, whining, ridiculing, and giving the silent treatment (Johnston & Campbell, 1988; Rudd, 1996). In the same vein, there is now strong evidence that intense marital conflict is the single strongest predictor of poor postdivorce child adjustment (Irving & Benjamin, 1995, Chapter 3).

Furthermore, independent of the functionality of relations in conflict are the approaches or strategies that groups have evolved to deal with conflict and thus address the grievances that underpin it. Here, the literature recognizes five variations: avoidance, negotiation, mediation, litigation, and coercion.

Although we regard conflict per se as neutral, some groups characterize conflict as necessarily negative and thus seek to *avoid* it, sometimes at all costs. When conflict avoidance applies to specific family systems, it is typically regarded as a sign of dysfunction (Barsky, 2000; Reiss, 1981) because this strategy serves to perpetuate grievances and minimizes opportunities for relationship repair. In turn, avoidance can be the focus of therapeutic intervention (Nichols & Schwartz, 1995). Conversely, when conflict avoidance is characteristic of a cultural or ethnic group, it is typically regarded as normative (Augsburgher, 1992; Barnes, 1994; Gulliver, 1979). For example, among both Hispanics (Irving, Benjamin, & San-Pedro, 1999) and Asians (Benjamin, 1996), there are strong prohibitions against addressing grievances through direct confrontation. Among Asians, avoidance reflects the emphasis common to three key Eastern religions—Buddhism (Gard, 1962), Confucianism (Wilson, 1982), and Taoism (Holt & Steinhard, 1990)—on balance, harmony, cooperation, and honor (Chang & Holt, 1994; Gao, 1996). Among Hispanics, such prohibitions stand as a hedge against the possibility of loss of control (Benjamin, 1996, Chapter 4).

A second strategy for dealing with conflict involves informal, direct, face-to-face interaction among the parties, that is, *negotiation* (Goldberg, Sander, & Rogers, 1992; Lewicki, Litterer, Minton, & Saunders, 1998). Without question, this is the strategy of choice for most people and applies as much to relations between spouses (Carter, 1996) as it does to relations between nations (Deutsch, 1991). Consequently, negotiation processes have been the focus of intensive study and, in turn, generated a voluminous literature, both academic (Breslin & Rubin, 1995; Pruitt, 1981; Sandole & van der Merwe, 1993) and pragmatic (Fisher, 1997; Fisher, Ury, & Patton, 1997).

Despite good intentions, efforts at informal negotiation are not always successful. Consequently, throughout history, different groups have sought the assistance of third parties who themselves have no stake in either the dispute or any possible outcomes, that is, *mediation* (see Axelrod, 1984). This strategy is typically defined as that process by which "an impartial person, the mediator, facilitates communication between the parties to promote settlement of a dispute between them" (James, 1997, p. 205). In the 20th century, although mediation had been widely used in labor-management negotiation, its rising popularity can be traced to the late 1970s and early 1980s, when the unprecedented rate of divorce and the clogged family court system confronted justice administrators and state officials with a serious problem (Irving & Benjamin, 1995, Chapter 2). This first application of family mediation to couples undergoing divorce offered the real possibility of court diversion and a fruitful way of resolving issues in dispute (Coogler, 1978; Folberg & Taylor, 1984; Haynes, 1981; Irving, 1980; Saposnek, 1983). As of this writing, at the dawn of the new millennium, the literature has exploded, both with respect to family mediation (Boulle & Kelly, 1998; Ellis & Stuckless, 1996; Haynes & Haynes, 1989; Kruk, 1997; Landau, Wolfson, Landau, Bartoletti, & Mesbur, 2000) as well as the mediation of other social and commercial disputes (Beer, 1997; McLaren & Sanderson, 1994; Slaikeu, 1995). Key advantages of the mediation strategy are that it is relatively fast, inexpensive, and effective (Irving & Benjamin, 1995, chap. 10). It empowers parties to resolve their own disputes while holding them responsible for the consequences of any settlement they reach. The result is that relitigation is uncommon (Cohen, 1998). The key disadvantage of mediation is that it is not universally applicable. Parties must be able to engage in productive negotiation. Those who, for a variety of reasons, are unable to do so are best referred elsewhere (Barsky, 1983; Mathis & Yingling, 1990).

For those unable to resolve their differences through informal negotiation or mediation, an alternate strategy involves the use of a third party invested with the authority to impose a settlement, that is, *arbitration or litigation* (Bossy, 1983). In this approach, adjudication involves the impartial application of an abstract set of rules and procedures, with the parties themselves typically represented by lawyers who are ethically committed to zealously presenting their client's position in the most favorable light possible (Mnookin & Kornhauser, 1979). The key advantages of this strategy are that it includes a variety of safeguards to protect the vulnerable and that it strives to ensure a fair and unbiased outcome (Benjamin & Irving, 1992). However, this strategy has key disadvantages. One disadvantage is that these same procedures are poorly suited to family disputes, such as those that arise in divorce, which are rooted in complex family dynamics (Acland, 1990). Another disadvantage is that litigation disempowers the parties (Chornenki & Hart, 1996). As a result, they may have little commitment to any imposed settlement and may later feel free to disregard its terms and conditions. Despite these serious limitations, arbitration and litigation strategies will likely always be with us, for they are the only options left when parties cannot reasonably address their grievances by any other means.

Finally, in the heat of the moment, one or both parties in dispute may seek an immediate solution in which one party imposes its will on the other; that is, resolution may involve the use of *coercion* (Ellis & Wight, 1998). This will typically occur when the parties are unequal in regard to some combination of three factors. The first factor is gender. Both as a function of socialization and conversational style, men more than women will be interested in taking and keeping control (Dingwall, Greatbatch, & Ruggerone, 1998; Maxwell, 1992; Stamato, 1992). The second factor is relative power, that is, control over resources, especially financial resources (Ellis & Wight, 1998). At present, society is organized in such a way that men much more than women have control over resources and are more prepared to use such power to achieve their ends (Goldner, 1989). The third factor concerns the use of threats, intimidation, and violence. In spousal relations, men much more than women are willing to use violence to achieve and maintain control, both in White (Jasinski & Williams, 1998) and non-White (Tang, 1994) cultural groups. The use of mediation in power-imbalanced couples remains controversial. Although some authors argue that mediation with such couples is possible under certain conditions (Benjamin & Irving, 1992), others disagree (Goundry, Peters, Currie, & Associates, 1998).

Of these various strategies for managing conflict, the balance of this book will concentrate on *family mediation* and will advance a particular practice model we have called *therapeutic family mediation* or TFM (Irving & Benjamin, 1995). In three senses, the above discussion helps to place in context family mediation in general and TFM in particular. First, it is important to recognize that family mediation is only one of a variety of options. Most divorce-related disputes have and will continue to be resolved through informal negotiation between the parties, with or without the help of their lawyers (Kressel, 1985). Second, the notion that mediation offers divorcing couples in dispute a better alternative than litigation requires careful qualification. Mediation is reserved for couples who cannot resolve their disputes informally, voluntarily choose to work with a mediator, and are capable of or can be made ready for productive negotiation. Among those who cannot resolve their differences informally, there are many whose intense emotions (of anger, grief, depression, anxiety, or resentment) will render them unsuitable for mediation (Somary & Emery, 1991). Others, for various reasons, should make appropriate use of litigation, but still others will see themselves as unable to meet the real or imagined demands of mediation and so will reject this strategy. Finally, the above discussion makes clear that mediation does *not* stand separate and apart from other strategies but rather incorporates several strategies within it. Thus, mediation relies heavily on the parties' capacity to negotiate or their willingness to learn to do so. Mediation practitioners have developed techniques for dealing with conflict avoidance and see mediators and lawyers as members of the same team and working toward the same ends—namely, a fair and reasonable settlement that meets the needs of all parties. Furthermore, at least some mediation models speak to the special requirements of couples in which there is a significant power imbalance, including those in which at least one member has opted to employ a coercive strategy for managing conflict. This implies that in the hands of an experienced practitioner, family mediation can be an extremely powerful and effective strategy (Kolb & Associates, 1994; Tracy & Spradlin, 1994) for helping couples address and possibly resolve the differences between them.

What our discussion leaves unclear is the extent of variation *within* mediation. For example, Boulle and Kelly (1998) differentiate between four practice models, whereas Bush and Folger (1994) do the same with respect to four different models. In our reading, efforts to discriminate between various practice models have very limited utility. In effect, available texts fall into two broad categories. One category encompasses texts that concern mediation per se, that is, texts that are generic in character and advance a set of practice techniques that apply to all groups in conflict, including couples in divorce (Allen & Mohr, 1998; Beer, 1997; Susskind, McKearney, & Thomas-Larner, 1999; Umbeit, 1995; Wilmot & Hocker, 1998). The other category includes texts that concentrate on family mediation but treat the family like any other group in conflict, that is, by focusing on substantive issues while giving limited attention to affective or relational dynamics (Davis, Cretney, & Collins, 1994; Erickson & Erickson, 1988; James, 1997; Landau et al., 2000).

In fact, there are very few practice texts that regard family conflict as *different* from conflict in other groups (see Jones, 1994), that apply techniques designed specifically with the family in mind, and that therefore engage family affective and relational dynamics as integral to mediating disputes among its members (Emery, 1994; Haynes, 1994; Sasposnek, 1994). TFM is one such model, and it is grounded on the view that there are reasons for thinking that a therapeutic approach is likely to be more effective than its generic counterparts. The first reason concerns the character and complexity of relations among members in family as opposed to other social systems. This argument holds that family systems are unique as regards the meaning, intimacy, and intensity of family relations and that divorce marks the reorganization rather than the disintegration of such systems (Ahrons & Rodgers, 1987; Pam & Pearson, 1998). In that sense, conflict within family systems is unlike conflict between neighbors, landlords and tenants, or buyers and sellers. Unlike other groups, spouses do not get divorced *from* each other; they get divorced *to* each other, with mediation affording them a unique opportunity to consciously decide how they will relate to each other as parents in the future. It follows that if family system conflict stands apart from conflict in other systems, then the mediation techniques used to address such conflict should similarly stand apart, that is, be crafted with such systems in mind.

Another reason to believe in TFM's effectiveness concerns the range of families amenable to mediation. As their name suggests, generic models are designed with generic client populations in mind. Accordingly, these models are unsuited for clients with special needs who are rendered unable to negotiate productively. Unfortunately, that applies to a good many couples in divorce (Coy & Hedeen, 1998), thus limiting the range of couples likely to benefit from generic mediation. In contrast, therapeutic models (Silbey & Merry, 1986), including TFM, assess for the bases on which productive negotiation cannot occur and intervene to change interaction, thus increasing the likelihood that mediation can proceed to settlement. The obvious consequence is that TFM is useful in mediating disputes among a wider range of divorcing couples than would be the case among its generic counterparts.

Yet another basis for asserting TFM's effectiveness concerns the durability of settlements among clients who go through this process. By suppressing conflictual behavior and ignoring affectively charged responses, generic models can be effective in helping divorcing couples reach agreement. However, we suspect that in doing so, they not only increase the dropout rate but also place the durability of such agreements at risk. Clients drop out of mediation and mediated agreements break down because spouses feel that they have not truly been heard, underlying sources of conflict have not been addressed, dysfunctional ways of handling conflict have been left unchanged, or some combination of all three. By addressing these processes directly, we suggest that TFM maximizes the likelihood that clients who reach agreement have truly settled their conflict (if not necessarily their differences) and, having learned new and better strategies for managing conflict, will be better prepared to address these differences informally when they inevitably arise in the future. TFM also takes full advantage of the skills that mental health practitioners bring into mediation as they seek to be helpful to clients in need.

With these advantages in mind, the balance of this volume will be divided into four parts. Part 2 provides a comprehensive description of the TFM practice model. This begins with an overview of the model, with particular attention to the model's complex theoretical underpinnings (Chapter 2). These underpinnings help explain how TFM practitioners are thought to think and why they enact the various therapeutic strategies at the heart of the model. Next, we review in detail the set of practice skills and abilities that we think are requisite to effective mediation practice (Chapter 3). The next series of chapters (4-7, inclusive) walks the reader through each of the five phases in the model and describes the relevant issues, solution-oriented responses, and ongoing links to other phases. The final chapter in this part provides a full-length case history that shows what it is like to do family mediation from a TFM perspective (Chapter 8).

Part 3 addresses the two central issues for families going through divorce, namely, parenting (Chapters 9 and 10) and money (Chapters 11 and 12). The first part of our discussion of parenting (Chapter 9) presents a developmental approach to family mediation, including the ethical responsibilities of the mediator to protect the best interests of the children. Such responsibilities mean that under some conditions, the mediator may need to advocate for the children, a stance that calls into question traditional notions of neutrality and client self-determination. The second part of the discussion (Chapter 10) then explores in detail the elements, principles, and guidelines associated with the co-construction of a parenting plan. Turning to money, the first part of the discussion (Chapter 11) addresses a variety of technical issues associated with child support, spousal support, and the equitable division of property. Such coverage recognizes the fact that such material is available in few other texts and, by implication, suggests a rationale for comprehensive family mediation. The second part of the discussion (Chapter 12) explores the relational bases of conflict when the substantive issues in dispute concern money. This part of the chapter also includes a brief review that indicates that various literatures, including the mediation literature, have been remarkably silent when it comes to money and the marital conflict that can arise around this issue.

In Part 4, we turn to two special issues in family mediation. The first issue concerns cultural diversity (Chapter 13). This chapter is divided into two sections. The first section provides a general discussion of the issues, especially the neglect of this topic in the mediation literature, whereas the second section explores the use of TFM with families that are Hispanic (Latino) in origin. Next, we provide a decade review of the mediation research literature (Chapter 14), with the accent on identifying a series of trends among the findings in four areas of inquiry—namely, person, setting, process, and outcome.

In Part 5, we conclude with a final word (Chapter 15), which elaborates on the eight themes that run throughout the volume. In brief, those themes emphasize the central importance of the relationship in doing family mediation, the longstanding patterns of relating that constitute the spousal relationship, variation in the level or degree of intervention based on the level of family dysfunction, the central importance of the mediator's authority to shape mediation processes and outcomes, the expression of that authority in five clinical roles that collectively highlight the socially co-constructed character of the mediation process, the importance to mediation of effective practitioner cultural competence, the reliance of the TFM model on a collection of theoretical and practice models, and, finally, the salience of a client-centered and feminist-informed approach that continuously seeks the best possible fit between client need and service delivery and thus the absence of any standardized TFM procedure.

In the interests of clarity, two aspects of our treatment of TFM deserve special mention. First, although the primary focus of this text is on practice, we also use the text as a forum to review and discuss the leading issues in the literature, show how they play out in the TFM model, and provide clinical illustrations of the model in action. Some readers may object that these discussions digress from the main purpose of the text, that they are too "academic" or "theoretical" or that they serve as a distraction from the book's primary themes. Readers who hold such views are encouraged to skip these sections and move on to the practice material. To others, we argue that the mediation field is still in flux, finding and defining itself through ongoing debate and discussion. Indeed, we predict that the shape of family mediation in the 21st century will emerge through discussion of these various issues. We therefore offer no apology for addressing these issues here, for we would be remiss had we done otherwise.

Second, from the use of the word *therapeutic* in the title, some readers may be misled into thinking that we advocate doing therapy in mediation. To avoid any misunderstanding, let us be clear at the outset that enacting the TFM model does *not* involve doing therapy. Rather, it does involve using therapeutic techniques *to advance the objectives of family mediation*. As noted already, family dysfunction may block productive negotiation. In such cases, intervention is used to make only those changes necessary to allow negotiation to occur. In short, this is an approach to mediation that merely recognizes the obvious—namely, the affective and relational dynamics of divorcing families and the occasional need to adjust these processes in order that mediation proceed.

Finally, and more generally, this text is intended to be interesting and accessible to anyone who wants more information about family mediation, including those who have themselves been affected by divorce. However, it will be of special interest to *three* professional groups. With the recent explosion in the availability of mediation training courses and programs, the first group consists of established professionals who see family mediation as a potential career path and who want to add family mediation to their roster of established skills. The second group will consist of mediation professionals who want to upgrade or enhance their existing family mediation skills in search of new and better ways of serving their clients. The third group will consist of mediation students who are interested in basic information about the TFM approach. With them in mind, descriptions of all rationales, procedures, techniques, and phases are detailed and further supplemented with illustrative clinical material.

References

Acland, A. (1990). *A sudden outbreak of common sense: Managing conflict through mediation.* London: Hutchinson.

Ahrons, C. R., & Rodgers, R. H. (1987). *Divorced families: A multidisciplinary view.* New York: Norton.

Allen, E. L., & Mohr, D. D. (1998). *Affordable justice: How to settle any dispute, including divorce, out of court* (2nd ed.). Encinitas, CA: West Coast Press.

Augsburgher, D. (1992). *Conflict mediation across cultures.* Westminister, BC: John Knox Press.

Axelrod, R. (1984). *The evolution of cooperation.* New York: Basic Books.

Barnes, B. E. (1994). Conflict resolution across cultures: A Hawaii perspective and a Pacific mediation model. *Mediation Quarterly, 12*(2), 117-133.

Barsky, A. E. (2000). *Conflict resolution for the helping professions.* Toronto: Brooks/Cole.

Barsky, M. (1983). Emotional needs and dysfunctional communication as blocks to mediation. *Mediation Quarterly, 2,* 55-66.

Beer, J. E. (with E. Stief). (1997). *The mediator's handbook* (3rd ed., rev.). Gabriola Island, BC: New Society.

Benjamin, M. (1996). *Cultural diversity, educational equity and the transformation of higher education: Group profiles as a guide to policy and programming.* Westport, CT: Praeger.

Benjamin, M., & Irving, H. H. (1992). Towards a feminist-informed model of therapeutic family mediation. *Mediation Quarterly, 10*(2), 129-153.

Bossy, J. (Ed.). (1983). *Disputes & settlements: Law & human relations in the West.* Cambridge, MA: Cambridge University Press.

Boulle, L., & Kelly, K. J. (1998). *Mediation: Principles, process, practice* (Canadian ed.). Toronto: Butterworths.

Breslin, J., & Rubin, J. (Eds.). (1995). *Negotiating theory & practice.* Cambridge, MA: Program on Negotiation, Harvard Law School.

Burton, J. W. (1987). *Resolving deep-rooted conflict: A handbook.* Lanham, MD: University Press of America.

Bush, R. A. B., & Folger, J. P. (1994). *The promise of mediation: Responding to conflict through empowerment and recognition.* San Francisco: Jossey-Bass.

Carter, B. (with J. K. Peters). (1996). *Love, honor and negotiate: Making your marriage work.* New York: Pocket Books.

Chang, H.-C., & Holt, G. R. (1994). A Chinese perspective on face as inter-relational concern. In S. Ting-Toomey (Ed.), *The challenge of facework: Cross-cultural and interpersonal issues* (pp. 95-132). Albany, NY: SUNY Press.

Chornenki, G. A., & Hart, C. E. (1996). *Bypass court: A dispute resolution handbook.* Toronto: Butterworths.

Cohen, I. M. (1998). Postdecree litigation: Is joint custody to blame? *Family & Conciliation Courts Review, 36*(1), 41-53.

Coogler, O. J. (1978). *Structured mediation in divorce settlement.* Lexington, MA: Lexington Books.

Coy, P. G., & Hedeen, T. M. (1998). Disabilities and mediation readiness in court-referred cases: Developing screening criteria and service networks. *Mediation Quarterly, 16*(2), 113-127.

Davis, G., Cretney, S., & Collins, J. (1994). *Simple quarrels: Negotiating money and property disputes on divorce.* Oxford, UK: Oxford University Press.

Deutsch, M. (1973). *The resolution of conflict: Constructive and destructive processes.* New Haven, CT: Yale University Press.

Deutsch, M. (1991). *Education for a peaceful world.* Amherst, MA: National Association for Mediation in Education.

Dingwall, R., Greatbatch, D., & Ruggerone, L. (1998). Gender and interaction in divorce mediation. *Mediation Quarterly, 15*(4), 277-285.

Donohue, W. A. (1991). *Communication, marital dispute, and divorce mediation.* Hillsdale, NJ: Lawrence Erlbaum.

Ellis, D., & Stuckless, N. (1996). *Mediating & negotiating marital conflicts.* Thousand Oaks, CA: Sage.

Ellis, D., & Wight, L. (1998). Theorizing power in divorce negotiations: Implications for practice. *Mediation Quarterly, 15*(3), 227-244.

Emery, R. E. (1994). *Renegotiating family relationships: Divorce, child custody, and mediation.* New York: Guilford.

Erickson, S. K., & Erickson, M. S. M. (1988). *Family mediation casebook: Theory and process.* New York: Brunner/Mazel.

Fisher, R. (1997). *Interactive conflict resolution.* New York: Syracuse University Press.

Fisher, R., Ury, W., & Patton, B. (1997). *Getting to yes: Negotiating agreement without giving in* (3rd ed.). New York: Penguin.

Folberg, J., & Taylor, A. (1984). *Mediation: A comprehensive guide to resolving conflicts without litigation.* San Francisco: Jossey-Bass.

Gao, G. (1996). Self and other: A Chinese perspective on interpersonal relationships. In W. B. Gudykunst, S. Ting-Toomey, & T. Nishida (Eds.), *Communication in personal relationships across cultures* (pp. 81-101). Thousand Oaks, CA: Sage.

Gard, R. A. (1962). *Buddhism.* New York: Braziller.

Goldberg, S., Sander, F., & Rogers, N. (1992). *Dispute resolution: Negotiation, mediation & other processes* (2nd ed.). Boston: Little, Brown.

Goldner, V. (1989). Generation and gender: Normative and covert hierarchies. In M. McGoldrick, C. M. Anderson, & F. Walsh (Eds.), *Women in families: A framework for family therapy* (pp. 42-60). New York: Norton.

Goundry, S. A., Peters, Y., Currie, R., & Associates. (1998). *Family mediation in Canada: Implications for women's equality.* Ottawa: Status of Women Canada.

Gulliver, P. H. (1979). *Disputes and negotiations: A cross-cultural perspective.* Orlando, FL: Academic Press.

Haynes, J. (1981). *Divorce mediation: A practical guide for therapists and counselors.* New York: Springer.

Haynes, J. (1994). *The fundamentals of family mediation.* Albany, NY: SUNY Press.

Haynes, J. M., & Haynes, G. L. (1989). *Mediating divorce: Casebook of strategies for successful family negotiations.* San Francisco: Jossey-Bass.

Holt, G. R., & Steinhard, D. (1990). The merely known mediator: Taoism and the metaphoric analysis of mediator behavior in divorce and custody mediation. *Mediation Quarterly, 7*(3), 251-284.

Irving, H. H. (1980). *Divorce mediation: The rational alternative.* Toronto: Personal Library.

Irving, H. H., & Benjamin, M. (1995). *Family mediation: Contemporary issues.* Thousand Oaks, CA: Sage.

Irving, H. H., Benjamin, M., & San-Pedro, J. (1999). Family mediation and cultural diversity: Mediating with Latino families. *Mediation Quarterly, 16*(4), 325-339.

James, P. (1997). *The divorce mediation handbook: Everything you need to know.* San Francisco: Jossey-Bass.

Jasinski, J. L., & Williams, L. M. (Eds.). (1998). *Partner violence: A comprehensive review of 20 years of research.* Thousand Oaks, CA: Sage.

Johnston, J. R., & Campbell, L. E. G. (1988). *Impasses of divorce: The dynamics and resolution of family conflict.* New York: Free Press.

Jones, T. S. (1994). A dialectical reframing of the mediation process. In J. P. Folger & T. S. Jones (Eds.), *New directions in mediation: Communication research and perspectives* (pp. 26-47). Thousand Oaks, CA: Sage.

Kolb, D., & Associates. (Eds.). (1994). *When talk works: Profiles of mediators.* San Francisco: Jossey-Bass.

Kressel, K. (1985). *The process of divorce: How professionals and couples negotiate settlements.* New York: Basic Books.

Kruk, E. (1997). *Mediation & conflict resolution in social work and the human services.* Chicago: Nelson-Hall.

Landau, B., Wolfson, L., Landau, N., Bartoletti, M., & Mesbur, R. (2000). *Family mediation handbook* (3rd ed.). Toronto: Butterworths.

Lewicki, R. J., Litterer, J., Minton, J., & Saunders, D. (1998). *Negotiation* (3rd ed.). Burr Ridge, IL: Irwin.

MacFarlane, J. (1999). *Dispute resolution: Readings and cases.* Toronto: Edmund Montgomery.

Mathis, R. D. (1998). Couples from hell: Undifferentiated spouses in divorce mediation. *Mediation Quarterly, 16*(1), 37-49.

Mathis, R. D., & Yingling, L. C. (1990). Recommendations for divorce mediation with chaotically adaptable family systems. *Mediation Quarterly, 8*(2), 125-136.

Maxwell, D. (1992). Gender differences in mediation style and their impact on mediator effectiveness. *Mediation Quarterly, 9*(4), 353-363.

McLaren, R. H., & Sanderson, J. P. (1994). *Innovative dispute resolution: The alternative.* Toronto: Carswell.

Mnookin, R., & Kornhauser, L. (1979). Bargaining in the shadow of the law. *Yale Law Journal, 88,* 950-997.

Moore, C. W. (1996). *The mediation process: Practical strategies for resolving conflict* (2nd ed.). San Francisco: Jossey-Bass.

Nichols, M. P., & Schwartz, R. C. (Eds.). (1995). *Family therapy* (3rd ed.). Boston: Allyn & Bacon.

Pam, A., & Pearson, J. (1998). *Splitting up: Enmeshment and estrangement in the process of divorce.* New York: Guilford.

Pruitt, D. G. (1981). *Negotiating behavior.* Orlando, FL: Academic Press.

Pruitt, D. G., & Carnevale, P. C. (1993). *Negotiation in social conflict.* Pacific Grove, CA: Brooks/Cole.

Reiss, D. (1981). *The family's construction of reality.* Cambridge, MA: Harvard University Press.

Rubin, Z., Pruitt, D., & Kim, S. (1984). *Social conflict: Escalation, stalemate and settlement* (2nd ed.). New York: McGraw-Hill.

Rudd, J. E. (1996). Communication effects on divorce mediation: How participants' argumentativeness, verbal aggression, and compliance-gaining strategy choice mediate outcome satisfaction. *Mediation Quarterly, 14*(1), 65-78.

Sandole, D. J. D., & van der Merwe, H. (Eds.). (1993). *Conflict resolution theory and practice: Integration and application.* Manchester, UK: Manchester University Press.

Saposnek, D. T. (1983). *Mediating child custody disputes.* San Francisco: Jossey-Bass.

Saposnek, D. T. (1994). *Mediating child custody disputes* (2nd ed.). San Francisco: Jossey-Bass.

Silbey, S. S., & Merry, S. E. (1986). Mediator settlement strategies. *Law & Policy, 8,* 7-32.

Slaikeu, K. (1995). *When push comes to shove: A practical guide to mediating disputes.* San Francisco: Jossey-Bass.

Somary, K., & Emery, R. E. (1991). Emotional anger and grief in divorce mediation. *Mediation Quarterly, 8*(3), 185-197.

Stamato, L. (1992). Voice, place, and process: Research on gender, negotiation, and conflict resolution. *Mediation Quarterly, 9*(4), 375-386.

Susskind, L. E., McKearney, S., & Thomas-Larner, J. (Eds.). (1999). *The consensus building handbook: A comprehensive guide to reaching agreement.* Thousand Oaks, CA: Sage.

Tang, C. (1994). Prevalence of spousal aggression in Hong Kong. *Journal of Family Violence, 9,* 347-355.

Tracy, K., & Spradlin, A. (1994). Talking like a mediator: Conversational moves of experienced divorce mediators. *New Directions in Mediation* (pp. 110-132). Thousand Oaks, CA: Sage.

Umbeit, M. (1995). *Mediating interpersonal conflicts: A pathway to peace.* Concord, MN: CPI Publications.

Wilmot, W. W., & Hocker, J. L. (1998). *Interpersonal conflict resolution.* Boston: McGraw-Hill.

Wilson, E. (1982). *The wisdom of Confucius.* New York: Avenel.

PART 2

THERAPEUTIC FAMILY MEDIATION

2

The TFM Approach

Overview

Practice models, such as *therapeutic family mediation* (TFM), are no different than the professionals who create them; both evolve, change, and grow through time. Initially developed in the late 1980s, the model has retained its basic structure but has become increasingly sophisticated in its theoretical underpinnings, the conceptualization of its phases and their interrelation, the roles the mediator is asked to play, and the practice skills needed for their enactment.

The task of this and the next six chapters will be to provide a detailed account of the model. What follows will be divided into five sections, which will deal with the rationale for the model, its theoretical roots or underpinnings, its underlying practice principles, a basic description or overview of the TFM model itself, and the different professionals and settings with whom and in which it is routinely applied.

Rationale

Irrespective of the particular practice model being advanced, there is general agreement in the literature as to the fundamental goals of family mediation:

- to create a fair and cooperative process for divorcing/divorced spouses in conflict,
- to set out and clarify the issues in dispute between them,
- to give spouses an opportunity to consider the possibility of reconciliation,
- to encourage parents to put the best interests of their children ahead of their own self-interests,

- to assist the partners in negotiating the issues in dispute between them,
- to arrive at a settlement on each of these issues that is mutually acceptable and both fair and equitable in light of their circumstances.

As we have seen in the previous chapter, mediation practitioners have developed a variety of models in an effort to achieve these goals. Here, TFM stands out by its emphasis on relationship processes and thus the additional goals we seek to achieve in mediation.

Although all spouses can give a variety of reasons for their decision to separate, beneath this rhetoric is an abiding sense of deep dissatisfaction with the relationship that is no longer tolerable for one or both of them. Such dissatisfaction speaks to dysfunctional patterns of relating between them that have been in place for some time and that they have been unable to change. Mutual blame for this state of affairs is commonplace and almost always associated with feelings of enmity, including recrimination, fault, anger, and bitterness. Even so, many couples separate with some ambivalence, in remembrance of positive experience in the past. Such ambivalence is quickly burned away on involvement with the adversary system, which may encourage parties to take inflexible positions in their effort to "win" against the other. In short, the dysfunctional conduct that characterizes partners in conflict does not cease on separation but rather carries on long afterward. Indeed, unless such conduct and the feelings associated with it are addressed in some way, these partners may be locked in combat long after their divorce has been ratified. Such combat, moreover, undermines their personal growth and development and may stultify their relations with all others in their life, including their children and any future relationships.

All of this is central to family mediation. Spouses bring their various forms of dysfunction with them. It drives their conflict, affects their ability to negotiate, and predicts the likelihood that they will reach agreement. In TFM, the task of the mediator, then, is to address couples' dysfunction in such a way as to allow them to take full advantage of the opportunity provided by mediation. Accordingly, to the standard goals listed above, the TFM model superimposes several additional goals:

- to understand the subtext of couples' unresolved conflict,
- to help couples make the transition from marital roles and relations to parental roles and relations,
- to block or change patterns of conduct that are likely to interfere with productive negotiation in mediation,
- to encourage the parties to resolve any feelings of enmity toward their former partner, and
- to reframe divorce in positive terms, that is, as a form of family reorganization that affords members an opportunity for a new beginning and for personal and/or family transformation.

Theory

In light of the standard goals noted earlier, most models of mediation practice give little emphasis to the role of theory. That is, most practice models are grounded on experience, with many practitioners characterizing themselves as "eclectic," another way of saying that they are wedded to no model or theory but rather borrow freely from various sources as the need arises.

There are several difficulties with this position. First, the family processes that unfold in mediation can be complex. Theory provides practitioners with some basis for understanding what is going on in front of their eyes, what role they can and should play in that process, and what they can do to achieve the goals set out above. Second, theory helps practitioners achieve some degree of consistency; in its absence, practitioners are likely subject to varying influences through time and consequently are inconsistent in their practice. Finally, in our experience, theory provides a ready way in which students can enter mediation. Theory renders it understandable and approachable, such that students can see themselves in the role of mediator. In the absence of theory, mediator conduct becomes difficult to understand and nearly impossible to emulate without a great deal of hands-on experience. For these reasons, we regard theory as essential to good mediation practice, with the incidental advantage that it renders TFM more accessible to testing and research than its theory-free counterparts.

For ease of presentation, the theoretical underpinning of TFM will be divided into two parts, the first concerning meta-theory and the second concerning substantive theory.

Meta-Theory: The Systems Approach

The TFM model derives much of its logic of practice from *systems "theory."* Known variously as general system theory, systems theory, open-systems theory, ecosystems theory, or ecological theory, this approach originated with the seminal work of biologist Ludwig von Bertalanffy (1950, 1975, 1968). We place the word *theory* in quotation marks advisedly because systems "theory" is *not* a theory in the usual sense that it concerns a particular phenomenon or body of substantive work. Rather, it is a meta-theory. In the words of Katz and Kahn (1966), "Open-systems theory is rather a framework, a meta-theory, a model in the broadest sense of that over-used term. Open-systems theory is an approach and a conceptual language for understanding and describing many kinds and levels of phenomena" (p. 63). Consequently, from its roots in biology in the 1930s, it has since been taken up by various disciplines (Bateson, 1979), from physics and engineering to psychology, sociology, anthropology, family therapy, and, most recently, family mediation. Its use in mediation has been the focus of some debate, both pro (Blume, 1993) and con (Roberts, 1992).

Full explication of the systems approach would be quite beyond the scope of the current work. Instead, we will focus on a handful of its basic assumptions to demonstrate its influence on TFM. These assumptions include the following:

1. *Relational entities.* The things or "entities" in the world that are to be regarded as real are relational in nature; that is, they involve two or more interacting units.

2. *Isomorphy.* All systems involve the same basic structural arrangement of parts, such that systems at different levels of complexity—from atoms to persons, from dyads to families, organizations, or nation-states—are isomorphic.

3. *Arbitrariness.* No level of complexity is to be seen as more real than any other; rather, all systems must be regarded as arbitrary organizational abstractions—a particular "punctuation" in the way one views the world—that are more or less useful in terms of the purpose(s) of the observer.

4. *Wholeness.* The system or whole is necessarily more complex than the sum of its parts; the characteristics of the whole are thus not reducible to the attributes of its constituent elements.

5. *Circular causality.* Causality within system is nonlinear, involving circular processes that reflect the reciprocal interaction among and between components through time.

6. *Patterning 1.* Interactions among system elements are patterned or organized and thus display repetitive sequences of interaction.

7. *Emergence.* These patterns are not determinate; rather, they emerge out of the interaction among the elements. In social systems, such interaction involves negotiation among the parties.

8. *Homeostasis (also known as morphostasis).* These patterns are self-correcting (homeostatic), operating automatically or routinely to maintain established patterns within specified limits and thus resist change despite perturbation within and/or outside the system. In social systems, such processes typically operate outside the awareness of the participants.

9. *Context.* Each system operates within some context consisting of other systems external to it and with which it interacts; no system can exist in isolation, independent of some context.

10. *Patterning 2.* Patterning not only characterizes relations between system components but also the relations between those components

and/or the systems and elements in its environment, that is, elements or systems external to it.

11. *Interdependence.* Due to the reciprocal interconnection between system elements, a change in one element will be associated, directly or indirectly, with a change in the relationship between all other elements; thus, relations between elements within a system can be described as interdependent (though not necessarily equal).

12. *Heterostasis (also known as mophogenesis).* Under some conditions, all systems have the capacity for adaptive self-organization, changing the organized relationship between the components in response to changes in the components, the environment, and/or the relationship between the two.

Implications

These assumptions hold a number of implications for the TFM model of family mediation practice. First, families in mediation are systems, that is, organized wholes rather than discrete individuals with divergent interests. This perspective suggests that they can be expected to display attributes when the spouses are together that are not apparent when the spouses are seen alone. It also points to the importance of identifying system components by virtue of their influence with regard to given problems or issues. In some cases, this will be confined to the partners and/or their children. However, in many cases, such description will point to the importance of third parties, including extended family members (such as grandparents), extramarital partners, and professionals (such as therapists and/or lawyers). Moreover, the influence of these various elements is seldom equal, with one or more individuals having more influence ("leading part") than others. Further still, the systems perspective suggests distinguishing between the interests of the system and those of its members. In many cases, the mediator, as a third-party observer, is the only one to "see" the system as a whole and is thus uniquely positioned to recognize those aspects of the larger system that are healthy and should be preserved or unhealthy and should be changed.

Second, through time, spouses in mediation will have evolved patterns of conduct that are both outside their awareness and stable, that is, resistant to change. In most cases, these patterns will be irrelevant to the practitioner because they pose no threat to the mediation process. However, patterns that actively interfere with the couples' effort to negotiate the issues in dispute cannot be ignored. These patterns must be addressed in mediation, either by blocking their emergence or, more likely, by disrupting or changing them pursuant to productive negotiation. It is in this sense that *therapeutic* family mediation gets its name, that is, by the willingness of its practitioners to intervene therapeutically to make it possible for the partners in question to negotiate productively. One of the roles of the mediator in TFM, then, is that of *therapist*, albeit only in pursuit of the goals of mediation. One consequence of such intervention efforts is that these new patterns carry on beyond mediation and increase the likelihood that couples will negotiate changes to their agreement informally, without the need either of future mediation or litigation. Another consequence of such efforts is that a minority of couples have cause to rethink their decision to divorce and may elect instead to reconcile, often by switching from family mediation to marital therapy, either using the same practitioner or being referred out for that purpose.

Third, divorce represents a major life transition. As such, it is a time when the family system is least stable, typically oscillating between stability and change. The problem is that partners, most of whom are divorcing for the first time, understand none of this. Rather, they experience this period in their life as an emotional roller coaster, feeling euphoric one moment, depressed the next, and angry the next. Normalizing such experiences can be enormously helpful to them. Moreover, even small interventions can have significant effects in unstable systems. Family mediation, then, can truly be an opportunity for transformation.

Finally, the circular form of causality in systems helps account for the recursive character of the TFM model. Whereas other models walk clients through their various steps in linear fashion, the TFM model is organized in the form of a series of feedback loops or circles. This means in practice that the model is enormously flexible, allowing the practitioner to make changes in the process that precisely match progress in client couples.

Substantive Theories

Systems theory, then, provides the basic scaffolding of the TFM model and also addresses several but not all of its substantive concerns. Various families of substantive theory fill in any remaining gaps. Accordingly, in what follows, we will touch briefly on 12 bodies of theoretical work, each of which informs the TFM model in one way or another.

Attachment Theory. Originally developed by Bowlby (1969), in simplified form attachment theory argues that the survival of the infant is dependent on his or her attachment to one or more parenting figures. The power of that attachment is such that it shapes children for life and can significantly affect adult attachments (Bartholomew & Horowitz, 1991; Mikulincer, Florian, & Wesler, 1993). Although in practice the quality of attachment varies over a continuum, most writing in this area tends to focus on the ends of this continuum. One end involves individuals who were *securely attached* to their parents and thus come into adulthood with a mature sense of self. At the other extreme are individuals who were *insecurely attached* to their parents and consequently emerge into adulthood with an immature sense of self. The likelihood of divorce is predicated on the match between spouses. Marriage between two securely attached individuals would be least vulnerable to divorce, whereas that between two insecurely attached individuals would be most vulnerable. Moreover, divorce may reactivate attachment fears, especially among the insecurely attached, and can lead to situational conduct that is starkly out of character for one or both spouses, that is, behavior that is frankly irrational or at least unreasonable and is triggered by the divorce process. For example, the postseparation period may involve the first instance of domestic violence (Johnston & Campbell, 1993).

Stress Theory. A related concern is with the way in which individuals and family systems recognize and manage stress. Given the universality of stress, it is important to realize that all of us are vulnerable to stress effects. As circumstances induce everyday stress to rise to the level at which it becomes *distress*, all of us will begin to display some combination of physiological and psychological signs of stress. Physiological signs include dry mouth, heart palpitations, sweaty palms, increased blood pressure, and increased heart rate. Related psychosomatic signs may include headache, stomach upset, and/or gastrointestinal disruptions, whereas psychological signs may include tunnel vision, disorganized thinking, erratic behavior, and emotional lability (see Goldberger & Breznitz, 1993).

Stress responses are relevant to family mediation for two reasons. First, next to the death of a loved one, divorce is the single most stressful event in the life of a family. Second, individuals vary widely in what they perceive as stressful and how they respond to stress. Thus, two different individuals may respond quite differently to the same set of stressors. Stress that may push one individual into crisis may leave another barely affected. Following the family adjustment and adaptation response (FAAR) model (Patterson, 1989), family stress responsiveness varies as a function of the resources available to cope with the different demands of short-term crises and long-term adjustment. Crisis-related resources may include experience, mental toughness, social support, and materials resources (money). Adjustment-related resources may include family flexibility, expectations regarding the character of the stressor(s), the number of simultaneous change events, and the character of the social network.

In light of these insights about stress, a couple's amenability to the demands of family mediation will vary as a function of their individual and collective stress level, their coping and adjustment resources, and whether they are both at the same or different phases of the stress response. That is, a couple in which one spouse is in crisis while the other is coping with adjustment will be less amenable to mediation than one in which both spouses are in the adjustment phase. In both cases, couples with ample resources are likely to fare better than their counterparts with few or no resources.

Structural Models of Divorce. Another set of theoretical models is concerned with understanding divorce as a social phenomenon, particularly in explaining the fact that variation in divorce rates through time is a highly systematic or regular phenomenon. Such models tend to be structural in character; that is, they explain changes in divorce rates in terms of changes in major social institutions (Irving & Benjamin, 1995, chap. 2). For example, in industrialized nations around the world, the past half century has seen major changes in several institutions, including the law (liberalization as regards divorce and women's rights), the labor force (rapid influx of women, globalization of trade), the family (reduced size, increased affluence, less quality time), technology (the information revolution), culture (recognition and support for diversity), and medicine (increased longevity), to name only a few. Moreover, such models point to a range of interaction effects. For example, women's increasing involvement in the workforce means that more women than ever are financially independent and thus perhaps more willing to consider divorce should they become unhappy in their marriage. Similarly, the technological revolution has had the unintended consequence of raising the minimal standards for employment, thus marginalizing workers based on ethnicity, social class, education, and gender.

Such models are relevant to mediation by expanding our gaze beyond the narrow confines of the family to include those larger social forces that act on it. Accordingly, assessment and negotiation efforts may now need to include information about changing marital roles, potential conflicts between work and family, and the character of spousal work patterns. These models also help explain why, generation after generation, settlement patterns in mediation have gradually become more complex as they take into account work-family links, legal options, forms of work, and types of assets that simply did not exist a scant generation ago. In turn, this expanding vision places the onus on practitioners to keep up to date on a rapidly expanding range of topics.

Models of Mate Selection and Marital Stability. A fourth set of theoretical models relevant to mediation concentrates on the bases on which spouses selected each other as mates and the factors that determine whether they stay together (Burr, Hill, Nye, & Reiss, 1979; Gottman, Coan, Carrere, & Swenson, 1998). Central to mate selection is the notion of *homogamy*, that is, the tendency for individuals to select as spouses those who are similar to them in one or more ways. The fact is that most people "fall in love" with mates with whom they share a variety of demographic attributes, including social class, ethnic group, religious affiliation, and educational attainment. This perspective implies that couples who are very different across these attributes may prove particularly problematic in family mediation. Moreover, these models highlight the role of in-laws and other extended kin in ensuring that offspring marry only those who are acceptable to the family. In family mediation, this implies inquiry into the involvement of extended kin in the formulation and maintenance of ongoing disputes between the spouses—for example, spouses who themselves may be inclined to compromise but may be pushed into continued conflict based on their loyalty to parents, extended kin, and/or new intimate partners (Johnston & Campbell, 1988).

As to marital stability, these models emphasize two sets of factors. The first set includes factors we have already encountered in models examined already, such as family size, homogamy, the extended kin network, and family resources (psychological, social, and fiscal). The second set of factors focuses on the quality of the marital relationship, such as communication effectiveness, problem solving, conflict management, and satisfaction. This second set of factors is central to mediation because it is precisely here that couples typically reach an impasse in negotiation. The TFM model emphasizes the importance of understanding these processes well and of being prepared with intervention strategies designed to block or alter those processes that interfere with productive negotiation. In addition, these factors highlight a role of the mediator as *educator*. That is, one way of helping couples overcome poor problem-solving skills is to teach them better and more effective ways of dealing with problems.

Models of Normal Family Processes. Statements referring to marital, parenting, or family dysfunction are always relative to normal standards of conduct. An expanding body of work sets out the empirical basis for judging conduct within a certain range (from "normal" to "dysfunctional") and for classifying parenting and child conduct as developmentally appropriate (Walsh, 1993). Such data are directly relevant to mediation because clients justifiably look to mediators as "experts" and "educators" in these areas. This is appropriate both with respect to the practitioner's professional training as well as the ready availability of such information, either on CD-ROM and/or online. In most cases, such information can simply be presented in a neutral way, as a counterweight to the client's lack of information or misinformation. In cases in which the settlement options under consideration are unconscionable or inconsistent with the children's best interests, the practitioner may use such "expert" information to *advocate* for different, more reasonable options (see "Practice Principles," below).

Feminist Models of the Family and Other Systems. The modern feminist movement began in the 1960s and has since been enormously influential in raising awareness of the various ways in which society disadvantages women (Goldberger, Tarule, Clinchy, & Belenky, 1996). This is so, these authors argue, across a range of social institutions, including systems of law, mental health, education, work, and family life (McGoldrick, Anderson, & Walsh, 1989), with the latter rendering women especially vulnerable to intimidation and violence. With some exceptions (Hernstein, 1996; Lichtenstein, 2000), feminist writers have been especially opposed to the family mediation movement, arguing that women's rights are better protected through the courts (Benjamin & Irving, 1992). Although we reject this last line of argument, taken as a whole, this body of work continues to be relevant to TFM in at least three ways: First, it stresses the importance of having practitioners who are thoroughly familiar with local family law statutes and regulations; second, it highlights the importance of power-balancing processes to ensure that any settlements in mediation are fair and equitable; and finally, it has been extremely valuable in underlining the need for vigilance in detecting evidence of violence and intimidation. The issue of violence and mediation remains controversial, with some authors arguing that any signs of violence, past or present, immediately render the case contraindicated for mediation, whereas others, ourselves included, prefer to reserve judgment by exploring each case on its merits.

Models of Conflict. Still another body of work has sought to characterize forms of conflict (Breslin & Rubin, 1995). Traditionally, family conflict was understood in negative terms, and its presence was indicative of dysfunction. More recently, conflict among family members has come to be understood as virtually inevitable. Indeed, it is the absence of conflict—that is, conflict avoidance or denial—that is now seen as a possible sign of dysfunction. This perspective has led theorists to distinguish between different forms of conflict, specifically between constructive versus destructive conflict (Deutsch, 1973, 1991). Destructive conflict is characterized by a lack of resolution, a diffuse focus that may involve several topics, a tendency to mix past and present events, and a tendency toward character assassination rather than a concentration on the issue in contention. Conversely, constructive conflict is characterized by issue resolution, as well as flexibility and clear and consistent communication. It may also involve the use of humor and the avoidance of name-calling.

With respect to family mediation, the clients' conflict style will be a central issue in deciding whether they are amenable to mediation and, if so, what techniques will be useful in moving the parties from destructive to constructive conflict.

Exchange Models of Negotiation. Yet another body of work relevant to mediation concerns efforts to apply exchange theory to the process of negotiation or bargaining. Proponents of these models tend to rely on an economic model of man that emphasizes the rational character of such an exchange, as the parties each pursue their self-interests. In doing so, each party is seen to weight various factors to determine how best to get what it wants out of the exchange (Deutsch, 1991).

From the perspective of family mediation, much of the work in support of the exchange model has relied on artificial tasks or "games" involving students who were strangers to each other. The results are therefore problematic when applied to families whose members have an ongoing relationship and who bring strong feelings to any exchange. This limitation notwithstanding, these perspectives are important to mediation by calling our attention to issues of fairness, equity, and balance in assessing both the way spouses negotiate for what they want as well as the bases on which parties accept or reject various offers. For example, in their role as *facilitators*, it is important that mediators know in advance what they regard as "fair" or "equitable" in their circumstances.

The Harvard Model of Negotiation. Perhaps the best-known model of negotiation is based on research done at Harvard University. Proponents of this model make a key distinction between *positions* and *interests* (Fisher, Ury, & Patton, 1991). Positional bargaining does not take into account what each party needs, only what each wants to get out of any exchange (i.e., the party's position). This approach to bargaining can be problematic because the positions of each party are often far apart, such that there may be little room for compromise or negotiation. Such limited maneuverability changes, however, when the focus shifts from wants to needs. Here, the parties are asked to speak to their shared interests, as in "providing for a safe and secure future for our child." In turn, this shift transforms the bargaining process from a struggle over divergent positions to a shared problem-solving exercise and thus one in which settlement becomes possible. Even so, not every negotiation will lead to agreement. In advance, each party is asked to consider its BATNA, that is, its "best alternative to a negotiated agreement." For example, one party's best offer may fall short of what it can expect to get in court, thus making litigation more attractive than mediation.

This model has been tremendously influential in alternative dispute resolution (ADR) circles and has been especially useful in commercial or civil mediation. However, it remains problematic for family mediation. Like the family of exchange models, the research for the Harvard model has relied on artificial problems, using students who are strangers to each other. Furthermore, it assumes that parties can be persuaded to act rationally by appealing to their self-interests. In contrast, the history of relations between family members means that they can be expected to act in accordance with patterns that preceded their divorce and that may vary from highly functional to highly dysfunctional. Accordingly, appeals to their rational self-interests may or may not be successful and may be inconsistent with the interests of other family members or, indeed, the family system per se in terms of their ongoing relations following divorce. Even so, the Harvard model remains germane to family mediation by calling attention to underlying issues, motives, goals, and/or concerns. These "hidden" concerns are, by definition, seldom expressed openly for a variety of reasons, including fear that they will be dismissed, rendering them vulnerable to others' scorn or ridicule of which they themselves may be consciously unaware. Bringing such concerns to light can be enormously helpful in promoting productive negotiation and in moving the spouses closer to settlement.

Models of Communication. Human communication practices are at the heart of the social sciences, such that any complete review is much beyond the scope of the present section. However, three clusters of studies have specific relevance to our concerns. The first cluster involves early studies in human communication and family therapy that established a handful of basic principles (Bateson, 1972, 1979). For example, one such principle established that all human communications involve at least four components, in which (a) I am (b) communicating a message (c) to you (d) in this context. This principle was qualified by a series of distinctions between cognitive as opposed to affective context, verbal versus nonverbal modalities, and communication versus meta-communication (i.e., communication *about* communication). Related principles emphasized that all interaction, even failure to communicate, constituted a form of communication (in interaction, one cannot *not* communicate) and that the energy for communication was as much in the receiver as it was in the sender (e.g., silence on the part of the sender can communicate a message to the receiver). Finally, it became readily apparent to family researchers that communication was highly patterned and varied on a continuum from highly functional to highly dysfunctional. This work also highlighted the social construction of meaning in family systems and the importance of context.

The second cluster of studies, originating with the work of Gottman (1979, 1994), dealt with communication among satisfied and dissatisfied married couples. Data collection involved an elaborate process of monitoring couples as they discussed conflictual and nonconflictual topics and included audio and video recordings as well as various physiological measures. These studies revealed that specific patterns of interaction coupled with particular physiological measures predicted with 94% accuracy which couples were likely to get divorced within 5 years and which couples were not. In particular, these patterns included harsh startup, criticism (as opposed to complaint), contempt, defensiveness, stonewalling, and emotional flooding. Research also showed that men were much more likely than women to find conflict uncomfortably arousing to the point of being aversive; in addition, repeated conflict without closure and exchanges characterized by contempt of the other spouse were particularly corrosive of the marital bond.

The final cluster of studies focused on the application of communication principles to the process of family mediation (Folger & Jones, 1994). For example, such work has demonstrated that certain patterns of communication are more consistent with agreement than with nonagreement, the parties' meaning structures and shapes their conduct as negotiators, and changes in context alter the way that parties and mediators interpret their interaction, including mediators' background, culture, training, gender, language use, and the organizational constraints under which they operate (see also Chapter 12, this volume).

These various models are all relevant to mediation by highlighting patterns of behavior and meaning that may undermine a couple's ability to engage in productive negotiation and thus are prime targets of intervention. For example, if contempt is corrosive of marital relations, then such behavior is likely to have the same effect on efforts at postdivorce cooperative parenting. Contempt and related behaviors cannot be allowed to continue if the couple is to have any hope of reaching a settlement in mediation and maintaining a viable parental relationship over the long term.

Models of Cultural Diversity. Cultural diversity is a fact of life in North America. International travel, coupled with immigration, ensures that this is ever more true. The result was unthinkable only 50 years ago—namely, states in which the White population is in the minority.

On one hand, such diversity has spawned a family of models concerned with understanding both the dynamics of social relations within such groups and the character of relations between such groups and the majority community. The former speak of transition, adjustment, and conflict as first-generation populations struggle to find their place in the immigrant and larger communities, whereas second and later generations search for identities and roles that connect to both. Some are successful, but others are not, with rising divorce rates as one indicator of the process. The latter speak to the short- and long-term effects of discrimination, racism, unemployment, and poverty.

On the other hand, cultural diversity has enormous implications for family mediation, and there is a growing need to ensure that such practitioners demonstrate cultural competence. This can be problematic in the absence of clear standards.

Models of Family Intervention. The therapeutic character of TFM means that we are interested in methods for inducing various forms of change in clients, including change that is behavioral (in the ways partners relate to each other), cognitive (in the way they understand their relationship to each other and their children or others they care about), and/or affective (the way they feel about themselves and their relationship to others). Toward these ends, several models of family therapy are relevant to our concerns, most notably models of solution-oriented, narrative, and strategic practice (Benjamin, 1995a, 1995b; Favaloro, 1998; Nichols & Schwartz, 1998). These are relevant to the TFM model both for their similarities and their differences.

These models are similar in at least three respects: All are oriented to short-term intervention, emphasize the importance of the client-therapist relationship, and concentrate on asking questions as the primary basis for collecting information. Not coincidentally, these attributes correspond closely to the requirements of the TFM models.

However, these models are also different from each other in ways we see as complementary. For example, both solution-oriented and narratives approaches focus on cognitive change and thus rely heavily on language, whereas the strategic approach is concerned with behavior and thus relies more on tracking interaction sequences. Similarly, solution-oriented and narrative approaches assume a collaborative relationship between client and therapist, with the accent on a client's resources, strengths, and positive experiences. In contrast, the strategic approach is more directive, with the therapist as outside expert and with the accent on pathological or negative events. Further still, whereas solution-oriented and narrative approaches emphasize the meaning of events and thus their susceptibility to changes in meaning through reframing, the strategic approach acknowledges the role of affect, especially negative affect, such as anger, in characterizing relations between partners. The latter is an especially important difference, given Johnson and Lebow's (2000) observation that "there is now clearer recognition that the regulation of emotion and emotional expression and responsiveness are defining features of close relationships and constitute what systems theorists call 'leading elements' in the couple system" (p. 32). Finally, given their common roots in systems theory, both solution-oriented and strategic approaches focus on processes in the present. In contrast, in keeping with the postmodern character of the narrative approach, emphasis is given to family history (life narratives) and to the socially constructive nature of these stories. Thus, the strategic approach serves as a counterweight for the tendency of solution-oriented and narrative approaches to ignore family conflict, relationship dynamics, and negative affect. Conversely, solution-oriented and narrative approaches serve to counterbalance the tendency of the strategic approach to ignore the hopeful, positive, resourceful, and satisfying or "successful" aspects of clients' experience.

Summary

Whereas most available practice models of family mediation are typically grounded on practice wisdom, with or without any theoretical input (cf. Schwebel, Gately, Milburn, & Renner, 1993), the TFM model reverses the order of things. It is heavily grounded on theory, which may or may not be modified by practice wisdom. Thus, the first layer of that base is derived from systems meta-theory, which asks practitioners to see the world in terms of organized wholes and commits them to a series of assumptions that serve as conceptual tools. Seeing the client couples as a family system is thus the first prerequisite of the TFM model and helps practitioners get "above" these partners' individuals complaints, concerns, or demands. Superimposed on this systems base is another layer of theory drawn from several disciplines. Here, 12 substantive models serve four functions. First, they sensitize practitioners to a range of issues that are critical to effective mediation practice. These issues include attachment and the possibility of nonrational conduct, stress, and the extent of related resources (psychological, social, and fiscal), the role of extrasystemic elements (both familial and societal), ongoing functional and dysfunctional patterns of relating (especially regarding conflict management), the developmental needs of the children (as a function of age and gender), the salience of gender and related rights and vulnerabilities (including the past or present use of intimidation and/or violence), the use of naive models of equity and fairness, the role of local family law statutes, the importance of vigilance for underlying processes and hidden agendas, and the bases of communication effectiveness in mediation, both on the part of clients and mediators. Second, the models collectively call attention to the five roles of the family mediator in TFM, including facilitator, expert, educator, therapist, and advocate. Third, these models highlight the importance of range and flexibility in the use of various clinical techniques and stress the importance of balance in exploring clients' strengths and weaknesses, their behavior and the meanings they attach to it, their current pattern of relating, and the "stories" of how they evolved to the present, as well as the importance of the practitioners' ability to be directive or collaborative at different times, in keeping with session or case goals. Finally, these models highlight various substantive areas in which it is important that practitioners be current, including child development, the dynamics of divorce, changes in family laws and procedures, and the changing face of the family and the consequences to it of changes in society, such as the changing organization of the labor markets. TFM, then, entails a comprehensive approach to family mediation that makes significant demands on its practitioners that go well beyond the narrow confines of family mediation per se.

Practice Principles

There is general agreement in the literature concerning at least seven principles of family mediation practice. Of these, five are seen as basic and thus generate limited discussion, whereas the remaining two are the focus of debate and thus are seen as controversial.

Basic Practice Principles

Five principles fall into the "basic" category: self-determination, confidentiality, fairness and equity, full disclosure, and safety and security.

Self-Determination. The adversarial system comes complete with a complex set of statutes, rules, procedures, and precedents. Knowledge about this system is something lawyers acquire in training and in their day-to-day professional lives, but it is something about which clients are almost entirely ignorant. In entering that system, then, clients are almost always dependent on representation by their lawyers and so have little or no independent voice.

However, what clients have and lawyers do not is an intimate knowledge of their family situation, their own motives and objectives, and their feelings about their situation. It is these attributes that are given value in mediation, as clients are given back their voice and asked to tell their story in their own words. That voice, that story, and those feelings are the essence of self-determination, on the understanding that clients know their situation best and it is they who must live with the consequences of any decisions arrived at in mediation. Self-determination, then, is about empowering spouses to take responsibility for the decisions that will shape their lives and the lives of their children for the foreseeable future.

Confidentiality. Although the communication between lawyers and clients is protected by privilege, everything else that transpires in court is on the public record, for all to see. In one sense, the same is true of mediation because any final settlement will become part of the public record. However, in another sense, mediation stands in sharp contrast to litigation because the *process* of arriving at that settlement is off the record, being held in confidence in "closed" mediation. It is closed not only in the sense that there is no record of exactly what transpired in mediation but also in the sense that the mediator is barred from appearing in court as a witness or from having his or her process notes entered as evidence.

Critics of mediation have argued that such informal justice can compromise clients' rights, relying too much on the good conduct and technical expertise of the practitioner and not enough on established procedures and a public record of events. As fallible practitioners, we must accept the possibility of error and/or abuse, and developments within the profession are beginning to address these important issues. Against such risks, however, are the advantages to the process of confidentiality. Such advantages include openness, frankness, trust, and cooperation, as clients need no longer fear for the consequences of their utterances or reprisals for their openness. In short, the principles of confidentiality speak to the different premises that underpin mediation as opposed to litigation. The latter assumes, as its name suggests, that the spouses are adversaries and as such have divergent interests. In contrast, mediation assumes that the spouses are partners in a joint enterprise, their family, and thus have many interests in common. Mediation, then, is not a battle for an unequal share of spoils but rather a joint problem-solving exercise in which confidentiality serves to facilitate process effectiveness and efficiency.

Fairness and Equity. Fairness and equity suggest a level playing field in which both spouses have an equal opportunity to present their perspectives and advance their proposals and in which any settlement will take account of their respective claims. Although all forums that address the needs of divorcing spouses strive to achieve these goals, some are more successful than others. In litigation, for example, all clients are, in principle, equal before the law. In practice, however, the unequal distribution of resources across spouses may result in an unfair process and an unequal result. Unequal resources are far less telling in mediation because the use of a professional third party, the mediator, tends to level the playing field. Far more important are the complex issues clients seek to negotiate, often involving difficult, even impossible, choices. For example, although both parents are equally responsible for the care and control of their children, the practical demands of work, family, and logistics often make for only one primary parent, irrespective of the parents' desire for an equal division of time and labor. In a similar vein, mediators have developed a variety of techniques for achieving balance between spouses in which one is more powerful than the other. Despite such efforts, absolute fairness and equity are more an ideal than a reality, even in mediation. However, relative fairness and equity in the *eyes of the clients* are often achieved in mediation because the settlement is negotiated between the clients and not imposed on them. Although clients in mediation will often grumble that they did not get exactly what they wanted, most will nevertheless agree that their settlement was reasonable—that is, fair and equitable—under their circumstances.

Full Disclosure. In striving for fairness and equity, both in process and outcome, it is universally agreed that full disclosure by both spouses is essential. Indeed, most mediation contracts say as much. Here, critics of mediation charge that in the absence of anything resembling the process of discovery, mediation may inadvertently be associated with injustice. There is some truth in these charges; clients can lie in mediation. Practitioners, however, are not without resources in constructing some version of the truth. For one thing, the principle of confidentiality discourages deceit. This is especially true among practitioners who rely on the TFM model, which encourages openly addressing underlying motives for oppressive conduct, including incomplete or distorted disclosure. Furthermore, both spouses can be asked to document their claims when this is appropriate, and both are free to request the involvement of outside experts, including their own lawyers, if there is good reason to think that this would advance the process. Although it is impossible to know how often mediation clients "get away" with less than full disclosure, in our experience the processes noted above ensure that this is seldom a major problem.

Safety and Security. As with disclosure, the safety and security of both clients are simply a prerequisite to fairness and equity. All clients must be assured of their physical safety from assault or other forms of attack, and all must feel secure psychologically, that is, free from intimidation, threats, or other forms of psychological abuse. Indeed, this is more likely to be an issue in mediation than in litigation because mediation sessions will often involve only the three parties, with no one else available to supervise or monitor the process. Later, we will detail some of the considerations and techniques used to ensure client safety. Here, it will be sufficient to note that safety and security in mediation involve separate issues as regards amenability to mediation as opposed to the establishment of a supportive environment in which to negotiate an equitable settlement.

Controversial Practice Principles

There are two additional practice principles about which there is considerable debate: the child's best interests and neutrality.

Child's Best Interests. Family law in all jurisdictions across North America recognizes the "best interests" standard in making decisions about child custody and access or, more recently, in creating parenting plans. As applied in most mediation practice models, "best interests" is less a standard than it is a sensitizing idea (Kelly, 1997). This idea seeks to encourage practitioners to raise issues and suggest options when dealing with client proposals that seem not to be consistent with the child's "best interests." In many cases, however, it yields a passive position on the part of practitioners, with their own concerns limited by notions of neutrality (see below) and client self-determination.

In contrast, as proponents of the TFM model, we take a more proactive stance, framing one of the mediator's roles as that of child advocate. That is, with regard to "best interests," mediators and clients are asked to distinguish between marital and parenting issues. Although client self-determination will apply to both, mediators will be more prepared to intervene in the latter than the former, especially when parenting proposals are seen as inconsistent with "best interests." Mediator judgments about "best interests" will be based on a number of concerns, including the following:

- the developmental needs and requirements of children as related to their age and gender,
- the mediator's knowledge of the research literature and what it shows about the impact of various parenting arrangements on children as related to the children's age and gender,
- the mediator's experience of the sorts of time-sharing and other arrangements that have worked well in the past,
- the mediator's global assessment of the client family system and the circumstances under which they currently operate,
- the network of extended family and extrasystemic attachments, and
- the likely immediate and long-term consequences for these children of the proposals in question.

In turn, intervention may involve any combination of the mediator's major roles. That is, as experts, mediators may provide information; as educators, they may provide parenting training; as facilitators, they promote communication that is open and clear; and as therapists, they may select from a range of intervention techniques, from confronting to reframing to suggesting options and alternatives. In any or all of these roles, however, a strictly neutral stance would represent an abrogation of their responsibility as child advocates. (For further discussion, see Chapter 9, this volume.)

Neutrality. Most definitions of mediation characterize the mediator as a "neutral third party." Following Boulle and Kelly (1998, p. 21), this general reference to neutrality may encompass a wide range of concerns, notably that mediators have no direct interest in the outcome of the dispute, no prior association with the parties, and no prior knowledge of the issues in dispute between them. The mediator will not sit in judgment of clients, will not use his or her substantive expertise to influence their decision making, but will act fairly and without bias toward the parties. Thus, mediators may be expected to act in ways that demonstrate that they are both *disinterested*, having no direct interest in the outcome, and *impartial*, treating both parties fairly and equitably.

There is general agreement that mediators should be impartial. Mediators are expected to be fair, even-handed, respectful, and supportive in their dealings with clients. Each client expects to be heard and understood by the mediator and to be given sufficient time to have his or her say. Conversely, the mediator is not expected to show bias or favoritism, with side taking clearly proscribed and adversarial conduct in language or conduct equally frowned on. In the words of Boulle and Kelly (1998), "Impartiality must be regarded as a core requirement in mediation, in the sense that its absence would fundamentally undermine the nature of the process. It is inconceivable that the parties could waive the requirement that the mediator act fairly" (p. 22).

As to neutrality or disinterestedness, there is growing consensus in the literature that neutrality in any absolute sense is untenable (Balto, 1990; Cobb & Rifkin, 1991; Cooks & Hale, 1994; Kolb & Kressel, 1994), especially in recent years (Cohen, Dattner, & Luxenburg, 1999; McCormick, 1997; Smoron, 1998; Taylor, 1997). Rather, on twin considerations, neutrality will necessarily be situational.

One consideration refers to the authority that inheres in the mediator role. Although the mediation process necessarily involves mutual influence (Bodtker & Jameson, 1997), mediator process control ensures that the interaction is unequal, with mediators invested with the power to shape decision making and thus dispute outcomes. Furthermore, mediators also possess expert power, having much greater substantive knowledge than clients, most of whom will be divorcing for the first time. On both substantive and procedural grounds, then, the power invested in mediators is one that research shows they exercise routinely (Greatbatch & Dingwall, 1994).

The second consideration is that, on moral and ethical grounds, mediators have a responsibility to pursue outcomes that are fair and equitable. Such a pursuit derives not only on principled grounds but also on the need to protect the interests of vulnerable parties not at the table, such as the children (see "Child's Best Interests," above).

Thus, we argue that mediators can and should be prepared to deviate from disinterestedness *as the need arises*. That is, the mediator's willingness to intervene will vary as a function of the parties' functional conduct. For example, so long as parties are exploring proposals about their children that are sensitive to their best interests, the mediator's only commitment is to ensure procedural fairness while otherwise abstaining from any substantive comment or intervention. As parenting proposals become increasingly dysfunctional in relation to the children's best interests, the mediator will feel more and more willing to intervene by advocating for more reasonable and developmentally responsible parenting options.

To fail to intervene on the grounds of neutrality would be to misinterpret the five major roles of family mediation. Rather, the TFM alternative is *focal neutrality,* in which the mediator remains disinterested so long as the couple is doing good work in shaping their agreement; the mediator only intervenes, through some combination of his or her roles, when that is not happening. In effect, the mediator enters into partnership with the clients, their shared goal being to create a settlement that will serve the family well, at least over the short term. In that sense, the mediator enters the system as much or as little as necessary to help clients reach their goals.

Therapeutic Family Mediation: Brief Overview _____

Although available practice models vary in terms of the number of phases (from 3 to 12), they share a linear structure in which clients proceed through the phases in sequence. In contrast, the TFM model, with its systemic roots, is recursive in structure. Thus, Phases 1 to 3 form a series of feedback loops, and clients move back and forth between phases in keeping with the extent to which they can engage in productive negotiation. Detailed exposition of the five phases of the TFM model will be deferred to the next series of chapters. What follows will concentrate instead on a brief overview, with the emphasis on the links between phases as the means to achieve the greatest likelihood of productive negotiation, comprehensive settlement, and agreement durability. For a graphic overview, see Figure 2.1.

Phase 1: Client Assessment

Following self-referral or referral by a lawyer or the court, mediation clients enter the *assessment phase* of family mediation. This usage is somewhat misleading because assessment as an activity and a sensibility is

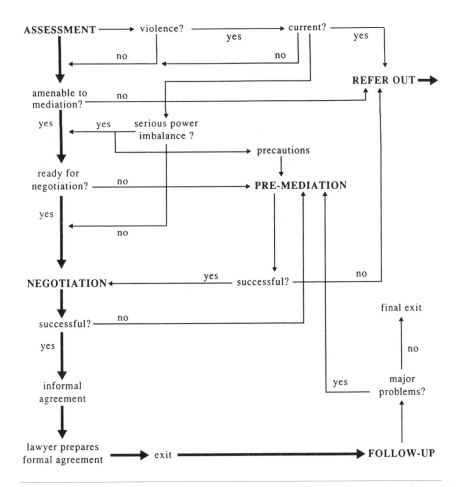

Figure 2.1 Therapeutic Family Mediation: An Overview

ongoing throughout the mediation process. It would, however, be correct to say that assessment is most concentrated in this phase, with two immediate concerns in mind.

The first and most salient concern is the extent to which these clients are amenable to mediation. The following must be answered:

- Does each client have a clear understanding of the issues in dispute?
- Can each client articulate specific proposals regarding these issues?
- Is each client capable of separating marital from parenting issues?
- Can each client control his or her feelings?
- How well or poorly do the clients communicate with each other?
- Can they distinguish between their self-interests and the best interests of the children?
- Can they together negotiate issues to closure?
- Can they together focus on one issue at a time?

- Can they together stay in the present (without repeatedly trying to refight old marital battles)?
- Can they together begin to consider what sort of future they want to create for their family?

If the answer to these and related questions is a clear or at least substantial yes, then they are probably good candidates for family mediation. We say "probably" because the assessment process is ongoing, such that initial evidence of amenability may later prove incorrect as they address specific issues. Conversely, if the answer to these questions is a clear or at least substantial no, then they are poor candidates for mediation *at this time*. Such clients may be referred on for litigation or for short-term therapy, after which they might wish to return to mediation for another assessment. On average, 80% to 90% of the clients we see in private mediation are found amenable for family mediation.

Of these clients, the second concern is whether they should move on to Phase 2, *premediation*, or to Phase 3, *negotiation*. The decision turns on whether there are processes present that would very likely produce an impasse. Such processes include relational dysfunction (such as a high level of uncontrolled conflict), poor affective control (either generally or with regard to specific affectively charged issues), or rigid positions. In such cases, clients would enter Phase 2. In their absence, clients would move on to Phase 3.

Phase 2: Premediation

As noted earlier, premediation presumes that productive negotiation is unlikely at this point, such that any such effort would probably fail. Instead, in this phase, therapeutic methods are applied to prepare clients for negotiation. What distinguishes such efforts from therapy proper is our much more limited goals. Rather than permanent change, our concerns are with change sufficient to allow these clients to fully engage in mediation by being able to negotiate productively.

However, as will shortly be apparent (see "Practice Skills," below), in terms of the methods used, premediation and therapy are very similar. Where they may diverge is in terms of the five major roles of mediation. That is, intervention approaches vary across those roles. As the expert, the mediator may simply impart information aimed at filling in gaps in the clients' knowledge base, including, for example, information concerning the impact of divorce on adults and children. Normalizing the emotional ups and downs commonly associated with divorce may help calm the fears of clients who secretly thought they were going crazy. As the educator, the mediator may teach skills that interfere with productive negotiation, including, for example, skills associated with clear communication. Such weak communication skills may have been a major reason for high conflict levels in some couples. Indeed, in a handful of cases, such skills training has been sufficient to cause couples to reconsider their decision to divorce, moving them from family mediation into family therapy. As the facilitator, the mediator may help each spouse understand the other by clarifying statements, summarizing proposals, or suggesting settlement options. Often, these options will not be particularly new or innovative but merely reflective of the mediator's wide experience with divorcing couples. In contrast, for clients who are getting divorced for the first time, these suggestions may strike them as both new and innovative and may be sufficient to suggest the basis for settlement. As the therapist, the mediator may intervene to block dysfunctional patterns of relating, including, for example, patterns of conflict in which both lack a single issue focus and seldom, if ever, reach resolution. For instance, in one couple, conflict episodes produced such anxiety in both spouses that they lasted less than 3 minutes. Simply instructing them to continue their exploration of a given issue allowed them to reach resolution for the first time in 30 years. Such interventions—some quite simple, others more complex—can be very helpful in increasing the likelihood that negotiation can occur and be productive. Finally, as an advocate, the mediator may challenge prevailing beliefs by one or both spouses, including, for example, the stereotype that women are "too emotional to bargain effectively." Such beliefs foreclose efforts at negotiation soon after they begin. Although changing these belief systems cannot guarantee either productive negotiation or a negotiated settlement, it gives such couples a running start where previously they had no chance at all.

These various intervention efforts do not always succeed, with such couples referred out to litigation, therapy, or some other community resource. In most cases, however, the effort is successful, and the couples move on to Phase 3, negotiation.

Phase 3: Negotiation

In Phase 3, couples are asked to negotiate the issues in dispute on a face-to-face basis. Given their history of failed negotiation, issues are usually arranged so that the least contentious issues are addressed first, with the most contentious issues dealt with last. This arrangement is intended to have them experience success in negotiation and begin filling the trust vacuum that has arisen between them—trust that will be essential when the more difficult issues come to be dealt with.

Throughout this phase, assessment efforts continue. Couples who moved directly from assessment to negotiation may confirm the initial assessment by negotiating all the issues in dispute, thus achieving settlement and then moving on to Phase 4, *termination*. The same may be true of clients who came to negotiation via premediation. However, in some cases, information will come to light suggesting an assessment error: Either the couples prove that they are not amenable to mediation after all and ought to be referred out, or the premediation effort was unsuccessful or, more likely, incomplete and further such effort is required. In this case, couples cycle between pre-mediation and negotiation until they achieve partial or comprehensive set-tlement, or until it becomes clear that settlement is unlikely and any further effort would be unproductive, leading to referral out.

Phase 4: Termination

Termination, then, can occur in one of three ways: Settlement proves impossible, leading to referral out; partial settlement is achieved, leaving some issues clarified but unresolved; or all issues in dispute are resolved, leading to a comprehensive settlement. In the latter two cases, termination then focuses on preparing the written "memorandum of agreement" that will be for-warded to respective counsel for finalization, signing, and inclusion in the court record. These clients will then move on to Phase 5, *follow-up*.

Here, TFM practitioners vary somewhat. In some cases, the mediator pre-pares the "memorandum," based on process notes, having no contact with the client in the process. Others prefer to have the clients draft the text of the memorandum. This serves several purposes: It helps ensure that both spouses have the same clear understanding of the content of their agreement, provides an opportunity to renegotiate issues still in contention, underlines their success in completing this important task, reinforces the point that the spouses have a reasonable deal that they can live with, and, in the end, extends the durability of the agreement over the short term. In either case, production of the memorandum brings the mediation to a formal close.

Phase 5: Follow-Up

The aims of the previous phases are to prepare the clients to negotiate pro-ductively, give them whatever information and skills they need to complete the task, address any relational processes likely to interfere with the negotia-tion process, facilitate negotiation of all issues, and encourage the clients to emerge with a comprehensive agreement. The aims of the follow-up phase, which occurs roughly 6 months after termination, is to evaluate how well or poorly their agreement is functioning and to intervene, if required.

In some cases, the agreement has proven so successful that they decline the follow-up session on the grounds that it would be superfluous. In other cases, follow-up involves a routine review of issues and relationships. This provides the former partners with the opportunity to pinpoint any difficul-ties they might be having in enacting their agreement, but it also provides the chance to celebrate their many small successes, patting them on the back for their persistence, ingenuity, and courage under trying circumstances. In still other cases, more serious difficulties will emerge, and this phase is an opportunity to briefly reenter mediation and thus forestall an impasse that might result in litigation. In all of these cases, follow-up provides an opportunity to reinforce several ideas—namely, that in reaching agreement and avoiding litigation, they have retained responsibility for their affairs, protected their rights, promoted the development of their children, and acquired the skills to deal effectively with any problems that may come up. However, it should also be emphasized that clients can call on the mediator in the unlikely event that the need should arise.

Different Professionals, Different Settings

Finally, application of the TFM practice models extends across different professionals and different settings.

Different Professionals

The professionals who have sought training in TFM distribute across disciplines but, in general, fall into two groups: those with a clinical background (including psychology, social work, and family therapy) and those with a legal background. Each group brings with it specific advantages and disadvantages.

The advantages of students with a clinical background include skill and comfort in the use of clinical intervention techniques, familiarity with many of the topics concerned with assessment, and the ability to step in should clients be willing to move from mediation to family therapy or separation counseling. Commensurate weaknesses include very limited knowledge of family law, some difficulty in being proactive in session, and little experience dealing with the limited time frame and objectives typical of family mediation. In addition, many lack direct experience of families in divorce and so may initially be taken aback by their lability.

The advantages of students with a legal background are that they are comfortable from the start with being proactive, have a thorough knowledge of family law statutes, have excellent negotiation skills, and can shift easily into the role of advocate. Conversely, they must learn intervention skills from the ground up, must relearn many of their interviewing skills, lack knowledge in important areas such as child development, must develop a conception of settlement that goes beyond available statutes and respects client self-determination (within reason), and must refer out when confronted with clients who need family therapy or divorce counseling.

On balance, professionals in both groups experience TFM as equally challenging, although for quite different reasons. With some direct experience under their respective belts, professionals in both groups have equal potential of becoming excellent practitioners.

Different Settings

As to practice settings, TFM has been applied in private practice, social service agencies, and court-based service. Although equally applicable in all three settings, some modifications are required as one moves away from private practice. That is, TFM was originally designed for private use in which there are relatively few time restrictions. In that context, an average of 12 service hours will be required to move clients through the model's first four phases, with an agreement rate of about 80%. However, in difficult cases, time requirements can increase dramatically, to as much as 30 service hours or more.

Agency settings typically involve more restricted time requirements but bring with them advantages of practical support and supervision. Agency settings, then, can provide excellent training opportunities as student move from course completion into the field. Unfortunately, unlike programs in social work or family therapy, few family mediation training programs include a practicum component. Consequently, even though mediation students will be well grounded in the principles and techniques of TFM, they lack direct experience, which agency work can provide.

Finally, the TFM practice model has been applied in a number of court-based settings. These settings impose the most stringent time requirements, typically limiting the practitioner to a total of 9 hours or less of service time. This leaves less time for assessment and puts the emphasis on negotiation. Even so, the therapeutic sensibility that TFM students bring to this setting has served them well. That is, although the likelihood of settlement is only slightly higher than mediation using ADR-based models, the range of issues dealt with tends to be much higher in TFM-based service, as is the durability of TFM-based settlements.

Discussion

In overview, this chapter serves to display the flexibility of the TFM practice model, the opportunities for change and agreements it offers clients, and the demands it makes on clients and mediators. As we have seen, mediators are expected to remain current across a range of substantive topics touching on family life and family law, be knowledgeable about developments across 12 theoretical topics, achieve a basic grounding in systems theory, and demonstrate mastery of at least 30 practice skills distributed across four clinical tasks. As if this were not enough—indeed, more than enough—students who seek training in the TFM model may originate from widely disparate disciplines and be expected to apply their expertise and knowledge across a range of practice settings. Following Barsky (2000), these various requirements suggest that TFM practitioners must become "reflective" practitioners—thoughtful, caring, and sensitive but also well rounded, knowledgeable, and highly expert—rather than merely qualified technicians.

These demands on TFM practitioners are, in turn, visited on their clients. Clients are told at the outset that application of this practice model intentionally goes well beyond simple problem solving to address underlying relational concerns and problems. Although this approach is rationalized on the basis of effectiveness and durability, its extra demands may be sufficient to dissuade some clients. For the majority who persist, the demands it makes correspond to the advantages it offers. In keeping with client variation, in the process of achieving settlement, clients may also acquire new communication and other relational skills, discover ways of resolving conflict, gain a better understanding of underlying relational issues, be informed of various matters relevant to their circumstances, and receive a great deal of support. The result is that TFM practitioners not only tend to experience a high settlement rate but can have confidence that few of these agreements are likely to break down, at least over the short term (6-12 months).

References

Balto, B. (1990). Mediator directiveness in child custody mediation: An exploration of alternatives and decision making. *Mediation Quarterly, 7*(3), 215-227.

Barsky, A. E. (2000). *Conflict resolution for the helping professions.* Belmont, CA: Brooks/Cole.

Bartholomew, K., & Horowitz, L. (1991). Attachment styles among young adults. *Journal of Personality & Social Psychology, 61,* 226-244.

Bateson, G. (1972). *Steps to an ecology of mind.* New York: Ballantine.

Bateson, G. (1979). *Mind and nature: A necessary unity.* New York: Dutton.

Benjamin, M., & Irving, H. H. (1992). Towards a feminist-informed model of therapeutic family mediation. *Mediation Quarterly, 10*(2), 129-153.

Benjamin, R. D. (1995a). The constructive uses of deception: Skills, strategies, and techniques of the folkloric trickster figure and their application by mediators. *Mediation Quarterly, 13*(1), 3-18.

Benjamin, R. D. (1995b). The mediator as trickster: The folkloric figure as professional role model. *Mediation Quarterly, 13*(2), 131-149.

Blume, T. W. (1993). Update on systemic practice. *Mediation Quarterly, 11*(2), 195-197.

Bodtker, A. M., & Jameson, J. K. (1997). Mediation as mutual influence: Reexamining the use of framing and reframing. *Mediation Quarterly, 14*(3), 237-249.

Boulle, L., & Kelly, K. J. (1998). *Mediation: Principles, process, practice* (Canadian ed.). Toronto: Butterworths.

Bowlby, J. (1969). *Attachment and loss: Vol. 1. Attachment.* London: Pelican.

Breslin, J., & Rubin, J. (Eds.). (1995). *Negotiating theory & practice.* Cambridge, MA: Program on Negotiation, Harvard Law School.

Burr, W. R., Hill, R., Nye, F. I., & Reiss, I. L. (Eds.). (1979). *Contemporary theories about the family: Research-based theories* (Vol. 1). New York: Free Press.

Cobb, S., & Rifkin, J. (1991). Practice and paradox: Deconstructing neutrality in mediation. *Law & Society, 16*(1), 201-227.

Cohen, O., Dattner, N., & Luxenburg, A. (1999). The limits of the mediator's neutrality. *Mediation Quarterly, 16*(4), 341-348.

Cooks, L. M., & Hale, C. L. (1994). The construction of ethics in mediation. *Mediation Quarterly, 12*(1), 55-76.

Deutsch, M. (1973). *The resolution of conflict: Constructive and destructive processes.* New Haven, CT: Yale University Press.

Deutsch, M. (1991). *Education for a peaceful world.* Amherst, MA: National Association for Mediation in Education.

Favaloro, G. J. (1998). Mediation: A family therapy technique? *Mediation Quarterly, 16*(1), 101-108.

Fisher, R., Ury, W., & Patton, B. (1991). *Getting to yes: Negotiating agreement without giving in* (2nd ed.). New York: Penguin.

Folger, J. P., & Jones, T. S. (Eds.). (1994). *New directions in mediation: Communication research and perspectives.* Thousand Oaks, CA: Sage.

Goldberger, L., & Breznitz, S. (Eds.). (1993). *Handbook of stress: Theoretical and clinical aspects* (2nd ed.). New York: Free Press.

Goldberger, N., Tarule, J., Clinchy, B., & Belenky, M. (Eds.). (1996). *Knowledge, difference, and power: Women's ways of knowing.* New York: Basic Books.

Gottman, J. M. (1979). *Marital interaction: Experimental investigations.* New York: Academic Press.

Gottman, J. M. (1994). *What predicts divorce? The relationship between marital processes and marital outcomes.* Hillsdale, NJ: Lawrence Erlbaum.

Gottman, J., Coan, J., Carrere, S., & Swenson, C. (1998). Predicting marital happiness and stability from newlywed interactions. *Journal of Marriage & Family, 60* (1), 5-22.

Greatbatch, D., & Dingwall, R. (1994). The interactive construction of interventions by divorce mediators. In J. P. Folger & T. S. Jones (Eds.), *New directions in mediation: Communication research and perspectives* (pp. 84-109). Thousand Oaks, CA: Sage.

Hernstein, B. H. (1996). Women and mediation: A chance to speak and be heard. *Mediation Quarterly, 13*(3), 229-241.

Irving, H. H., & Benjamin, M. (1995). *Family mediation: Contemporary issues.* Thousand Oaks, CA: Sage.

Johnson, S., & Lebow, J. (2000). The "coming of age" of couple therapy: A decade review. *Journal of Marital & Family Therapy, 26*(1), 23-38.

Johnston, J., & Campbell, L. E. G. (1988). *Impasses of divorce: The dynamics and resolution of family conflict.* New York: Free Press.

Johnston, J., & Campbell, L. E. G. (1993). A clinical typology of interpersonal violence in disputes in child custody divorces. *American Journal of Orthopsychiatry, 63*(2), 190-199.

Katz, D., & Kahn, R. L. (1966). *The social psychology of organization*. New York: John Wiley.

Kelly, J. B. (1997). The best interests of the child: A concept in search of meaning. *Family & Conciliation Courts Review, 35*(4), 377-387.

Kolb, D. M., & Kressel, K. (1994). Practical realities in making talk work. In D. M. Kolb (Ed.), *When talk works: Profiles of working mediators* (pp. 69-80). San Francisco: Jossey-Bass.

Lichtenstein, M. (2000). Mediation and feminism: Common values and challenges. *Mediation Quarterly, 18*(1), 19-32.

McCormick, M. A. (1997). Confronting social injustice in a mediation. *Mediation Quarterly, 14*(4), 293-307.

McGoldrick, M., Anderson, C. M., & Walsh, F. (Eds.). (1989). *Women in families: A framework for family therapy*. New York: Norton.

Mikulincer, M., Florian, V., & Wesler, A. (1993). Attachment styles, coping strategies and post traumatic psychological distress. *Journal of Personality & Social Psychology, 64*, 817-826.

Nichols, M. P., & Schwartz, R. C. (1998). *Family therapy: Concepts and methods* (4th ed.). Boston: Allyn & Bacon.

Patterson, J. M. (1989). A family stress model: The family adjustment and adaptation response. In C. N. Ramsey, Jr. (Ed.), *Family systems in medicine* (pp. 95-118). New York: Guilford.

Roberts, M. (1992). Systems or selves? Some ethical issues in family mediation. *Mediation Quarterly, 10*(1), 3-19.

Schwebel, A. I., Gately, D. W., Milburn, T. W., & Renner, M. A. (1993). PMI-DM: A divorce mediation approach that first addresses interpersonal issues. *Journal of Family Psychotherapy, 4*(2), 69-90.

Smoron, K. A. (1998). Conflicting roles in child custody mediation: Impartiality/neutrality and the best interests of the child. *Family & Conciliation Courts Review, 36*(2), 258-280.

Taylor, A. (1997). Concepts of neutrality in family mediation: Contexts, ethics, influence, and transformative process. *Mediation Quarterly, 14*(3), 215-236.

von Bertalanffy, L. (1950). An outline of general system theory. *British Journal of the Philosophy of Science, 1*, 139-164.

von Bertalanffy, L. (1968). *General system theory: Foundations, development, applications* (Rev. ed.). New York: Braziller.

von Bertalanffy, L. (1975). *Perspectives on general systems theory: Scientific-philosophical studies* (E. Taschdjian, ed.). New York: Braziller.

Walsh, F. (Ed.). (1993). *Normal family process* (2nd ed.). New York: Guilford.

3 Family Mediation Practice Skills

Established professions, such as medicine and law, involve a set of practice skills about which there is consensus and an elaborate curriculum to ensure mastery. In a developing profession such as family mediation, this is not the case. There is little consensus about what constitutes an appropriate set of practice skills. Worse, of the texts we consulted in preparing this volume, few provided a list of practice skills, and even fewer described such skills in any detail (see Barsky, 2000, pp. 45-51, 149-157; Boulle & Kelly, 1998, pp. 163-196). It would appear that many authors in family mediation simply assume that practitioners know and have mastered the requisite practice skills and therefore are content to reserve their descriptions for the process itself (Folberg & Taylor, 1984; Landau, Wolfson, Landau, Bartoletti, & Mesbur, 2000; Leviton & Greenstone, 1997; Moore, 1996).

In contrast, in our experience, although many students have some or most of the requisite skills, few have integrated them into a family mediation context, and even fewer have attempted to apply such skills to mediation clients. Listing and describing these practice skills in detail, then, will benefit practitioners, especially given the five roles that they will be expected to enact in the therapeutic family mediation (TFM) practice model. Accordingly, as set out in Table 3.1, this chapter will focus on 32 practice skills organized in four task-related clusters. We will also explore the comediation option.

Connecting With Clients

Family mediation can be a difficult, trying, and emotionally demanding process. For clients to stick with the process and resist the temptation to drop out, it is crucial that they feel connected to the mediator. That is, it is crucial that clients trust that he or she understands them and their situation

Table 3.1 Mediation Practice Skills

Connecting with clients (7 skills)
- Listening (active)
- Normalizing
- Questioning
- Clarifying
- Summarizing
- Supporting
- Interpreting

Maintaining control (9 skills)
- Explaining rules and procedures
- Choosing who has the floor
- Listing standards of practice
- Blocking disruptive behavior
- Defining and selecting issues for discussion
- Moving between joint sessions and individual caucusing
- Maintaining a safe environment
- Terminating sessions/service
- Referring out to an appropriate source

Making informed choices (5 skills)
- Exploring underlying needs, interests, and expectations
- Stating professional biases
- Teaching new/enhanced skills
- Informing by adding to their knowledge base
- Reality testing (re: BATNA)

Intervening (11 skills)
- Maintaining a solution-oriented focus
- Generating options and suggesting trade-offs
- Defining and narrowing issues
- Role enactment
- Reframing
- Identifying/summarizing areas/issues of agreement
- Balancing power
- Storytelling
- Using metaphor
- Preempting
- Confronting

Comediation option

Total skills: 32

and is fair and evenhanded, competent and knowledgeable, and the sort of person to whom they would be willing to cede authority over the mediation process. Creating and sustaining such feelings of trust and connection require practitioners who have mastered at least seven skills, including active listening, normalizing, questioning, clarifying, summarizing, supporting, and interpreting.

First, perhaps the most fundamental of these skills involves *active listening*, for at the heart of every situation, there are at least two and more often several stories. Hearing those stories, with all their nuances, feelings, and multiple layers of meaning, is at the heart of connecting with clients and is one of the key bases on which clients come to trust and rely on the mediator. Without that trust, it is a highly likely that these clients will drop out the moment things become difficult in mediation.

Second, clients often come to mediation with the mistaken belief that their experience in divorce is unique and therefore one that no one else can possibly understand, including the mediator. *Normalizing* is the mediator's way of giving the client several interrelated messages, among them that their experience, though unique in particular ways, is similar to that of many families undergoing divorce; their emotional ups and downs do *not* mean they are going crazy but rather are typical of the divorce process they are currently undergoing; and the mediator is sensitive to their needs, having assisted many other families in a similar situation. In short, normalizing acknowledges the clients' unique experience while linking it to the similar experience of other divorcing families. Thus, normalizing encourages the development of trust in the mediator-client relationship while reassuring clients that they will survive this ordeal.

Third, it is not always easy for clients to tell their story, remember to include all relevant details, clearly articulate a set of proposals, examine the pros and cons of each proposal, and so on. The mediator helps clients to achieve these objectives by *questioning* them. In doing so, it should be acknowledged that questions can have a variety of functions, including the following:

1. Getting information (On what date did your spouse move out of the house?)

2. Identifying objectives or concerns (What would it take for you to feel secure in your relationship with your children?)

3. Exploring options (What, if any, are the possibilities of a reconciliation between you and your partner?)

4. Showing concern, support, and empathy (Discovering that your husband was unfaithful must have been very painful for you.)

5. Doing reality testing (How much do you think you would get for your house if you sold it now?)

6. Exploring in detail a tentative parenting plan (Exactly what sort of time-sharing plan would be practical given your respective work schedules?)

The diverse functions enacted through questioning help make clear just how important questioning is in mediation. That importance suggests a distinction between good and poor question construction. In general, questions should be short, specific, and clear in form, as well as nonjudgmental, evenhanded, and sympathetic in tone. That is, they should convey a genuine interest in understanding the client's point of view and should assume (unless the evidence indicates otherwise) that the client's involvement in mediation is intended to resolve the issues in dispute. By contrast, poor questions tend to be long and rambling, lack clarity, touch on two or more topics at once, and contain elements of the answer (leading questions), and they may be judgmental, biased in favor of one spouse, or harsh and unsympathetic in tone. Good questioning should be complemented by body language that projects openness and acceptance as opposed to closure or rejection and includes steady eye contact and close reading of the clients' verbal and nonverbal responses. Good questioning skills, then, require both training and experience. The consequences of poor questioning skills are an incomplete or distorted picture of the case and an increased likelihood that the client will simply drop out.

Fourth, the emotionally charged character of the divorce process can easily interfere with the clients' efforts to provide a coherent account of their situation. *Clarifying*, then, involves a variety of skills that the mediator can use to help the client be coherent. One of these skills, questioning, has already been noted. Other skills involve developing illustrative examples, using analogies and metaphors (see below), providing instructions that focus on one issue at a time, using a linear time line, separating behavior from feelings, and distinguishing between "you" and "I" statements. In short, clarifying skills involve helping the client communicate clearly, both with the mediator and, as important, with the partner. This task can be more difficult than it first appears if confused or fuzzy communication reflects a dysfunctional pattern of interaction involving both partners. Here, clarifying goes much beyond specific instances and involves a major intervention intended to teach clients the fundamentals of clear communication. Blocking interruptions, showing patience in allowing the client time to tell his or her story, and asking clarifying questions, for example, can yield revelations that are as much a surprise to the client telling the story as to the partner hearing it.

Fifth, although clients may tell their story as completely as they know how, they may still provide an account in which key points are scattered throughout their narrative. *Summarizing* is one way the mediator can help clients be clear. This skill involves pulling together these various points in one clear statement (So what I hear you saying so far is . . . one, two, three.). Such a summary assists in moving the client to the next step in the process, and it also proves to the client that the mediator has been attending closely to what he or she has been saying. Such attendance can be very satisfying for clients who may have felt chronically unheard or misunderstood by their partner and helps promote a sense of connection between the client and mediator. Note, however, that the fact that the mediator can summarize the client's perspective is not the same as saying that the mediator necessarily accepts this account at face value. Rather, depending on his or her objective(s), the mediator can point out contradictions in the summary or use the summary to suggest underlying processes or hidden issues to which the client has not explicitly referred. In short, summarizing can be a simple mechanical process to aid client clarity, or it can be much more than that.

Sixth, the process of divorce can be extremely stressful and difficult. One of the things that makes it so is that it often involves doing many things at once, including changes in child care, housing, community, self-image, and so on. Clients will often report feeling overburdened and completely alone. Even when support is abundant, clients may still feel that no one *really* understands what they are going through. Here, the mediator may be in a unique position to provide *support*, having previously dealt with tens, hundreds, or even thousands of divorcing families over the years. Just knowing that someone else truly understands what the clients are going through can be an important source of emotional support. Providing such clients with an outlet—someone to talk to and with whom to explore options, plans, expectations, and the like—can be vital to their emotional stability and thus their ability to go through the mediation process. The mediator's capacity for empathy, warmth, and sensitivity, then, is an important skill that helps create a strong bond between the two.

Finally, try as they might, many clients are just not clear in their own mind as to exactly what they are trying to convey to the mediator. They may be trying to express feelings they do not normally put into words. They may be trying to understand concepts that are foreign to them. Whatever the case, their efforts to express themselves may be inadequate or incomplete. Here, the mediator's efforts to understand take the form of an *interpretation* (I think what you're trying to say is . . .) that puts into words what the client cannot. When the mediator gets it right, there is a leap of recognition on the part of the clients, who are typically grateful for the release and satisfied that the mediator has made this effort on their behalf. As in questioning, the mediator's interpretations assure the clients that they have been heard. Indeed, such is the case even when the mediator gets it wrong and must try again, for at least he or she is trying to understand, and that alone is seen by clients as important. Finally, there are instances in which the interpretation moves beyond what the clients have said to what the mediator thinks are implicit in their words, to some underlying thought or insight. On one hand, such efforts promote a strong connection between the mediator and the client. On the other hand, such efforts mark the point at which, as therapists, practitioners following the TFM model diverge from those following other models. TFM gives the mediator license to advance such interpretations and to pursue them in the effort to uncover processes that are otherwise hidden from view—even outside the client's awareness—and that may be salient to the ongoing conflict.

Combining narrative and solution-oriented perspectives, the interplay between clients and the mediator involves the co-construction of the client's story or narrative within a larger "solution" frame. The client's original version often suggests that the dispute is intractable, typically due to the character and/or behavior of the other partner. The revised version, co-constructed with the mediator, involves a reformulation in which the dispute is redefined as a joint or common problem ("how both parents can contribute to and ensure the future well-being of their children") and then rendered "solvable" through cooperative negotiation (see Phillips, 1999).

Maintaining Control

Without exception, clients tell of having tried long and hard to resolve their differences informally, between themselves, and failed. The latter can be explained in a variety of ways, but salient among them is their inability to engage in an orderly process of negotiation, one that both partners regard as fair and equitable and in which they both feel safe and secure. Mediation thus imposes on the parties what they themselves cannot create or maintain— namely, a process of negotiation that is orderly, fair, and equitable and in which both parties have the same opportunity to tell their story in a safe environment. To achieve these ends requires that the mediator exercise at least *nine* related skills.

The first skill involves having the mediator explain the rules and procedures he or she intends to follow in simple, straightforward terms. Such explanations typically make reference to some or all of the following:

(a) An overview of the entire process within TFM
(b) The purposes of TFM-based family mediation
(c) The rights and responsibilities of the parties, including their right to have their say, place on the table any issues they wish to pursue, and be treated fairly and with respect
(d) The rights and responsibilities of the mediator, including his or her responsibility to control the mediation process
(e) The principles that underpin the process, including client self-determination, confidentiality, and impartiality, and our bias favoring the child's or children's best interests
(f) The sorts of conduct that are to be avoided, including shouting, swearing, interrupting, accusing, belittling, threatening, intimidating, and acting violently
(g) The fee schedule
(h) The mediation contract
(i) The difference between the parenting plan, the financial plan, and the memorandum of understanding

The explanation of the rules sets the stage for clients who typically do not know what to expect either in mediation or from the mediator. It sets up realistic expectations and makes clear that the mediator is in charge of the process, whereas the clients are in charge of the content, at least within reason. This explanation is then followed with a written contract that sets out many of the same terms and conditions.

The next practice skill involves *choosing who has the floor*, that is, indicating who may talk and for how long. For some, this may appear intrusive and insensitive. In fact, it is a necessary exercise of authority because in the absence of such control, client interaction often breaks down into the sort of squabbling that defeated their informal effort to resolve their differences. By controlling floor time, the mediator ensures an orderly process in which both parties have the same opportunity to tell their story. Such equality will often be quite at odds with their "normal" way of managing conflict, in which one party, typically the husband, is dominant, whereas the other party, typically the wife, feels under the other's control and unable to speak freely. In this sense, having the mediator in control can be a liberating experience and both rewarding and anxiety provoking at the same time. In most cases, such control is routine; the mediator simply behaves *as if* he or she has the authority to do so, and client compliance is automatic. However, there are exceptions in which one or both parties challenge the mediator's control, in which case the mediator must adopt a more assertive approach, reaffirming control over the process. In more extreme cases (see below and Chapters 5 and 6), still other measures may be required, up to and including termination.

Another approach to control involves having the mediator *list his or her standards of practice*. This aids in control by lending credibility to the mediator's statements and by making clear that the mediator knows what he or she is doing and deserves the clients' respect and compliance. One variation on this theme is provided by the following "clients' bill of rights" (Allen & Mohr, 1998, p. 146):

(a) You have the right to make fully-informed, completely voluntary, decisions.

(b) You have the right to take as much time as you need, in order to make decisions that will work for you and your children in the long run.

(c) You have the right to leave mediation any time, if the process is not working for you.

(d) You have the right to know the mediator's fees, before you begin.

(e) You have the right to be treated with respect, by the mediator, as well as the [other] participants.

(f) You have the right to be assisted by a mediator who is neutral and uninvested in the outcome of your dispute, and who has no stake in the terms of your settlement or in whether or not your case settles.

(g) You have the right to get outside legal advice at any time during the mediation.

(h) You have the right, in divorce mediation, to full disclosure from your spouse on all financial issues.

On one hand, such instructions suggest that the mediator is a person of integrity and character who is committed to certain standards of ethical practice. On the other hand, it makes abundantly clear who is in charge of the mediation process.

A related aspect of control involves *blocking disruptive behavior*. Across clients in mediation, disruptive behavior varies on a continuum of severity. At the extreme end, the practitioner will encounter behavior that makes productive negotiation simply impossible. A typical example of such conduct is uncontrolled conflict, with both parties shouting at each other at the same time. Slightly less problematic is behavior in which one spouse repeatedly interrupts the other or makes disparaging remarks. Less disruptive still is conduct that is not so much provocative as distracting or annoying, such as the party who cannot sit still, rattles keys, or repeatedly expels air noisily while looking at the ceiling. Such descriptions could be extended indefinitely, but what they have in common is that they divert the couple from the issue at hand and their intention to resolve their differences about it. As varied as such behavior is, the mediator's attempts to block it may be equally varied and innovative. Parties may be reminded of the initial instructions and their agreement to abide by them. The mediator may be assertive in insisting that each party has an equal right to tell his or her story as he or she sees fit and without interruption. The mediator may confront the behavior as inappropriate to the context or may repeatedly remind the offending party or parties to attend to the task at hand. The mediator may interpret the conduct as part of some larger dysfunctional process and intervene to uncover its underlying roots. As noted below, the mediator may elect to shift from a joint session to an individual caucus, where he or she may admonish the offending party that the conduct must stop if mediation is to proceed, or the mediator may insist that one party apologize to the other for making offensive remarks. Finally, the mediator may terminate the session entirely, noting that multiple repeats of this disruptive behavior will place the mediation process itself in jeopardy. Irrespective of the specific maneuver, it should be clear that unless and until the mediator can regain and maintain control of the process, he or she simply cannot be effective in any roles and may as well terminate the process.

Another aspect of process control involves having the mediator *select and define the issues for discussion*. Having the mediator select the order in which the issues are to be discussed is typically rationalized as giving the couple the opportunity to succeed where before they had repeatedly failed. As noted already, this usually means addressing the minor and less contentious issues first and leaving the bigger and most contentious issues for later. At the same time, this selection process is another means by which the mediator asserts his or her control over the process. The logic underlying the definition of the issues is related but less obvious. Put simply, clients' definitions of the substantive issues are often negative and tend to incite conflict. For example, a husband may define a property division task as having his spouse "give me the pension money that I earned by my hard work." Similarly, a wife may define a parenting task as "caring for the children that he never cared about while we were married." Clearly, both approaches to defining the task are highly judgmental and thus likely to generate an equally critical response, in keeping with the ongoing conflict the couple brought with them into mediation. The more useful alternative is for the mediator to provide a definition conducive to cooperative problem solving. Examples might include "sharing the assets that you accumulated together" or "deciding how you can best express your shared responsibility for child care."

Such definitions not only move the parties in a more appropriate direction but also reaffirm the mediator's right to define the issues and control the process. Note, however, that in so doing, the mediator has highlighted the arbitrary character of the distinction between content and process. Whereas some mediators treat the distinction as absolute (Haynes, 1992), the above example demonstrates that the mediators' need for control forces their involvement in both process and content. That is, by defining the problem, the mediator has necessarily begun to shape the range of possible outcomes or solutions.

Above, we touched on another control maneuver—namely, *moving between joint sessions and individual caucusing*. Here, individual caucusing may refer either to a time-out period during a joint session or entire sessions, first with one party and then with the other. In the previous example, we alluded to shifting to individual caucusing as a way of controlling conflict. This maneuver can also serve other functions. For example, caucusing may be used to give the parties a break from a grueling session, address one or both parties' intense feelings, clarify the underlying basis for conflict around a particular issue, or give one or both parties some needed support. These examples have three things in common—namely, that shifting contexts is intended to advance the mediation process in some way, enhances the clients' trust in the mediator's professional expertise, and reinforces their control over the mediation process.

A variation of the theme of control concerns the mediator's efforts to *maintain a physically safe and psychologically secure environment* for both parties. The need for safety and security underscores several features of the mediation process, including the equality of the parties, their ability to negotiate productively, and the likelihood that their efforts will yield an outcome that is fair and equitable. In all cases, these objectives would be compromised should one or both parties feel unsafe. Indeed, such logic extends also to mediators because their effectiveness would be compromised in a similar fashion if they too did not feel safe. Maneuvers used to maintain safety and security will vary as a function of the sources of threat. Threats to safety and security may be countered in ways that are limited only by the mediators' imagination and the limitations of their physical circumstances. By way of useful examples, the mediator may stagger the parties' arrival and departures times, sit between the parties throughout all joint sessions, shuttle between the parties seated in different rooms, shift to an in-session caucus at the first sign of difficulty, behave in an authoritarian fashion in emphasizing prohibitions against violence or intimidation, or allow one party (typically the wife) to be accompanied by another person who provides moral and other forms of support. Selection of these and other maneuvers is the choice of the mediator, thus highlighting his or her control over the process.

These efforts to maintain safety and security may and often do succeed, thus allowing for a process that is fair and equitable. In a minority of cases, however, they do not succeed, and the mediator may then be forced to *terminate the session or the service.* Termination is the ultimate expression of the mediator's control of the process. Termination of the session may occur for positive or negative reasons. Positive reasons include the emergence of new facts or proposals that require careful consideration, some breakthrough in understanding, or some agreement but with little time or energy left in the session to pursue any new issue(s). The main negative reason for session termination is that one or both clients have failed to comply with the mediator's control efforts. However, other negative reasons include lack of progress in negotiation, the emergence of an impasse, or evidence of some underlying process that requires a return to premediation. Whatever the specific reason(s), session termination reaffirms the mediator's control over the process and signals the need for clients to rethink their commitment to mediation in general, their willingness to consider other alternatives (including litigation), and their interests with respect to a specific issue. Should session termination occur with regularity, especially if it results from client noncompliance, then negative termination of the service would need to be seriously considered. This sort of termination typically signals an assessment error, with clients who were judged amenable to mediation having turned out not to be so. Such errors should not be discounted because they represent valuable learning opportunities. Of course, the alternative is positive termination occasioned by a partial or complete settlement, and this should be seen as a tribute both to client motivation and flexibility, as well as to practitioner skill and perseverance.

Finally, practitioner control over the process may be reflected in the decision to *refer the client out to an appropriate source.* Although there are a variety of reasons for such referrals, all fall into one of two categories. The first category concerns unfinished business, including continuing attachment or deep enmity. In either case, such feelings are clearly dysfunctional because they involve remaining connected to a person from whom one is getting divorced. Failure to address such connections can have dire consequences for the family, as conflict can be ongoing for years, if not decades, blocking the spouses from fully engaging new partners and placing the children at risk into the bargain. Although such processes can be identified in mediation and partly addressed in TFM, only divorce counseling can lay such feelings to rest permanently, hence the referral out, with counseling to run concurrently or following mediation termination.

The other reason for referral out derives from an impasse in mediation. In such cases, an assessment error is implied, for these are couples who were simply not ready to negotiate productively and thus not amenable *at that time* for family mediation. In some cases, clients may be referred back to their lawyer and then to litigation, or they may be referred for marital therapy, after which they may be reassessed for mediation. In either case, referral out signals the termination of mediation, a decision that is typically made by the mediator as a final marker of his or her control over the process.

Making Informed Choices

Pursuant to their roles as expert and educator, the third task of mediators is to ensure that clients *make informed choices*. Enacting this task requires mastery of at least five practice skills.

The first of these skills involves *exploring underlying needs, interests, and expectations*. Clients come to the mediator prepared to tell their story. That account can often be incomplete, confused as to the sequence of events, and unclear as to their underlying concerns, interests, or needs. For example, a wife may be eloquent as to her desire to get back at her philandering spouse, but this account leaves unsaid that she is quite insecure about the future now that he is finally gone. Her unstated need, then, is to arrive at a financial settlement that will secure the future for herself and her children. Similarly, a husband may expound at length at the many and varied faults of his wife but leave unsaid that he is quite insecure about the future character of his relationship with the children. His unstated need, then, is to arrive at a parenting plan that will secure that relationship in a form and with a frequency that is comfortable for him and that meets the developmental needs of the children.

Similar reasoning applies to their respective expectations regarding a host of related matters. For example, one or both spouses may have little knowledge about family law (e.g., the status of the matrimonial home), the tax implications of any possible financial settlement, and the differences between sole and shared parenting, which may result in correspondingly unrealistic expectations about the content of any future settlement.

By being able to discriminate between the clients' positions and interests, their wants and needs, and their realistic and unrealistic expectations, the mediator makes them subject to discussion, debate, correction, or revision. In so doing, the mediator advances the mediation process by increasing the likelihood that future client decisions will be realistic and informed and thus involve goals that are achievable.

A related aspect of helping clients make informed choices includes being clear about one's own *professional biases*. Such self-revelation at the beginning of the process will help prevent misunderstandings later and reduce the likelihood that clients will perceive the mediator as favoring one client over the other. The nature of one's professional biases will vary widely across practitioners. Some biases, such as client self-determination, are germane to the field, but others, such as impartiality, may reflect adherence to one or another practice model. Still other biases may be more personal, such as a preference for or an avoidance of cases involving violence or infidelity.

Having discussed practice principles above, little would be served by repeating that discussion here as regards TFM. More important is the notion that it is reasonable for mediators to have biases so long as they are transparent to the clients, who can elect or refuse service on that basis. Indeed, in the intake interview, it would not be uncommon for clients to report seeking a mediator with one or another bias. Female clients, for example, often prefer a mediator who is "pro-feminist," whereas male clients often prefer a mediator who is "father friendly." Whatever the biases in question, making them transparent to the clients is key to their informed choices. For example, in TFM, we routinely report to clients that we are both pro-feminist and father friendly and are clearly biased in favor of the best interests of children, up to and including advocating for them if necessary.

A related skill involves *teaching clients new and enhanced skills* relevant to mediation. Clients may be heir to a host of problems and difficulties. Some of these problems will be addressed and perhaps resolved through negotiation. Others will be such that they actively interfere with negotiation and thus *must* be addressed if mediation is to proceed with any hope of resolution. Problems with communication are a case in point because communication is fundamental to the entire mediation process. Skill deficits in this area not only contribute to the dysfunctional ways in which clients attempt to negotiate but also help explain their relational dysfunction in the first place. Efforts to ameliorate these deficits may take place over one or more sessions and may involve one or both spouses (depending on the problem).

In one case, for example, a client couple presented with a conflict style in which issues were never resolved. Failure to resolve, in turn, generated not only a host of issues in conflict but also a great deal of frustration and resentment, with each client accusing the other of having a personality disorder. Having witnessed this process several times, the mediator intervened to prolong the discussion because premature termination was at the root of their problem. The result was resolution of a relatively minor issue. For the couple, however, it was a revelation because this was the first time they could recall resolving an issue together in more than 30 years of marriage. Other similar instructions regarding clear communication so changed the tone of the interaction that they seriously considered dropping out of mediation and entering marital therapy. In the end, they decided to carry on with their divorce and completed mediation with a generous settlement with which both parties were very satisfied. The more general point is that teaching clients the skills they need can dramatically enhance the mediation effort, sharply increasing the likelihood of settlement. As important, new and enhanced communication skills may carry on long after mediation is over, providing them with resources they can use later to negotiate the changes that their agreement will inevitably need over the long term.

In a related vein, *informing clients*—that is, giving clients information that they need in areas in which they are ignorant—can have similar benefits. Such information may apply to virtually any aspect of mediation, including, for example, family law, child development, financial principles, tax principles, and so on. Moreover, that information may take various forms (e.g., books, pamphlets, videotapes, tape recordings, oral presentations), and although they will typically be provided by the mediator, alternatives are also available by referral to various outside experts, including the clients' own lawyer. Because we routinely provide information to clients in mediation, we have developed short "canned" lectures on a number of topics. More generally, it is essential that clients make informed choices and decisions because much will hang in the balance, not only about themselves but also about their children. It therefore behooves the mediator to ensure that his or her clients have access to all the information they are likely to need to make the decisions that are necessary to secure their best interests, the best interests of the children, and the best interests of their larger family system.

Finally, in the interests of decisions that are realistic, a related skill involves *reality testing*, or what others would refer to as the clients' best alternative to a negotiated agreement (BATNA). With respect to child access and custody, reality testing calls on the mediator's knowledge of recent court decisions, the developmental requirements of children by age and gender, and past experience of the sorts of arrangements that have proved practical as opposed to impractical. For example, it is commonplace for a father to demand a 50% share of the child's time despite the fact that he works a 40-hour week and the mother is not employed. Similarly, a mother may attempt to severely restrict the father's access to the child despite numerous court rulings to the contrary. Raising these issues helps clients realize what is likely to occur if they do *not* settle through mediation but try to achieve their objectives through litigation.

This is not to say that clients will always do what is in their best interests or those of their children; feelings can run so high or their dysfunction is so severe that they may behave nonrationally despite the mediator's warnings. In cases of parental alienation, for example, parents may convince themselves that they are acting for their children when all the evidence before the mediator points to the contrary—namely, that their conduct is harmful. Indeed, on many occasions, children in this situation have told us how much they miss the other parent while cautioning that they cannot say that to the resident parent as it would hurt him or her very much. Similarly, the mediator's reality testing may reveal that the financial proposal being advanced is wildly unrealistic in light of recent court rulings, only to have the client seek satisfaction through litigation. These examples, however, are more the exception than the rule. The typical example is one in which, in the face of the mediator's reality testing efforts, the client is forced to rethink his or her objectives, thus increasing the likelihood of reaching a settlement that is fair and equitable. For example, in a recent case, a mother was livid at her husband's blatant infidelity. Accordingly, she proposed that his contact with their son, then age 2, be limited to two afternoons per month. Further questioning revealed that father and son had a very close relationship in which the father put the son to bed every night. When the mother was asked to describe in detail what would happen to the son if his father suddenly disappeared for 2 weeks at a time, she burst into tears. In caucus, she acknowledged that the access schedule was designed to punish the father for the pain he had caused her, but she had not thought through what effect it would have on the child. In subsequent discussions between sessions, the parents decided to drop out of mediation and enter marital therapy instead, in the hope of reconciliation.

Intervening

Pursuant to their roles as facilitator and therapist, the fourth and final task of mediators is to *intervene* as needed, either to block or otherwise alter conduct or patterns of relating that interfere with productive negotiation or to advance the process by introducing new ideas and maintaining a level playing field. Enacting this task requires mastery of at least 11 practice skills.

The essence of negotiation in mediation involves defining issues in dispute as shared problems that are solvable through cooperative negotiation. The most generic of the mediator's practice skills, then, is that of *maintaining a solution-oriented focus*. The ease with which this is done is directly related to the couples' level of interactional dysfunction. Severe dysfunction is typically associated with a diffuse communication style that erratically blends past and present, thoughts and feelings, and spouses and others. Conflict can concentrate on events that occurred 20 years ago, those that occurred last week, or both in the same conversation. Maintaining a solution focus with such couples requires dogged persistence on the part of the mediator, who must select the issue for discussion, define it as one that involves a shared but solvable problem, and block any and all digressions that might shift the focus from the construction of such a solution.

For example, the mediator may begin by indicating that "a key issue for all parents is how best to share the task of caring for their children." By stating this, the mediator selects an issue and immediately frames it as a shared task. The mediator might then further define the issue by saying,

"One aspect of that shared responsibility concerns the amount of time the children spend with each of you. Given your circumstances and your shared commitment to your children, what do each of you propose?" This statement expands the problem definition by focusing on time sharing, making the effort sensitive to context, and implying that differences in time do *not* reflect differences in either parental caring or commitment. Finally, the mediator may help the couple maintain a focus on this issue by comments such as, "The issue at hand concerns time sharing . . ." or "Let's get back to the key issue here . . ." or "What would be practical under your circumstances?" or "It seems to me that that is a marital issue; let's put it aside and I promise to get back to it another time."

A related skill involves *generating options and/or suggesting trade-offs.* Here, it is important to remember that couples are typically novices in divorce, trying to negotiate emotionally sensitive topics at a time when both parties are often under a great deal of stress. These circumstances do not encourage client creativity or flexibility. Initially, both attributes may need to come from the mediator, who has the advantage of experience with all of the issues with which the couple is grappling. Thus, when the couple gets "stuck," the mediator can get them unstuck by suggesting options or trade-offs specific to the issues in question.

A typical example has already been noted above—namely, the father who has had little prior involvement with the children but, on divorce, wants to be involved in their care half the time. This demand is often posed as a "take it or leave it" option, with no room for discussion and, more important, little thought or planning as to how this objective might actually be achieved. One impediment is the mother's lack of faith in the father's parenting ability, coupled with her resentment that it took a divorce to get him to wake up about the children. Another impediment is the options that are impractical under their respective circumstances. Alternative options, then, might involve some sort of graduated time-sharing schedule. Other options include having the father take the children to medical and dental appointments and after-school activities or to have him become involved in morning busing arrangements, all tasks that would be one less thing for the mother to do. Similarly, clients can be urged to accept trade-offs of *like kind.* That is, although it would be inappropriate for parents to trade money for time with the children, it would be entirely appropriate for them to trade times and activities ("If you will take them to school in the morning, I will pick them up at the end of the day.").

These examples could be expanded indefinitely and make clear that the range of options and trade-offs is limited only by the clients' and the mediator's imagination under a specific set of circumstances. That imagination, however, is importantly assisted by experience, such that the mediator may have an advantage over the clients in coming up with practical suggestions.

A third practice skill involves *narrowing and/or defining the issues* under discussion. This skill is important because clients often approach issues in ways that are counterproductive. One such problem involves clients who diverge in the initial definition of the problem, often in ways that are continuous with processes that characterized their life together prior to divorce. A case in point concerns what constitutes a fair financial settlement, with the wife going "high" because of all the grief he caused her and the husband going "low" because of all the money she has squandered over the years. This definition mixes marital affairs with legal entitlements and is unworkable on its face. As so defined, the issue is unresolvable and can only lead to litigation. The alternative advanced by the mediator is that the couple is here to "divide the assets you have both accumulated during the course of your marriage together." This definition of the problem disqualifies the concerns of neither party, focusing instead on the shared task—namely, a division of assets that is both fair and equitable. The next hurdle involves narrowing the issue because the division of assets per se is simply too broad and encompassing to be workable. In this regard, clients are often at sea and can offer no plan or procedure, or they may jump in and start arguing about who owns the dining room table. These approaches are impractical and quickly break down. The alternative is for the mediator to immediately impose an orderly procedure for addressing the issues. This will typically involve distinguishing between different classes of money or property ("A financial plan can have up to four components concerned with child support, spousal support, the equal division of assets, and tax implications.") and the order in which these classes will be addressed ("I suggest we begin by discussing child support. What would be fair under your circumstances?").

This approach avoids getting bogged down by unproductive conflict and instead breaks down the larger issue into a series of manageable parts that will be worked through using a process that is orderly, systematic, and yet sensitive to context. This approach may be further enhanced if it is also sensitive to underlying or hidden agendas. Bringing these agendas into the open makes them available for inclusion, discussion, debate, or intervention. For example, the mediator might say to a wife, "I get the impression that this money is important to you as a way of securing your financial future?" This is one way to sensitively address an underlying issue—namely, that with her husband no longer there to support her, she may be extremely anxious about the future on her lower income (see Chapter 11, this volume, for a discussion of financial plans).

Redefining and/or narrowing the issues will be useful in many cases but may not be sufficient in the face of a client conflict management style that is dysfunctional. Here, *role enactment* can be a powerful tool for changing patterns of behavior. As the name suggests, this skill requires that couples do something in session, in front of the mediator, thus making it subject to reinforcement or intervention. One variation involves *staging a failure*, in which the couple is asked to negotiate some issue, with the mediator knowing full well that their conflict style will make this impossible. Having thus achieved their usual end, failure, the mediator can then intervene by saying,

"Your usual approach doesn't seem to work very well. Would you like me to show you another and more productive way to negotiate?" Alternately, the mediator may intervene while the enactment is unfolding, to change the dynamics. For example, simply blocking their repeated and mutual interruptions can dramatically alter their interaction. Now, each partner can actually complete his or her thought before the other responds *to that thought*, rather than going off on a tangent or mounting an attack in terms of past conduct. A third variation involves *role reversal*, in which each partner is asked to play the part of the other and answer and behave as each thinks the other would. Taking the part of the other can give the partner insight into the other's underlying motives or feelings that can change how they relate to each other about the issues in dispute.

Another practice skill involves *identifying and summarizing areas of agreement*. This skill relates to the negative feelings that are commonplace in family mediation. So prominent are such feelings that clients can lose sight of the extent to which their efforts to reach agreement have been successful. That is, each partner may be using different words to say exactly the same thing, but neither is really listening to the other. By stepping away from their feelings and attending to the meaning of their words, the mediator can highlight agreement that neither partner was aware of previously. In a related vein, mediation can be so stressful and tiring that it is easy for clients to lose a sense of where they are in the overall mediation effort and thus how close or distant they are from the end.

On both counts, it is important for the mediator to repeatedly inform clients how far they have come, what has yet to be done, and, most important, the areas and topics about which they have reached agreement. This may occur in regard to a session just ended ("You've done some fine work today. You've put in place three key elements of your parenting plan: how you will share in decision making, how the two of you will split the time you will spend with your children, and who's going to do what around the busing issue. Great!"), or it may apply to two or more sessions devoted to a particular topic, such as the disposition of the matrimonial home ("That was certainly a tough nut to crack, but you've done it, and in a way that gives each of you a fair share of this asset. Just so we are perfectly clear, let me briefly summarize exactly what you've agreed to, as I understand it. First . . .").

Note that these agreements are framed as an achievement of the first order, typically after much hard work. This is consistent with how the clients themselves perceive the negotiating process and true also in regard to their informal efforts prior to mediation. In other words, such summaries not only praise the clients' efforts, thus rendering the process rewarding for them, but also imply that mediation has made a significant difference in moving them toward their settlement goals. They also locate where the clients are on the initial list of issues in dispute. That is, if the mediator has informed them that a financial plan involves four elements, then the periodic summary suggests that they only have so many elements left before they are finished. Clients can then pace themselves emotionally so that they do not become emotionally exhausted before all issues have been addressed. For highly conflicted couples, for whom mediation can be protracted, the mediator may need to give them frequent breaks and much support while periodically summarizing their progress to date, to avoid their becoming emotionally exhausted before the process is complete. Without time to recharge their emotional batteries and in the absence of hard evidence of progress, there is the real chance that mediation will terminate prematurely, with a partial agreement, simply because the couple has run out of steam. Finally, failure to provide such summaries dramatically increases the risk of client dropout, for in the absence of the rewards such summaries bring, clients can become depressed, tired, and increasingly hopeless.

It would be rare in mediation to find families for whom power is evenly balanced between the partners. More often, power—defined as the ability of one person to control the behavior of another—is unequally distributed, typically on a consensual basis. That is, partners have often fallen into an arrangement that involves a particular division of roles, with wives typically in charge of family and household duties and husbands typically in charge of household maintenance and matters external to the family, often including work and finances. Although the influx of women into the workplace has changed this traditional arrangement in some families, it remains quite prevalent in our experience, with working women assuming a domestic "second shift" at home after a long day at the office. Furthermore, we suggest that couples have "fallen" into such an arrangement because the details have typically not been discussed but have simply evolved, based on shared assumptions of the traditional roles of men and women. In these cases, divorce arose because growing dissatisfaction with the arrangement led to conflict that could not be satisfactorily resolved. Alternately, in some families, the imbalance does not depend on marital consensus but rather is imposed by one spouse on the other. This imposition may be done through force of personality, as a function, for example, of husbands' control over family resources and/or through the use of force (i.e., through intimidation and the use of physical violence). In such families, divorce arose because growing dissatisfaction at the oppressive character of the arrangement led either to conflict that could not be resolved or one spouse escaping the relationship, often (though not always) taking the children with him or her.

Whatever the case, significant power imbalances cannot be allowed to continue because mediation is designed to ensure and, if necessary, impose a roughly equal playing field. Such balance is crucial because sharply imbalanced couples are likely to yield sharply imbalanced settlements, that is, settlements that are neither fair nor equal. *Power-balancing* skills are used to achieve that end. This practice skill is unusual because it is synthetic, the result of using a variety of other skills in some combination. For example, in practice, power is expressed in session by one party's effort to dominate the other by controlling the floor, that is, by talking in ways that prevent the other from doing so. Such behavior is not only counterproductive in relation to negotiation (because this requires a dialogue) but also directly challenges the mediator's control over the process. Power balancing is achieved by having the mediator take charge of who has the floor and for how long, often by saying something as simple as, "I'm sorry to interrupt, Mr. (Mrs.) Smith, but I would like to hear what your wife (husband) has to say on that topic." Related efforts may involve invoking the rules and procedures stated at the outset, using body language (holding up a hand to say, "Stop!"), going to individual caucusing, confronting (see below), reframing (see below), informing the couple about the negative effects of oppressive behavior on spouses and children, and so on.

The effects of these power-balancing efforts can be dramatic. For clients who have previously been oppressed, being free to speak up can be liberating, exhilarating, and anxiety provoking. Given the latter, such clients may need the mediator's help in formulating their thoughts, expressing them in words, and overcoming their fear of the consequences of directly challenging their partners. Furthermore, a client's difficulty may stem *not* from fear but rather from a lack of expertise because the other spouse had always been in charge of the area in which he or she is now being asked to express an opinion or advance a proposal. As for the other spouse, the oppressor, power balancing can be much more than an opportunity to learn to listen to what the other spouse has to say. It may also offer this person a window on why it is so important for him or her to be in charge at all times and why lack of that control in mediation can be so uncomfortable. Therapeutic intervention may reveal, for example, a spouse who feels deeply insecure; this person may fear that in giving up control, the other spouse will think of him or her as being less masculine or feminine. This sort of revelation places the mediation in a whole new light that may either cause the spouses to rethink their intention to divorce or greatly enhance their efforts at negotiation.

We have now alluded several times to the next practice skill, that of *reframing*. This is a widely used technique that may be defined quite simply as "changing the frame in which a person perceives events in order to change the meaning. When the meaning changes, the person's responses and behaviors also change" (Bandler & Grindler, 1982, p. 1; see also Bandler & Grindler, 1979). In the context of mediation, reframing is used to promote productive negotiation among clients by shifting how they see and/or define their own conduct (including their motives and intentions and the consequences of their acts) and that of the other spouse. Often, clients enter mediation with a frame that is either adversarial (winning or losing), conflictual (one against the other), or characterological (good or bad). All of these frames will be counterproductive in mediation because they define the task in oppositional as opposed to cooperative terms. Describing parenting as based on "shared responsibility" shifts the meaning as something both parents *must* do together, thus making it consistent with the goals and procedures of mediation. Similarly, describing a father's intense anger as a "marital issue," which has nothing to do with his feelings for his children, made it much easier for him to negotiate an equitable parenting plan. In still another case, a mother was livid that the father returned the child in T-shirt and jeans when she had been sent in a beautiful color-coordinated outfit. The mother framed such conduct as "irresponsible" and "insensitive." The mediator reframed each parent's conduct as involving a "lifestyle choice" that exposed the child to no risk and that was entirely in keeping with "family boundaries," which give each parent license to raise the child in accordance with his or her values. Having both parents accept this reframing reduced their conflict by 90% and dramatically changed the tone of subsequent negotiation. Repeatedly, then, we have seen that reframing can be an extremely potent way to promote cooperative problem solving by changing the way clients perceive and understand their situation and the behavior of both parents in that situation.

The same is true of a closely related practice skill, that of *storytelling*. Experience indicates that humans seem to have a natural affinity for stories, beginning in earliest childhood and extending into old age. Stories capture attention, entertain, instruct, and bond the teller and listener through shared experience. In mediation, they are used primarily to instruct, either as an easy or nonconfrontational way to convey a message that clients cannot or will not hear more directly. The other features of storytelling are an added bonus, as is the possibility that the story will unlock client memories, thoughts, and feelings that may facilitate subsequent mediation efforts. Although these stories may, literally, come from anywhere (books, movies, personal anecdotes, jokes, etc.), for the mediator, his or her experience with previous clients is a gold mine of relevant material that has immediate resonance with current clients. Moreover, it matters little whether these stories are genuine or fictional, refer to past or present events, or are realistic or fantastic. What matters most is the extent to which they allow the clients to identify with the characters, as well as the events or the outcomes, and so get the point.

Over the years, we have spun many a tale for clients. Indeed, an entire book might be written about teaching tales (see Wallas, 1985). Instead, consider the following story as a representative example and how it might be used by a mediator to resolve an impasse:

> In the jungle, there lived a troupe of monkeys. These monkeys were much like all others save that they loved to eat a particular local fruit. When the local villagers stumbled on this fact, they devised a means of capturing these monkeys to add them to the local zoo. To do so, they built traps of a local wood that resembled birdcages. The bars of these cages were built close together so that a determined monkey might insert his flat hand to grab a piece of the fruit he loved so much but, having done so, could only remove his hand by letting go of the fruit. This is how the villagers eventually captured many of the

monkeys, for even when they saw a villager coming at them with a net, so great was their love of the fruit that rather than release it and escape, they held on to the fruit and were captured.

Metaphor is used in a closely related fashion and represents another practice skill. A figure of speech in which one thing is likened with or compared to another, the use of metaphor is a staple of fiction, as in Shakespeare's notion that "all the world's a stage." As in fiction, the ideas being conveyed can be and often are stated directly. However, there are times when, wishing to highlight or otherwise call attention to important thoughts or feelings, authors may prefer means of expression that are dramatic, arresting, and memorable. Such is also the case in mediation, and hence practitioners might prefer the use of metaphor as an indirect form of reframing. Characterizing a wife as a "burnt twig" captures her sense of exhaustion and emptiness and provides a dramatic way for the mediator to convey sensitivity and understanding. Similarly, describing a man as a "draft horse" suggests strength and reliability and thus implies that much of value is not immediately apparent on the surface. To characterize the heated conflict between spouses as an "intimate ballet" suggests complicity in a dysfunctional pattern that either or both are free to change; they need only step outside the dance.

Such examples might be extended indefinitely. The point is that metaphor represents a deceptively simple way for the practitioner to get across a powerful message. Properly fashioned, such messages have a way of stopping clients in their tracks, forcing them to ponder an unfamiliar image and, having deciphered it, consider what it means for them. Of course, clients are free to reject the message, as they might have done anyway had it been conveyed directly. More often, metaphors alter the way clients perceive or understand a person, idea, or problem, thus suggesting ways around impasses or new approaches to difficult problems or issues.

A related skill involves *preempting*, a strategic maneuver used to diminish the likelihood of a given behavior by predicting it. For example, by telling a client that in their subsequent conversation (between sessions), he or she will be sorely tempted to be sarcastic but will successfully resist this temptation, the mediator is trying to stop this behavior. Similarly, predicting conflict over a given issue will tend to underline that behavior when the issue arises. Thus, preempting maneuvers have a particular form: They always refer to events or behaviors in the future, and they always predict behavior the mediator knows is very likely to occur because it is has occurred frequently in the past. The onus is then on the client to prove the mediator wrong by behaving differently, typically in a way that is constructive as opposed to destructive.

The final intervention skill is that of *confronting*. We place it last, not because it is least important but rather because it must be used with special care. Given the emphasis in mediation on cooperation and mutual problem solving, practitioners will tend to rely on methods of persuasion. Alternately, confrontation, if it is to occur at all, will be left to joint conversation between clients. There are, however, some ideas or proposals that are so offensive or obviously destructive that they cannot be left unaddressed. To do so through the clients would be to promote conflict between them. Similarly, there may be occasions when both parties hold to the same offensive ideas or position.

Examples include derogatory or inaccurate generalizations (women don't belong in the workforce, women and men can't work together, men are smarter than women, smart-mouthed kids deserve to be smacked, kids who are breast-fed grow up smarter than those who are bottle-fed) or ideas that are rationalized by "what everybody knows," as in "everybody knows that organic milk is better than ordinary milk."

Clients are free to hold whatever ideas they wish. When ideas such as those listed above are propounded in mediation or, worse, become the fundamental basis for a parenting or a financial proposal, then confrontation becomes an option, especially when other, less direct methods have already been tried without success. Confrontation can take a number of different forms. One approach is based on information sharing, either requested from the client ("That's interesting. How do you know that?") or provided by the mediator in his or her role of "expert" ("Available research shows that . . ."). Another approach is based on experience ("As someone who has helped many families, I can tell you from experience that that approach is simply impractical."). A third approach is based on values universally upheld in mediation, including notions that all clients are equal (in mediation), all clients are equally deserving of respect, children have rights, violence is wrong (irrespective of the provocation), each person is responsible for his or her actions, and so on.

Irrespective of the approach selected, the underlying issue is that mediators cannot allow themselves to be a party to a process and/or an outcome that is unconscionable. To avoid doing so, one may need to take on an advocacy role, even if this means advancing a bias and even at the risk of terminating the service. To do otherwise would involve doing a disservice to one or both partners, one or more children, or oneself as a professional.

Comediation Option

The majority of family mediators are sole practitioners. This is often so for a number of reasons: They have been taught to do so, they prefer working alone, the trouble required to work with a partner is not worth the effort, they know no one they would like to work with, the sorts of cases they have do not warrant more than one mediator, they prefer to rely on their personal judgment, or they enjoy the one-on-one relationship with clients. In short, there are good reasons why solo practice is so common.

However, even the most satisfied solo practitioner will, if pushed, acknowledge that there are disadvantages associated with this choice. These disadvantages are worth noting:

- Solo practitioners have no one to hand off to should they become tired, confused, and/or feel "stuck."
- Solo practitioners have no one to observe their conduct or stop them should they be headed into error, and thus they have no one to learn from should they conclude, in retrospect, that they committed an error.
- Solo practitioners seldom have anyone to call on should they feel unsafe or insecure in session.
- Solo practitioners are limited by their own background and expertise and have no one to call on should issues arise in session that are beyond their expertise.
- Solo practice is not an option for students or practitioners who are just starting out and have had no direct experience with real clients.
- Solo practice may encourage clients to feel at a disadvantage in terms of gender, with either two males (spouse and mediator) facing a female or two females (spouse and mediator) facing a male.
- Solo practice opens the possibility, real or perceived, of an alliance between a client, male or female, and the mediator of the same gender.

Many solo practitioners are clearly content to live with these difficulties. Some may prefer another practice option either from time to time or on a full-time basis. That option is comediation (Boulle & Kelly, 1998, pp. 124-128; Emery, 1994, pp. 123-124, 136)—that is, mediation involving two mediators, usually a male and a female, and often with divergent backgrounds, such as a social worker and a lawyer.

Practitioners who are trained in the same mediation practice model can offer several advantages over solo practice. Comediation

- achieves gender balance, the appearance of impartiality, and the means to avoid the appearance of any client-practitioner alliances and also may make it possible for one practitioner to "see" something the other would otherwise have missed;
- allows the practitioners to role model effective communication and other examples of functional interaction;
- allows for the enactment of a coordinated plan, based on the distribution of roles, including the means to play "good cop, bad cop" and/or other relational techniques;
- creates an extra pair of eyes, allowing one practitioner to take the lead while the other observes and takes notes, and vice versa, thus increasing the likelihood of avoiding errors (e.g., redirecting attention to an overlooked issue) or at least understanding their basis in retrospect;

- provides the enormous advantage of a postsession debriefing as the basis for identifying errors and planning strategies and structures for the next session;
- maximizes clinical effectiveness by taking best advantage of the practitioners' divergent areas of expertise, with, for example, a social worker taking charge of the parenting plan and the lawyer taking charge of the financial plan;
- creates a "hand over" option should one practitioner become tired, confused, or "stuck" and increases patience and perseverance of the mediation team by sharing the burden of mediating;
- provides a creative and intensive training method for students and inexperienced practitioners who may have no direct experience with real clients; and
- allows the team, through added resources and synergistic creativity, to take risks they might not have taken had they been working solo.

These advantages, however, come at some cost. There are disadvantages to comediation:

- In terms of the fee rate, it is twice as costly as solo practice, cost that is probably not justified in cases that are simple and straightforward.
- It takes time and experience for the practitioners to "jell" as an effective comediation team; during this process, the comediation pair may be ineffective, may compete with or be in conflict with each other, and/or may hesitate to do what is required.
- Gender and other differences may encourage clients to adopt a manipulative "divide-and-conquer" strategy of their own, with gender-based differences between partners mirrored in differences between the comediators.
- To be effective, comediation requires greater preparation and structure than solo practice; it is logistically more expensive and requires greater substantive and process expertise than sole practice.
- Incomplete coordination between practitioners may establish the basis for negative role modeling.

The choice of sole practice versus comediation is a matter of judgment and individual preference. Some mediators thrive in comediation, where the presence of another mediator creates synergistic opportunities for creativity, professional growth, and clinical effectiveness. Others find that they prefer to work alone and report that the time and energy required to create an effective comediation team undermine their interest in this option. Still others move back and forth between solo practice and comediation, as a function of opportunity and case requirements. The latter is our preferred option, but practitioners must weigh the advantages and disadvantages for themselves, in their own best interests and those of their clients.

Discussion

From a layman's perspective, the mediator's job must appear quite straight-forward: One goes back and forth between the parties until they either agree or do not. Students of mediation soon learn otherwise that family mediation is a complex endeavor that depends in no small part on the practitioner's mastery of an array of practice skills. In the interests of clarity, as above, these skills should be presented in orderly fashion, one by one. Indeed, such is typically the case for teaching purposes, which are usually associated with a role-play or exercise designed to promote mastery.

In practice, however, these skills are used in bundles or clusters that are constantly changing in response to clients, circumstances, or problems. That is, their effective use requires full and complete integration because during a session, practitioners will have little time to ponder on whether this or that skill might be the best choice under these circumstances. Rather, the choice of skill set must be an automatic expression of practice wisdom. Indeed, the contrast between the student's halting efforts and the seamless conduct of the experienced mediator makes the latter's behavior appear both magical and unattainable.

The good news is that mastery of the individual skills will, sooner or later, lead to their full integration. That integration reflects mastery of yet another skill—or, better still, a meta-skill—we call *selection*, that is, the ability under any particular set of clients or circumstances to select and enact an appropriate set of practice skills. The bad news is that mastery of selection takes time and experience, first under the expert guidance of an experienced mediator and, later, in the hurly-burly of mediation practice, under the inexpert but effective guidance of one's clients, for their responses provide the best measure of what works and what does not.

References

Allen, E. L., & Mohr, D. D. (1998). *Affordable justice: How to settle any dispute, including divorce, out of court* (2nd ed.). Encinitas, CA: West Coast Press.

Bandler, R., & Grindler, J. (1979). *Frogs into princes: Neuro linguistic programming* (J. O. Stevens, ed.). Moab, UT: Real People Press.

Bandler, R., & Grindler, J. (1982). *Reframing: Neuro-linguistic programming and the transformation of meaning* (S. Andreas & C. Andreas, ed.). Moab, UT: Real People Press.

Barsky, A. E. (2000). *Conflict resolution for the helping professions.* Belmont, CA: Brooks/Cole.

Boulle, L., & Kelly, K. J. (1998). *Mediation: Principles, process, practice* (Canadian ed.). Toronto: Butterworths.

Emery, R. E. (1994). *Renegotiating family relationships: Divorce, child custody, and mediation.* New York: Guilford.

Folberg, J., & Taylor, A. (1984). *Mediation: A comprehensive guide to resolving conflicts without litigation.* San Francisco: Jossey-Bass.

Haynes, J. M. (1992). Mediation and therapy: An alternative view. *Mediation Quarterly, 10*(1), 21-33.

Landau, B., Wolfson, L., Landau, N., Bartoletti, M., & Mesbur, R. (2000). *Family mediation handbook* (3rd ed.). Toronto: Butterworths.

Leviton, S. C., & Greenstone, J. L. (1997). *Elements of mediation.* Pacific Grove, CA: Brooks/Cole.

Moore, C. W. (1996). *The mediation process: Practical strategies for resolving conflict* (2nd ed.). San Francisco: Jossey-Bass.

Phillips, B. (1999). Reformulating dispute narratives through active listening. *Mediation Quarterly, 17*(2), 161-180.

Wallas, L. (1985). *Stories for the third ear: Using hypnotic fables in psychotherapy.* New York: Norton.

4 The TFM Approach: Step-by-Step Guide

Phase 1: Intake/Assessment

Given the sweep and complexity of the TFM approach, an overview was a prerequisite for clarity and intelligibility. However, by definition, such material omits the detail necessary to have any sense of *how* the models work on the ground, in practice. In this and subsequent chapters, we fill in these gaps by examining in detail each of the model's five phases, including the practitioners' goals, their bases for the selection of one or another practice technique, their criteria for evaluating process and outcomes, and their thinking as to whether to move forward to a new phase or feed backward to a previous one. This treatment will make clear that the key strengths of the model are its fluidity and flexibility. Its fluidity derives from the ability of the mediator to move seamlessly between phases in pursuit of particular goals, whether relational (better communication) or substantive (fair settlement). Its flexibility derives from the range of requisite practice skills at the mediators' disposal, thus allowing them to fit the process to the particular requirements of the client rather than insisting that the client adapt to a fixed procedure. Although these strengths inhere in the model's design, their emergence will depend on practitioners who are themselves fluid and flexible—that is, practitioners who are able to attend to and go with whatever process is then unfolding, comfortable with a high level of uncertainty and thus able to defer closure, and able to do both while never losing sight of their relational and substantive objectives.

Phase 1: Intake/Assessment

As noted previously, the first phase of the model involves intake/assessment. As seen in Table 4.1, this is a complex phase involving multiple goals

72

Table 4.1   TFM: Intake/Assessment

General
- Amenability
- Suitability
- Phase at entry

Goals
- Establish rapport with clients as individuals and as a couple
- Identify patterns of interaction
- Specify dysfunctional patterns likely to block negotiation
- Evidence of violence and/or intimidation
- Evaluate potential for reconciliation
- Evaluate amenability to family mediation
- Evaluate suitability for agency/practitioner
- Contracting
- Select entering phase
- Contact lawyers as legal team members

Procedure
- Initial contact
- With lawyers
- With clients
- Introduction to mediation
- Marital history
- Current events
- Issues in dispute and preferred solutions

Indicators

Interpersonal skills and attributes
- Communication skills
- Social support

Intrapersonal skills and attributes
- Affect: Type and intensity
- Subjective stress
- Cognitive functioning
- Psychological resources
- Individual problems
- Future orientation

Life circumstances
- Objective stress (life change events)
- Life resources (social, financial)
- Litigation history

Relationship quality
- Spousal conflict
- Spousal attachment
- Spousal violence and/or child abuse
- Critical incidents
- Living arrangements
- Extrasystemic involvements
- Parenting
- Balance of power

and assessment criteria. It is also crucial in three senses: It is here that the mediator must decide whether clients are *amenable* to mediation, whether they are *suitable* to the resources available to the practitioner or the agency, and, if so, whether they should *enter the process* via premediation (Phase 2) or negotiation (Phase 3).

The first decision, amenability, is crucial for the client and mediator but for different reasons. For the client, it will determine whether he or she proceeds to litigation, attempts mediation, seeks therapy, or engages in some alternative process (such as arbitration). Because each of these choices is very different and likely to affect clients and their children in very different ways, the mediator's decision can have significant consequences. For mediators, their decision is equally important on different grounds: in committing their resources to this couple and not to another; in terms of their reputation in the professional community, for those with good outcome records will be preferred; as regards the ease or difficulty with which they are likely to form a good working relationship with the lawyers in question and with a judge who may have sent this couple for mediation; and in reference to balancing their income requirements against their ability to manage their overall caseload without becoming exhausted or burned out. Thus, as will shortly become apparent, although the decision as regards amenability will always be made first and foremost on clinical grounds, other nonclinical considerations routinely come into play.

As to suitability, this criterion points to the intersection between resources and expertise. In both regards, agencies and practitioners vary. Court-based services, for example, are typically marked by high demand and limited resources. Consequently, such services routinely restrict the number of service hours available to any given client couple, such that these services are best suited to cases involving a limited number of highly focused issues. Put differently, this is to suggest that court-based services allow few complex cases to enter their service. The situation is different when the practitioner is in private practice and has no limit on the number of service hours. Here, suitability refers primarily to practitioner expertise. Those with a mental health background often feel comfortable dealing with cases centered on parenting planning, whereas those with a legal background often feel comfortable dealing with cases centered on financial planning. Only a minority of practitioners do comprehensive family mediation. Service agencies fall somewhere between court-based and private services, depending on the nature of their funding, the size of their staff, the nature of their demand, and a number of other factors. Thus, cases may be deemed suitable or not based on the mix of factors that apply across a range of service settings.

Finally, among cases thought both amenable to and suitable for family mediation, the decision that clients enter the process at Phases 2 or 3 is a statement about their degree of dysfunction and thus the extent to which some preliminary intervention efforts will be required before productive negotiation is likely to occur. We detail the bases for selecting one option or another later in this section.

Goals

Before we address the engagement between clients and mediator in the intake phase, it is first important to clarify the goals of the assessment phase. As in all professions, including mediation, it is easy for practitioners to be overwhelmed by the behavioral data being enacted right in front of them. Remaining focused on their objectives provides a basis for practitioners to interpret these data and to manage the session to ensure that the information that the clients provide is adequate for clinical decision making.

During this first phase of the mediation process, the practitioner strives to match data against 10 objectives. The first objective is *to establish rapport with these clients, both as individuals and as a couple.* Relying primarily on the range of connection techniques, the quality of their rapport will often be the key basis on which clients stay in the process or drop out. One aspect of this process concerns connecting with each spouse separately. Each has a different story to tell and often a different perspective on the issues in dispute. To maintain the substance and appearance of impartiality and have each client feel that the mediator understands his or her point of view, the mediator must establish a relationship of trust with each of them.

However, it is fascinating to observe how the behavior of clients changes from individual to joint contact. That is, in interaction, what emerges unbidden and often out of awareness is the organized or patterned way in which these spouses relate with and to each other. These patterns will facilitate or undermine their efforts at negotiation and thus, in part, determine the outcome of mediation. Consequently, the second goal of this first encounter will be *to identify and describe these patterns of interaction* based on their individual accounts. To this end, practitioners will rely heavily on their questioning and active listening skills and on their trained powers of careful and detailed observation. What should emerge as one product of the assessment is a series of hypotheses about their relationship and thus the hidden dynamic underneath their substantive positions. These hypotheses will be put to the test during their first joint session and thus either be confirmed or require revision. In turn, these insights will provide the basis for the mediator's intervention and facilitation strategies in mediating this case to settlement.

Although we are interested in the full range of organized relations that characterize the couple in question, of special interest are those patterns that are likely to facilitate or impede negotiation. Thus, the next goal of the assessment process is *to identify and describe patterns of relating that will be likely to promote or impede productive negotiation.* This will involve different clusters of indicators whose description will be deferred to a later section, with special attention paid to indicators of *family violence and intimidation.*

Here, however, it is noteworthy that those patterns likely to promote productive negotiation may also suggest a viable relationship that need not end in divorce. The fifth goal of assessment, then, is to evaluate the client couple's *potential for reconciliation.* In some couples, the decision to divorce may have been impulsive and thus ill considered. In others, ongoing conflict may reflect rudimentary communication skills that could be dealt with easily in therapy. In still others, divorce may reflect pressure from extended family members. In all of these cases, family mediation affords couples an opportunity to slow down and think carefully about what they really want to happen in their relationship. As we note routinely, nothing is official until one or both of them make it so. Help with their marriage is available so long as it is on consent, the proviso being that it requires two people to make a marriage but only one person to end it. Although obvious, this statement needs to be said publicly, for it will be commonplace for one spouse to affirm a desire to save the relationship while the other affirms a desire to end it. Roughly 5% of couples entering mediation will drop out in an effort to seek reconciliation.

In this context, the next assessment goal is *to evaluate the couple's amenability to family mediation.* Detailed discussion of the several indicator clusters that confirm that a couple is or is not amenable will be deferred to a later section. However, more generally, two aspects of this part of the process are noteworthy. First, amenability criteria tend to vary across practice models, typically becoming *less* restrictive as one moves across a continuum from structural models, at one extreme, to therapeutic models, at the other extreme. This is so because therapeutic models, in general, and the TFM model, in particular, claim that intervention practices can significantly improve the readiness of couples who would otherwise be unable to negotiate productively on intake. Put differently, this is to suggest that alternative dispute resolution (ADR) and therapeutic family mediation (TFM) practice models employ different intake criteria, with TFM models much less restrictive than their ADR counterparts. Consequently, couples who are assessed as unable to benefit from mediation with a TFM practitioner would be those who display significant dysfunction, either at the individual or the couple level. Couples such as these would be referred out either for litigation or some form of counseling or both. Assuming they would still be interested, couples who complete a course of counseling could then be reassessed for family mediation.

A related goal concerns the need *to evaluate the couple's suitability for the agency and/or the practitioner.* This goal is distinct from the issue of amenability because couples amenable to mediation may or may not be suited for a given agency and/or practitioner. At the agency level, suitability is often a function of available resources or operative policies. As to policy, there may be a number of reasons why an agency might deem a given case unsuitable. For example, couples seeking comprehensive mediation may be seen as unsuitable by an agency that only does parenting plans. Related policy reasons for turning away a given case may include case content (evidence of family violence), catchment area (the couple is not within the agency's area), language issues (the agency cannot provide service in the preferred language), or payment issues (the agency provides service only to couples who can pay something for the service). As to resources, additional reasons to see cases as unsuitable include a full caseload (some agencies have wait lists whereas others do not), room for simple but not complex cases, and cases associated with requirements the agency cannot meet (such as the request for transportation or day care). Many of the same concerns apply to private practitioners. For personal reasons, specific mediators may prefer not to take on certain types of cases, for example, those involving a history of violence against women or spousal infidelity. Both at the agency and individual levels, then, there may be a number of reasons why couples who are otherwise amenable to mediation may or may not be deemed suitable for mediation service.

Among cases deemed both amenable to and suitable for mediation, the proximate goal will be *to establish a service contract* of the sort seen in Appendix 4.1. Across North America, such contracts contain a number of standard clauses indicating the following: The couple is entering mediation voluntarily to address a specified number of issues with the assistance of a mediator who has no interest in the outcome(s) (i.e., one who is impartial), will not give legal advice, and will not select among available settlement options. Each spouse is represented by a lawyer, who agrees in advance to disclose all information necessary for the parties to make an informed choice and for the mediator to do his or her job properly as part of a process that is, with specific exceptions (e.g., child abuse), strictly confidential.

In this context, two areas of variation in contract content are noteworthy. The first source of variation concerns the fee schedule. This typically turns on the forum for service. Some court-based services offer their services at no cost because they are fully subsidized by the state. Other court-based services charge a user fee, either a flat fee or on a sliding-fee scale tied to the clients' income. In contrast, and almost by definition, private practitioners charge an hourly rate but may require payment up front (as a retainer), at the end of each session, or even billed at the end of each month.

The other source of variation is jurisdictional and specifies whether mediation will be *open* or *closed*. In almost all jurisdictions in North America, mediation is automatically closed. That is, in the event that the mediation is unsuccessful, the mediator cannot be called as a witness, and his or her records are sealed. The key advantages of this approach are that it encourages openness and frankness because clients need have no fear that anything they say or do in mediation can be used against them in court. Such openness promotes cooperation and disclosure and thus increases the likelihood of settlement. However, the disadvantage of this approach is that any gains in mediation are lost should they fall short of a full settlement. In that event, the mediator may report only that he or she has seen the couple in question so many times for so many service hours and that the couple could not reach agreement. These restrictions are consistent with the latest draft of the U.S. Uniform Mediation Act, which prohibits mediators from making any recommendations, for fear that mediators may coerce couples into agreement. Accordingly, couples who return to the mediator or move on to litigation must do so with a clean slate.

The alternative, open mediation, is only available in Ontario, Canada. Here, for couples who cannot achieve full settlement, everything said throughout the mediation process is "on the record," the mediator may be called to testify in court, their process notes may be entered into evidence, and, on consent, the mediator may be asked to write a report that records what agreements have been reached, what issues are still in dispute, how the parties have conducted themselves, and what recommendations the mediator might make as to the resolution of any remaining issues. The key advantage of open mediation is that any gains in mediation carry over to subsequent efforts at mediation or litigation, and intransigent parties may be held accountable for their actions. Such accountability is especially important in cases involving significant family dysfunction or in which one party is deliberately staging a failure for later use in court. The obvious disadvantage is that it may inhibit openness, making it slightly easier for the practitioner to abuse his or her authority. In practice, both would be quite rare. Rather, open mediation is typically reserved for couples with a long litigation history and whose likelihood of reaching agreement is judged *by the referring agent* as relatively low. In our experience, the closed or open status of the case makes little practical difference to the process and, in a handful of cases per year, may make a slight difference to the outcome.

Irrespective of these content variations, *contracting* per se is an integral part of the intake and assessment process, setting out the terms and conditions of the mediation service that tie client and mediator together. The contract also serves the dual function of lending credibility to the mediator while formalizing the clients' commitment to the process. Finally, it serves to protect the mediator in the event of untoward client conduct, including payment refusal (including checks returned "NSF" [not sufficient funds]), concurrent court action, or subsequent litigation in which the mediator may be called as a witness.

Of course, contracting is necessarily reserved for clients who are deemed both amenable to and suitable for family mediation. It remains for the mediator to *select the phase of service* at which these clients will begin the mediation process. The majority of clients are able to begin negotiation immediately and so enter mediation in TFM at Phase 3. However, for a significant minority, as much as 40%, this is not the case. Rather, these clients are sufficiently dysfunctional that direct entry into Phase 3 would ensure an impasse, that is, an inability to negotiate productively such that the likelihood of their reaching agreement would be vanishingly small. In ADR models of mediation, there would be no alternative, such that these clients would likely be turned away. In TFM, they enter mediation in Phase 2, premediation, which is designed to block or alter those patterns of conduct that prevent constructive negotiation. If such interventions are unsuccessful, these clients would be referred out. However, in most cases, such intervention efforts are successful, and clients move on to Phase 3.

In either case, selection of the entry phase is subject to later confirmation or refutation, in keeping with the circular structure of the TFM model. Unlike other models, refutation recognizes a possibility long acknowledged in family therapy (Coleman, 1985)—namely, that the mediator may have made one or more assessment errors. The notion of "error" is an extremely important one for a least two reasons. For one thing, it highlights the related notion of lifelong learning. Although mediators may not be able to reduce their error rate to zero, through continuing education and experience, they minimize clinical errors. For another thing, "error" calls our attention to the co-constructed (Phillips, 1999) or coproduced (Hasenfeld, 1992) character of all mediation processes and outcomes. Although the mediator may have more authority than the client in some contexts, mediation always consists of the dialogue between them. In this sense, "error" refers not to what the mediator did or did not do but rather to a course of mediation that is not in keeping with the mediator's intentions.

Finally, whether they enter mediation in premediation or negotiation, clients are expected to have or acquire representation by a lawyer. The final goal of the intake process is *to involve the lawyers as team members.* Lawyers play an important role in the lives of clients. They typically provide clients with their first exposure to family law, inform them of their rights and obligations, provide emotional support at a time when many clients feel extremely vulnerable, and can be an important source of reality testing in regards to both parenting and financial planning. In addition, lawyers are clearly and unequivocally on their clients' side. For all of these reasons, it is important for mediators to see lawyers as team players and to treat them accordingly. In most cases, the team approach comes naturally because most family law lawyers seek to do what is in the best interests of the children and are interested in working cooperatively toward settlement. Such cooperation not only serves clients well but is also of mutual benefit to both professionals because mediators provide a resource to lawyers, whereas lawyers refer clients to mediators.

Procedure

Achieving these goals requires a procedure that is structured enough to give the client a sense of order but flexible enough to ensure that the mediator can collect all the information he or she needs. This involves five steps enacted in the sequence set out as follows.

The first step encompasses *initial contact,* either with the lawyers or with the clients. Contact with the lawyers concerns case referral, which can take two slightly different forms. One form involves a direct referral, with both lawyers in the cases having agreed on their selection of the mediator. Here, discussion, typically on the telephone, centers on how each perceives the issues in the cases and what outcomes each would think reasonable. These formulations are important for future reference because they may or may not correspond to the client's account of the case. When they do not correspond, the mediator may need to bring the lawyers around if the client's settlement is to be viable. In turn, these processes highlight the friendly but sometimes ambivalent relationship between mediators and lawyers, its cordiality being complicated by the mediator's need for referrals.

The second form of case referral is one in which the lawyers have *not* selected a mediator but rather are searching for one among several potential candidates. Here, telephone contact can be complicated. On one hand, the lawyers' intentions are to provide the prospective mediator with minimal information about the case, obtain a copy of the mediator's curriculum vitae (CV), and feel out the mediator to see if he or she might be suitable under the circumstances. On the other hand, the mediator's intentions are to obtain a sketch of the case, figure out what the lawyers might be looking for in a mediator, provide them with a copy of the mediator's CV, and establish contact for future cases even if the mediator is not selected for this one. This mix of divergent intentions can make for a guarded and awkward conversation, although it does get easier with experience, especially if the mediator has worked with them in the past.

The final four steps in the intake process occur during separate sessions with each spouse, with each session lasting between 1 and 2 hours. We prefer individual sessions for several reasons: to hear the client's account without interruption, encourage complete openness and frankness, form some sort of relationship with each client separately and apart from his or her partner, and work together to create a problem formulation that is "solvable" in mediation.

The salience of the last reason cannot be overstated. Following Phillips (1999), clients frequently present an account of the case that is not amenable to mediation. For example, they may picture themselves as innocent victims of partners who are variously described as crazy, unreasonable, dangerous, or incompetent. From a systemic perspective, such accounts are untenable because they leave out the storyteller; that is, they are static. To create a dynamic account and thus assess for amenability, the mediator must include the storyteller. This is always a joint effort. For example, a client, the father, recently provided an account that pictured his partner, the mother, as abusive toward their son. Further questioning about the husband's role in this process implied that if abuse did indeed occur, he must have been complicit in it because he did not intervene to stop it. What gradually emerged was an account in which the parents had widely divergent standards of child care, which was the focus of repeated conflict between them. The client then gradually amended his account to suggest that he disapproved of the mother's more physical style of play but acknowledged that the child had never been physically injured in this process. This new account was, in turn, supported by mother's account, which pictured the father as passive and ineffective. This new account would likely be amended still further, when the parents came together for their joint sessions, but for purposes of assessment, this provided a preliminary account that the mediator could work with.

Constructing this account involves four steps: introducing the clients to mediation, taking a marital history, describing current events in their relationship, and listing the issues in dispute together with each spouse's preferred solution. The introduction to mediation is typically quite short, lasting between 10 and 20 minutes, and briefly covers a number of standard topics:

- commending the clients for their willingness to seek a cooperative solution to their problem(s);
- describing the litigation option;
- contrasting the litigation option with the mediation option;
- defining family mediation and the mediator's roles;
- describing TFM and its dual focus on substantive issues and underlying relationship processes;
- affirming the mediator's impartiality;
- emphasizing the mediator's bias favoring the children's best interests and describing the advocacy option;
- describing the mediator's control over the process and the client's control over the content (at least within reason);
- characterizing the mediator's contribution to the process, including the status as an "expert" in various matters relevant to mediation, including divorce, financial affairs, family law, and child development;
- affirming the mediator's years of experience in the field and thus his or her practical expertise in conducting the mediation process and assisting the parties in reaching settlement;
- describing mediation procedures, including the four components that make up the first session;
- explaining the notion of caucusing;
- defining the limits of confidentiality;
- describing the fee rate, payment method, and the mediation contract;
- distinguishing between open and closed mediation options (where applicable);
- answering any questions posed by the client; and
- affirming a joint commitment to begin the mediation process.

This brief introduction is intended to serve three functions: to ensure that family mediation is an informed choice for this client, affirm the mediator's expertise and authority, and reduce or eliminate any anxiety or confusion the client may be experiencing.

Following the final affirmation, it is the clients' turn to take center stage by providing a brief history of their marriage "from the very beginning," that is, from their meeting. This is often a difficult task for clients, not only because it means trying to remember events in the past (sometimes the far past) but also because it involves briefly reliving a mixture of pleasant and unpleasant experiences. As important, how they handle the task is telling for the mediator. That is, a complete history will be impossible. Rather, clients are forced to select those events and experiences that were most salient for them. Which events they highlight says much about how they see the partner in the present, just as comparing the partners' accounts speaks to their different perceptions of events they experienced in common. Moreover, as noted earlier, this account is co-constructed. The mediator's questions and the clients' responses slowly create a three-dimensional portrait of the clients' marriage and life circumstances that is coproduced and renders it, to varying degrees, mediatable or "solvable."

The process by which this is achieved makes different demands on the clients and the mediator. The clients' memories, their way with words, and their ability to organize events into coherent wholes are all put to the test. Not surprisingly, clients vary widely across all three dimensions. For example, as a group, men tend to present accounts that are well organized and place great emphasis on a chronological account of "facts." However, these accounts tend to lack detail and are often very thin as regards affective content. They also tend to focus almost exclusively on events within the immediate family and thus omit reference to extended family members, family friends, and professionals. By contrast, as a group, women tend to present accounts that are highly detailed, are affectively charged, and include extended and extra-family members. However, they are often chronologically confused and mix facts and feelings. The affective character of these accounts also often requires pauses, as women become briefly overwhelmed by the feelings they are reliving.

These contrasting styles of presentation place the onus on the mediator. He or she must ask good questions and do so in a way that is neither intrusive nor disruptive. The mediator must also listen carefully for what is said or omitted or implied between the lines. Where appropriate, the mediator must be sensitive to what the client is saying and feeling while showing support for the client's pleasure or distress. Furthermore, the mediator must be mindful of the assessment agenda, systematically gathering the data pertinent to his or her various concerns. This can often be done unobtrusively by simply following on from openings the client provides. On occasion, however, the mediator may be forced to digress from an unfolding account to have the client speak to an issue that is relevant to the assessment, for example, as regards violence in marital relations or abuse in parenting the children. Furthermore, divergences in emphasis will often be salient in identifying points of tension that can be expected to emerge later in negotiation. For example, where a father may describe himself as having been involved in parenting "as much as possible," the mother may characterize him as having "dumped" the parenting task "entirely on my shoulders." Later, when they begin to negotiate a parenting plan, the mother can be expected to resist the father's demand for shared parenting, characterizing his newfound interest in the children as "too little and too late."

As this account slowly comes up to the present, it is a simple matter to have the clients describe current events in their relationship. If the clients do not naturally describe their current parenting and financial arrangements, this is an opportunity for the mediator to ask them to do so. Other relevant topics include their experience with their lawyer and/or litigation, their current living arrangements (including the presence of a partner, live-in or otherwise), their employment status (especially any recent changes), their financial status, their support network (including relations with their parents), their health status (including any medication they take regularly), their involvement with any professionals (such as a counselor or psychologist), and any other aspects of their current circumstances that might be of interest to the mediator.

Finally, the client is asked to list the issues in dispute together with their preferred solutions. Some clients have considerable difficulty with this task. They have been so wrapped up in the events of their lives and their feelings about them that they have given little thought to the substantive issues. For them, the past and, to a lesser extent, the present are more real or vivid than the future, which seems clouded, uncertain, and fraught with anxiety. They may also get confused in trying to distinguish between what they want and think is fair and what their understanding of the law says are their entitlements. Such clients need a great deal of support, as the clients and mediator slowly walk through the parenting and financial issues and their preferred outcomes. They may also benefit from education about several issues, such as the difference between litigation and mediation, the notion of client empowerment, the basic thrust of the family law statutes in their jurisdiction, and the novel idea that, as adults, as long as they are in agreement (on consent), they and their partner are free to arrive at just about any solution to the issues in dispute, whether or not they are consistent with the prevailing statutes in their jurisdiction.

Other clients may approach the task with a preprepared list, including their preferred solutions and perhaps even a fallback position. In one sense, such clients make the mediator's job easier; rather than having to tease out the list of issues, one is already available. Even with such clients, however, the mediator should move forward cautiously, checking to see to what extent the clients have thought through their choices. It would not be uncommon, for example, for a father to indicate a desire to fight for sole custody of "his" children. Brief discussion, however, may reveal a man who has previously left much of the parenting to his wife, works a 60-hour-a-week job, lives with his parents or in a one-bedroom apartment, and is terrified that his wife will take the children away from him entirely. Such information would suggest that the father has a hidden agenda (to take a tough bargaining stance to increase the time he spends with his children) and that his position is either not intended seriously or is quite unrealistic.

An additional concern is the extent to which the client's list of concerns is negotiable. That is, some clients advance lists that they intend to be used as the mediation agenda, and they are unwilling to discuss any issues other than those on "their" list. In effect, such clients challenge the mediator's authority, presenting as determined, assertive, and even combative. Here, the mediator's response should be to highlight the notions of fairness and equity that are the hallmarks of mediation and to insist they will only proceed on the understanding that *both* parties are free to put on the table any issues they find problematic. Then and only then is there any possibility that both parties will emerge with an agreement they find reasonable and satisfying. At this time, the mediator might also note the consequences of selecting the litigation option while carefully probing for some hidden agenda. It would not be surprising if the client's rigid stance reflects some underlying fear or anxiety—for example, that fathers will lose their children or that mothers will end up on the street without a penny. In addressing these concerns directly, clients' fears often can be allayed and alternate solutions explored—first in the intake session and again later in their joint sessions. We say "often" to imply that there are exceptions when this is not the case. Clients do occasionally present who have no hidden agenda as such, but their need always to be in control is so central to their relationship with their partner (and often others) that they are unwilling to relinquish it, no matter what the consequences. Such clients would typically be judged as not amenable to mediation.

These various responses to the construction of a list of substantive issues, co-construction of a case formulation, and the clients' accounts of the various processes currently ongoing in their lives represent an enormous amount of information. That information is then subject to interpretation, both as to the amenability of this couple to the demands of family mediation and/or their initial placement either in Phase 2 (premediation) or Phase 3 (negotiation). In TFM, both decisions are based on the mediator's assessment of the couple, that is, their performance on a range of indicators, to which we turn next.

Indicators

Client assessment is based on a total of 19 indicators organized in four clusters concerned, respectively, with (a) interpersonal skills and attributes, (b) intrapersonal skills and attributes, (c) life circumstances, and (d) relationship quality. Collectively, these indicators are drawn primarily from the 11 sets of substantive models reviewed in Chapter 2. However, 2 indicators (personal problems and future orientation) are drawn from clinical experience.

Cluster 1: Interpersonal Skills and Attributes. Family mediation is demanding on clients' *interpersonal communication skills*, especially their ability to own their own thoughts and feelings (without attributing thoughts and feelings to the other), articulate them clearly, and put themselves in the place of the other, that is, demonstrate a capacity for empathy. Clients who attribute all of their problems to the other, have great difficulty articulating their own thoughts and feelings, and are often highly egocentric and thus unable to place themselves in the place of the other are poor candidates for mediation. A related interpersonal attribute, the degree to which they are a part of a network of others who can provide *social support*, speaks to the intense demands of the divorcing process. Social support is important in buffering stress and can assist clients in participating in mediation. Thus, the presence of such a network would be a positive indicator as regards mediation, whereas its absence would be a negative indicator.

Cluster 2: Intrapersonal Skills and Attributes. Family mediation also places demands on a range of clients' intrapersonal skills and attributes. For example, the divorce process is an *affectively charged* one, with both negative and positive feelings commonplace. At low to moderate levels, such feelings are useful in mediation, providing the motive to address issues and persist when negotiation is difficult. However, at very intense levels, affect—especially negative affect—becomes debilitating by interfering in joint efforts at negotiation and planning and individual efforts at thinking and reasoning.

Similarly, the *subjective experience of stress* is universally associated with divorce. The capacity to cope with and adjust to stress is an important intrapersonal skill. At low to moderate levels, stress per se is manageable and would not interfere with the clients' ability to participate meaningfully in mediation. As stress levels rise, however, this becomes less and less true. At high or very high levels, clients report feeling overwhelmed and unable to cope, a contraindication as regards mediation.

In turn, both affective intensity and subjective stress affect clients' *cognitive functioning*, that is, their ability to think clearly, logically, and coherently. Because they will be asked to address complex issues and formulate and modify plans concerning parenting and finances, clear thinking is important. Their ability to display such thinking would be a positive indicator for mediation, but their inability to do so would be a negative indicator. In particular, their ability to think and plan for the future would be a salient positive indicator, just as their obsessive preoccupation about the past would be a salient negative indicator.

In a related vein, their *intrapersonal resources* represent another indicator of amenability. Here, we are thinking of resources such as flexibility, adaptiveness, mental toughness, and self-confidence—that is, indicators of their ability to negotiate on their own behalf, yet put their own interests aside on behalf of their children. An abundance of such psychological resources would be a positive indicator for mediation. Conversely, clients who are bereft in this regard may be poor candidates for mediation.

Finally, clients may come to mediation with a variety of *individual problems* that may compromise their ability to participate fully in mediation. Examples of the sort of problems we have in mind include a history of psychiatric problems, one or more forms of learning disability, one or more medical conditions, or a history of substance abuse. One or a combination of these problems may interfere with clear thinking, promote inappropriate affective responses, undermine their flexibility or self-confidence, and/or reduce their stamina and energy level. However, we should caution that the presence of one or more of these problems per se would *not* automatically mean that they could not participate effectively in mediation. With appropriate medication, patients with psychiatric disorders can perform within the normal range. Some forms of learning disability would be irrelevant to mediation, but others can be compensated for in a variety of creative ways. Clients with medical conditions may participate with some accommodations, such as shorter sessions, whereas substance abuse need not be continuous, such that alcoholics may do fine in mediation so long as they agree not to drink within at least 24 hours before the sessions. Accordingly, even when clients present with problems, for purposes of assessment, each case should be examined on its own merits.

The final indicator in this cluster concerns clients' *future orientation*—that is, their ability to consider, conceptualize, plan, and negotiate around parenting and financial matters in the future. This is important because much of any mediated settlement will pertain to couples' visions of a desirable or at least acceptable future. Most couples can do so—some easily (having thought it through before coming to mediation) and some only with help from the mediator. Their future orientation, then, is a positive indicator for mediation. Some clients, however, cannot or will not engage in constructing such a vision. Rather, they remain obsessed with the past, either in laying blame on the other partner or themselves, trying to understand what went wrong, or imagining ways to set things right. In many cases, various interventions may be employed to move them from this position and help them understand that, for their sake and for the sake of their children, they must leave the past in the past and move on. In such cases, although the absence of a future orientation is a negative indicator, it is not fatal to mediation. In a minority of cases, clients' obsession with the past is simply unmovable, and they are best referred out for separation counseling.

Cluster 3: Life Circumstances. A third cluster of indicators concerns a variety of life circumstances that may affect the ability of one or both clients to participate in mediation. One such indicator concerns the number and type of *life change events.* Such are widely understood as indicative of stress (see Chapter 2, this volume). Such events are especially pertinent to divorce that is characterized by such events, including possible changes in residence, employment status, income level, relationship network, school catchment areas, and living arrangements. Some divorcing families will encounter many such changes all at once and may find themselves overwhelmed in the process. Others will encounter few such changes or will be more resilient in response and so report adequate or superior coping under conditions others would find distressing. Such life change events are seldom, if ever, fatal *on their own* to involvement in mediation. But they can be part of a larger array of indicators that *together* may contraindicate a particular client couple.

A related set of indicators concerns *life resources*. Here, we are especially concerned with social and financial resources. The intensely stressful character of divorce means that this is a particularly poor time to be alone. Even so, clients vary widely in their available social resources. For example, it would be unusual for women to be without parents, siblings, and friends at this time. In contrast, many men rely on their wives for much of their social life. In divorce, many men report encountering loneliness for the first time in their lives. In a related vein, many women are financially dependent on their partners' income, such that divorce may see a sharp drop in their income. Although men may show no change in income related to divorce, this is not always the case. Preoccupied by their failing marriage, their drop in performance, coupled with an increased absentee rate, may lead to job loss and thus a sharp drop in income.

In both cases, recent changes in the level of social and financial resources *alone* will seldom be fatal to mediation, but they represent another set of indicators that may undermine client performance and thus need to be taken into account in the assessment process.

Finally, clients vary widely as regards another indicator, namely, their *litigation history*. Some self-referred clients may arrive having had virtually no involvement in litigation and may or may not even be represented by a lawyer. Others may have an extensive history of litigation and, indeed, may have had several lawyers in the process. In our experience, an extensive litigation history is a negative indicator for several reasons. Financial resources may be limited precisely because they have already spent their savings on litigation. Enmity between the spouses will typically be intensely negative, as will the level of interpersonal conflict, with litigation having promoted both. In some cases, prolonged litigation can also promote a relationship of dependence between lawyers and clients, such that clients can have difficulty formulating their own plans or even thinking independently. That said, litigation is fatal to mediation only in extreme cases, whereas those with no litigation history or who have just begun litigation represent positive indicators for mediation.

Cluster 4: Relationship Quality. The final cluster of indicators, and perhaps the most important, concerns the quality of marital and family relationships. Here, key indicators of mediation amenability are the *frequency and intensity of marital conflict* and the degree to which both are under some degree of conscious control. The fact that spouses were unable to resolve their differences explains their presence in mediation, so that some degree of marital conflict is given. However, among clients seeking to enter mediation, the extent of conflict varies widely. We have found Garrity and Baris's (1994, p. 43) Conflict Assessment Scale particularly helpful (see also Aldarondo & Straus, 1994; Straus, Hamby, Boney-McCoy, & Sugarman, 1996). Based on their extensive clinical experience, Garrity and Baris offered the scale as a "guideline" only, acknowledging that a couple's position on the scale may change through time. The scale encompasses five points or positions, as follows:

- *Minimal Conflict (1):* Cooperative parenting and the ability to separate child and parental needs; each parent validates the importance to the child of the involvement of the other parent and affirms the parenting competence of the other parent. Conflicts are resolved with only the occasional expression of anger, and negative emotions are quickly brought under control.
- *Mild Conflict (2):* One parent occasionally berates the other parent in front of the children, and verbal quarrels occur in front of the children. One parent questions the children about personal matters in the life of the other parent and may attempt to form a coalition with the children against the other parent.
- *Moderate Conflict (3):* Verbal abuse but no violence and loud quarrelling between the parents; one parent denigrates the other parent and may threaten to limit the other parent's access to the children. One or both parents may threaten litigation, and there is an ongoing attempt by each parent to form a coalition with the children against the other parent.
- *Moderately Severe Conflict (4):* Parents are a danger to each other, and there are mutual threats of violence. Parents may slam doors or throw things and exchange verbal threats of physical harm or child kidnapping. There is continual litigation, and one or both parents may attempt to form a permanent coalition with the children against the other parent (alienation syndrome). The parental relationship emotionally endangers the children.
- *Severe Conflict (5):* Parents endanger the children through physical and/or sexual abuse, drug/alcohol abuse to the point of impairment, and/or severe parental psychopathology. The parental relationship places the children in emotional and physical danger.

Most clients in family mediation display conflict patterns that fall somewhere in the mild to moderate range, with couples characterized by moderately severe or severe conflict contraindicated for family mediation. Furthermore, this conflict scale is complementary with our own experience of variation in client conflict by topic area. That is, clients fall into one of three groups: Clients find negotiation of parenting issues easy but financial issues difficult, they move through the financial issues with little problem and find parenting issues conflictual, or they are conflictual across both sets of issues. Furthermore, the level or intensity of conflict around these topics may vary through scale positions 1 to 3. For clinical purposes, then, it will be useful to think about client conflict in terms of the interaction between topic and intensity. Conflict that is mild to moderate in intensity and confined to one topic area represents a positive indicator for mediation. Conversely, conflict that is severe in intensity and includes both topic areas—that is, high-conflict couples who are out of control—represents a negative indicator for mediation.

Much the same variation applies to issues of *spousal attachment*. Given that in most cases, the divorce is initiated by one partner, it would be commonplace for the other partner to display some degree of unresolved attachment. In the majority of cases, mild attachment can be a positive indicator because it will positively dispose these clients in how they perceive other partners and in their willingness to cooperate with them. Conversely, extreme or even obsessive attachment is a strong negative indicator. Typically, such clients experience difficulty in advancing a plan independent of partners or in negotiating with them, for their hidden agenda concerns reconciliation rather than divorce. In extreme cases, mediation becomes impossible because the client is either lost in thought about the other ("he [or she] is everything to me; I can't go on without him [or her]"), is searching desperately for some way to get the other back ("he [or she] just doesn't understand how much I love him [or her]"), or is in passive ("he's [or she's] just confused") or active denial ("I won't let him [or her] go") about the impending divorce. Although those in active denial may represent a real threat to the partner, all forms of intense attachment are contraindicated for family mediation. Such clients are best referred for separation counseling, after which they may be reconsidered for mediation. More generally, differences in attachment speak to differences in *readiness* to engage in mediation (see Fuhr, 1989). The greater the discrepancy in attachment or readiness, the less likely are clients to engage in productive negotiation and thus reach agreement. These speculative comments about the relationship between readiness and outcome in family mediation have been confirmed in a recent empirical study (Bickerdike & Littlefield, 2000).

A third variant that is contraindicated for family mediation involves *some form of abuse*, whether directed at a spouse, a child or children, or both. Although physical violence is the most overt form of abuse, various forms of emotional or sexual abuse may be equally destructive, especially of the partners' ability to think, feel, or act independently (see Jasinski & Williams, 1998). When such conduct is discovered in the assessment process, the practitioner's statutory obligation to report is clear and simply precludes mediation. However, in our experience, it is far more common for such conduct to be part of the reported family history and thus will have occurred some time in the past. Here, we do *not* regard that aspect of the couple's history as necessarily fatal to mediation; to do so would be disrespectful of the clients' right to choose the means by which their differences are resolved. Rather, we assess each case on its merits.

One aspect of that assessment concerns the occurrence of any number of *critical incidents* in the recent past. Such incidents vary widely in content but have two features in common: that the client reporting them attached great significance to the incident(s) in question and that, as a consequence, these events represent a potential source of impasse in mediation. Such incidents thus represent a negative indicator for mediation, though seldom a fatal one.

Another relational indicator concerns the clients' *current living arrangements*. In most cases, by the time the client couples have sought family mediation, they are living "separate and apart," as called for in family statutes as one of the grounds for divorce. However, in a minority of cases, in practice, living "apart" means living on different floors of the same house. In some cases, this happens because the partner built the house "with his [or her] own hands" and refuses to relinquish it for any reason whatsoever, including divorce. In other cases, partners may have been advised by a lawyer that moving elsewhere would be seen by the court as "abandonment" and might lessen his or her claims regarding custody of the children. Whatever the reasons for their remaining together, such conduct is typically a negative indicator for mediation, suggesting either a high level of ambivalence or a high level of conflict.

The *involvement of extrasystemic others* calls attention to another set of indicators. Such others typically include extended family members and friends as well as the possible inclusion of a new romantic partner. Extrasystemic involvement can be a positive indicator to the extent that it is a source of social support. That involvement becomes negative, however, to the extent that it puts pressure on one or both partners to take extreme positions that they would otherwise not take. Much the same is true of the involvement of a romantic partner. The presence of such a person invariably complicates matters in mediation by influencing the conduct of one or both partners. Even so, such involvement can be a positive indicator if this person entered the picture *after* the separation, and his or her influence is confined to providing support. When such involvement occurred *before* the separation, or if this person's influence extends to pushing a partner to take an extreme position, that involvement is invariably a negative indicator. This is so because infidelity immediately suggests a trust vacuum between the partners that may make it very difficult for them to negotiate productively. The sense of betrayal involved may also suggest intense negative feelings on the part of the injured partner, with the same result. That said, from the perspective of TFM, mediation can provide partners with the opportunity for transformation through mutual forgiveness. Consequently, although infidelity is a potent negative indicator, it need not be fatal to the mediation process if handled from a therapeutic perspective.

Another set of indicators concerns the issue of parenting and parenting competence. In this regard, as in so many others, clients vary widely. Here, it will be important to distinguish between parenting prior to and after divorce, for the latter creates a unique situation in which clients may behave quite differently than before. In some cases, that difference will suggest a striking improvement. Fathers, for example, may see the divorce as a wake-up call and become far more involved in child care than while they were still married. Alternately, parents may be more cooperative and mutually supportive than before, fearing that the divorce may otherwise place their children at risk. In other cases, the difference will suggest a striking deterioration. Overwhelmed by the changes associated with the divorce and the subsequent litigation, clients who were competent parents while together now begin fighting with each other through the children. In extreme cases, parent alienation may occur, with one parent poisoning the minds of the children against the other parent. In still other cases, little will have changed over time; parents were and remain either equally competent or equally incompetent. In considering these various indicators, the mediator's first responsibility must be to act in the best interests of the children. In most cases, this will mean inclusion in mediation, for only then will the mediator have some opportunity to act to preserve or improve the situation of the children. In a small number of cases, typically where the mediator is powerless to act in situations destructive of the children, this will mean referring couples out for counseling and/or litigation, in the hope that someone else can act where the mediator cannot.

The final set of indicators concerns the quality of the marital relationship as regards the *balance of power*. We highlight this dimension as distinct from conflict, attachment, or abuse because of the particular demands of family mediation. Most mediators, ourselves included, work on the premise that the likelihood of achieving a fair and equitable settlement is directly related to creating a level playing field in which both partners are roughly equal. In fact, that is often the case, typically with women having some advantage as regards parenting and men having some advantage as regards family finances. This arrangement represents a series of positive indicators for mediation because it renders both substantive areas subject to education and negotiation. The reverse is increasingly true the more power sharing is imbalanced. In traditional couples, a typical example involves a wife who has total control over the home but knows virtually nothing about the family's finances, whereas the reverse is true of the husband. A related example is one in which one spouse is extremely powerful and controlling but the other spouse is weak and dependent, with both displaying rigid expectations and a very limited response repertoire. Although such imbalances reflect a series of negative indicators, only in very extreme cases are they fatal to mediation. That is, in most cases, power-balancing techniques are successful in creating a playing field that is sufficiently level to ensure an equitable settlement.

Taken together, these four clusters of indicators yield a mediation amenability checklist, as seen in Figure 4.1 (see also Tan, 1988, 1991). This

Item	Indicator				
	Very Positive	Positive	0	Negative	Very Negative
Interpersonal Skills					
• Social support					
Intrapersonal skills					
• Affect, type, and intensity					
• Subjective stress					
• Cognitive functioning					
• Intrapersonal resources					
• Individual problems					
• Future orientation					
Life circumstances					
• Objective stress (life changes)					
• Life resources					
• Litigation history					
Relationship quality					
• Spousal conflict					
• Spousal attachment					
• Family abuse					
• Critical incidents					
• Living arrangements					
• Extrasystemic involvement					
• Parenting					
• Balance of power					

Figure 4.1   Mediation Amenability Checklist

checklist is intended to provide a systematic means for a mediator to review his or her impressions, based on one intake session with each partner. It should *not* be seen as a psychometrically sound instrument in which a derived score is used for clinical decision making. On the contrary, clinical decision making in TFM remains a judgment call based both on the evidence gathered at intake and the mediator's clinical experience. In practice, between 80% and 90% of clients seen at intake will be judged amenable to mediation. The percentage reduction on the basis of suitability will vary widely across service sites. In private practice, amenability and suitability are almost always one and the same. The situation in not-for-profit agencies and in court-based services may be quite different, both as a function of available resources and agency policy. Although some indicators, such as ongoing abuse, are simply fatal to mediation, in most cases the decision about amenability will turn on the mediator's judgment concerning intervention effectiveness. Cases in which negative indicators are subject to intervention will, in turn, be seen as amenable to mediation. However, when intervention efforts will very likely prove futile, then cases are best judged nonamenable to mediation and referred out, either to counseling, litigation, or some other option (such as arbitration).

The majority of cases, then, will confront the mediator with a second decision—namely, should the couple in question enter mediation in Phase 2 (premediation) or Phase 3 (negotiation)? Here, as noted earlier, the decision turns on the mediator's judgment concerning the couple's ability to engage in negotiation. The latter requires reasonable skills as regards communication, reasoning, affect control, stress management, future orientation, and empathy. Couples who show evidence of these skills and attributes should be moved on, at least on a provisional basis, to Phase 3. Those who show some evidence of these skills and attributes, but at a level insufficient for productive negotiation, *and* who are amenable to intervention should be moved on, at least on a provisional basis, to Phase 2. Irrespective of their initial placement, assessment should be continuous throughout their involvement in mediation. Accordingly, in keeping with the circular character of the TFM model, couples' stay at a given phase will be performance based. Couples who respond to intervention efforts move on to Phase 3; those that do not are referred out, with the mediator accepting that they have made an assessment error. Couples who negotiate effectively will move on to Phase 4; those who do not move back to Phase 2, to which we turn next, following a brief summary.

Summary

Phase 1 of the TFM model is crucial to all that follows in family mediation. It is here that the mediator establishes a relationship of trust and authority with the client couples, decides if these couples are amenable to mediation and suitable to the practitioner or the agency, and assigns amenable couples to premediation or negotiation; the clients and the mediator co-construct a formulation that will guide the mediator's action, at least into the next phase of mediation.

Properly handled, what the client couple should experience is a serious but sensitive and supportive discussion with an experienced professional who they believe can assist them in resolving their differences. But much needs to be accomplished in a relatively short period of time: only 2 hours in court-based service and up to 4 hours in private service. Thus, the full assessment described here may be practical in some settings but may need to be modified or scaled down in others. However, irrespective of setting, intake sessions are demanding of the full range of the mediator's skills, both in the present and in planning for the future. They should reflect the mediator's experience and careful planning, as demonstrated by the fact that both should be invisible, woven seamlessly into a casual discussion that should be a positive experience for all concerned.

Appendix 4.1

Sample Family Mediation Contract

THIS IS AGREEMENT BETWEEN:
Applicant No. 1 _____ and
Applicant No. 2 _____ and
Family Mediator _____

1. AGREEMENT TO MEDIATE

The parties will participate voluntarily in mediation in an effort to resolve their differences arising from a domestic matter. This agreement sets out the terms and conditions under which the mediation will proceed. Either party or the mediator for any reason may terminate or suspend the mediation process at any time.

2. ISSUES

The parties have agreed to mediate the following issues:

(a) care, control, and parenting of the children;
(b) spousal support;
(c) child support;
(d) possession, ownership, and division of their property; and
(e) such other issues as are made known by the parties during mediation.

3. IMPARTIALITY AND NEUTRALITY OF THE MEDIATOR

The parties acknowledge that the mediator is a professional who will assist them to communicate and will not make recommendations or give legal advice. The parties acknowledge that the mediator has had no previous or personal relationship with either party and that the mediator has no personal interest in the outcome of the mediation.

4. INDEPENDENT LEGAL ADVICE

The parties acknowledge that they have been advised to retain independent legal advice regarding their rights and obligations under the law and, by not doing so, risk making decisions without being fully aware of legal rights and obligations, as well as not having full knowledge of the possible legal implications and ramifications of their decisions. The parties acknowledge that the mediator will not prepare a final and binding agreement for them and that if they wish to have a mediated understanding made legally binding on each other, they will need their lawyer's assistance for that purpose. The parties agree not to make any unilateral changes to ownership or possession of property or to the status quo in relation to the child or children while mediation is in progress, unless ordered by the court or by mutual consent. Furthermore, the parties agree, on their instruction to their lawyers, not to initiate or take any new steps in any legal proceedings between them while mediation is in progress.

5. DISCLOSURE

The parties agree to provide each other and the mediator full disclosure of all relevant information and the required documents to ensure success of the mediation process.

6. CONFIDENTIALITY

The parties agree that any communication in the mediation process, written or verbal, will not be voluntarily disclosed to anyone who is not a party to the mediation. The only situations where there would be exceptions to this understanding are as follows:

(a) responding to a party's lawyer;
(b) responding to any order of the court;
(c) complying with any obligations imposed by law (e.g., child or elder abuse);
(d) protecting the lives, safety, and well-being of any persons; or
(e) contributing to mediation research, education, or training, provided that the identities of the parties are not disclosed.

The parties agree that anything said or any admission or communication made while participating in the mediation process cannot be used in current or subsequent court proceedings. The parties acknowledge that the mediator may request to meet privately with each party during the mediation or request to see the child or children or other interested parties, and the mediator will only inform the other party of such information where, in the sole discretion of the mediator, such information is relevant to the issues in dispute and the disclosure would assist in the resolution of the issues.

The parties agree that they will not call the mediator as a witness in any legal proceeding to their opinions or to disclose any admission or communication made to him or her in the course of mediation. If, however, the mediator is subpoenaed, then the client is responsible for all legal costs and the mediator's fees and expenses.

7. USER FEES

Court-Based Service: The parties acknowledge that the mediation is not a free service and that they must make a contribution toward the cost of mediation based on their incomes and the sliding-fee scale, which has been explained to them. This fee is the sole responsibility of the clients. Fees will be due at the end of each session.

Private Service: We agree to share equally or proportionately (husband   %, wife   %), or _____ alone agrees to pay the fees and disbursements for the mediation services provided, for preparation of any documents or reports, including but not limited to time for interviews; reading reports and documentation; telephone conversations with the clients, lawyers, or other collateral sources; preparing correspondence; and other relevant activities. Disbursements and other out-of-pocket expenses incurred by the mediator, such as photocopying, long-distance telephone calls, facsimile transmissions, and messenger services, will be billed additionally. Travel time (if any) will be billed at half the normal rate.

We agree to pay an hourly rate of $___ per hour, subject to change upon notice by the mediator. We also understand that we will be billed for appointments that are cancelled if there is less than 24 (twenty-four) hours' notice prior to cancellation.

We agree to pay this rate at the end of each and every mediation session.

8. CONSULTATION, INTERNS, AND OBSERVERS

The parties understand and agree that the mediator may have interns, an observer, or a comediator in the mediation process. These above persons would have completed mediation training and would be obtaining practical experience under the supervision at the mediation center. The participation of interns, comediators, and observers in the mediation process will be subject to the same duty of confidentiality as the mediator.

9. OPEN/CLOSED REPORTS

The parties have been advised that they must choose a closed or open mediation report before mediation begins. The parties acknowledge that they fully understand the difference between the reports and, after careful consideration, have agreed to select the following:

A "closed" or limited report indicates the number of interviews, the persons who attended the interviews, and the terms of any agreement reached as well as any issues on which agreement was not reached.

DATED at _____, ON this Day of

Witness	Signature
Witness	Signature
Witness	Mediator

References

Aldarondo, E., & Straus, M. A. (1994). Screening for physical violence in couple therapy: Methodological, practical and ethical considerations. *Family Process, 33,* 425-439.

Bickerdike, A. J., & Littlefield, L. (2000). Divorce adjustment and mediation: Theoretically grounded process research. *Mediation Quarterly, 18*(2), 181-201.

Coleman, S. B. (Ed.). (1985). *Failures in family therapy.* New York: Guilford.

Fuhr, J. (1989). Mediation readiness. *Family & Conciliation Courts Review, 27*(2), 81-101.

Garrity, C. B., & Baris, M. A. (1994). *Caught in the middle: Protecting the children of high-conflict divorce.* San Francisco: Jossey-Bass.

Hasenfeld, Y. (1992). The nature of human service organizations. In Y. Hasenfeld (Ed.), *Human services as complex organizations* (pp. 3-23). Newbury Park, CA: Sage.

Jasinski, J. L., & Williams, L. M. (Eds.). (1998). *Partner violence: A comprehensive review of 20 years of research.* Thousand Oaks, CA: Sage.

Phillips, B. (1999). Reformulating dispute narratives through active listening. *Mediation Quarterly, 17*(2), 161-180.

Straus, M. A., Hamby, S. L., Boney-McCoy, S., & Sugarman, D. B. (1996). The revised Conflict Tactics Scale (CTS2): Development and preliminary psychometric data. *Journal of Family Issues, 17*(3), 283-316.

Tan, N. T. (1988). Developing and testing a family mediation assessment instrument. *Mediation Quarterly, 19,* 63-67.

Tan, N. T. (1991). Implications of the Divorce Mediation Assessment Instrument for mediation practice. *Family & Conciliation Courts Review, 29*(1), 26-40.

5 The TFM Approach: Step-by-Step Guide

Phase 2: Premediation

That a client couple may be assessed as amenable to mediation does *not* mean they are immediately ready to begin negotiation. It *does* mean that, in the mediator's judgment, they have the potential to do so. To realize this potential, however, one or several blockages must first be removed, hence their entry into mediation via premediation. As seen in Table 5.1, the ultimate goal of the premediation phase is make whatever changes are necessary so that the couple in question may engage in productive negotiation, thus allowing them to participate meaningfully in the family mediation process.

The problems couples bring to mediation that might block productive negotiation fall into four categories. First, couples often lack *basic information*, either about mediation itself or about the substantive problems about which they disagree. Next, the information they do have may be *incomplete or incorrect*, or their attitudes toward or their values about some area of dispute may be inimical to cooperative action or joint problem solving. Such couples need to be *taught an alternative perspective* more in keeping with the requirements of mediation. Third, their ideas about some preferred solution may be inconsistent with the mediator's understanding of what is in the *children's best interests* under their circumstances. From the mediator's perspective, a parenting plan containing these provisions would be unconscionable. Within therapeutic family mediation (TFM), under these conditions, the mediator would *advocate* for provisions of a parenting plan in keeping with the children's best interests. Finally, and most frequently, the couple displays one or more *dysfunctional patterns of interaction*, especially as regards conflict, that make efforts at joint problem solving or negotiation simply unproductive. Such couples need therapeutic intervention designed to induce change sufficient to make productive negotiation possible.

Table 5.1   Premediation

Goals
- Prepare the client couple for productive negotiation
- Inform as needed
- Educate as needed
- Advocate as needed
- Intervene as needed

Indications
- Affect: Type and intensity
- Logical clarity
- Communication effectiveness
- Interaction effectiveness
- Problem accommodation
- Client responsiveness

In what follows, we will elaborate on three of the four areas of blockage—discussion of advocacy will deferred to a later chapter (Chapter 9) focused on the construction of parenting plans—and detail the indications we use to determine whether clients should (a) be referred out for further action regarding their dispute; (b) be sent on to Phase 3, negotiation; or (c) would prefer to reconcile, perhaps with the assistance of marital therapy. Before doing so, however, it will be important to clarify our use of therapeutic methods in family mediation.

Therapeutic Methods in Family Mediation _____

The use of therapeutic methods in family mediation is controversial on several grounds. First, it might be argued that mediation is *not* therapy, and the two ought not to be confused. Alternately, one might argue that client couples contract for family mediation rather than therapy, and therefore therapeutic efforts are inconsistent with both the contract and the notion of client self-determination. Finally, one might suggest that therapeutic methods augment the already considerable power and authority of the mediator, and in the hands of an inexperienced person, therapeutic efforts might further abrogate clients' rights and lead to settlements that may not be in keeping with their best interests. Below, we speak to each of these arguments in turn.

Mediation Versus Therapy

This often repeated argument is based on a fundamental misunderstanding of the use of therapeutic methods in family mediation. Individual psychotherapy may be described as an approach to construct a relationship between therapist and client, which is intended to allow the client to develop insight into his or her problems and make long-term changes to his or her identity, conduct, and relationships to reduce or eliminate the presenting problem(s). In complementary fashion, marital therapy is an approach to construct a relationship between a therapist and couple intended to stabilize the couple's marital relationship and to improve their quality of life by helping them develop new and more effective ways of relating to each other. In short, both psychotherapy and marital therapy focus on effecting long-term fundamental changes in individuals or couples.

In contrast, as seen in the introduction to this volume (Chapter 1), mediation is intended to assist couples in resolving disputes. However, couples' ability to resolve disputes assumes both the presence of certain underlying skills and the absence of certain patterns of relating inimical to negotiation. Many couples meet these criteria and require no intervention. Others have the potential to achieve these criteria but need help in doing so. The use of therapeutic methods is one way of providing that help. In this sense, the use of therapeutic techniques serves the purposes of mediation rather than those of therapy per se. As such, such intervention efforts are short-term, specific, and limited to those processes likely to interfere with clients' efforts to negotiate productively. That is, such efforts are congruent with client goals in mediation; by bringing to the surface underlying feelings and inter-actional dynamics, clients are given the power to alter that which would otherwise block their best efforts at resolution. The further benefit of such intervention is that it sets the stage for postdivorce relations after mediation is over, including the freedom for each spouse to get on with his or her life, the opportunity to select a different life path, and the skills to fully engage in cooperative parenting, in the best interests of their child or children.

Mediation Contract and Client Self-Determination

These arguments require two slightly different responses. As regards the contractual character of the relationship between the mediator and client couple, in TFM this routinely involves explicit disclosure of the typical course of service. Such disclosure includes reference to the phasic structure of the TFM approach and the intention of the mediator to address *both* substantive and relational issues. The inclusion of the latter is explained as serving the former. That is, conflict over substantive issues is often, if not always, tied to conflict over underlying marital and/or parenting issues. Explicitly addressing relational issues, then, reduces conflict over substantive issues, reduces the over-all duration of the process, and substantially increases the likelihood of compliance with the terms of settlement. All of this is made absolutely plain to client couples *before* they sign a standard mediation contract and thus gives informed consent to the two-level approach we use.

As to the issue of client self-determination, this is fully supported in TFM but with an important qualification. It is an old saying in mediation that the client is in charge of the issues, whereas the mediator is in charge of the process. As we have argued already, this perspective is misleading in light of the co-constructed character of the process of issue formulation. Unless issues are cast in forms that are amenable to shared problem solving, the mediator's efforts will be fruitless. The co-construction process ensures an appropriate form, such that client self-determination might better be rephrased in practice as "mutual determination," as client and mediator work together to solve the problems they have co-constructed.

Moreover, it would be naive to think that the problem and process are not interconnected. In coming into mediation, clients implicitly concede that their informal efforts at problem resolution have failed and that they need help. In coming to mediation, clients relinquish control of the process to the mediator. Doing so voluntarily can here be construed as an expression of client self-determination, as is their right to terminate mediation any time they wish. TFM, then, involves a partnership between clients and mediator characterized by a *moving balance* between mediator authority and client self-determination. Clients cede to the mediator control over the process and negotiate with the mediator a case formulation amenable to joint resolution. In turn, clients retain ultimate authority over the terms of settlement, which they can accept or reject, the same being true of the opportunity that mediation affords them of personal transformation.

Abuse of Authority and Unconscionable Agreements

This argument, typically advanced by feminist writers (see Benjamin & Irving, 1992), affords three responses. First, in all forms of human service, including family mediation, clients voluntarily cede to the service provider authority they would not have otherwise. On one hand, such imbalance is explicitly intended to advance the best interests of the clients by giving them the opportunity to effect some change or achieve some outcome that they would be unable to do or achieve by their own effort. On the other hand, this unequal balance of power opens the possibility of the abuse of authority. Daily newspaper reports of such abuse by doctors, lawyers, psychiatrists, psychotherapists, and others make two things readily apparent: Wherever such imbalances occur, abuse will inevitably follow; however, such abuse will typically be quite rare, will usually be detected, and will be associated with heavy sanctions against the abuser. As the popularity of family mediation continues to increase, the likelihood that instances of abuses will occur will approach certainty. However, as with other human service professions, the benefits that accrue to clients from their involvement in family mediation in general, and TFM in particular, far outweigh the slight risk of abuse.

Second, that said, there is a clear and discernable trend in family mediation that further reduces any risk to clients. That trend refers to the growing efforts to ensure that all mediators are bound by organizational standards of conduct and ethics. Throughout North America and internationally, professional organizations have come into being whose members uniformly meet standard measures of training and continuing education and who agree to be bound by related standards of conduct and ethics. All such members must further display evidence of liability insurance and agree to respond to consumer complaints by peer review. Furthermore, training programs have sprung up across North America—some private, others university based—whose methods continue to improve, in some cases including provisions for a practicum or internship. Despite these safeguards, there is at present no basis for mandatory accreditation, such as that in medicine or law. As a result, it is still possible for individuals to offer mediation service who are affiliated with no professional organizations and thus formally unqualified. However, as we have seen above, even with such qualifications, the risk of abuse can never be reduced to zero.

Finally, arguments concerning the risks associated with family mediation have been helpful in raising awareness of this issue. That awareness has been reflected in a growing research literature, with particular reference to the experience of women in mediation. Although detailed discussion of the findings will be deferred to a later chapter (Chapter 13), it will be sufficient here to indicate that there is little evidence of abuse. On balance, women more than men tend to be satisfied with their experience of mediation, and review of settlement documents indicate that neither gender is disadvantaged by their participation. Such reports in the literature reflect our own experience providing TFM-based mediation services.

We conclude, therefore, that opposition to the use of therapeutic methods in family mediation is based more on misinformation than direct experience. What merit such arguments have derives less from the available technology than on human fallibility. Conversely, we suggest that the use of therapeutic methods offers significant advantages both to clients and practitioners by

- expanding the range of clients amenable for service,
- improving the quality of the process by addressing those underlying processes likely to generate conflict and by addressing such underlying causes,
- improving the likelihood of client compliance with the terms of settlement, and
- improving the likelihood that client postdivorce conflict will be resolved informally, thus reducing the rate of litigation or relitigation.

Premediation

As noted earlier, premediation involves four classes of intervention—namely, giving information, providing education and training, intervening to improve performance, and advocating for different provisions. Thorough review of these three classes would require book-length treatment because the number of possible examples is very large indeed. Instead, in the interests of space, in each case we will focus on a handful of typical examples.

Giving Information

Most people who marry, whether formally or common law, intend to remain married; relatively few plan for their divorce. The result is that most divorcing couples are very poorly prepared for what follows, either in terms of their marital or parent-child relationships, the procedures and statutes concerning family law, or expectations of family mediation. Consequently, giving information to clients involves a series of mini-lectures covering a wide range of topics. These lectures may be delivered routinely or only if they would appear to serve some service in aiding the mediation process. In either case, these lectures are intended to serve a series of interrelated purposes:

- promote informed decision making;
- affirm the mediator's credibility and competence in the clients' eyes;
- provide a neutral forum for dialogue between clients;
- create a neutral forum in which the clients may exchange information and explore thoughts and feelings;
- help co-construct a mediatable frame, that is, formulate issues in ways that render them solvable through mediation; and
- promote the value of cooperation, negotiation, flexibility, and the construction of win-win solutions.

Brief reviews of the following five topics are all consistent with these goals and give some idea of how simply giving information can advance the mediation process.

The Principles of Family Mediation. As noted previously (see Chapter 3), it is imperative that the mediator be in control of the process. One way to do that is to have the practitioner in charge of the principles of mediation. One example of such principles is provided in Table 5.2. A printed list of these 16 "principles" would be handed out at the first joint session, with each point subject to brief discussion on the understanding that these rules would be in force throughout the mediation process and either applied or enforced by the mediator. In practice, Principles 3, 4, 5, and 6 invariably prove the most problematic and require the most attention, especially during the first few joint sessions. The utility of the other principles is not obvious at first, but their importance becomes increasingly apparent by the time the couple has entered into negotiation.

Child Development and Divorce. Most parents can see the effect of their separation on their children. But their judgment on this matter is often

Table 5.2   Rules of Family Mediation

1.	Beware of *emotional* logic; my pain in return for your assets.
2.	Be clear about the motives underlying your position; who is the *real* beneficiary?
3.	Be clear about your priorities; focus on the *best interests* of the children.
4.	Act with good will; give the other the benefit of *your* doubts, suspicions, or fears.
5.	Show mutual *respect* in language and conduct.
6.	Keep your feelings in check; stay *cool*.
7.	Own your own thoughts and feelings; only *I* statements allowed.
8.	Remain flexible; be prepared to *compromise*.
9.	Present well-considered positions; do your *homework*.
10.	Break large, complex issues into smaller, *manageable* chunks.
11.	Be *patient*; workable agreements take time.
12.	Look for *common interests*.
13.	Think of the present but consider the future; good agreements *last*.
14.	No one can foresee the future; build in mechanisms for *change*.
15.	Consider the costs of *not* reaching an agreement.
16.	In good agreements, everybody *wins*!

clouded by their own emotional turmoil and the absence of any systematic knowledge in this area. Moreover, many parents perceive children as small adults. That is, although immature, children are often seen as operating with much the same logic and thought processes as adults. In this context, discussion of child development and divorce is intended to highlight three aspects of children's experience: It is set in terms of a normal trajectory of developmental milestones; these milestones can be seriously disrupted by the divorcing process, with effects likely to vary systematically by age and gender; and until about age 12, children experience the world very differently than adults, such that their conduct must be understood in terms of children's motives and intentions and so can be easily misunderstood when seen in terms of adult motives and intentions (for details, see Chapter 9, this volume). If they are interested, clients may also receive supplementary readings, such as Saposnek (1998, pp. 156-167).

The thrust of this presentation is that the responsibility for the impact of their divorce on their children rests with them. Merely having one parent move out of the home will have some impact. However, through time, if handled properly, by muting conflict, talking openly with their children, and developing a business-like parental relationship, the impact on the children may be minimal. Conversely, handled poorly, especially in terms of spousal conflict, the impact on the children may be profound and long lasting. There is a choice, and it is theirs. In our experience, many parents duck the issue, with a substantial minority, for example, having reported that they had *not* talked to their children about the divorce or the fact that one parent had left the home. Most explained that they were fearful of doing more harm than good, had no idea what to say to the children or how to respond to their questions, felt uncomfortable being in the same room with the other parent, or some combination of reasons.

Adult Adjustment During and After Divorce. Divorce is an extremely stressful life process. It is small wonder, then, that many people going through it report a wide variety of symptoms—some psychological, such as emotional lability or difficulty in concentration, and others physiological, such as headaches or fatigue. These various symptoms can interfere with the mediation process, and, as important, clients suffering from them often do not associate these symptoms with the divorcing process. It can therefore be very helpful for them to understand the short- and long-term consequences of divorce and what they can do to respond to them.

In premediation, information giving involves discussing the consequences of high stress levels for psychological and physiological functioning. Such effects are not pictured as limited to the individual but affect their relations with others, their functioning on the job, and even their performance in driving a car. Most important, it is emphasized that these effects are temporary—and entirely normal under the circumstances—and that mediation can help reduce stress levels by empowering clients to take charge of their lives. (Discussion of things they can do to deal with stress will be deferred to the next section, concerned with teaching and training.) Moreover, as clients gain better control and stress levels begin to fall, not only will their performance in mediation improve, but they will also be in a better position to parent their children.

Shared Parenting in Divorce. Parents in mediation confront the urgent need to make decisions about the care of their dependent children. One basis for doing so is to continue with arrangements in place prior to the decision to separate. For the parent, typically the mother, whose primary task was to look after the children, that choice is reinforced by the involvement of a lawyer steeped in the traditional language of custody and access. For the other parent, usually the father, involvement with a lawyer or, more recently, with fathers groups often means pushing for joint custody.

In mediation, as part of the process of softening the conflict between clients on this issue, we often introduce them to the notion of shared parenting. As explained to clients, this idea works on three different levels. First, it involves a shift in language. Because the language we use affects how we think about things, this shift is a very important one. Shared parenting means that neither parent *owns* the children, but rather that both parents are equally *responsible* for their care. Second, shared parenting is a way to approach the construction of a time-sharing arrangement. This need not involve a 50-50 split in time. *Shared legal parenting* may or may not coincide with *shared physical parenting*. Parents may share decision making, even though the children spend most of the time with one (primary) parent. What it does involve is a split made on the basis of what is best for the children and what is practical for their parents. Whatever that split, it means that both parents will continue to be involved in caring for the children and in making decisions about their welfare. Finally, this issue speaks to available research. This shows unequivocally that children do best when both parents are fully involved in their care. It also shows that children's needs in relations with their parents vary by age and gender. For example, young children (younger than 5 years of age) need frequent contact with both parents to develop a secure and healthy attachment, whereas older children can sustain their sense of attachment with less frequent contact (see Chapter 14, this volume). Finally, it shows that mothers and fathers each have important but different things to contribute to their children's development and that both are capable of learning the skills needed to be good parents. Taken together, these different approaches to shared parenting suggest a new way of thinking about parenting in divorce. It would now be up to the clients to decide whether to embrace this new perspective and how, if at all, it would affect their decisions in constructing a parenting plan. However, the immediate effect of this mini-lecture is to undercut any ongoing conflict on this issue, as both parents are now forced to reconsider what they now think best for their children.

Monetary Issues in Divorce. Parenting issues speak to clients' direct experience and are thus an area about which many clients already feel empowered. Monetary issues in divorce are another matter altogether and often one in which clients feel overwhelmed. From their contact with their lawyers, clients know that this is a complex area of law, such that many come into mediation feeling unequipped to make competent decisions and thus are inclined to leave the entire matter to their lawyers. The mini-lecture we provide in response involves two components. The first component speaks to the advantages of comprehensive mediation with the same practitioner. Here, we emphasize the link between good child care and the frequency and intensity of spousal conflict. It matters little to the children if their parents are fighting over them or over money. All they know is that when they are fighting, the parents are less available. It follows that relationship gains made in negotiating the parenting plan should, if possible, be preserved in negotiating a financial plan. This is most likely in mediation, whereas the adversarial approach of the lawyers may erode any relationship gains, as conflict between them escalates. Indeed, we prefer to think about such negotiations as a team effort, in which their respective lawyers are team members who continue to work on their behalf but within the larger context of mediation.

The second component of this presentation is to de-mystify the financial issues that need to be addressed. The details will be deferred to a later chapter (see Chapter 11). Here, it will suffice to say that we emphasize that none of the issues in question are beyond the grasp of anyone with at least a high school education. Moreover, they will not be asked to do this on their own. Rather, the mediator will be present to walk them through every step of the process, explaining matters as needed and assisting them in negotiating a fair and reasonable deal. Throughout the process, we explain, the clients will be free to consult with their lawyers at any time, and other experts can become part of their process as necessary. Because it is they, the clients, who must live with the consequences of any deal they reach, it is they who should be in charge of negotiating the details. Finally, even if a full settlement proves elusive, mediation does not foreclose the litigation option; it will only cost them a little time, money, and sweat to do what needs to be done themselves, and they should consider how good it will feel if they succeed, despite their present doubts.

The empowering message at the heart of this presentation is not lost on clients. Despite their ongoing doubts, especially among women, most clients decide to go ahead and try mediating their financial issues. In our experience, none, especially the women, are sorry that they did so. Many succeed in achieving a full settlement, having acquired, often for the first time, a complete picture of their financial situation. Even if they do not succeed or only arrive at a partial settlement, most clients report that they were much better prepared to actively participate in litigation than would otherwise have been the case. Finally, as is their choice, a small proportion of clients decline our offer and prefer to have the monetary issues handled through their lawyers, a decision we respect and support.

Education and Training

Productive negotiation in family mediation makes certain demands on clients. Among other things, these demands include effective communication skills, a shared understanding of their parenting task, and a shared understanding of the difference between their ongoing commitment to parenting and the termination of their spousal relationship. When couples demonstrate in assessment that they lack such skills or understandings, one or more premediation sessions can be used for purposes of providing education and training, typically through the use of short exercises. The four examples reviewed below are illustrative of the exercises in question.

Shared Parenting. A case in point concerns the issue of shared parenting in divorce. This can be highly problematic, as enmity around marital issues interferes with parenting efforts. Parallel parenting is therefore quite common, with no discussion about basic issues and only brief and highly strained discussion concerning logistical issues. Such efforts may be further undermined by ongoing litigation that encourages each parent to characterize the other as incompetent and blocks direct communication between the parents and redirects it through the lawyers. As a result, many mediation clients report no or very little direct communication about parenting between them in the past 3 to 6 months—in some cases, much longer—with

Table 5.3   Shared Parenting in Divorce

A. First Principles
1. Shared responsibility
2. Mutual respect
3. Shared love and concern
4. Children first (best interest)
5. Respect boundaries
6. Respect differences (values, lifestyle)

B. Rules of Cooperative Parenting
1. *Competent care:* love/affection, food, clothing, cleanliness, discipline, education
2. *Boundaries:* time, value differences, styles of parenting
3. *Schedule compliance:* predictability, trustworthiness, reliability
4. *Due notice:* change, unexpected, unforeseen
5. *Informing the other:* child safety, mutual respect
6. *Parental communication:* separating parental and marital roles, conduct when child is present
7. *Special circumstances:* flexibility

neither parent having any knowledge of the children's experience when with the other parent. Such discontinuity in parenting is clearly not in the best interests of the children. For example, such arrangements make it very difficult to follow through on drug regimens, homework, discipline, extra-curricular activities, and school trips. Because events and experiences that are important to the children are not passed on, children can soon come to believe that neither parent cares about them because they repeatedly fail to acknowledge such significant events.

One way to reverse this process is to engage the parents in dialogue about the basic principles of parenting, taking apart the nuts and bolts of daily parenting. An exercise designed to create such dialogue is displayed in Table 5.3. Mainly, this is an opportunity for parents to explore one of the few areas that they have in common—namely, the love and affection they both have for their children. In this sense, this discussion can be both positive and enjoyable. However, it is also an opportunity to discuss, sometimes heatedly, problems in shared parenting. Although sometimes painful, such discussions are often very fruitful, especially in uncovering difficulties that stem primarily from the previous lack of discussion and dialogue. By initiating such a discussion, not only are solutions to these difficulties often readily apparent, but they begin the process of coming to terms with the fact that some differences must simply be accepted. This exercise can also afford the mediator the opportunity to introduce parents to the new language of parenting that will be used throughout subsequent sessions and that forms the fabric of their "Memorandum of Understanding." Although notions of *executive decision making, family boundaries, best interests,* and *due notice* will initially be foreign, they will also be essential to the construction of a

Table 5.4   Positive and Negative Intimacy

Positive Intimacy	Negative Intimacy
Acceptance	Rejection
Positive assumptions, expectations	Negative assumptions, expectations
Trust, respect, loyalty	Distrust, disrespect, disloyalty
Privacy, informality, confidences protected	Privacy, informality, confidences not protected
Implicit agreements and assumptions are positive	Implicit agreements and assumptions are negative
Healthy interdependence	Unhealthy dependence
Supportiveness, understanding	Competitiveness
Disclosure is nurturing	Disclosure is destructive
Good give-and-take	All take or all give
Security, comfort	Insecurity, discomfort
Maximum intensity of emotions	Maximum intensity of emotions

parenting plan within TFM. Thus, the exercise serves dual functions, initiating the dialogue that must be in place for effective shared parenting and teaching the language that speaks to a new conceptual approach to parenting. On one hand, both will be necessary to productive negotiation of their parenting plan. On the other hand, both will serve to bring order to what was previously unorganized, if not chaotic. Many parents subsequently report that an unexpected, even shocking, by-product of that discussion was a dramatic reduction in tension and conflict between them, either on the telephone, at the doorway, and/or at pickups or drop-offs. So delighted are the children that they often become boosters of mediation, encouraging their parents to attend.

Spousal Relations in Divorce. The patterns that characterize the ways clients relate to each other as spouses have evolved over a period of years and do not stop just because the partners now live apart. That these patterns will be displayed in mediation can be assumed. However, such patterns can be highly problematic because they serve to maintain a relationship, the spousal relationship, which should end with the impending or previous divorce. The maintenance of these patterns explains why these clients have been unable to negotiate a settlement informally and will actively interfere with their ability to be effective in a shared parenting relationship in the future. Premediation, then, is intended to do two things—namely, help parents understand the destructive character of their current relationship and picture for them the new business-like relationship they will need to develop to be effective shared parents.

With respect to the former, Ricci (1997, p. 83) makes a distinction between positive and negative intimacy, as seen in Table 5.4. These two sets of attributes are typically apt in characterizing the couple's relationship when it was still "good" and how it operates in the present. Further

Table 5.5   From Intimacy to a Business Relationship

Dimension	Intimate	Business
Legal status	Formal (married)	Informal
Emotional intensity	High	Low
Boundaries	Unclear (merging)	Clear
Sexual relations	Yes	No
Exclusive	Yes	No
Inhibitions	Low	High
Affect	Love	Respect
Obligations	High	Low
Sense of self	Dependent	Independent
Growth potential	High	Low
Stakes	High	Low
Focus	Involvement	Task

discussion of negative intimacy shows how the current pattern keeps the partners at a distance but still locked together. Finally, negative intimacy is explored in terms of parallel parenting and the various ways in which the latter interferes with effective parenting.

To help the couple move from negative intimacy to a business relationship, we use another exercise displayed in Table 5.5. Here, we review a range of dimensions and indicate what changes as one moves from an intimate to a business relationship. In each case, such a review moves in the direction of less intensity and involvement as well as greater distance and interaction limited to specific topics, issues, and especially tasks—in this case, tasks specific to their mutual involvement in parenting.

Understanding Conflict. In giving information to parents, we stress the destructive impact of engaging in conflict in front of the children or, worse, making them participants in the process. Such information is intended to make them aware of what they are doing and their potential consequences. To move their relationship still further, we need to make a distinction between different types of conflict. For this purpose, we use an exercise displayed in Table 5.6. Walking client couples through this exercise serves a number of related functions.

First, it qualifies previous information about conflict, making clear that conflict is inevitable and thus cannot be bad in its own right. Rather, the partners have a choice in how they handle issues in dispute between them. This is an important idea because mediation is *not* intended to eliminate conflict but rather to afford partners the opportunity to achieve workable solutions that they see as fair and reasonable.

Second, it suggests that different styles of conflict are associated with quite different outcomes. These partners will already be familiar with destructive conflict and can readily recognize their own conflict style. Discussion of

Table 5.6   Constructive and Destructive Conflict

Assumptions
- Conflict is a useful, necessary, and unavoidable part of parenting.
- Conflict can be handled in ways that are constructive or destructive.
- Everyone can learn to deal with issues in dispute in constructive ways.
- Constructive conflict involves a search for workable solutions to a shared problem, pictures the partners as team members, and achieves closure.

	Constructive	Destructive
Similarities		
Strong feelings	Yes	Yes
Sincere beliefs	Yes	Yes
Short/longstanding issue	Yes	Yes
Differences		
Closure on issue(s) in dispute	Yes	No
Attitude toward partner	Respect	Contempt
Engage in mind reading	No	Yes
Focus on issue(s)	Specific	General
Speak of past hurts	No	Yes
Hair trigger	No	Yes
Character assassination	No	Yes
Turn taking	Short/long	Short
Laughter	Yes	No
Reference to other (e.g., mother-in-law)	No	Yes
Clear objective	Yes	No
Attribution to partner	Positive	Negative
Check out assumptions	Yes	No
Closeness/distance (in closing)	Close	Distant

the notion of constructive conflict raises the possibility that this is something that they can and must learn to do, if not for themselves, then in the best interests of their children. Clients typically respond with ambivalence. Cognitively, they know that constructive conflict is desirable. Affectively, their relationship, characterized by negative intimacy, is such as to make it difficult for them see how this might be possible for them. Indeed, in some cases, this discussion merely feeds into an existing cycle of mutual blame.

Third, even if they do not know how to engage in constructive conflict, it affords them the opportunity to indicate publicly that they think it desirable and would gladly do so if only they could be shown how to do it. Such positive indications contribute to a mediatable frame and may themselves be enough to inhibit or curtail their negative intimacy. For example, Mathis (1998) refers to "couples from hell" in which "[undifferentiated] couples delude themselves that they communicate well, but what they are doing is actually *pseudocommunication*. Pseudocommunication is indirect, misleading, frequent but ineffective, and based mostly on negative skills like sending double messages, disguising criticism, and mind reading" (p. 43). Most couples in premediation will not be as extreme. Many will benefit from information giving and/or instruction to the point where they may begin negotiation. In more extreme cases, further intervention will be required before negotiation can begin.

Intervening to Improve Performance

Intervention in premediation is intended to alter a destructive pattern of interaction, reduce intense conflict (a "blockage") around a particular issue, and/or avoid an impasse. Separately and together, these various processes stand in the way of productive negotiation and thus make it impossible to resolve issues in dispute. In this regard, client couples vary widely. A helpful way to picture this distribution of couples is by means of their position on Garrity and Baris's (1994, p. 43) Conflict Assessment Scale. Qualified as only a "guideline," the scale recognizes five degrees of destructive conflict, including minimal, mild, moderate, moderately severe, and severe. Most couples who enter premediation fall in the first three positions. Couples displaying minimal conflict can distinguish between the needs of parents and children, can validate each other as parents, and have good control over expressions of negative intimacy. Those displaying mild conflict may fight in front of the children, question the children about the other's lifestyle, and attempt to form a coalition with the children against the other parent. Couples displaying moderate conflict may be verbally abusive but engage in no physical violence, quarrel loudly in front of the children, denigrate the other to the children, exchange verbal threats, and strive to entice the children into a coalition with one parent against the other.

Intervention with couples displaying this range of behaviors can take a variety of forms. For illustrative purposes only, we briefly explore five intervention techniques in common use, which are presented in no particular order of importance.

Reframing. Once mastered, reframing is a simple but powerful intervention technique. With couples in conflict over parenting, we often use a linked series of four reframing statements to create a mediatable frame. The first and most important intervention involves shifting their view of the children from *"mine to ours."* This obviates initial disputes over custody with the notion of shared responsibility. In the typical scenario in which a mother has done most or all of the parenting, the logic of the reframe rings true. Although she may have done most of the work, she clearly recognizes the importance of the father to the children's development. Frequently, she may have begged him to become more involved with their care, to no avail. Consequently, she is apt to hear the notion of shared responsibility as a form of vindication. For their part, fathers typically accept the reframe easily because they are often fearful that in divorce they will lose contact with their children completely.

The "shared responsibility" reframe is then linked to a second reframe, namely, *"each to his own."* This reframe is especially useful with couples struggling over child care practices. Many report longstanding conflict over this issue, with the mother insisting that her standards are best and the father insisting that his standards are better. This reframe cuts through this futile debate by validating both parents as competent and equally committed to responsible and supportive child care, even if their respective parenting styles vary ("there are 1,000 different ways to raise a healthy child"). This reframe is also consonant with the theoretical notions of systems and boundaries discussed previously (see Chapter 2). Although it can take some persuasion, given the longstanding character of this power struggle, it is often effective *so long as basic parenting competence is not itself an issue* (see below).

Objections to the "each to his own" frame are typically rooted in a marital complaint rather than a parenting concern. That is, the mother will typically resist the reframe on the grounds that it took a divorce to finally get the father to pay attention to the children. "How then," she asks, "can I be sure that it is genuine and not just a temporary flash in the pan?" The answer is in the third reframe, namely, *"better late than never."* This reframe builds on the mother's nearly universal recognition that the father's involvement is good for children's healthy development. Further questioning typically reveals that the children have responded positively to the father's recent but sincere efforts and wish for him to continue. The reframe thus asks the mother to be patient, now that her longstanding request for the father's involvement is beginning to occur, and to feel satisfied that the children are getting what she knew all along that they needed. It also asks the father to continue his new interest in child care while being vigilant as to his dependability—that is, keeping to an agreed-on schedule, giving due notice about changes, and so on—because both parents must learn to work together about parenting over the long term.

An alternate objection to these sequential reframes concerns the issue of basic parenting competence. As the argument goes, the mother questions the father's competence on the simple ground that his lack of previous involvement suggests that he may lack the requisite skills. The final answering reframe is that *"it takes time to learn to do things well."* This goes beyond asking both parents to be patient in parenting and speaks to a range of practical issues. Although one or the other is learning the appropriate skills, a graduated schedule may serve the children well. The newly involved parent may agree to take a parenting course or ask his or her mother (the children's grandmother) for help or, more rarely, accept advice from the other parent. Whatever their particular course, the reframe establishes the principle that both parents will become equal in parenting, even if one parent may need some additional time to do so. At that point, the first two reframes would then become operative, providing the basis for cooperative parenting over the long term.

Enactment. This is a technique in which the client couple is asked to discuss an issue in conflict in front of the mediator. This allows the mediator to map the precise sequence of interaction, pinpoint areas of dysfunction, and design an intervention intended to alter that sequence. In premediation, this typically involves two variations. The first variation involves "staging a failure." That is, the mediator asks the couple to discuss a contentious issue, knowing from past experience that their discussion will rapidly deteriorate into destructive conflict and thus accomplish nothing. That failure allows the mediator to argue that their usual method of problem solving is patently ineffective and that it is time for a change.

The second variation is identical to the first, except that in this instance, the mediator introduces some change in the sequence, in the hope that this will lead them to a different outcome. In a recent case, for example, a couple displayed a markedly dysfunctional approach to conflict management. The wife would normally begin by advancing a specific proposal in regard to an issue in dispute. After about 90 seconds, the husband would make a slashing motion with his hand, and the wife would stop, ending the sequence, with the issue obviously unresolved. In the enactment, the sequence unfolded as always, with the wife ending in silent frustration. In this instance, however, the mediator asked the wife to continue. When she could not, looking stunned and confused, the mediator leaned over and, in a staged whisper, asked the wife if the husband had a gun in his pocket with which he would shoot her if she continued. Wife shook her head "no." "Perhaps he has a knife?" the mediator continued. Again, the answer was no. "Surely, if you continue, he will leap across the table and beat you with his fists?" the mediator asked melodramatically. Now, with both spouses smiling, again she answered no. "Well, then," said the mediator, "by all means continue, and I will keep you safe." She did continue, and within 10 minutes the couple had resolved the issue. Although the issue was a minor one, it marked a turning point in the case, for according to them, it was the first time they had been able to achieve closure in more than 30 years. The couple went on to achieve a complete settlement.

In this case, a single enactment was sufficient to produce a breakthrough in the case. In more dysfunctional couples, repeated enactments may be required to achieve the same degree of change. In another case, after 24 years of marriage, a wife had had a blatant affair with a much younger man, leaving the husband enraged, confused, and feeling vaguely guilty. Their conflict style was characterized by repeated angry outbursts, multiple issues, and character assassination. After doing the conflict exercise (see Table 5.6), repeated enactments were run, with the mediator labeling destructive elements, keeping them focused on a single issue, and giving much support. In time, their conflict style gradually evolved from entirely destructive to primarily constructive, that is, at least positive enough to allow for productive negotiation.

In a third example, a couple had ended a brief marriage on an explosive note and had barely spoken since, despite sharing in the care of a toddler. Efforts at communication had been further exacerbated by repeated court appearances, police involvement, and the intervention of both sets of in-laws. Despite bitter feelings and a distinct lack of trust, assessment indicated that poor communication and the lack of communication were the key problems. By connecting enactments around specific parenting issues, maintaining a singular focus, and blocking premature closure, the couple resolved several minor issues and were much clearer about the major issues that would be the later focus of negotiation. In subsequent caucusing with the mediator, each spouse reported that the sessions had gone much better than expected, and both felt much less negative about their in-laws.

Microanalysis. If enactments focus on behavior, microanalysis focuses on insight. After seeing a particular pattern unfold repeatedly, the mediator comments on it explicitly, offering the couple an interpretation that is then discussed. The aim of the intervention is to pinpoint misunderstandings rooted in each party's perception of the other's behavior and intent.

In a recent case, a couple displayed the following pattern. The wife would advance a proposal, and the husband would begin asking questions about it. The wife would feel attacked and would defend herself by referring to some past offense by the husband. The husband would respond in kind, at which point the mediator would intervene to stop the process. After seeing this pattern repeat several times, the mediator engaged in microanalysis, closely questioning each party in front of the other as to his or her intentions and feelings as the process was unfolding. What emerged was that the parties had different styles of decision making. The wife was a generalist who focused on the big picture and whose proposals were accordingly quite broad. The husband was a specialist who focused on the details and whose questions were intended to supply him with the specifics he needed before he could make any decision. When their relationship involved positive intimacy, these two approaches worked well because they were complementary. Now, in a state of negative intimacy, these same approaches yielded a competitive outcome that blocked closure and promoted conflict. The mediator reframed both approaches as "efforts at being helpful" and as "different, with each neither better nor worse than the other." The parties were asked to refrain from slipping back into the past, to focus on one issue at a time, and to have patience in arriving at an agreement, with it being perfectly reasonable to come back to a particular issue several times before they were both satisfied. Gradually, over three sessions, their efforts at negotiation became steadily more effective. Note that in this case, as in many others, there is no fine line between premediation and negotiation. Rather, one may merge into another, sometimes in a single session, sometimes over several sessions.

Speaking and Listening. Speaking and listening are especially useful when dealing with couples whose listening skills are poor and/or who have difficulty making statements that are clear and easy to understand. To improve their communication skills, the couple is asked to discuss an issue in dispute. Each partner is asked to make a short statement on the issue, couched in respectful terms, that advances one or more suggestions for change. As each partner speaks, the other partner is expected to remain silent (no interrupting allowed) but attentive. As one partner finishes his or her statement, the other partner is asked to summarize what he or she heard and to check with the other partner to make sure that he or she got it right. The partners take turns being speaker and listener, and then the entire process is discussed for lessons in which the couple can learn from the experience.

A variation on this intervention involves *role reversal*. Here, each partner is asked to play the role of the other, as he or she goes through the speak and listen process, and to check out if he or she has correctly articulated the other partner's position in regard to the issue in question.

These interventions are typically foreign to clients in mediation, who feel awkward and uncomfortable in enacting them. Nevertheless, the results can be impressive. Speakers often find that they were much less clear than they thought they had been, and listeners often find that they were so busy formulating their response that they had stopped listening. Speakers often find that the effort to be clear often means saying new things (i.e., articulating thoughts that are new to them), offering a new slant on an old issue. Similarly, listeners often find that in really listening, they actually hear new things—that is, come to understand the other person's plans and intentions in a new way—and are more sympathetic than they were before. In short, teaching improved communication skills increases the likelihood that the parties will come closer to settlement.

Trauma. Some marital relationships end quietly, but others end in some form of trauma. Trauma can take various forms, including violence to a person, violence to property, infidelity, and the misappropriation of funds. Sometimes trauma is unidirectional, involving a partner who does something that hurts the other. Sometimes it is mutual or sequential. Consider the case in which a wife had an affair with her husband's best friend, in response to which the husband emptied out their bank accounts, leaving the wife penniless and forced to beg for support from her parents, a process she found utterly humiliating. Sometime clients are cognitively aware that their affective fixation with the traumatic experience is irrational but feel powerless to block the intrusion of these thoughts or feelings. More often, clients show no such awareness, hidden shame, or guilt or resentment at the root of their ongoing rage at the other (Retzinger & Scheff, 2000). In either event, trauma is especially problematic for mediation. This is so because the fixation of one or both partners with the traumatic experience(s) dramatically increases the likelihood of impasse, as all roads seem to lead back to the trauma.

Several intervention techniques have been found helpful with such clients. One possibility involves the use of a forgiveness ritual (Schneider, 2000). It is striking how often what the injured party wants most is for the other to simply acknowledge the harm, accept liability, and ask for forgiveness. The compliance of both parties can be problematic. It can be difficult for the injured party to say explicitly that he or she seeks forgiveness, both because the party may find such an admission humiliating and may be afraid that doing so may somehow let the other party off the hook. Similarly, it can be difficult for the offender to accept blame, either because of denial (he or she blames the other party's rejection for the affair), guilt, or fear that doing so will undermine his or her bargaining strength in mediation. This process can be especially complicated when both parties were involved in the trauma. However, with patience and sensitivity, and sometimes movement between joint and individual sessions, these admissions can often be teased out and a forgiveness ritual planned between them. For example, the offender may agree to literally go down on bended knee and say, "I'm sorry," in a form acceptable to both parties. Most important, enacting such a ritual can mark the turning point in the case.

In a recent case, the parties were at impasse regarding a particular issue. Individual caucusing revealed that the wife felt victim of a trauma that followed her voluntary departure from the matrimonial home. It also showed that the husband, without the wife's knowledge, had kept track of her welfare through the wife's mother, felt considerable guilt at what had befallen her, and was indeed willing to say, "I'm sorry." The greatest obstacle was overcoming the wife's reluctance to ask for forgiveness, based on her own weak self-esteem. When, with the support of the mediator, the wife did articulate her request and the husband did ask for forgiveness, the issue that had initiated the process in the first place was resolved in 10 minutes flat, to their mutual surprise.

In some cases, "sorry" alone is not enough to satisfy the injured party's abiding anger. In such cases, an ordeal of some sort (Haley, 1984) may be required as a tangible form of penance. The nature of the ordeal is limited only by the imagination of the parties and the canons of ethics. In mediation, ordeals that might involve pain, suffering, or injury are ruled out of bounds. Instead, ordeals must carry symbolic weight for *both* parties. For example, if transporting the children is an issue in dispute, as it often is, the offender may agree to drive the children back and forth between homes for the next 6 months. Alternately, the offender may agree to a cash settlement, based on third-party payments for the other party's medical or dental care, car insurance, or still other symbolically important payments. The offender may agree to tutor the children in mathematics or read to them before bed (at his or her home), neither of which had been done prior to the separation. Whatever the details of the ordeal, the central issue is whether it satisfies the injured party's sense of justice and fair play and begins the process for both of them of healing and recovery.

Still another option involves the use of a technique designed to diminish the trauma. One innovative technique involves a thought experiment first described in Bross (1982). In simplified form, this asks clients to imagine that their pain and anger are contained in a knapsack filled with rocks. The knapsack is very heavy and painful, as the straps cut into the shoulders. "How wonderful it would be," the mediator asks, "if you could find a way to take off the knapsack. If I could show you a way to do this, would you want to take off the knapsack?" When the clients say yes, as they typically do, they are told to imagine a small box, open, empty, and waiting. The client is to imagine easing off the knapsack for the first time in years and to feel the relief through his or her entire body. The client then sets the knapsack down and begins transferring the rocks from the knapsack to the box, each rock shrinking so that they all fit easily into the small box. The box is then sealed and taken to the client's car. The client then drives to a local sports stadium, enters, and carries the box to the bleachers at the very topmost row of seats. The box, containing the bitter and angry feelings of the trauma, is deposited behind one of the seats. The client returns home, without the box, or the knapsack, or the feelings. He or she has not been asked to forget these events or the feelings attached to them. Rather, these remain safe in the box in the stadium. But the client no longer has to carry these feelings every day; these memories and feelings have been diminished in importance, shrunk to the size of a small box, now far away. Accordingly, the client can now get on with the task of negotiating a fair settlement with his or her partner (for an alternative cognitive restructuring approach to trauma, see McIsaac & Finn, 1999).

Indications and Contraindications

This review of premediation methods has only scratched the surface of the full range of possibilities and options in TFM. Even so, whether through giving information, teaching and instruction, and/or clinical intervention, the premediation phase of TFM is intended to prepare clients for productive negotiation. These methods are likely to be effective to the extent that they address weaknesses, blockages, or dysfunctions that, left untouched, would predict an impasse in negotiation. The indications listed in Table 5.1 constitute those criteria by which we determine if premediation efforts have or have not been successful. For clients to move on to Phase 3, negotiation, they should:

- have some conscious control over the type and intensity of their feelings;
- be able to advance an organized and logical proposal;
- be clear and effective in their communication (i.e., communication should address specific issues, one at a time, in the present, and express a clear preference or position);
- be responsive to the other partner, that is, speak to him or her respectfully, make eye contact, allow for reasonable turn taking, consider the other's ideas (without dismissing them outright), and show that he or she has heard what the other has had to say;
- show some willingness to accommodate issues in dispute, that is, display some flexibility and willingness to compromise or at least consider alternate perspectives and solutions; and
- be responsive to the mediator, both as regards managerial (who speaks, turn taking) and substantive instructions and suggestions.

About 80% of client couples will achieve these criteria within two to three 2-hour premediation sessions and will then enter the negotiation phase. Another 10% will eventually achieve these criteria over a longer process, whereas the remaining 10% will show, usually early on, that premediation efforts are futile. The latter will either be referred for longer-term counseling or be returned to their lawyers for litigation.

Discussion

Of the phases in the TFM practice model, premediation is the most likely to be misunderstood. Such misunderstandings may arise in three areas. First, given the therapeutic character of the model, one may conclude that TFM practitioners do therapy. As this chapter shows, that conclusion would be reasonable but incorrect. Rather, practitioners use therapeutic *techniques* in pursuit of mediation objectives, particularly in ensuring that clients possess the requisites for productive negotiation in family mediation. Doing so has two important consequences: It permits many clients to participate in and benefit from family mediation who would otherwise be turned away as unmediatable and, by addressing underlying relationship problems, dramatically increases the likelihood that those who reach agreement will be able to avoid impasse in the future and thus have no need to turn to the court.

Second, the therapeutic character of the model might suggest that premediation efforts involve an exclusive reliance on therapeutic techniques. As this chapter makes abundantly clear, the model is therapeutic in the generic sense of inducing change. Although change can result from clinical intervention, it can also occur in response to giving information, teaching new skills, or some combination of all three. In turn, this perspective suggests a broader sense in which mediation clients need help. In many, dysfunction refers specifically to ineffective and often destructive patterns of interaction that may predate mediation by years, if not decades. In others, dysfunction refers to situational difficulties specific to the divorce and thus of recent origin. Such difficulties may include confusion, emotional distress, and simple ignorance, especially as regards the impact of divorce on adults and children. In such cases, complex clinical interventions may *not* be called for; active listening, support, empathy, information, and some instruction may be quite adequate to prepare them for negotiation.

Finally, the notion that TFM involves five phases suggests that they would normally be enacted sequentially. In fact, such a conclusion significantly underestimates the flexibility of the model, which recognizes several different variations, including the omission of premediation, its one-time sequential use, its repeated use as clients alternate between premediation and negotiation, or its repeated but declining use as blockages are addressed and the focus shifts exclusively to negotiation. More generally, the use of premediation illustrates one of the central tenets of the model—namely, the importance of fitting the model to the changing needs of the clients. In practice, this means that practitioners intervene with clients as much or as little as is deemed necessary to allow and maintain productive negotiation, with *intervention* defined generically to encompass anything likely to be helpful for clients, given their attributes and circumstances.

References

Benjamin, M., & Irving, H. H. (1992). Towards a feminist-informed model of therapeutic family mediation. *Mediation Quarterly, 10*(2), 129-153.

Bross, A. (1982). The family therapists reference manual. In A. Bross (Ed.), *Family therapy: A recursive model of strategic practice* (pp. 218-242). Toronto: Methuen.

Garrity, C. B., & Baris, M. A. (1994). *Caught in the middle: Protecting the children of high-conflict divorce.* San Francisco: Jossey-Bass.

Haley, J. (1984). *Ordeal therapy.* San Francisco: Jossey-Bass.

Mathis, R. D. (1998). Couples from hell: Undifferentiated spouses in divorce mediation. *Mediation Quarterly, 16*(1), 37-49.

McIsaac, H., & Finn, C. (1999). Parents beyond conflict: A cognitive restructuring model for high-conflict families in divorce. *Family & Conciliation Courts Review, 37*(1), 74-82.

Retzinger, S., & Scheff, T. (2000). Emotion, alienation, and narratives: Resolving intractable conflict. *Mediation Quarterly, 18*(1), 71-85.

Ricci, I. (1997). *Mom's house, Dad's house: Making two homes for your child.* New York: Fireside.

Saposnek, D. T. (1998). *Mediating child custody disputes* (Rev. ed.). San Francisco: Jossey-Bass.

Schneider, E. D. (2000). What it means to be sorry: The power of apology in mediation. *Mediation Quarterly, 17*(3), 265-280.

6 The TFM Approach: Step-by-Step Guide

Phase 3: Negotiation

Although some clients will be referred out during Phases 1 and 2, most will enter Phase 3, negotiation. For our purposes, we will follow Antsey (1991, pp. 91-92, cited in Boulle & Kelly, 1998, p. 50) in defining *negotiation* as (a) an interaction process (b) involving two or more parties (c) who seek to reach agreement (d) over a problem, issue, and/or conflict of interest between them (e) in which each seeks as far as possible to preserve his or her self-interest but is willing to adjust views and/or positions in the joint effort to achieve an agreement.

This definition is interesting in two respects and serves to foreshadow much of our difficulty with the treatment of negotiation in the mediation literature. On one hand, this definition is useful in capturing key elements of negotiation in mediation—namely, that it is a dynamic and thus highly variable process; involves parties whose involvement is motivated, at least in part, by a desire to reach agreement; and concerns issues or problems that are defined in common, at least broadly so. On the other hand, this definition is problematic on several grounds. First, as with all alternative dispute resolution (ADR) models, it makes no assumptions about the history or character of the relationship between the parties, either in the past, the present, or the future. However, in family mediation, especially in therapeutic family mediation (TFM)–based efforts, the character of the relationship between the parties is simply integral to negotiation between them. Indeed, insofar as the majority of cases involve parenting issues, it is clearly in the interests of the children that the parties, their parents, find a way to interact that is cooperative, mutually supportive, and mutually respectful. Second, this definition leaves the "problems" in conflict unspecified and, by referring to "interests," implies that those problems are substantive in character. In family mediation in general, all substantive problems fall into two broad categories having to do with parenting and/or financial plans. Moreover, in TFM in particular, negotiation will not be restricted to substantive issues alone but will also encompass relational issues and processes. Thus, the question of "How should we get along?" during and after mediation is at least as important—if not more so—than the question of "How shall we solve this or that problem?" Finally, in referring to "interests," the definition offers a perspective restricted to the interests of the parties at the table. However, as we have noted already, this perspective is too narrow, omitting reference to the family system as an "interested" party in its own right, to the best interests of the children, which may or may not coincide with the self-interests of their parents, and to the interests of extended family members, such grandparents, whose involvement with the children may hang on the outcome of the negotiation between the parents. These various considerations suggest a reformulation of negotiation more in keeping with both family mediation in general and TFM in particular. Thus, negotiation in TFM-based family mediation may be defined in terms of the following core elements: a dynamic verbal and behavioral interaction process involving both partners and possibly others (a) who are in conflict over parenting, financial, and relational issues affecting them, their children, and possibly others and (b) who seek to achieve agreement over these issues to realize their self-interest(s), meet their individual needs, protect the best interests of their children, preserve their relationship as parents, and otherwise get on with their separate lives.

Although somewhat cumbersome, this definition captures the sense of negotiation in TFM-based mediation—that is, a complex process driven by multiple motives, the outcome(s) of which will likely importantly affect the lives and relationships of the people making up the two family systems brought together by the marriage of the partners.

From this perspective, this section will describe the negotiation process in TFM while constructing a model of negotiation in family mediation (see Table 6.1). Such a model does not now exist in the family mediation literature, and it is badly overdue. Instead, practitioners have been content to borrow from the ADR literature. Although we will also feel free to borrow from the good work done there, we will also be at some pains to point out its limitations when applied uncritically to family mediation. Thus, what follows will begin with a brief overview of the four most prominent negotiation models currently in use.

Models of Negotiation: Overview and Critique

Four models currently dominate the ADR and mediation literatures (for other models, see Pruitt & Carnevale, 1989; Rifkin, Millen, & Cobb, 1991;

Table 6.1   Negotiation

Goals

Substantive issues
- Clarify issues
- Expand the stock of options
- Submit preferred options to reality check
- Full disclosure
- Achieve settlement

Relationship issues
- Accept the divorce
- Put hard feelings in the past
- Establish a working relationship
- Put the children first
- Display constructive negotiation skills
- Create a level playing field
- Make a commitment to comply with terms of settlement

Family mediation
- Client satisfaction

Principles
- Equity
- Fairness
- Functionality
- Satisfaction

Methods

List issues in dispute
- Rejoin in public
- Create a mediatable frame
- List the issues in dispute
- Set the agenda
- Break complex issues into smaller, more manageable chunks
- Identify subtexts and hidden agendas
- Maintain an even playing field: power balancing
- Move between relational and substantive issues
- Create options and alternatives: brainstorming
- Trade off
- Evaluate options: reality check
- Avoid impasses
  - Relational options ($n = 10$)
  - Substantive options ($n = 5$)
  - Generic options ($n = 3$)

Indications

Relational
- Frequency and intensity of positive affect
- Frequency and intensity of negative affect
- More effective conflict management skills
  - Enhanced focus on the issues and not the parties
  - Greater flexibility and openness
  - Improved focus on the present and future
  - Greater tolerance of differences

(Continued)

Table 6.1 (Continued)

- Enhanced communication skills
  - Improved communication clarity
  - Improved assertiveness and sensitivity to verbal and nonverbal cues
  - Enhanced mutual attention, listening, respect, and empathy
  - Improved listening accuracy
- Reduced frequency of common dysfunctions

Substantive
  - Settlement: complete, partial
  - Fair, equitable under the circumstances
  - Thorough review

Processual
  - Client satisfaction

Slaikeu, Pearson, Luckett, & Myers, 1985). Below, we describe and evaluate each model in turn for its utility in illuminating processes in family mediation.

Power Negotiation. Following Barsky (2000, p. 64), the first dominant model is the power negotiation model. As such, it is the focus of a large popular literature, with titles such as *Winning!* (Nelson, 1997), *Negotiate to Win* (Schoonmaker, 1989), *How to Argue and Win Every Time* (Spence, 1995), and *How to Get What You Want* (Cohen, 1980). Using labels such as *positional bargaining* and *distributive justice,* it is also the focus of a scholarly and research literature (Druckman, 1993; Menkel-Meadow, 1984; Pruitt & Carnevale, 1989; Raiffa, 1982).

As these popular titles would suggest, this is an approach in which the parties compete for an unequal share of a limited single resource, such as money. Negotiation is based on zero-sum logic, with any advantage to one party a disadvantage to the other party. Parties are thus encouraged to take extreme opening positions in the hope that eventual accommodation somewhere between these extremes will offer them some advantage (Ellis & Stuckless, 1996). To reach that accommodation, parties are further encouraged to use various tactics and strategies to coerce, persuade, and/or delude one side to give in to the other side's demands. Research has shown that such efforts can be counterproductive and wasteful (Menkel-Meadow, 1984), in that the parties can find themselves in locked-in positions (Burton, 1987). Finally, power-based negotiation gives a clear and decided advantage to the party with greater power and resources. In family mediation, power-based tactics are apparent when one spouse makes outrageous monetary demands or the other party advances parenting demands based on a subtext.

Evaluation. A positive feature of this approach to negotiation is that it encourages parties to be confident, self-assured, and absolutely clear about their objectives. Otherwise, this is an approach to negotiation that is unsuitable for family mediation. The prime reason for this is that power-based negotiation shows no regard whatever for the previous and ongoing relations between the spouses. Strategic conduct merely exacerbates the "trust vacuum" between them, a condition that is antithetical to cooperative problem solving or respectful coparenting over the long run. Furthermore, by promoting an uneven playing field, it tends to advantage men at the expense of women and may promote settlements that are unconscionable. Finally, although one might conceive of family assets in distributive terms, that would certainly not be true of parenting. Indeed, recent efforts in the field have moved decisively away from notions of ownership or property in favor of shared responsibility and coparenting. On balance, then, power-based negotiation is *not* an approach likely to be useful in family mediation.

Rights Negotiation. The rights approach to negotiation is based on the rule of law in which the parties' claims are rooted in legal entitlements, procedural conventions, and/or judicial precedents (Bossy, 1983; Conley & O'Barr, 1990; Menkel-Meadow, 1984; Mnookin & Kornhauser, 1979). These bases for negotiation seek to ensure that all parties—whether rich or poor, male or female—are equal before the law. If one set of claims prevails over another, it is primarily because they are based on stronger legal arguments. Furthermore, the rights approach is buttressed by discovery procedures in which respective claims are held to a rigorous standard of truth and in which statutory changes seek to ensure that laws reflect current conditions and perspectives. These safeguards place limits on the illegitimate use of power and provide a standardized adversarial system for resolving disputes.

Evaluation. The positive features of this approach to negotiation are that parties are required to meet known standards of truth and advance claims in a context in which all parties know the rules and in which there are clear sanctions for rule breaking. These features are likely to promote rational thought and curb behavioral extremes. Perhaps most important, it is the model of choice for those couples who cannot or will not enter mediation. Among divorcing couples in dispute, the rights model accounts for the majority of settlements and will likely continue to do so for the foreseeable future. That said, this model of negotiation remains highly problematic for family mediation. Among its various limitations, perhaps the most prominent is that this approach favors rules over relationships (Conley & O'Barr, 1990). The adversarial logic of this approach remains zero sum, thus generating winners and losers who are unlikely to look kindly on each other after the proceedings are over. Clients are encouraged to take extreme positions and may be enjoined by their lawyers not to speak directly to each other while the proceedings are ongoing. Despite the rules, or perhaps because of them, the use of positional tactics and strategies is widespread (Nelson, 1997), and there is much room for the abuse of power. Such abuses extend to the use of children as pawns or game pieces, as each partner jockeys for position and advantage. The entire process is extremely taxing in emotional and financial terms and exacerbated by client disempowerment, as major decisions revert to the lawyers and the judge. Finally, in adjudicated cases, imposed settlements may be unacceptable to the parties, such that continued conflict and repeated returns to court (relitigation) are both commonplace. Although we may not dispense with rights-based negotiation, this model is clearly not suited to family mediation except as an alternative should the parties reach an impasse.

Interest-Based Negotiation. An alternative approach is variously known as collaborative negotiation, integrative bargaining, problem-solving negotiation, principled bargaining, or interest-based bargaining. Championed by Fisher and Ury of the Harvard Negotiation Project (Fisher & Brown, 1988; Fisher, Ury, & Patton, 1997; Ury, 1991; see also Ellis & Stuckless, 1996) and highly influential, the model is centered on four features.

First, separate the people from their problems or issues. In an effort to promote a working relationship among the parties, they are encouraged to recognize each other's feelings, treat each other with respect, and avoid blaming each other. Acknowledging feelings in this way allows the parties to put their feelings aside and focus clearly on the substantive issues in dispute.

Next, the parties are asked to go beyond their positions and focus instead on their underlying needs and interests. These interests are both the real reason for the conflict and the real bases for settlement. In exploring these interests, the discovery of overlapping or complementary needs would be commonplace.

Third, the parties are asked to be creative—that is, think outside the box—in exploring settlement options. This means moving beyond the narrow confines of legal solutions to options that make full use of available resources while addressing respective interests. This approach to negotiation, then, frames the effort in terms of cooperative problem solving and the satisfaction of mutual interests.

Finally, settlement options should be explored in terms of objective criteria rather than subjective preferences or perceptions. This focus is based on the notion that it is easier for parties to accept an objective standard than concede to the others' subjective demands. Parties are thus encouraged to consider market values, expert opinions, industry standards, or commercial conventions. They are also asked to consider their BATNA, their best alternative to a negotiated agreement. That is, compared to objective criteria, settlement should be considered only if it offers the parties a better deal than could be obtained elsewhere, such as through litigation or arbitration.

Evaluation. This model of negotiation has much to recommend it. As others have noted (Adler, Rosen, & Silverstein, 1998; Boulle & Kelly, 1998, p. 56; Barsky, 2000, p. 79), this model deals with real conflict by addressing the parties' needs and interests, is efficient in encouraging creative problem solving, preserves relationships by addressing feelings and encouraging mutual respect, provides legitimate standards for evaluating and accepting settlement options, promotes rationality among the parties, and encourages noncoercive modes of influence.

These advantages notwithstanding, the interest-based approach remains highly problematic in terms of family mediation. Perhaps the most salient of these limitations is that it fails to account for the previous, ongoing, and future relations among the parties. With a focus on commercial issues and problems, there is no mechanism to correct prevailing dysfunction in relations among the parties. For the same reason, the parties may be unwilling or unable to act rationally, rendering the model ineffective when quick decisions may be needed. Similarly, there is no mechanism to address power imbalances between the parties and thus means to avoid unconscionable settlements when one party is being exploited by another, more powerful party. Furthermore, the advanced social skills required by the model may not be in evidence among the parties, just as the requirements of rationality and individual decision making may not be in keeping with parties who derive from communal cultures. Thus, although elements of the model may be transferable to family mediation, the model per se is better suited to ADR nonfamily matters than family mediation.

Transformative Negotiation. Transformative negotiation is the approach advanced by Bush and Folger (1994) and since supported by their advocates (e.g., Lang, 1996). This model is centered on two key notions, that of empowerment and recognition. In this context, empowerment refers to improved self-awareness, confidence, and self-efficacy. Partners are intended to develop a clearer sense of their goals and interests, the options and choices available to them, their interpersonal skills, their available resources, and their conscious decisions. Recognition is an extension of each partner's interpersonal skills, with specific emphasis on developing an empathic understanding of the other. These efforts are intended to reduce anxiety, anger, and defensiveness while becoming more open, sympathetic, and aware of the other person's situation. Clearly, empowerment and recognition interact. Recognition by the other is empowering, whereas empowerment makes it easier for each party to recognize the other. As both parties are empowered and recognized, they are better able to work cooperatively and resolve their differences. However, whether they do so is not the central focus of transformative efforts. Even though the parties may continue to disagree, each may still have shown personal growth in engaging in the process.

Evaluation. Both empowerment and recognition are important elements in TFM, suggesting that these elements of the model transfer well to other models. However, as a model of negotiation per se, this model remains problematic for family mediation. Perhaps the central difficulty with the model is its idealism. The central premise of the model is that clients are offered empowerment and recognition because they are inherently good things, not because they are expected to engender reciprocity. Although these may be appropriate goals for some clients, most come to mediation seeking more pragmatic outcomes, such as how to share time with their children or how to apportion their accumulated assets. These outcomes may be realized using this model, but they are clearly not its central focus, such that many clients may simply reject the opportunity for transformation. Furthermore, the model has little to say about the negotiation process per se and thus fails to address a variety of related issues, including power imbalances, the child's best interests, or high-conflict couples. In reference to the latter, the model places inordinate emphasis on rational discourse and thus is unclear about methods for inducing such discourse among clients who display intense anger, depression, anxiety, or grief. It may also provide a poor fit with clients from communal cultures who may reject individualistic, insight-oriented psychotherapy. Finally, the time required for clients to develop insight about self or other may be out of step with the urgent and immediate needs of clients undergoing divorce. Thus, although the transformative model displays several useful features, we conclude that it is not an appropriate choice as a model of negotiation in family mediation.

More generally, then, it will now be apparent that none of the predominant models of negotiation will serve as models of negotiation in family mediation. Although several models provide elements that can usefully be incorporated into a mediation model, such a model does not exist. In turning to the TFM approach to negotiation, we attempt to fill that gap in the literature by advancing a model of negotiation specific to family mediation.

Phase 3: Negotiation

Discussion of negotiation within TFM is divided into four parts, concerned respectively with goals, principles, methods, and indications.

Goals

As noted already, negotiation in TFM is concerned with resolving differences about both relationship and substantive issues. This duality is reflected in the various goals of mediation.

As to the *substantive issues*, the goals of mediation are as follows:

Clarify the Issues. On one level, this goal involves helping each partner describe his or her various proposals in sufficient detail to ensure that he or she has thought it through in practical terms *and* is well understood by the other partner. Because the former is often *not* the case, walking through a proposal is a way of teaching the client and his or her partner how to approach proposals in ways that are logical, orderly, and practical. As to the former, checking one partner's proposals with the other partner is a way of ensuring that both can display the listening skills needed when they are asked to negotiate their proposals.

On another level, clarifying the issues involves co-constructing the issues to ensure that they are mediatable. This will have been done already among couples who require premediation, for this will be their first *public* airing of their respective proposals. For the same reason, it occurs during the negotiation phase among couples who enter it directly after intake/assessment.

Expand the Stock of Options. On entry into mediation, clients typically advance diametrically opposed proposals. Expanding the stock of options gives clients room to maneuver and dramatically increases the likelihood that one or more of these options will make sense to both parties.

Submit Preferred Options to Reality Check. Just because given options are preferred by one or the other client does not automatically mean that they are reasonable or better than options that might be obtained elsewhere, that is, through litigation or arbitration. Before they can be considered for inclusion in any settlement, they should first be evaluated against some standard. In some cases, that standard may be objective, including comparable options available through the court and the market value for specific assets or expectations based on a child's age, gender, and developmental level. In other cases, those standards may be common sense, logical consistency, or the mediator's common experience. In any event, before selecting any option for inclusion in the settlement, both clients must demonstrate informed consent.

Full Disclosure. To be effective, the mediator must have access to any and all facts relevant to the issues in dispute. This applies equally to parental and financial issues, for the absence of either may mislead the mediator and perhaps give one party an unfair advantage. So central is this objective that it is a standard feature of all mediation contracts.

In most cases, such disclosure will not be difficult to achieve because the facts themselves may not be complex and both parties are more than willing to be open and honest in response to the mediator's questions. Moreover, each spouse can provide a reality check against the other, thus filling in inadvertent omissions and correcting errors.

In some cases, however, disclosure can be problematic. The most common reason for such problems is lack of knowledge, based on the distribution of family roles. In traditional families, for example, mothers care for children, and fathers are in charge of the money. Although there will always be some overlap, mothers in this arrangement may not be fully informed about the family's finances, just as fathers' knowledge about the children may be incomplete. In such families, discussing parenting and money can be a revelation for both spouses. In a small proportion of cases, additional problems arise through overt efforts at concealment and subterfuge. Given that mediators have no powers of discovery and rely on a trust relationship with clients, their ability to ensure disclosure is limited. They may legitimately ask to see relevant documents, may call in the respective lawyers, and, rarely, may call on outside experts, such as forensic accountants. However, the closer mediation comes to look and feel like litigation, the less effective it becomes at inducing trust and promoting cooperative problem solving among the parties. If reasonable efforts on the mediator's part do not leave the parties satisfied that all relevant facts have been disclosed, the mediator will have little choice but to terminate service. That said, we should note that we have never terminated a case for lack of disclosure.

Achieve Settlement. Finally, clients arrive in mediation reporting that they are "stuck," unable to move forward in their lives because they cannot arrive at an agreement by informal means. They come to mediation, hoping that the practitioner will help them get "unstuck," that is, help them reach agreement so that they can move on. Settlement is especially crucial for the children who may find themselves in interim arrangements that are *not* in their best interests. Such arrangements may arise by chance, as a function of the circumstances under which the parents separated, or they may reflect a court order that was intended to stabilize matters temporarily but has outlived its usefulness. Achieving settlement, then, is important for all concerned, ensuring the best interests of the children but also empowering the parents to make the necessary decisions that will allow them to move on with their lives. They are further empowered by the fact that, once signed, their settlement supercedes any existing court order(s) and, with specific exceptions, may go beyond various family law statutes.

With the exception of the co-constructed character of mediation formulations, mediation of substantive issues appears very much like ADR mediation and leans heavily on the interest-based approach to mediation. As noted earlier, however, TFM negotiation pursues an additional agenda concerned with *family relations*. The goals in this area are as follows.

Accept the Divorce. Much current conflict over substantive issues originates in the couple's history of marital conflict. The substantive issues come to symbolize old sources of conflict, pain, and anger. That is, to some extent, ongoing conflict reflects these partners' unwillingness to accept the reality of their impending or previous divorce. That divorce renders most, if not all, old arguments moribund. Consequently, an important relational goal of family mediation is to encourage partners to accept their divorce on an emotional level on the assumption that once they have done so, much of the conflict surrounding substantive issues will begin to dissipate.

Put Hard Feelings in the Past. Failure of couples to accept their divorce is typically manifested in their repeated return to past events that engendered "hard" or negative feelings. When such feelings are intense, couples will be referred to premediation. In negotiation, these past references will often surface occasionally. Such past references can be problematic in two respects: by interfering with ongoing negotiation and by undermining each partner's commitment to the terms of settlement, thus reducing the likelihood of future compliance. In either event, a relational goal of mediation is to help couples get past these hard feelings by attaching them to events that are in the past and thus no longer relevant. This goal is often expressed as a stock phase, namely, that "we can do nothing about past events, only learn from them."

Establish a Working Relationship as Parents. Negotiating a settlement involves cooperative problem solving and constructive conflict management. Moreover, this is not only true of the mediation process but will become even more important after mediation is over and the couple must work together to enact a settlement that, by its very nature, will need regularly to be amended informally. For both reasons, establishing a working relationship among the parents is perhaps the key goal of the negotiation phase.

Put the Children First. That aspect of their settlement that concerns the children is called the parenting plan. Creating that plan requires parents to place the interests of the children ahead of their own self-interests. It also requires that they be able to clearly distinguish between marital issues and parenting issues. Under the stress of their divorce and in grappling with hard feelings and past events, the goal of putting the children first can be a challenging one. This can be especially so when the shock of the divorce has induced dramatic changes in one or both parents' behavior toward the children. In some cases, for example, the parent who has been least involved in child care (typically the father) now, in divorce, demonstrates sharply increased involvement. This behavior conflicts with the other parent's involvement, can be perceived as manipulative and controlling, and can be a source of resentment for the other parent (typically the mother). In contexts such as this, putting the children first can be simultaneously crucial and very difficult.

Display Constructive Negotiation Skills. Constructive negotiation skills center on communication (listening, summarizing, communicating), cognition (logic, organization, clarity), cooperation, flexibility, and compromise. An important goal of mediation, then, is to encourage clients to develop and consistently display such skills. On one level, this goal relates to the skill level of the clients in question. On another level, irrespective of their skills, clients' willingness to display such skills will relate to the extent to which they have developed a positive working relationship. Thus, although we see negotiation skills and relational quality as distinct, these goals clearly interact, with clients with sophisticated negotiation skills unable or unwilling to access them unless they can get past their hard feelings for each other.

Create a Level Playing Field. Negotiating assumes that each partner is equally free to advance proposals and negotiate settlements that are acceptable to both of them. For this to happen with any likelihood and to ensure that both process and outcome meets the mediator's ethical standards, it is essential that the mediator ensure a level playing field in which both partners are roughly equal, that is,

- equally free to develop and advance proposals;
- equally free to articulate their thoughts and feelings;
- equally free to object to or otherwise challenge the other's proposals;
- equally free to advance evidence and otherwise develop an argument;
- equally free to leave the mediation process, either temporarily or permanently;
- equally free to consult experts, such as lawyers, their accountants, or others; and
- equally free to accept proposals and ratify the terms of settlement.

In this context, the mediator can only achieve this objective within the confines of the mediation process. In most cases, this will be sufficient to ensure both a fair process and a fair settlement. If this is not the case, a return to pre-mediation may be required or, in extreme cases, case termination and referral out may be unavoidable. In other cases, unequal control of resources external to mediation may skew the process and again force termination. However, such cases will be rare and only serve to reinforce the point that achieving and maintaining a level playing field is an important objective.

Make a Commitment to Comply With the Terms of Settlement. In most cases, family mediation will achieve a comprehensive agreement, settling the issues in dispute. To the extent that this was arrived at through cooperative negotiation, clients already have some degree of commitment to comply with its terms and conditions. However, such agreements, especially when they concern dependent children, have a relatively short shelf life of perhaps a year or two. Subsequent regular revisions are a certainty. Clients' commitment to the terms of settlement, then, must extend well beyond the terms of their agreement to encompass their working relationship for years, perhaps decades, into the future. It is that long-term commitment that is an important goal of TFM-based family mediation.

Client Satisfaction. Finally, developing a working relationship and making that long-term commitment will, at least in part, reflect the extent to which the mediation process itself was a satisfying experience for both clients. Given the contentious character of the mediation process, this is seldom easy to achieve. It is difficult also because it depends on several different features of the process:

- the extent to which the mediator is perceived as fair and evenhanded,

- the extent to which clients receive the different and changing levels of support that each needs as the process unfolds,

- the extent to which clients feel that their concerns have been heard and that they have had sufficient time to air their grievances,

- the extent to which they can put aside their hard feelings and begin the arduous process of reestablishing trust in each other,

- the extent to which each truly feels empowered relative to their past experience of litigation and in terms of their own sense of worth in the marital relationship just ended, and

- the extent to which they achieve settlement, the terms of which are seen as fair and equitable under the circumstances.

This complex mix of features makes client satisfaction a precarious outcome to achieve, yet the overall success of the family mediation effort makes client satisfaction very important.

Principles

With these objectives in mind, negotiation in TFM-based family mediation is guided by four overarching principles—namely, equity, fairness, functionality, and satisfaction.

Here, *equity* refers to the extent to which both partners share in similar measure the advantages and disadvantages of the mediation process and have had a similar say in any final settlement. On these grounds, the partners can reasonably place their trust in the mediator and have confidence in the outcome. That trust is essential if clients are to disclose their intimate thoughts and feelings, an openness without which the objectives of mediation would be impossible. That confidence—in the mediator, oneself, and the other—is a key basis on which clients are likely to commit to and comply with the terms of settlement.

Fairness, unlike its more formal referent in law, is here seen in common-sense terms and is thus highly subjective. Prior to mediation, that subjectivity had blocked agreement because it was based on conflict and hard feelings. In contrast, within mediation, its variability is limited by the co-constructed formulation negotiated between the mediator and the client couple, with emphasis on cooperative problem solving and mutual trust. Thus, fairness is typically construed in plural rather than singular terms, on the assumption of ongoing relations between the partners. Any settlement will be judged fair, then, if and only if it satisfies both short-term and long-term concerns.

As to *functionality*, this refers to the pragmatic character of the mediation process. The mediator is there to be helpful to couples with substantive and relational problems. The mediator's purpose is not to impose solutions—even when they are readily apparent—but rather to engage in a joint effort to discover solutions. One set of solutions addresses immediate concerns: How can this couple get along in such a way as to resolve their disputes around these issues? Another set of solutions addresses medium-term concerns: What set of skills and understandings does this couple need to allow them to get along in the future in such a way that they can solve as yet unforeseen problems? Still another set of solutions is optional and addresses long-term concerns: What set of skills and understandings does each client need that will allow him or her to get on with his or her separate life and make choices that will enhance each person's future potential? In short, TFM-based family mediation strives to offer client couples a range of solutions that extend from immediate concerns to future concerns to personal transformation. In each case, these choices are co-constructed in negotiation between client and mediator.

Finally, the mediator strives to construct a process that is *satisfying* for all concerned. This typically means different things to the different participants. For the mediator, it attaches to change, movement, and outcome. Change refers to the clients' ways of relating to each other such that they meet or exceed the criteria for amenability and suitability. In these senses, change is always relative. Some clients will need to make considerable changes before their involvement in mediation will be productive, whereas others will need to change very little, if at all. Movement refers to their approach to the substantive and relational issues that brought them into mediation. Prior to their involvement, their informal efforts proved unsuccessful. In mediation and with the changes noted already, their efforts now prove successful; that is, they are able to achieve settlement. Substantive resolution of their differences is a desirable outcome. Over the medium and long term, resolution of their relational problems may prove far more important. Thus, speaking more generally, for the mediator, satisfaction will be associated with a positive and productive relationship with clients in which they make the changes needed to solve their substantive and relational difficulties.

These outcomes are important to clients too, for they are thus freed up to get on with their lives and to parent their children without the constant drag of conflict and dissension. However, in our experience, there are other aspects of the mediation process that are equally important for client satisfaction. Being heard is certainly one of them. In practice, this means being given the time, opportunity, and attention to tell their story and be acknowledged in such a way that they feel understood, if not necessarily by their partner then at least by the mediator. Next, feeling supported is another central basis for client satisfaction. The divorcing process is so difficult in itself that the added stress associated with mediation can seem unbearable without support from the mediator. Such support highlights the special relationship between service provider and client seen in the various helping professions, including mediation. It is that specialness that, in turn, allows for the co-constructed formulations at the heart of effective mediation service. Finally, clients value settlement results as the acme of their effectiveness. This is not just another reflection of that special relationship but is an indication of the divorcing process in which clients often label themselves as social failures. In this sense, settlement results in mediation represent an act of redemption or character reform, positive evidence of a new start as an unmarried person. Conversely, their new identity is typically precarious and fragile, with failure in mediation more salient even than adversity in litigation, for it is more personal and more painful. For these reasons, client satisfaction is a central principle underlying TFM-based family mediation.

Methods

The negotiation process in TFM-based mediation involves no specific subphases. However, it does proceed in a more or less linear fashion. This is "more or less" true due to movement between relational and substantive issues. The ordered list of issues below reflects that linear process.

Listing Issues in Dispute. Listing the issues in dispute is a deceptively simple process. In fact, it involves five interrelated tasks.

1.   *Rejoining with each partner in public.* The first task involves rejoining with each partner *in public*, that is, in front of the other partner. This sets the tone of all subsequent sessions, reflecting the mediator's intention to be fair and even-handed with each client. It also reestablishes the mediator's control over the process because moving between partners reinforces the notion that the mediator selects who will speak and in what order. The actual process of rejoining begins with the opening greeting and some initial talk. This occurs as the clients take their seats and get comfortable and is designed to give them a few minutes to get over their initial anxiety, both over entering this next phase of the process and of sitting in the same room as their partner. This can be especially upsetting if there has been a history of dominance, intimidation, and/or violence. The mediator's control over the process is crucial to reassure these clients and to establish a safe, caring, and supportive environment for both clients. Additional efforts along these lines may involve brief discussion of the ground rules in mediation, the ritual of signing the mediation contract in sextuplicate, a brief overview of the negotiation process and what will follow should they reach agreement, an opportunity for either client to ask any questions, reaffirmation of the voluntary character of the mediation process, brief review of the mediator's intention to move back and forth between relational and substantive issues, reaffirmation from the clients that they have no interest in reconciliation,

engagement with the clients in the parenting exercise noted in premediation, and perhaps a brief discussion of the sort of relationship they would prefer to have after the mediation process is concluded (no contact, business-like, or friendly). All of these efforts help to reduce client anxiety, rejoin with the mediator, and reaffirm the mediator's voluntary control over the process.

These efforts can also serve to highlight areas of tension and foreshadow areas of conflict. For example, although most partners affirm their intention to divorce, this is not always the case; one partner may indicate a willingness to consider reconciliation. Indeed, in a small number of cases (about 5%), mediation leads to eventual reconciliation, typically associated with a referral for marital therapy. Similarly, these ice-breaking efforts may reveal greater similarity in parenting attitudes and values than either client had thought possible, divergence that reflects their lack of communication as opposed to any real substantive differences. Conversely, such discussion can reveal areas of resentment, anger, and distance. These differences can be diffuse and general or specific and linked to particular issues. In either case, they help prepare the mediator for the negotiation process with this couple.

2.   *Constructing the mediatable frame.* The next task involves establishing what we have previously referred to as the "mediatable frame" (see Chapters 2, 4, and 5)—that is, a general interpretive framework designed to encourage cooperative problem solving and mutually respectful talk. This frame involves a number of components:

- sharing responsibility for parenting and assets acquired during the marriage;
- leaving the past in the past—all we can do now is learn from it;
- looking to the future, both as individuals and as coparents;
- cooperating around parenting tasks because the children need you to do so;
- creating a fair settlement under their circumstances;
- considering what it would be worth to the partners to have all of this over, once and for all; and
- weighing the consequences of not reaching a settlement in mediation.

Taken separately and together, these interrelated themes provide the rationale for much of the mediator's conduct in session. Variations on these themes will be repeated over and over again by the mediator to block unnecessary or unproductive conflict, prevent efforts to refight old marital battles, divert the use of legalistic standards and language, and avoid impasse over minor issues. They will similarly be used to remind clients of their painful experience in court, of the enormous stress associated with ongoing conflict, and of seeing beyond their failed marriage to the best interests of their children, including the fact that ongoing conflict between them does a disservice to their children.

3.   *Listing the issues.* It is in the context of this frame that the next task, listing the issues in dispute, is accomplished. In practice, creating such a list might better be characterized as co-constructing a set of solvable or mediatable problems. In some cases, clients present problems that are already framed in mediatable terms. Examples include the following: "I only want my fair share of the assets," "I want both of us to be involved in caring for our kids," "I want more time with my kids," or "The TV should come to me, but he can have his precious CD collection." In each case, the clients present a problem in which there is room for the give-and-take that is the essence of negotiation. Alternately, some clients frame problems as nonnegotiable positions. Examples include the following: "Just give me my kids. She can have the house." "That pension is mine. I worked for every dollar." "He never lifted a finger for those kids while we were married. He doesn't deserve to have them now." "I built that house with my own hands. It's mine." In each case, the clients present a problem in which there is no give-and-take, no room to maneuver. In that form, it is not mediatable and thus cannot be allowed to stand. Application of the mediatable frame is intended to recast such formulations in ways that make them negotiable. For example, "give me my kids" becomes "let us discuss how the children can share time with both their parents"; "the pension is mine" becomes "we are here to discuss the fair division of all of the assets both of you worked so hard to accumulate throughout your marriage, including the pension"; and "he doesn't deserve them" becomes "let us discuss what arrangements we can make to meet your children's immediate needs, especially their need to know every day that Daddy and Mommy love them and will always be there for them."

In each case, these restatements reflect the mediatable frame noted earlier. Furthermore, and as important, they highlight the crucial importance of the sensitive use of language. In positive terms, such usage includes the shift from singular to plural, from past to present or future, and the use of words and phrases consistent with the mediatable frame, including the following: *cooperation, fair, equitable, responsible, best interests, options, alternatives,* and so on. In negative terms, consistent efforts should be made to block the use of words and phrases inconsistent with that frame, including accusations, name-calling, swearing, threats, and all efforts at intimidation, domination, humiliation, and the like. Having established that all exchanges between the parties should be respectful and typically mindful of the need to build trust pursuant to ongoing relations, it is important that these rules be enforced consistently. Failure to do so can have serious consequences for the mediation process, including loss of respect for the mediator, suspicion of bias, unproductive negotiation, and the increased likelihood that the parties will drop out of the process.

4. *Setting the agenda.* Having established the frame and listed the issues, the next task is to set the agenda for the balance of the current and subsequent sessions. That is, the mediator indicates the substantive issues to be discussed and the order in which this is to be done, with the tacit understanding that relationship issues will be included as needed. In most cases, clients merely adjust to the order without comment, a tribute to their acceptance of the mediator's acknowledged control over the process. However, although the agenda is the mediator's choice, exceptions or variations are routinely discussed if circumstances warrant. For example, issues related to school or holiday schedules, the timing of paid work, or crisis events may all legitimately require that the agenda be varied in favor of urgent or time-related issues.

Failing such a rationale, client requests for changes may need to be blocked, as they may reflect power or control issues. This is especially true when, as is commonplace, the mediator has elected to begin with the less contentious issues, whereas clients may prefer to begin with the issue that is most contentious for them. Apart from seeing such a request as a challenge to the mediator, clinical experience indicates that without some experience of success in negotiation, beginning with highly contentious issues is a recipe for failure. Politely but firmly, then, the mediator should block such requests: "I understand why that issue is important to you, and I do promise to get back to it when the time is right, but starting here [with the minor issues] will offer you a better opportunity to get used to the mediation process and develop some positive experience with issues about which you agree."

As to the substantive order of issues, mediators vary. In comprehensive mediation, some prefer to begin with the financial issues, especially the distribution of assets (see Chapter 11, this volume). Others feel more comfortable starting with parenting issues, on the assumptions that love for their children ensures at least some common ground. Our own personal preference is to begin with the parenting plan because the resolution of these issues is likely to endure long after the monetary issues have been forgotten. In the final analysis, however, the substantive starting point for negotiation is arbitrary and should be decided on the basis of whatever makes the mediator comfortable.

5. *Break complex issues into smaller, more manageable chunks.* Part of the task of setting the agenda involves breaking complex issues into smaller, more manageable chunks. Thus, the mediator does not deal with "child custody" per se but rather with routine and holiday time-sharing schedules, decision making around major and minor issues, and parental communication. Similarly, property divisions break down in a series of smaller issues, such as the valuation of the family business or the matrimonial home and the listing of assets and liabilities. Depending on the level

and character of the conflict, even these issues may need to be further subdivided or "fractionated" to maximize the likelihood of achieving settlement. With relatively functional couples, we might take the time to explain the logic of this process and deliberately address larger issues. With relatively dysfunctional couples, even after premediation, the process of subdivision would be done automatically, with no explanation, and address a series of small issues, only later reassembling these small issues into the larger issues used in parenting or financial plans.

Identifying Subtexts and Hidden Agendas. In the TFM model, identifying and addressing subtexts and hidden agendas are the primary focus of the premediation phase. Even so, unless these issues have been eliminated entirely, the likelihood that they will recur during the negotiation phase is high and should be expected.

Identifying these issues typically involves spotting a discrepancy between the size or importance of an issue and the clients' responses to it. That is, when objectively "small" issues get large or heated responses, the chances are that a subtext or hidden agenda is driving the process. Such discrepancies may arise concerning any conceivable issue, from splitting the CD collection to swearing a document, or from the exact pick-up or delivery time to money for the children's lunches. Each becomes a screen onto which one or the other client projects his or her fears, disappointments, or angry feelings. Such issues are important because they impede the negotiation process, interfere with the ongoing effort to build trust and put the past behind them, and, if left unattended, may even threaten the mediation process itself.

Here, it will be important to distinguish between minor and major problems. Minor issues are those that were previously dealt with in premediation and recur in negotiation. Having dealt with them already, the mediator is well prepared to deal with them again. This is often done by referring to the previous discussion and reinforcing any conclusions reached then. A typical example involves anger about some past event about which the parties disagree. Such "he said, she said" issues are unproductive in mediation. There is no way in which the mediator can sort out what actually happened—each client will simply have different truthful recollections of the events—and there is little purpose in doing so because one cannot change past events, only learn from them. Thus, the mediatable frame is used as a generic intervention, with each client asked to forgive the other's transgressions in the interests of cooperative parenting, getting past their current dispute, getting on with their respective lives, and avoiding future litigation. That interpretation is used again when subtexts and hidden agendas reappear in negotiation. By now, it should be apparent to the parties that such emotionally charged issues are both destructive and unproductive. The result is that only brief intervention at this stage is required to get them back on track. Indeed, the speed with which clients themselves recognize these outbursts as unproductive and are willing to move on is indicative of the extent to which the mediator's therapeutic efforts have begun to bear fruit. To ease movement back into productive negotiation, the mediator may supplement the frame interpretation with normative and preemptive interpretations:

> "Giving up negative feelings from the past is hard to do. That these feelings come back to you from time to time is only normal. It takes time and practice to get past them entirely. You can expect such feelings to recur with less and less frequency over months or even years. Focusing on what is happening now in your relationship and on your joint commitment to the children is the way to rid yourself of such feelings for good."

For most clients, interventions such as these will be sufficient to return to productive negotiation. For a small minority, however, these efforts will be insufficient and indeed may infuriate them still further. Such clients will become adamant, insisting that the children's future turns on whether they are given $5.25 in lunch money as opposed to the $4.75 being offered by the other party. Such clients may be willing to return court, turning their backs on a deal worth tens of thousands to them, merely because the other party refuses to swear an income statement about which there is no dispute. Such examples could be multiplied indefinitely and turn not on any substantive issue but rather on their postdivorce adjustment (Irving & Benjamin, 1995).

In this regard, partners can vary widely, with the partner who initiated the divorce (typically the wife) having a clear advantage over the other. This information is not new and is routinely the focus of premediation efforts directed at improving the readiness of the other partner. However, in some cases, this difference in readiness appears to go underground and only surfaces in response to a particular issue about which the partner is especially sensitive. Until that issue comes up for discussion, both parties appear reasonable, and much productive work can be accomplished. When the triggering issue arises, however, a large discrepancy occurs. A client who has been calm and cooperative turns unexpectedly surly and loud or becomes visibly upset and tearful. Furthermore, the standard interventions noted above are notably unsuccessful, and the mediation reaches an impasse. Although couples can reach an impasse for other reasons (see below), the usual techniques for overcoming this impasse will typically be unsuccessful here, with return to premediation required either in joint session or often by way of individual caucusing (see below). If successful, the couple will return to negotiation thereafter. However, such differences in readiness or adjustment are difficult to overcome and may force case termination and referral.

Maintaining an Even Playing Field: Power Balancing. Mediation seeks to ensure that any settlement will be fair and equitable relative to each couple's circumstances. It is therefore essential to establish and maintain a level playing field between the partners. Because most couples will be imbalanced in some respects, the task of establishing a level playing field will occur primarily in premediation, whereas that of maintaining it will occur through the negotiation phase.

Two means to that end have already been noted—namely, the mediator's control over listing the issues and setting the agenda. Together, such control imposes severe restraints on either partner's efforts to take unfair advantage of the other. However, perhaps most salient of the mediator's tools is his or her control over client talking time, that is, who speaks, for how long, and on what topic. The ideal is that this control be virtually invisible, the clients having been socialized early in the process to follow the mediator's lead, with each partner given roughly the same time to speak to the selected issue.

Even with the most cooperative couple, however, some talking out of turn is all but unavoidable, as one party reacts to something the other has said. The typical response will be to gently block such interruptions: [with hand upheld in a "stopping" motion] "He didn't interrupt you while you were speaking. Please give him the same courtesy. I promise to give you ample time to respond when he's finished." Several repetitions of this sequence are usually enough to get clients to respect the rules. This is especially true when coupled with admonitions against improper or disrespectful comments and with explicit praise for real accomplishments achieved by the end of each session.

In a minority of cases, these efforts will be insufficient to curb disorderly conduct in session. Repeated breaches of the mediation rules, including the "no interruptions" rule, may need to be addressed in an individual caucus. There, the mediator needs to discover if such breaches reflect relational issues between the parties or a control issue between the partner and the mediator. In the case of the former, the options are brief intervention in caucus or return to premediation, with the former clearly favored at this stage in the process. In the case of the latter, the mediator may need to "read the riot act," for without the client's respect for the mediator and his or her control over the process, the mediator cannot be effective. The issue, therefore, is a crucial one for the mediator. "Reading the riot act" centers on the mediator's control over the process and the benefits of an agreement as opposed to the costs of a return to litigation. In addition, the threat of termination should be explicit. Improved client compliance usually follows, with case termination over this issue possible but rare.

Moving Between Relational and Substantive Issues. All models of mediation are committed to facilitate discussion and negotiation between clients in conflict, with the aim of helping them reach agreement. Some models, including TFM, take a long view, also helping clients learn to interact in ways conducive to effective problem solving and cooperative parenting.

This emphasis extends virtually throughout the process, although such efforts tend to be more intense during premediation and less so through the negotiation process.

Such teaching efforts are enacted by moving between relational and substantive issues. In generic terms, this involves the mediatable frame. In more specific terms, such efforts emphasize communicational skills, with explicit praise for increasing success in such efforts.

For example, common communication errors are identified and corrected. Such errors include attributing motives to the other ("What he's really trying to do is . . ."), mind reading ("She always thinks the worst of people . . ."), name-calling ("Mama's boy!"), or characterization ("She's a selfish person who only cares about herself. You can't change it. It's the way she's always been."). Such errors undercut efforts at negotiation by exacerbating the trust vacuum between the clients while failing to address the substantive issues at hand. By the time the couple has entered negotiation, many of these errors will have begun to fall away. However, to the extent that this communication pattern was characteristic of them prior to mediation, such errors can be expected to recur. It is incumbent on the mediator to continue to be vigilant and to block and correct such errors as and when necessary.

As the frequency of such errors lessens and their efforts at communication gradually become more efficient, related training (as required) in negotiation skills can then be added. Developing realistic proposals, evaluating offers, learning to articulate needs and concerns, getting in touch with underlying interests, and developing a shared vision of their future as coparents are all skills that are necessary not only to effective negotiation in mediation but also to effective conflict management long after mediation is over. In this regard, couples vary widely. Some couples will need minimal support in negotiating issues in dispute, whereas others will need extensive coaching. In either case, the rationale for such assistance is provided by the mediatable frame, which insists that couples see their negotiation efforts as working toward a sustainable relationship over the long term.

Creating Options and Alternatives. All mediation clients have one thing in common: They have tried—often repeatedly—to resolve their differences and failed. Earlier, we identified a number of relational bases for such failure. There are, however, substantive processes that have contributed to this outcome. Key among these substantive reasons is the limited range of options the parties bring to the table, often one each.

As regards parenting, for example, it is commonplace for each parent to demand care and control of the children. In the words of one client, "Just give me my children." These are "zero-sum" choices, for anything one parent "wins," the other parent "loses." Moreover, in the absence of any concerns about parenting competence, this is a marital dispute centered on control and has very little to do with what is best for the children. As such, these clients have very little to talk about, with any effort at negotiation foreclosed before it even begins. Shifting to the mediatable frame, however, with its emphasis on shared responsibility and children's best interests, changes things dramatically. Instead of who "owns" the children, the parents are asked to discuss how they will share the multiple tasks of parenting, *not* because that is what they want but rather because that is what their children need. Now, from only two options, the parents are faced with 15 or 20 choices attached to issues such as time sharing, decision making, competent care, household boundaries, scheduling compliance, due notice, informing the other, parenting communication, and special circumstances. Now, parents have much to talk about and are forced to begin the process of dialogue that they will continue beyond mediation for the next 5 to 20 years (depending on the age of their children). Indeed, beyond the substantive issues, this dialogue is, in our view, the single most important contribution TFM-based mediation has to offer parents in dispute.

To a lesser extent, the same is true regarding the division of assets. We say "to a lesser extent" because such division need only occur once, whereas the parenting dialogue must become an ongoing process. Similarly, we accord children a greater value than the assets because the children represent the future, whereas the assets reflect the past, which is fast receding. Here, too, clients often present with a very limited range of options and, what is more, options that are often blatantly self-serving. This approach makes plain why they failed to agree in the past and is manifest in unproductive conflict that reflects past marital disputes. Shifting to the mediatable frame, with its emphasis on fairness and the future, makes a dramatic difference. From a series of zero-sum options, clients must now confront a range of settlement scenarios whose evaluation requires dialogue. For example, as regards the matrimonial home, they may sell it and divide the net equity, each may buy out the other, they may retain it as a rental property, they may retain it now (while the children are still young) and dispose of it later, and so on. Each choice is attached to multiple pros and cons and may, in turn, be linked to other choices to do, for example, with financing, tax implications, real estate markets, property evaluation, and so on. In addition, the clients may consider settling just for the sake of settling because the conflict has been draining and expensive and has prevented them from moving on with their respective lives. In short, expanding the range of options creates the requirement for dialogue, which dramatically increases the likelihood of settlement.

A way of further expanding available options turns on the distinction between interim and final agreements. Couples may find a particular option acceptable, but both may have qualms about whether it will work in practice. Forced to accept or reject the option, they may quickly reach an impasse as one pushes for its acceptance, thus strengthening the other's resistance to it. The alternative, often suggested by the mediator, is to call it an interim agreement and try it out for some reasonable period of time.

What may appear problematic in hypothetical terms may, in fact, work out smoothly. The mediator may try a preempting maneuver by adding, "Even if you do encounter minor problems, you can always make minor adjustments along the way. At the very least, this experience will give the information you will need to create new options if this one proves unworkable." There are several advantages of using interim agreements:

- They allow the party who was opposed to the idea in the first place to save face by retreating gracefully from an extreme position.
- They highlight the importance of teamwork if the option in question is to be given a fair trial.
- They typically constitute a small concession on the part of one or both parties, thus creating momentum toward settlement, and should be framed as such by the mediator.

Trading Off. As part of the process of expending their range of options, the couples may be introduced to the notion of *trade-offs*, that is, exchanges in which each client gives up something of value to get something of roughly equal value. The logic of trade-offs takes slightly different forms when applied to parenting or asset division.

With respect to parenting, trade-offs often involve exchanges of service. For example, one parent may be willing to take the children to appointments if the other agrees to take the children to school in the morning. They may agree to rotate particular child care duties or alternate certain privileges (such as Christmas or New Year's Eve) on an annual basis. Such examples can be multiplied indefinitely and reveal the creative side of constructing parenting plans. Indeed, almost anything goes here, so long as it is legal, not likely to harm the children, and on mutual consent. Furthermore, as noted earlier, such efforts can be agreed to on an interim basis, to give parents a short-term opportunity to try out various options. Such trial runs can be important as ways of overcoming a trust vacuum in which each parent pictures the other as unreliable and irresponsible.

The same is true as regards asset division. Indeed, trade-offs may be easier to create when dealing with assets that are concrete and physically divisible and can be accorded an "objective" value in the marketplace. An obvious example concerns chattel in which clients are encouraged to do a "walkthrough" of the matrimonial home, with each client indicating the things he or she wants to keep or is willing to give up. Related examples include pensions, retirement savings, investments, electronic equipment, motor vehicles, and so on. Again, the range of choices is limited only by clients' imagination and their specific circumstances. Apart from the fact that such trade-offs move clients to settlement, they force clients to engage in dialogue that breaks down emotional barriers, creates the basis of renewed trust, and sets a course for their relationship that will need to continue long after mediation is over.

Evaluating Options: Reality Check. Most clients are mediation amateurs who have limited experience in negotiation. In addition, their interaction is powerfully shaped by patterns rooted in their failed relationship. These dynamics suggest two bases on which clients' proposals may be unworkable: Their lack of experience may give rise to proposals that are out of keeping with available information, and their proposals may arise from their feelings rather than from available facts. In both cases, the mediator is responsible for providing a crucial reality check.

In the case of simple ignorance, consider two commonplace examples. The first example concerns parenting, specifically clients' time-sharing proposals. Among clients who wish to share their children on an equal basis, a week on, week off schedule is simple and convenient, offering the advantage of giving both parents time with the children on weekends, when the children are off school. With older children, this is often workable for the clients and consistent with the developmental needs of the children. However, with young children (younger than 6 years of age), this choice can be highly problematic. Research reviewed by Gordon, Donner, and Peacock (2000) and Kelly and Lamb (2000) makes clear that young children need frequent contact with both parents to ensure healthy attachment and good postdivorce adjustment. For them, a week on, week off schedule is likely to give rise to distress. Informing parents of such information allows them to make parenting decisions in their child's best interest.

In a similar vein, valuing property can be problematic. In a recent case, estranged spouses had not spoken to each other for more than 6 months. During that time, one spouse encountered severe financial difficulty. Unable to contact the other spouse, the spouse in distress elected to sell some of their jointly held property at an amount far below what the property originally cost. In mediation, the other spouse demanded that the property be replaced. In fact, in divorce situations, most property, including chattel, is assigned a price at market value (see Chapter 11, this volume), that is, at the price it would fetch were it sold on the separation date on the open market. This information is crucial in helping clients make claims that are fair and reasonable and thus more likely to be the subject of agreement.

As for claims rooted in relationship, these can be much more difficult for the mediator. Again, consider two commonplace examples. In the first instance, one basis for divorce is that arrangement in which the mother shoulders the entire burden of parenting, whereas the father's role is restricted to paid employment. The divorce serves as a "wake-up" call to father, who suddenly realizes that if he does not become more involved in parenting, he may very well lose contact with his children. From the mother's point of view, such belated involvement is seen as "too little, too late." In mediation, she demands complete control over the children, relegating the father to a brief, occasional visit, and reserves the right to schedule and cancel such visits as she sees fit. The father demands more time with the children, shows evidence of increased involvement, and proposes a time-sharing schedule that is workable on its face. Left as is, this case would be intractable and would be headed for litigation. In TFM, the mediatable frame provides an alternative perspective on the situation, with the focus squarely on the children's best interests and developmental needs rather than the spouses' longstanding conflict. Data reviewed by Gordon et al. (2000) and Kelly and Lamb (2000) make abundantly clear that, barring some challenge to parenting competence (such as abuse), dependent children at all ages benefit from ongoing involvement with *both* parents. Such findings favor time-sharing arrangements that ensure the meaningful involvement of both parents. Such reasoning is buttressed by frame elements that encourage emphasis on current rather than past events and on forgiveness rather than ongoing enmity. In most cases, parents' superordinate common goal of protecting their children's welfare provides the lever that allows them to compromise and reopen dialogue that will serve them well through mediation and beyond.

A related example concerns property, in this case spousal support. A couple lived a rich lifestyle, based primarily on the husband's six-figure income. For the wife, the problem was that the husband was virtually never home but always at work. In anger, she had a rather blatant affair with a much younger man that effectively ended their relationship. In mediation, she continued to be very angry about her husband's neglect, and he was very angry about the affair. The upshot of this dynamic was that wife asked for a very large sum of money by way of spousal support, primarily in compensation for her neglect. In response, the mediator initiated a public review in session of their financial situation. To the horror of both partners, this revealed that they had both been living far beyond their means, despite the husband's income, and that the best both could hope for on divorce was to minimize their common debt. Although the wife's claim and the husband's counterclaim may have made sense to both of them emotionally, it made little sense in the harsh light of reality. Although the wife still retained a valid claim for support, it would, of necessity, be far less than the large sum that she had initially proposed.

In short, in negotiation, the mediator's roles as educator and expert combine in the form of a reality check. The typical consequences are to moderate exaggerated claims, support reasonable positions, and open meaningful dialogue that serves as the primary route to settlement. In different situations, this may entail enriching the dialogue by introducing "expert" data or simply exploring family data in a public forum. Such objective standards not only provide a different perspective from which clients may consider the issues in dispute but also, and as important, give a voice to others, such as the children and/or the grandparents, who may not be in a position to come to the table.

That said, the effectiveness of any reality check is a function of the extent to which the parties are in touch with reality. For most couples, this is simply not an issue, as they make explicit their desire to reach settlement. For some, however, that explicit desire—sometimes expressed with tears in their eyes—is inconsistent with their attachment to the conflict. In a recent case, a marriage ended with sequential trauma, leaving both partners bitter and angry. Both were effective in containing these feelings when negotiating the parenting plan, but they emerged to create an impasse when mediation turned to the financial plan. Although the differences were significant, in the order of $10,000, they paled by comparison to the eventual costs of litigation and to the hard feelings that would likely arise from it and potentially interfere with their coparenting arrangement. Despite the reality check provided by the mediator and the couples' expressed desire to "put all this behind us," neither were ready to let go of their conflict over this issue. The case ended in impasse, with both parties adamant and prepared for litigation.

Avoiding Impasses. Despite the mediator's best efforts to facilitate give-and-take among the clients, it may not be enough; impasses may still occur. As in the above case, some impasses force termination of the mediation process. Most impasses, however, can be addressed successfully. To that end, the mediator has a range of options aimed at breaking the impasse. Choice of which option or combination of options will depend on whether the impasse arises from relational or substantive processes. In our experience, roughly 80% of impasses are rooted in relationship processes, compared with 20% whose character is essentially substantive. Although this distinction is somewhat arbitrary—relational and substantive issues can overlap—it is nevertheless useful in highlighting the distinctive character of family mediation. Below, this distinction is used as a way of organizing discussion of various impasse-breaking options.

Turning first to *relational options*, we routinely use at least nine variations.

- *Engage third parties.* In family mediation, third parties are always involved and encompass family members (especially children) and friends (personal third parties) as well as lawyers and others (accountants, real estate agents, business evaluators, psychiatrists, etc.). In some cases, involving third parties adds different perspectives to the mix that can have the effect of breaking an impasse. Lawyers, for example, can assure clients that the proposal on the table is a reasonable one and in frequent use among their clients. Accountants may come up with alternative proposals that continue the dialogue and increase the likelihood of settlement. However, in other cases, third parties may be directly responsible for the impasse, such that their influence needs to be blocked. Clients who might otherwise be inclined to settle may be reluctant to do so in the face of threats by a third party ("If you give in to that bum, I'll never speak to you again."). Inclusion of the third party in mediation is one option, whereas contact with them on the telephone may be another, in both cases with the aim of having them back off and allowing the parties themselves to make the decisions that will shape their future family.

- *Time-out.* The mediation process invariably acquires a certain momentum that can assist in achieving settlement or that may work against it. In this context, impasses may reflect situational dynamics. A negative statement by one client may increase resistance by the other partner, leading to impasse. Here, premature termination of the session may work in favor of settlement, with a proposal rejected in the heat of the moment appearing far more acceptable in the harsh light of reality the following day. In this instance, advising clients to "sleep on it" may result in a reversal leading to settlement. In a recent case, a client demanded complete control of the children, offering only a half day a week to the other parent. Following a discussion of shared responsibility in parenting, the session was ended a half hour early, and the clients were instructed to "go home and think about what is best for the children." The following week, brief discussion had them settle on a shared parenting arrangement. That said, there are other instances in which a similar delay would be fatal to the process. On the cusp of an agreement, a seemingly minor issue threatens to unravel the entire process. In such instances, the mediator is better advised to confront the couple, therefore increasing pressure to settle. In a recent case, a couple had endured 2 years of litigation before they entered mediation. Negotiation between them was very difficult in a virtual trust vacuum. Even so, they managed to construct a complex but viable parenting plan, save for a final issue on which they reached impasse. When thorough discussion revealed that their different positions were rhetorical only and had no practical consequences, the mediator refused to let them leave the room until one or both of them compromised. After 10 minutes of stony silence, a compromise deal was reached. Alternatively, the mediator might have given them a deadline beyond which mediation would be terminated.

- *Move on.* In many cases, the difference between "impasse" and "disagreement" is based solely on how the situation has been framed by the mediator. Labeling a disagreement as a "temporary problem" rationalizes moving on to discussion of other issues in which productive negotiation is more likely. Success in such efforts, coupled with the mediator's lavish praise of their hard work, can change perceptions. Accordingly, when the couple is asked to reconsider the original issue on which they disagreed, productive negotiation can now occur, such that the original label becomes a self-fulfilling prophesy. Settlement occurs when it would not have occurred before. A variation on this option involves dealing with several issues at the same time, that is, having several issues under active consideration. Moving between these issues has the advantage of keeping things fluid while increasing the possibility of small concessions by one of them. That concession then changes the mood and allows productive return to the original issue, thus avoiding impasse.

Reframing. Impasse often occurs because of how the clients perceive the issue. Changing those perceptions can often dramatically increase the likelihood of settlement. One variation on this theme refers to the mediatable frame whose consistent application is intended to shift clients from intractable positions to mediatable perspectives. "My property" to "the fruits of your (shared) hard work," "my children" to "your shared responsibility," and "what I want" to "what your children need" are all examples of the frame in action. In other cases, more specialized reframes will be needed. For example, in a recent case, a client characterized her partner's lack of involvement with the children as a result of his "selfishness" and "lack of concern." These character flaws were further labeled as permanent and provided the basis on which she demanded sole custody of the children. In response, the mediator reframed the father's current conduct, which showed sensitivity to the children's needs, in terms of his "growing maturity and responsibility," which fit with "their shared responsibility" for these children. In turn, she was asked if she was willing to "help" the father "learn to give the children what they need." She agreed to help. In effect, this reframe moved the couple from what the mother or father "wanted" to what the children "needed" and helped redefine "cooperative parenting" as the primary goal of their parenting plan.

• *Exploring assumptions.* Clients invariably enter negotiation with a variety of assumptions about the process, its purpose, their motives, the motives of the other parent, the motives of the mediator, and so on. Some of these assumptions can assist the process, but others may undermine or interfere with it. A case in point concerns each client's bottom line, that is, those outcomes that, for each client, are not negotiable. The more of these there are and the narrower their range, the less flexible each is, the less room to maneuver each has, and the less likely they are to reach settlement. Perhaps most important, these assumptions tend to change as client couples go through the stages of TFM-based mediation. Accordingly, it is wise to check out these assumptions from time to time. Impasse is one such time. An enactment is an especially useful form for such an inquiry. That is, the couple is asked to discuss two questions with each other: First, "why should the other parent accept your proposal?" Second, "why does the other parent's proposal not work for you?" The discussion that then unfolds helps flesh out the basis or bases of impasse and may suggest one or more new approaches that may lead past the impasse. In a recent case, a mother explained that the father's proposal was controlling and intruded on her private life. She went on to explain that she had not found this surprising because that is how he behaved when they were married. Some exploration with the father revealed that he was unaware of the mother's objections and was not adverse to changing his proposal accordingly. They then proceeded to negotiate a revised proposal that met both their needs.

• *Examining consequences.* Failure to agree comes with a price, sometimes a heavy one. Such costs include a return to litigation, renewed legal costs, and the emotional exhaustion and sense of helplessness that often accompany a court battle. Perhaps most important, consequences of litigation are *not* confined to the parents but can also adversely affect the children *and* the parents' continued willingness to cooperate with each other around the children. However, in the heat of negotiation, couples lose sight of these consequences, with each insisting that he or she is right and the other wrong. In impasse, it can be helpful to remind clients of these consequences, ask them to think carefully about them, and then return to mediation "to try to settle this issue one last time." In one case, conflict over splitting their meager assets had reached impasse. Had they settled, each would have walked away with less than $15,000 in hand. In contrast, a litigated solution would have seen both of them in debt. In response to this sobering analysis, they agreed to resume negotiation and eventually did settle. In another case, a couple was faced with a substantial community debt. This left them with two options: litigate and end up further in debt, with neither retaining ownership of the matrimonial home, or settle and have one partner take on additional debt but retain ownership of the home. After thinking it over for 2 weeks, they chose the second option.

• *Individual caucusing.* Although most efforts at breaking impasses involve working with the couple, there are contexts in which individual caucusing can be very helpful. One version of this approach involves caucusing with only one of the partners. This is useful in a number of situations, including trauma and ongoing attachment—in short, wherever the mediator suspects the problem "belongs" to one partner and not the other. Clear evidence of this situational interpretation is when one partner gives a very strong response to an objectively small issue ("Either she agrees to park no closer than 10 feet from the house on drop-offs or I'm going to court! This issue is NOT negotiable!") but the other party does not. In this circumstance, standard premediation techniques would be used to encourage the partner to let go of or diminish the feelings attached to the experience. The other and more typical version involves caucusing with both parties. In caucus, the mediator can say things to the client that he or she might not say with the other partner present, including exploring for areas of compromise, allowing the client to express his or her feelings, giving support or coaching, and examining risky solutions or even apparently crazy ones. The mediator can also shuttle between partners and make various nonbinding suggestions or recommendations, in an effort to find a way around the impasse. In rare cases, the mediator himself or herself may declare an impasse because of an aspect of the process that he or she finds problematic. For example, in a recent case, negotiation was going too well, as the husband accepted his wife's every demand. The result would have been inequitable, would not have been in the best interests of the children, and would inevitably have broken down in the near future. Individual caucusing with the husband soon revealed the basis of his behavior—namely, overwhelming guilt over an impulsive affair that had ended the marital relationship. To expiate that guilt, the husband was asked to go down on his knees to ask for his wife's forgiveness. In turn, this helped the wife see her husband in a new light. They were then able to renegotiate a parenting plan more in keeping with the best interests of their children.

•   *Exploring "what if" options.* Seen together, clients can be asked to engage in a kind of brainstorming by role-playing various "what if" options. "What if" options are exactly what their name suggests, possibilities that have already been rejected or that appear, on their face, impractical or "crazy." The advantages of role-playing these possibilities are that the partners have nothing to lose in doing so and, at least in fantasy, get a chance to try them out to see how they feel. Of course, they also create yet another opportunity for dialogue and exchange. The results are unpredictable in a positive sense. Attaching a sense of "play" to these role-plays gives clients license to be creative in a team effort. In the process, they may discover that an option previously rejected may in fact work, either "as is" or in some modified form. Alternatively, they may come up with options that no one had previously thought of, including the mediator! Furthermore, by exploring the implications of given choices, couples gain a deeper and more complete understanding of exactly what a given option would really mean, both for themselves and for their children.

•   *Return to premediation.* Finally, the mediator may conclude that one or more relationship issues are blocking settlement and return to premediation. Although doing so acknowledges an assessment error on the part of the mediator, it is the appropriate response in the face of evidence of an adjustment problem. In a recent case, a couple reached impasse over the division of property. Although the difference between them was not large (less than $3,000), both partners were adamant that their numbers, and only their numbers, were the correct ones and that the other partner was "trying to screw me around." Return to premediation revealed that the pain of mutual trauma had been exacerbated by lengthy litigations that had put both parties in debt, with each blaming the other for his or her distress. Microanalysis suggested that both parties were being inflexible because both refused to acknowledge their guilt and instead had transformed it into rage directed outward, toward the other. Exploration of this interpretation was coupled with a diminishing intervention. In the end, the couple agreed to abandon their futile debate about the "right" numbers and instead reached settlement based on splitting the difference.

As to *substantive matters*, there are at last four techniques we routinely use to break impasses.

•   *Increase the range of options.* Divorce is a difficult time for most clients, a time when they are under intense stress and likely not as flexible as they might otherwise be. Impasse, then, may mean nothing more than that the right set of options is not yet on the table. It follows that breaking an impasse may require a creative effort to expand the range of options. Although this can be the task of the mediator, experience shows that it is more useful to engage the couple and ask for their creative ideas. Time may be put aside for "brainstorming," whose purpose is to generate ideas, no matter how wild or crazy they may appear. Incidentally, such efforts also offer another opportunity for dialogue. The results are then processed for ideas that have some appeal to one or both clients. In turn, these new options generate discussion and, in many cases, an option that is finally acceptable to both of them. In a recent case, the mother had the children most of the time, but the father wanted more time with them. The mother acknowledged that the children were "a lot of work" but at the same time characterized them as "my life." She was adamant in refusing the father's request. It appeared they were at an impasse. Playing with these ideas, however, suggested several new options centered on the father "sharing some of the burden" by providing services to the children. For example, he might take them to school in the morning or to after-school activities. He might also have the children for dinner one night a week. With this free time, the mother was then asked how she might use this time to "pamper" herself. Subsequent discussion indicated the mother had few friends and that the price she paid for her devotion to her children was feelings of isolation and loneliness. She elected, with some trepidation, to join a social club. Thus, expanding the range of options provided the basis of settlement in which both parents' needs were met, his for more time with the children and hers for an adult social life.

• *Link the issue to others.* A related process applies when issues that have been dealt with in isolation are linked to others in an effort to break an impasse. The problem with dealing with issues one at a time is that available options may satisfy some client requirements but not others. Linking issues thus addresses multiple concerns and can lead to a satisfying settlement. In a recent case, a couple was at an impasse over ways to split the value of their matrimonial home. Because it is the main asset for most couples and often the only home the children have known, disposing of this asset can be difficult and complex. In this case, no matter what set of options the mediator came up with, either one or the other partner found a variety of reasons for rejecting it. In search of still further options, discussion of the reasons why the couple could not get past this particular issue revealed a concern over the husband's "fat" pension. The husband insisted the pension was "his," as he had been paying into it nearly all of his adult life. The wife indicated that as a "stay-at-home mom," she had no such retirement nest egg. This discussion made clear that the "house" had quite different meanings for each partner. To the husband, it was merely another asset to be split between them. To the wife, it was her "pension," her security against a rather bleak future alone. Linking the two issues allowed for a mutually satisfying trade-off in which the wife kept the house while the husband kept the pension.

- *Break larger issues into a series of smaller ones.* If linking issues is one method of breaking impasses, then breaking larger issues into smaller ones is another approach. For some couples, dealing with large issues, such as "spousal support," is perfectly acceptable. For others, such issues touch so many different "nerves" and generate such intense conflict that it is unworkable. For these couples, breaking large, complex issues into smaller ones is an effective way to avoid or break impasse. As noted previously, "child custody" encompasses a range of issues, including time sharing, decision making, communication, due notice, respect for boundaries, changing the schedule, and so on. Similarly, splitting the value of the matrimonial home encompasses issues such as home valuation, specifying the valuation date (i.e., the date of separation), buyout options, sale options, rental options, the distribution of chattel, and so on. Focusing on these minor issues can dramatically reduce conflict and has the advantage of providing a simple focus for dialogue. In turn, such dialogue dramatically increases the likelihood of settlement while allowing the mediator to isolate the issue or issues at the heart of the conflict, which may require a return to pre-mediation if it continues to lead to impasse.

- *Look for new trade-offs.* Trade-offs are simple and effective ways to achieve settlements that clients see as fair and equitable. However, not all trade-offs are created equal. Good trade-offs are those in which each client genuinely values his or her side of the deal and feels that the exchange involves items of roughly equal value. It is the latter more than the former that can be problematic and lead to impasse. One variation on this theme concerns the number of items being exchanged. Clients who insist that "if I get one, then you get one too" tend to ignore the relative value of the items in question. When the difference between items is large, then one or the other will likely cry "foul" and balk at the deal. This can get especially complex when the relative value is identical in objective or market value terms but differential in sentimental or subjective terms. Conflict may also result when both clients equally value the same item. In situations such as these, one solution is to look for new trade-offs that do not have the same emotional charge but still meet the criteria of a good trade-off. In a recent case, dispute centered on an item of chattel, namely, an antique table purchased at auction for a few hundred dollars. Each claimed to care about it "more" than the other. It was obvious to the mediator, if not to the clients, that the table had come to symbolize a longstanding marital dispute. One option was to return to premediation in an effort to resolve the underlying issue. Another option was to look for a different sort of trade-off mechanism. The couple would first trade off the items that were of roughly equal value and about which there was no dispute. The remaining items would be numbered, the numbers placed in a box, and each would take turns picking numbers out of the box, rather like winning at the lottery, with such choices then no longer negotiable. The couple was rather tickled by the game-like atmosphere created by the lottery analogy and spent an enjoyable hour dividing up their remaining chattel. Discovering another kind of trade-off avoided impasse.

Finally, there are three additional techniques that are *generic in character* and equally applicable to impasses rooted in relational or substantive issues.

- *Relentless persistence and optimism.* On entry into mediation, clients have typically repeatedly tried and failed to resolve their differences, either by their informal efforts or in litigation. Consequently, they often enter mediation with a sense of futility and hopelessness. This is all too apparent in the sorts of questions or statements clients are likely to ask of or make to the mediator: "Do you really think this can do any good?" "Can you help us?" "How long is this going to take?" "She will behave one way when she's with you but quite another when we are alone together." "He has to be in control, no matter what. You'll see." In light of this futility, it is imperative that the mediator instill in clients a sense of hope that mediation can be effective and that, within a specific time frame, there will be an end to the pain and frustration of their current relationship. To these ends, the mediator must be relentlessly positive, optimistic, hopeful, and highly persistent, even in the face of repeated failure. In effect, as negotiation begins, the mediator must supply the emotional energy to keep it going. Later, after some initial success, that energy will increasingly come from the clients. Accordingly, mediators should advise clients of the need for patience ("Good agreements take time to build."), perspective ("It took two years for you to get here. It will take some time to get past that negative experience."), flexibility ("Just because you didn't settle on the first try doesn't mean you won't succeed on the second try or the third."), and compromise ("In mediation, you're working toward a "good enough" agreement, not one in which you get exactly what you want."). Similarly, final summaries, as clients are getting up to leave, should be positive ("A lot of really good work today," or "Excellent effort from both of you," or "This is the sort of behavior that will keep you going for the next 20 years. Well done!").

- *Be satisfied with partial agreements.* Although mediators strive for a complete or comprehensive agreement, that is not always possible. Some issues may be intractable for some couples. Such couples belong in counseling, litigation, or both and should be referred accordingly. However, outcomes should *never* be considered in black or white terms. Rather, outcomes come in shades of gray, that is, in various degrees of agreement. For example, for reasons that are not entirely clear, some couples may have an easy time constructing a parenting plan but reach an impasse when it comes to negotiating a financial settlement. In other couples, the reverse may be true. In either case, their partial agreement is a real accomplishment and should be seen as such by both the couple and the mediator. Indeed, given sufficient time, the agreement in one area can generalize to the second area. In a recent case, the couple's parenting plan was a hard one to accomplish and reflected real changes in the quality of their interaction. By chance, one of the parenting issues that had been fiercely negotiated and resolved recurred after impasse was reached on their financial plan. In this case, directly as a result of mediation, the issue was handled smoothly and without upset. Both parents were so pleased, they agreed to reopen the financial issue and try again. Although their negotiation was occasionally heated, this time they reached agreement. The result is a mixed message: Be satisfied with partial agreements, but never stop looking for opportunities to extend the dialogue and thus hold out the hope of a full and complete settlement.

• *Mediation/arbitration.* When an impasse around a large issue cannot be resolved, the mediator has no choice but to refer out, either for counseling, litigation, or both. However, when an impasse pertains to a specific issue—such as a workable arrangement for Christmas holidays or whether to send the children to public or private school—then another option is available to couples in family mediation, namely, mediation/arbitration. It is called that because the process furthers the goals of mediation and has the mediator change hats to do the arbitration. In this context, arbitration is an adjudicative process that is intended to end conflict around the issue in question by having the mediator/arbitrator make a binding decision that is no longer subject to negotiation. The process involves three steps. First, the mediator seeks the consent of the lawyers in question. Their support will be essential because the final decision is intended to be legally binding on their clients. Second, each client is asked to submit what he or she regards as the best offer on the issue in dispute. Some mediator/arbitrators insist that such submissions be in writing. Others, ourselves included, allow for an aural presentation in keeping with the mediation process with which the clients are familiar. Finally, the mediator/arbitrator prepares a written report. This sets out the issue, summarizes the positions of the parties, and explains why a particular solution should be preferred. That solution may select among the parties' preferred choices, merge these choices to create some sort of hybrid, or prefer a third solution developed by the mediator/arbitrator. When the issue concerns parenting, the children's best interests provide the ultimate rationale for the final decision. When the issue concerns property, the decision must take account of local statutes and recent precedents (where appropriate) as well as factors connected to the relationship between the parties (past, present, and future), including (where appropriate) the interests of third parties not at the table, especially the children.

Indications

Finally, our treatment of negotiation would not be complete without some consideration of outcomes, particularly how we conceptualize what are popularly known as *win-win* outcomes. In its popular usage, the term suggests an outcome that is satisfying to both parties because each is able to walk away with something of value. That is, the outcome satisfies one or more of each party's interests. Such congruence is consistent with a TFM perspective, in which partial or comprehensive agreements on the substantive issues in dispute are clearly desirable. Similarly, we think highly of substantive efforts that clarify issues and pave the way for future efforts, including litigation. However, unless and until such agreements and/or clarifications also reflect concomitant shifts in relational processes, they are not adequate in and of themselves. This is so because in the absence of relational shifts, such agreements will not endure; in a year or two, these couples will be back in court, having learned little from their brief experience of family mediation. Indeed, it is not uncommon to have couples enter mediation who have been locked in mortal combat for 10 or more years *after* their divorce was finalized.

To avoid such outcomes, TFM sets out a series of relational criteria used to evaluate the quality of the outcome as follows:

- Increased frequency and intensity of positive affect
- Decreased frequency and intensity of negative affect
- More effective conflict management skills

    Enhanced focus on the issues and not the parties
    Greater flexibility and openness, including willingness to explore issues and options, use reality testing, and compromise where appropriate
    Improved focus on the present and future while coming to terms with the past
    Greater tolerance of differences in values, preferences, and attitudes

- Enhanced communication skills

    Improved communication clarity
    Improved assertiveness and sensitivity to verbal and nonverbal cues
    Enhanced mutual attention, listening, respect, and empathy
    Improved listening accuracy
    Reduced frequency of common dysfunctions, such as mind reading, attributing motives, stereotyping, name-calling, swearing, and the use of extreme language (*always, never*)

Such relational changes creation the foundation on which the clients and the mediator together co-construct a settlement that is fair and equitable under their unique circumstances. To ensure that this is so, a draft settlement should be very thoroughly reviewed with the clients. Here, two approaches may be distinguished: Either the mediator prepares the draft, based on process notes, or such notes are used to create a point-form summary, with the clients responsible for drafting the text. In either case, thorough review in session is important because disagreements can still arise. One client is sure that a given clause meant this, but the other client is equally sure that it meant that. This difference in interpretation is subject to continued negotiation. Even the final draft provided to the clients can be problematic because there is a real chance that all their hard work will be rejected by their respective lawyers, each zealous to protect and enhance the rights of their client.

To avoid this possibility, we routinely rely on two related approaches. The first is to encourage the lawyers to see themselves as team members in which all participants are working toward the same goal, namely, a fair and reasonable settlement. Toward that end, the lawyers need to be kept informed of the progress of the mediation and of the issues about which their clients have reached agreement. In turn, this gives the lawyers opportunities for input and dramatically reduces the likelihood that they will reject the final "memorandum." The other approach involves a preempting maneuver designed to prepare clients for their lawyers' possible response and suggests the importance of dialogue between clients and lawyers as to what the clients want to get out of the process (for a sample memorandum, see Appendix 6.1).

In addition, clients should be informed that the memorandum is non-binding; only when it has been reviewed and approved by their lawyers, redrafted to meet the requirements of the court, and then signed does their settlement become a legally binding contract. Even so, clients should be warned on several occasions that such agreement likely has a shelf life of only a year or two. That is so because their children are changing, as are the circumstances of the clients' own lives. To keep their agreement relevant, they can expect to make informal changes to it on a regular basis. Indeed, a well-functioning agreement will soon be forgotten entirely, left to gather dust in a drawer as the clients get on with their lives, making informal changes on the fly as needed.

It is this combination of relational change and substantive fairness that alone warrants the label *win-win*. Although this will be typical of TFM-based settlements, that is not always the case. Despite having reached settlement, in a minority of cases, the sort of relational change the mediator would like to see happen will not have occurred. Similarly, in some cases, the best the couple can manage is a partial agreement. Such incomplete outcomes reflect the reality of mediation practice. So long as mediators can honestly say they have done their best, they must be content with their clients' best performance, whatever that may be.

Finally, in light of relational change and substantive fairness, most clients will report that the mediation process has been a satisfying one. Both should feel that they have had their say and been given equal time to do so. Both should also agree that the settlement reached was the best they could have hoped for under their circumstances and that it does recognize and protect the children's best interests. In this context, most clients are deeply appreciative of the mediator efforts, and the mediator, in turn, offers congratulatory comments in recognition of all their hard work. Even so, such positive feelings are often bittersweet, for they occur in the midst of divorce, with the clients now free to confront the challenges of parenting across two households and often with inadequate financial resources to do so. Accordingly, even in parting, the mediator should be supportive and encouraging and available in light of the real possibility of future impasses.

Appendix 6.1

Sample "Memorandum of Understanding"

Parenting Plan

1. PREAMBLE

Children of divorce do best in the short and long run when they feel loved and cared for by *both* parents. This is most likely to occur when the children have ongoing contact with both parents and when those parents participate fully in their lives. Children feel more secure and better about themselves knowing both parents want them and want to be involved in their lives. Such parental commitment helps to diminish or eliminate any feelings children may have of abandonment or rejection. Children also need consistency and stability in their lives. Thus, children's need for regular contact with their parents must be balanced against their need for stability and consistency. The balance between the two will depend on many factors, including factors related to the children (e.g., their ages, developmental needs, and temperaments), the parents, and the circumstances.

2. INTRODUCTION

Parents will share parenting of their # children: (name, age), (name, age), and (name, age). Notwithstanding, the usual and holiday schedule, child-related decision making, and dispute resolution methods will be as per the following parenting plan.

The parents are committed to the spirit of the parenting plan, which recognizes the children's need for a good and ongoing relationship with both parents and calls for shared parenting, with both parents involved in all matters related to the children.

Shared parenting involves two major components: (a) how major child-related decisions are made and (b) the time the child spends with both parents. The primary goals of such a plan are to minimize factors that produce or promote conflict between parents, to ensure smooth implementation of the parenting plan, and to maximize healthy child adjustment. The decisions that typically and most frequently challenge families are those related to day-to-day family management. These decisions include but are not limited to those concerning parental values and morals, clothes and toys traveling back and forth, parent-child telephone contact, transportation between homes, discipline, consistency and routines, changes and flexibility, extracurricular activities, parental communication, holiday schedules, differences in parenting styles, and routine exchanges of information.

Shared parenting poses a challenge for most families, as ineffective communication, mutual animosity, and power and control issues contribute to impasses. To the extent that it minimizes factors that produce conflict, a structured and specific parenting plan is preferred. Such plans provide solutions to day-to-day family management dilemmas and a method for making child-related decisions. Toward these ends, both parents agree to conduct themselves in accordance with the *parenting guidelines* set out in Appendix 6.2.

Of course, all possible changes in a family's circumstances and management cannot be foreseen, no matter how comprehensive or thorough the plan. Children mature and change, as do their needs. Parents may move residence or change jobs, become involved with new partners, or become ill, such that periodic changes in living arrangements and family dynamics are a normal part of family life. Any parenting plan will therefore require revision from time to time.

In the interests of clarity, when the children are with their father, he will be referred to as the "resident" parent, and when the children are with their mother, she will similarly be referred to as the "resident" parent.

3. CHILD-RELATED DECISION MAKING

   A. HEALTH CARE

      i. Routine or Daily Health Care

         a. The parents will continue to use the services of Dr. _____ as the children's doctor and Dr. _____ as the children's dentist. The parents will provide each other with the names, addresses, and telephone numbers of all physicians, dentists, orthodontists, or other professionals providing care to the children.

b. The resident parent is responsible for making day-to-day medical decisions (such as giving over-the-counter medicines, keeping the children home from school due to minor illness, taking the children to see a doctor for minor illness, etc.).

c. The children will *not* be expected to travel between homes if, in the judgment of the resident parent, they are too ill to do so. The other parent will accept this judgment and will not expect any makeup time.

d. The children will *not* be expected to travel between homes if, in the judgment of the other parent, they themselves are too ill to receive them. The resident parent will accept this judgment, and the other parent will not expect any makeup time.

ii. Major Medical Decisions (including long-term medication/treatment, surgery, orthodontic work, etc.)

The parents will notify each other of an emergency child visit to a physician, specialist, and/or hospital. Both parents may attend.

Each parent will provide written permission to the children's physicians to release information to the other parent.

The parents will directly request any relevant records/information from the children's physicians and not expect the other parent to provide such records or updates.

Major medical decisions are usually infrequent. Because they are serious, it is in the children's best interest for both parents to be involved in major medical decisions, with the assistance of expert third parties, such as medical specialists, dentists, and so on. The parents will notify each other of any potential major medical decisions as well as provide the other with the name(s) and telephone number(s) of the attending physician(s). It is ideal for the parents to consult with the physician(s) together. However, if this is not possible, the parents may consult individually, adding second opinions as they think necessary. The parents will arrive at major medical decisions mutually. If they cannot, they shall abide by the consensus medical opinion, in consultation with the mediator, as outlined below in paragraph 10.

B. EDUCATION (including school selection, psychoeducational testing, remedial assistance, report cards, parent/teacher meetings, etc.)

    i. At present, the children are too young to attend primary school. However, when they begin doing so, it will be in their best interest if the parents attend parent-teacher meetings together. In doing so, the children will perceive that their parents are working together on their behalf. This may lessen the children's loyalty bind and curtail any effort on their part to "play both ends against the middle." If either parent prefers to have an individual meeting, each parent will be responsible for arranging with the school his or her own parent-teacher meeting. Any special meetings, involving board or school personnel (other than the teacher), are likely to require the parents to attend together, as time and resources usually do not allow for separate meetings.

    ii. Each parent will be responsible for staying up to date on any relevant educational matters and requesting involvement for any special meetings about their children. Each parent will request *from the school* that he or she be provided with all notices, report cards, and so on. If the school cannot accommodate such requests, each parent will continue to notify the other of all school events at the time he or she learns of them. The residential parent who first obtains the children's report cards will provide the other parent with copies of them.

    iii. It is in the children's best interests for both parents to attend school-related functions, such as open houses, plays, concerts, fund-raisers, and so on.

    iv. Major decisions related to the children's education include class placement, psychoeducational testing, remedial assistance, enrichment, and so on. Such decisions will be made in consultation with relevant experts, including teachers, principals, school or independent psychologists, and so on. It is ideal for the parents to consult with these professionals together. However, if this is not possible, the parents may consult individually, adding second opinions as necessary. The parents will make educationally relevant decisions mutually, in consultation with the relevant expert or experts, if there are different expert opinions. If the parents cannot agree, they will follow the dispute resolution mechanism outlined in paragraph 10, below.

v. The school will have both parents' names to call in case of an emergency. The resident parent will be called first. If he or she cannot be reached, then the nonresident parent will be called. The contact parent will notify the other parent as soon as possible.

C. RELIGIOUS INSTRUCTION

i. The parents will educate and expose the children to religious instruction in keeping with the Christian tradition in place prior to their separation and consistent with the children's best interests.

4. THE CHILDREN'S TIME WITH THEIR PARENTS

A. ROUTINE OR DAILY TIME-SHARING SCHEDULE

i. The children will live with both parents pursuant to the following rotating schedule.

Week 1

a. The children will live with father from Monday after day care/nursery school until Wednesday morning, when he will deliver them to day care/nursery school.

b. The children will live with mother from Wednesday after day care/nursery school to Friday morning, when she will deliver them to day care/nursery school.

c. The children will live with father from Friday after day care/nursery school to Monday morning, when he will deliver them to day care/nursery school.

Week 2

d. The children will live with father from Monday after day care/nursery school until Wednesday morning, when he will deliver them to day care/nursery school.

e. The children will live with mother from Wednesday after day care/nursery school to Friday morning, when she will deliver them to day care/nursery school.

f. The children will live with mother from Friday after day care/nursery school to Monday morning, when she will deliver them to day care/nursery school.

B. HOLIDAY TIME-SHARING SCHEDULE

On all personal, school, civic, and religious holidays or special days, the children will spend equal time with each parent. With the following exceptions, the parents will work out the detailed arrangements between them.

Easter

i. On Easter Sunday, the children will be with mother from 9 a.m. to 2 p.m. and with father from 2 p.m. to 8 p.m.

ii. This arrangement will rotate on an annual basis.

Christmas

iii. On Christmas, the children will be with father from Christmas Eve to Christmas Day at 2 p.m. and with mother from 2 p.m. to Boxing Day at 8 p.m.

iv. This arrangement will rotate on an annual basis.

Summer Holidays

v. During the summer holidays, the children will spend 2 nonconsecutive weeks with each parent.

vi. Each parent will give the other 4 weeks' notice of their holiday plans.

Travel

vii. When traveling away from either parent's residence, the phone number(s) of the children's whereabouts will be provided in writing to the nonresident parent in case of emergency.

C. TRANSITIONS

i. Pickup and/or Drop-Off

a. The nonresident parent will be responsible for picking up the children.

ii. Parental Conduct at Transition Points

a. At transition points, both parents will behave in accordance with the *parental guidelines* (see Appendix 6.2).

iii. Parenting Continuity

It will be in the best interests of the children if *both* parents are aware of the events and the experiences in the children's lives, including those that occur when the children are with the other parent.

a. At transition points and/or at another time mutually preferred, the resident parent will provide the other parent with a brief synopsis of the children's experience.

D. CHILDREN'S CLOTHING & BELONGINGS

i. It is preferable for both parents to have adequate clothing for the children. The clothes the children have worn en route to the time with the other parent will be returned (washed or not) and placed in the children's knapsacks when they return to the other parent.

ii. The children's belongings belong to them. The children will have the option of taking toys, computer games, and so on back and forth if they wish. As each of them becomes old enough, they will be encouraged to assume responsibility for these items by remembering to bring and return them as they desire.

iii. Major sporting items, dress clothes, and other expensive items will travel back and forth with the children as they desire and/or on the verbal request of the other parent. The items will be promptly returned with the children. If the item is damaged or broken, the parent who had it when the damage occurred is responsible for replacing the item. Depending on their age, the children may also be expected to assume some responsibility as determined by the resident parent at the time.

5. COMMUNICATION

A. PARENTAL COMMUNICATION

i. On a weekly basis, mother will telephone father, or vice versa, to communicate about the children's weekly experience (including upsets, special events, etc.). The children will benefit knowing both parents are aware of these significant events. Also, the children will be less likely to "play both ends against the middle" when they know their parents communicate regularly about them.

ii. In addition to weekly telephone calls, the parents may use a communication/information book that will travel back and forth with the children between each parent's home. This book may include, but not be limited to, the following: the parenting plan, names and addresses of the children's friends, names and addresses of coaches and instructors, schedules of lessons and sports, immunization record, health card number, dates and reasons for medical visits, other medical information, current prescriptions, discipline/structure routines, and any other child-related information. This book may be especially useful in that it provides one place to store relevant child-related information.

     iii. The children will not be asked by their parents to relay information from parent to parent.

B. PARENT-CHILD COMMUNICATION

     i. The children may call the nonresident parent on the telephone whenever they wish. The nonresident parent may call the children on the telephone whenever he or she wishes, with proper consideration given to mealtimes and bedtime.

C. PARENTAL COMMUNICATION WITH THE CHILDREN PRESENT

As part of their normal development, children identify with *both* their parents. When one parent says negative things about the other parent within earshot of the children, he or she undermines that part of the children that identify with that parent and thus undermines the children's identity and self-esteem.

     i. Within earshot of the children, both parents will conduct themselves in accordance with the *parenting guidelines*. In particular, they will be supportive of the children's relationship with the other parent and will scrupulously avoid overt conflict between them.

6. EXTRACURRICULAR EVENTS AND ACTIVITIES

A. SELECTION

     i. Each parent may enroll the children and/or participate in the activities he or she chooses, provided the activities do not overlap with the other parent's time with the children. The parents will consult and come to a mutual decision regarding extracurricular activities that *overlap both parents' time with* the children. Neither parent will enroll the child in activities that overlap with the other parent's time without that parent's consent.

     ii. The parents will obtain schedules and other necessary information directly from the instructor and/or coaches of the activities.

     iii. The parents may attend special events at school and extracurricular activities, such as games, concerts, recitals, shows, or performances.

7. UNEXPECTED EVENTS

Unexpected events are a normal part of everyday life. Traffic, inclement weather, traffic accidents, road closures, and sudden illness are to be expected but not predicted. Consequently, there will be occasions when such events interfere with routine and/or holiday time-sharing schedules.

A. CHANGING THE TIME-SHARING SCHEDULE

   i.   Should the need arise, the parents will communicate verbally and/or in writing as to a request(s) for a change to the usual or holiday schedule. They will do so with as much notice as possible. A verbal or written response will be provided within 48 hours.

   ii. Each parent will discuss changes to the schedule, first with the other parent and prior to mentioning anything to the children about a change and/or a special activity.

   iii. If additional time is required due to a special event or celebration, notice will be provided to the other parent when the need arises and/or 2 weeks in advance. A response will be provided within 24 hours.

   iv. As a rule, the parents will not be entitled to make up time if they request a change. Notwithstanding this rule, makeup time may be offered.

   v.   If, for any reason, one parent cannot be available to care for the children at scheduled times, the other parent will be given the "first right of refusal" to care for the children. If the other parent cannot accommodate the request, the resident parent is responsible for arranging alternate child care.

   vi. It is understood that traffic and inclement weather may cause delays. Notwithstanding, every effort (including allowing for more time when necessary) will be made by the parents to be punctual in their delivery of the children to the other parent, to day care, to nursery school, or to activities. If one parent cannot deliver the children within 15 minutes of the scheduled time, he or she will notify the other parent when the need for delays arises.

8. MOVING HOUSEHOLDS (MOBILITY)

A. MOVING

   i.   Two months' written notice will be provided to the other parent if a residential move is being considered.

   ii. Either parent may move freely within 20 miles of his or her current residence without the consent of the other parent.

   iii. For moves further than 20 miles, the parents will consult with one another as to any changes required to their time-sharing schedules. Neither parent may move without the express written consent of the other parent.

9. ANNUAL REVIEW

No parenting plan is permanent, and all plans require revision over time as the parents' and the children's needs change. Any aspect of the parenting plan may be revised by the parents on mutual consent. Accordingly, the parents will monitor the terms of the parenting plan in relation to the children's ongoing adjustment and will review their plan at least on an annual basis.

10. DISPUTE RESOLUTION MECHANISM

   A. BREAKING IMPASSES

   i.   When either parent has an issue he or she wishes to resolve with the other parent, he or she will indicate this to the other parent, either on the telephone or in person.

   ii. The parents agree that within 7 days of being informed of a problematic issue, or as soon after as is reasonable and practical, they will discuss the issue to see if they can resolve the conflict between themselves. The parents have every confidence that they will be able to do so.

   iii. However, if the parties alone cannot resolve the conflict, they agree that they will refer the problematic issue to mediation with Dr. Michael Benjamin, and he will assist the parents in reaching a resolution. If the issue is not resolved during mediation, the parties may submit the matter to arbitration with Dr. Michael Benjamin, on consent.

   iv. While the dispute is being resolved in mediation or arbitration, the residential parent will continue making such day-to-day decisions as are necessary but will take no substantial action in the area of disagreement that would prejudice or take unfair advantage of the other parent by use of their residential status to his or her own benefit.

City, State/Province

Month, Day, Year

_____ Appendix 6.2

Parenting in Divorce: Practical Guidelines

1. Parents should strive for a decent, business-like, working relationship with one another that meet the needs of their children (Ricci, 1997, pp. 51, 83, 89-92):

Watch your language; be courteous and mutually respectful.

Keep your feelings in check.

Respect the other parent's privacy and expect the same in return.

Act like a guest in the other parent's home.

Don't expect appreciation or praise from the other parent, but do acknowledge when your partner shows understanding, sensitivity, compromise, or flexibility and support and expect the same in return.

Keep a positive but realistic attitude.

Keep your sense of humor and encourage it in the other parent.

Be reliable; do what you say you're going to do and expect the same from the other parent.

Be flexible and supportive of the other parent and expect the same in return.

Be patient; Rome wasn't built in a day.

Expect to feel strange about this new relationship at first; give yourself time to adjust.

Though it may be difficult at first, don't give up; the effort is worth it.

2. In all interaction between parents, use good communication practices (Ricci, 1997, pp. 91, 95, 104, 108):

Be explicit with the other parent.

Direct communication between parents should be preferred at all times; do not communicate through third parties, especially the children.

Say what you mean and mean what you say; make no assumptions.

Double-check your verbal understandings; to build trust, don't take the other parent for granted.

Demonstrate you understand what the other parent is saying.

Try to ensure that verbal and nonverbal "messages" are the same and not in conflict.

Know the things that trigger conflict between parents and avoid them.

Confront only with great care.

Keep the other parent a person in your mind; don't make him or her into a "monster."

3. Parents should work to maintain a healthy, positive parenting pattern (Ricci, 1997, pp. 90, 95, 117):

Time with the children is time together, not baby-sitting.

Make your children's needs more important than your territorial rights or your independence; always, children before rules or procedures.

Respect the other parent's time with the children.

Respect the other parent's parenting style.

Interfere with the other parent's effort only if your children need your protection.

Share information about the children frequently with the other parent; parenting continuity is important as the children move between households.

Parents should compare notes on the other adults in your children's lives, including teachers, coaches, medical and dental professionals, and others.

Each parent should be supportive of the other parent's relationship with the children.

Don't use the children to carry messages to the other parent.

4. Parents should work to develop and maintain a healthy, positive relationship with their children (Ricci, 1997, pp. 125-130, 142-153):

Let your children know you are thinking about them and expect them to keep in touch with you.

Make regular contact with the other adults in your children's lives, including teachers, coaches, medical and dental professionals, and others.

Talk to your children regularly; young children especially need to understand the changes in their lives in ways that are seeable, touchable, and concrete.

Give children a say in the decisions that affect their lives based on their TLC; ensure that they feel heard, even though adults make all final decisions.

Don't "bad-mouth" the other parent in the presence of the children.

Don't participate in the children's angry feelings about the other parent.

Encourage the children to speak about any difficulties they are having with the other parent, but don't pursue it at length; suggest other adults with whom the child might wish to confide.

Don't ask the children about the other parent's life or circumstances; respect the other parent's privacy and give his or her motives the benefit of any doubt.

Don't tell the children to keep secrets about you from the other parent.

Be the grown-up.

Keep changes to a minimum during the first few years, especially in regards to young children.

Never threaten to abandon your children.

Know and respond to danger signals in your children and get help as required.

Provide your children with structure and predictability.

Don't lead your children to believe that you may reconcile with the other parent.

Calm your children's fears and help rebuild trust and security.

Frequently reassure the children of your love and that you will always be there to care for them and look after their needs.

5. To make wise, informed decisions, parents should be informed of advances in research concerning parenting in divorce.

- Lamb, Sternberg, and Thompson (1997), for example, show that on consent, various parenting arrangements can be effective in divorce, with shared parenting offering the best opportunity for children to have a meaningful relationship with both parents.[1]
- Kelly and Lamb (2000) show that children's requirements for a healthy attachment to their parents change with age: Frequent movements between parents and children are better for children younger than age 6, and less frequent movements are better for children older than age 6.[2] The authors also affirm that there is no evidence of harm in overnight visits, even with very young children.
- Warshak (2000) shows that the view that overnight visits with more than one parent are bad for children is an opinion based on no evidence whatsoever.[3] Available evidence, much of it indirect, suggests that even in very young children such visits promote a healthy relationship between children and both their parents.

Notes

1.   The effects of divorce and custody arrangements on children's behavior and adjustment.

2.   Using child development research to make appropriate custody and access decisions for young children.

3.   Overnight contact between parents and young children.

References

Adler, R. S., Rosen, B., & Silverstein, E. M. (1998). Emotions in negotiation: How to manager fear and anger. *Negotiation Journal, 14*(2), 161-179.

Barsky, A. E. (2000). *Conflict resolution for the helping professions*. Belmont, CA: Brooks/Cole.

Bossy, J. (Ed.). (1983). *Disputes and settlements: Law and human relations in the West*. Cambridge, MA: Cambridge University Press.

Boulle, L., & Kelly, K. J. (1998). *Mediation: Principles, processes, practice* (Canadian ed.). Toronto: Butterworths.

Burton, J. W. (1987). *Resolving deep-rooted conflict: A handbook*. Lanham, MD: University Press of America.

Bush, R. A. B., & Folger, J. P. (1994). *The promise of mediation: Responding to conflict through empowerment and recognition*. San Francisco: Jossey-Bass.

Cohen, H. (1980). *You can negotiate anything: How to get what you want*. New York: Citadel.

Conley, J. M., & O'Barr, W. M. (1990). *Rules versus relationships: The ethnography of legal discourse*. Chicago: University of Chicago Press.

Druckman, D. (1993). An analytical research agenda for conflict and conflict resolution. In D. J. D. Sandole & H. van der Merwe (Eds.), *Conflict resolution theory and practice: Integration and application* (pp. 91-108). Manchester, UK: Manchester University Press.

Ellis, D., & Stuckless, N. (1996). *Mediating and negotiating marital conflicts*. Thousand Oaks, CA: Sage.

Fisher, R., & Brown, S. (1988). *Getting together: Building relationships as we negotiate*. New York: Penguin.

Fisher, R., Ury, W., & Patton, B. (1997). *Getting to yes: Negotiating agreement without giving in* (3rd ed.). New York: Penguin.

Gordon, R. J., Donner, D. S., & Peacock, K. (2000). From infants to adolescents: A developmental approach to parenting plans. *Family & Conciliation Courts Review, 38*(2), 168-191.

Irving, H. H., & Benjamin, M. (1995). *Family mediation: Contemporary issues*. Thousand Oaks, CA: Sage.

Kelly, J. B., & Lamb, M. E. (2000). Using child development research to make appropriate custody and access decisions for young children. *Family & Conciliation Courts Review, 38*(3), 297-311.

Lamb, M. E., Sternberg, K. J., & Thompson, R. A. (1997). The effects of divorce and custody arrangements on children's behavior, and adjustment. *Family & Conciliation Courts Review, 35*(4), 393-404.

Lang, M. (Ed.). (1996). Transformative approaches to mediation [Special issue]. *Mediation Quarterly, 13*(4).

Menkel-Meadow, C. (1984). Toward another view of legal negotiation: The structure of problem-solving. *UCLA Law Review, 31*, 754-842.

Mnookin, R. H., & Kornhauser, L. (1979). Bargaining in the shadow of the law: The case of divorce. *Yale Law Journal, 88,* 960-997.

Nelson, N. C. (1997). *Winning! Using lawyers' courtroom techniques to get your way in everyday situations.* Paramus, NJ: Prentice Hall.

Pruitt, D. G., & Carnevale, P. C. (1989). *Negotiation in social conflict.* Pacific Grove, CA: Brooks/Cole.

Raiffa, H. (1982). *The art and science of negotiation.* Cambridge, MA: Harvard University Press.

Ricci, I. (1997). *Mom's house, Dad's house: Making two homes for your child* (Rev. ed.). New York: Fireside.

Rifkin, J., Millen, J., & Cobb, S. (1991). Toward a new discourse for mediation: A critique of neutrality. *Mediation Quarterly, 9,* 151-164.

Schoonmaker, A. N. (1989). *Negotiate to win: Gaining the psychological edge.* Englewood Cliffs, NJ: Prentice Hall.

Slaikeu, K. A., Culler, R., Pearson, J., & Thoennes, N. (1985). Process and outcome in divorce mediation. *Mediation Quarterly, 19,* 55-74.

Spence, G. (1995). *How to argue and win every time.* New York: St. Martin's.

Ury, W. (1991). *Getting past no: Negotiating with difficult people.* London: Penguin.

Warshak, R. A. (2000). Overnight contact between parents and young children. *Family & Conciliation Courts Review, 38*(4), 422-445.

7

The TFM Approach:
Step-by-Step Guide

Phases 4 and 5:
Termination and Follow-Up

Family mediation is intended as a short-term process. Termination is therefore a universal feature of all family mediation cases. Many texts picture termination as simple and straightforward (Acland, 1990; Allen & Mohr, 1998; Chornenki & Hart, 1996; Fisher, Ury, & Patton, 1997; Goldberg, Sander, & Rogers, 1992; James, 1997; Leviton & Greenstone, 1997; MacFarlane, 1999; Slaikeu, 1995; Weeks, 1992), so much so that Beer (1997) mentions it only in passing. There is much to be said for this approach, but it can be problematic in family mediation in at least two respects. First, the complexity of the process, which infuses each of the phases discussed above, continues in termination. Second, and equally salient, most of the authors noted above make no assumptions about the ongoing relationship between the participants. In contrast, in family mediation, such assumptions are simply mandatory, especially given the additional assumptions that underpin the therapeutic family mediation (TFM) model.

In turn, these assumptions require an approach to mediation that is more complex, recognizes several different variants of this outcome, and is mindful of the link between termination (Phase 4) and follow-up (Phase 5). Set out in Table 7.1, this approach distinguishes between goals and outcomes.

Goals

The termination process should be useful to both clients and mediators. To these ends, we distinguish five goals of termination.

Table 7.1   Termination

Goals

Achieve closure to the mediation process
- Complete a "memorandum of agreement"
- Evaluate for referral out
- Evaluate family dynamics and classify outcome
- Create links to follow-up

Outcomes

Positive Termination 1
- Agreement on all issues in dispute
- Clients satisfied with process and outcomes
- Complete "memorandum"
- Arrange for follow-up

Positive Termination 2
- Partial agreement
- Clarify issues that remain unresolved
- Complete partial "memorandum"
- Open mediation: offer to write report
- Refer out

Negative Termination 1: mediator initiated
- Client conduct makes meaningful agreement impossible
- Assess for mediator error
- Refer out

Negative Termination 2: client initiated
- Client(s) refuse to continue
- Early impasse
- Client dropout
- Assess for mediator error

Achieve Closure to the Mediation Process

From the clients' perspective, mediation is an emotionally and intellectually arduous, difficult, and tiring process. However it ends, these features of the process need to be acknowledged, as does the clients' need for some form of final closure. The latter derives from the fact that clients and mediators have invariably formed a close and intimate relationship that is coming to a close. That such an ending was a foregone conclusion makes it no less affectively charged. It follows that its termination must be handled with sensitivity. Furthermore, mediation is about working on resolving issues in dispute. It is rare that couples make no headway whatsoever in this effort. Indeed, in most cases, full resolution will have been secured. Such an achievement deserves to be highlighted and celebrated.

From the mediator's perspective, mediation is a process that often does not end with simple termination. Rather, the mediator's efforts to restructure the dynamic relationship between the partners is intended to carry forward into the short-term, if not the long-term, future. There is also the matter of follow-up to consider. Termination, then, is the mediator's opportunity to ensure that these processes carry on as they were intended.

Complete a "Memorandum of Understanding"

Although we do not believe that settlement is the only or even the most important outcome of family mediation, completion of a "memorandum of understanding" is important in at least two senses. First, it is salient in legal terms, forming the heart of the couple's separation agreement. Second, it is symbolic of the couple's efforts in mediation and is thus a tangible reward for them.

At the same time, the "memorandum" per se will ensure neither cooperative problem solving nor a ready solution to future problems. It is thus crucial to preempt any such unrealistic expectations. As a symbol of the clients' commitment to each other and to their children, it is important. But, like their children's toys, it is likely to be outgrown rather quickly and should be seen as a rough guideline only, not as a set of prescriptions that must be adhered to slavishly.

Evaluate for Referral Out

Divorce arises from dysfunctional marital and family processes. It may also have dysfunctional sequelae. Both forms of dysfunction will need to be addressed in TFM-based family mediation to ensure that they do not interfere with the process. Such efforts may be entirely successful, partially successful, or completely ineffective, with clear implications for outcome. All of these considerations suggest the need to evaluate terminating couples for the utility of some form of postmediation referral. A common referral target might involve some form of individual therapy, typically to address issues such as anger management, postdivorce attachment, adjustment, and/or parenting. Alternative bases for referral include arbitration or litigation. On balance, referral out will be more likely in couples with a negative as opposed to a positive mediation outcome (see below).

Evaluate Family Dynamics and Classify Outcome

In many cases, TFM-based mediation will involve some effort to shift family dynamics to promote cooperative problem solving, productive conflict management, and future-oriented planning. These outcomes in mediation will reflect the extent to which these efforts have been successful. Evaluation of both dynamic and outcome features of the mediation process is part and parcel of the mediator's commitment to lifelong learning and the pursuit of practice excellence. Although the mediator is always expected to do his or her very best for each and every couple, each practice experience offers the opportunity for professional growth.

Especially important here is the issue of clinical error (Benjamin & Bross, 1982; Coleman, 1985). The mediator may judge couples amenable to mediation when they turn out not to be. Their efforts to intervene during pre-mediation may prove ineffective or, worse, may be a source of distress for one or both partners, thus setting back the process. The same may be true of interventions made by the mediator during negotiation. Among some mediators, such errors may reflect inadequate training and thus may call into question their basic competence. In most mediators, such errors reflect judgment calls that were reasonable at the time under those circumstances but simply did not produce the intended result(s). In that sense, they are necessary to the mediation process by confirming or disconfirming the mediator's working hypothesis at the time. In a related sense, such errors may also be seen as a learning opportunity and thus as a source of growth as clients teach mediators what they need to know.

The latter point is salient. In our experience, beginning and seasoned mediators make different sorts of errors, suggesting different sorts of learning curves in these different subgroups. The key difference between them involves their respective degree of conscious control. Beginners tend to become overwhelmed with data and feel themselves under great stress. Consequently, their efforts at intervention tend to be more impulsive, less thought out, and naturally less based on experience than formal training. In contrast, seasoned mediators have developed filters to slow down the intake of data and are more relaxed and more self-confident. Consequently, their efforts at intervention tend to be more planful, thought out, based on experience, and thus often more creative. Although both groups continue to make errors, beginner errors tend to be avoidable, whereas the errors of seasoned mediators tend to be necessary.

Finally, in both groups, the mediator will typically act as a solo practitioner. The issue of error raises the related issue of the absence of on-site supervision as an independent source of feedback. Two sorts of response are typical, and both are warranted. The first involves a heightened sense of self-reflexivity, as mediators learn to operate at more than one level, engaging with clients while watching themselves do so. The second involves conferring with colleagues who act as informal supervisors, sharing cases and exploring options as they learn together. These efforts assist clients by improving the mediator's expertise while making for a rich learning experience.

Create Links to Follow-Up

Finally, the TFM model includes a follow-up phase. Informing couples of this opportunity must occur on termination. It is here that the utility and objectives of follow-up can be explained and the clients' questions answered.

It is here too that the mediator can book the follow-up session or sessions and warn clients to expect a call about 1 week prior to the session itself.

Outcomes

We recognize four outcomes in TFM-based mediation, two positive and two negative.

Positive Termination 1

This termination option is characterized by agreement on all issues in dispute, completion of a "memorandum," completion of arrangements for follow-up, and client satisfaction with both process and substantive and relational outcomes.

This is the best possible outcome in mediation and is associated with various congratulatory and supportive comments by the mediator. The former acknowledge how far the couple has come since entry into mediation, how hard they have worked to overcome initial blocks to agreement, and how much their final settlement means to them and to the mediator. The latter are essentially preemptive maneuvers intended to warn clients of the difficulties to follow, indicate the mediator's confidence in their ability to handle such problems well and informally, but note the availability of the mediator should intractable problems arise in the future, despite their best efforts. This is also a time to step back from the mediation process and encourage the clients to talk about what that experience was like, including the parts that were especially useful and those that were not. As part of their own efforts at closure, this is when clients often thank the mediator for his or her assistance, while divulging the time(s) when the clients may have doubted their support or felt they were leaning more toward the other side or felt pushed by the mediator to make difficult and uncomfortable choices.

Such talk helps achieve closure, a process that is important when any intimate relationship ends or undergoes transition from one form to another. Talk serving the same function, if having somewhat different content, can readily be observed at the bedside of terminal patients or as parents see their last child leave home for good. Such talk reaffirms a range of positive sentiments that speak of the meaning of the relationship to the participants and how it has effected a change in the lives of all of them. Although this is more true of the clients than the mediator, the mediator also should acknowledge genuine concern for the clients and pleasure in helping them overcome a difficult set of problems in their effort to move on with their lives. Such affirmations not only help achieve the mediator's own sense of closure in the case but also give yet another opportunity to paint a hopeful and positive picture for clients whose life challenges following divorce have just begun.

Finally, such affirmations not only create the link to follow-up but, more generally, leave the door open should future problems arise that the clients are unable to overcome on their own.

In most cases, the mediator's confidence in the clients' newfound competence will be justified, and the clients will have no occasion to return to mediation. In some cases, however, the limited interventions available in TFM-based mediation will clearly be inadequate to address the clients' needs, and referral out should be suggested. For example, it would not be uncommon for a client couple to achieve a Positive Termination 1 outcome despite ongoing problems in attachment or anger management. Such couples can do fine work with the mediator to help the process along but can be expected to have problems achieving the same outcome alone. Similarly, different clients can be expected to adjust to divorce at different rates. Parenting may be more difficult for some clients than others, whereas some clients may be willing to reenter the dating scene when others are simply not ready for a new intimate relationship and may seek assistance in overcoming their fears. In such cases, community resources will be available to which such clients can be referred for ongoing help. It is incumbent on mediators to maintain a current list of such local resources.

Finally, no discussion of Positive Termination 1 would be complete without brief comment about the role of the lawyers. On entry into mediation, all clients are required to have legal representation. On termination, clients are informed that mediation-generated "memoranda" are not legally binding unless they have been vetted and approved by a lawyer, prepared in accordance with court requirements, signed in the presence of a lawyer, and filed with the family court. That is, legal review is simply mandatory in order for the final agreement to be seen as valid and binding by the family court.

In this context, lawyers who are knowledgeable about and supportive of mediation can be enormously helpful. Initially, such lawyers can inform clients of the mediation option and make appropriate referrals. During the process, they can stand by as legal consultants, informing clients of their rights and helping them work through complex issues, especially those pertaining to finances and taxes, at which most lawyers excel. On termination, they can work to preserve the integrity of a hard-won mediated agreement while providing their clients (and the mediator) with a safety net in case of "memoranda" that are flawed or incomplete, in rare cases sending their clients back to the mediator for further negotiation or fine-tuning.

In contrast, lawyers who know little about mediation and/or disapprove of it can make life difficult for the mediator. Initially, they may fail to inform their clients of the mediation option, cast it in negative terms, or make inappropriate referrals, in some cases hoping to stage a failure in mediation as part of their larger litigation strategy. During mediation, they may work at cross-purposes with the mediator, giving their clients advice that exacerbates conflict. In one case, a lawyer advised a client to drop out of mediation because "I can get you another $40,000 in court." In another case, a lawyer advised a client to take the children out of the jurisdiction without advising the other parent in order to "put a scare" into the other parent. On termination, such lawyers may ignore the mediation process and assess the "memorandum" on its technical merits, that is, in terms of the advantages it offers to their client. In the absence of such advantages or the presence of various compromises, such lawyers may undermine such agreements and insist that the client return to litigation.

On balance, as mediation has become more widespread and as more lawyers get mediation training, lawyers have become far more supportive of mediation than at any time in the past. Even so, it is not inappropriate for mediators to engage in a preempting maneuver, indicating to the clients that they may need to make clear to their respective lawyers the extent to which the memorandum reflects their true feelings about the issues in question.

Positive Termination 2

The second form of positive outcome is typically characterized by a partial agreement, clarification of unresolved issues, the completion of a partial "memorandum," and the need to refer out.

In this outcome, it is important for the mediator and the clients to capitalize on whatever gains have been made in mediation. A key gain refers to the partial "memorandum," typically either a parenting plan or a financial plan, rather than bits and pieces of both (though that too is possible). Equally important will be any advances in clarifying the issues that remain unresolved, so that the couple may return to mediation with another mediator, negotiate with the assistance of their lawyers, or litigate these remaining issues.

Moreover, these options make clear the necessity of an outside referral following the termination of mediation. In general, anything less than litigation is preferred. This is so because of the enormous cost of litigation—financial, social, and psychological, especially its negative indirect impact on the children—and the likelihood that the parents will be less willing to cooperate with each other, whatever the imposed settlement. One option that is gaining popularity is that of mediation/arbitration. Here, the mediator may be asked to change hats, asking each parent to provide reasoned arguments favoring his or her preferred solution. After carefully considering these various arguments, the mediator prepares a settlement report that is final and binding.

Negative Termination 1: Mediator Initiated

Outcomes are judged as "negative" in relation to the goals of TFM-based mediation; they are not negative in and of themselves because they honestly reflect the state of the relationship between the clients. Here, negative termination may arise in one of two ways: Either it is initiated by the mediator or by the clients. Negative Termination 1 refers to case termination initiated by the mediator.

Boulle and Kelly (1998, p. 152), for example, list 10 bases on which the mediator would have little choice but to terminate, 8 of which are relevant to family mediation:

- One or both parties refuse to adhere to the mediation guidelines and are generally uncooperative.
- Either one or both parties display a lack of commitment to the process or appear to be using the process for some hidden agenda.
- One or both parties disclose, either directly or indirectly, that they have no intention of complying with the terms of settlement.
- One or both parties are unable to negotiate effectively or, for some other reason, are unable to participate meaningfully in making decisions.
- One or both parties indicate, directly or indirectly, that they can no longer trust the mediator.
- The mediator is unable to ensure the safety of one or both parties, or the terms agreed on between the parties is illegal in some respect(s).
- The power imbalance between the parties, including the threat of physical violence, is such as to preclude the free consent of one of the parties to the terms of agreement.
- The level of conflict between the parties is such that no meaningful negotiation is possible.*

Each of these bases for termination necessitates some sort of outside referral and raises the specter of a mediator error either at assessment or during the process. As regards the former, on assessment a couple presented, both individually and together, as well-spoken, thoughtful, reasonable, and mutually respectful. This carried over to the construction of a parenting plan. However, as the mediation turned to consider the financial issues, such intense conflict arose as to make meaningful negotiation virtually impossible. As to the latter, on closing an early but productive session, one partner quietly asked if her attendance was mandatory. Subsequent discussion made clear that she had only attended at her husband's insistence, that she was going through the motions to please him, but that she had no intention of complying with the terms of any settlement. In both cases, with the usual 20/20 hindsight, it would appear the mediator had missed serious underlying dysfunction that only manifested later. Neither couple should have been accepted into mediation, and neither benefited from their involvement in it. Although both cases yielded a negative outcome, both were nevertheless invaluable in developing what Lang and Taylor (2000) call "artistry" in professional mediation practice.

---

* Reprinted, with permission, from Boulle & Kelly, *Mediation: Principles, Process, Practice.* Toronto: Butterworths.

Negative Termination 2: Client Initiated

Clients terminate mediation by refusing to continue, either by reaching impasse early, having failed to agree on any issue, or dropping out of service, with no reason given. Although relatively rare, these outcomes are subject to multiple interpretations. An obvious possibility is that of mediator error, either in assessment or process. A second possibility concerns variation in mediation readiness: the partner who is attached and agrees to virtually anything or the partner who is still very angry and agrees to virtually nothing. A third possibility concerns situational complications that are outside the mediator's control:

- the partners who meet accidentally in a supermarket parking lot, have a screaming match, and refuse to return to mediation;
- the client whose mother dies while mediation is ongoing;
- the client whose boss is fired unexpectedly while mediation is in progress;
- the client who is abandoned by a live-in lover; or
- the clients whose poor communication leads to several mishaps in their effort to coparent.

These variations can occur separately or together. On one hand, they speak eloquently of the extraordinary stress associated with divorce and with litigation pursuant to it. In turn, such stress helps explain the emotional lability of clients who must live under these conditions, often for months or even years at a time. Timing, then, can be a crucial factor in determining the course of mediation; get them early enough and intervention can be helpful. Get them too late, and very little will be helpful. The difference between the two can be a very fine line and easily missed in assessment.

On the other hand, such processes speak to the special demands and difficulties of solo practice. Without another pair of eyes or a videotape machine, it is often hard to know if one or more clinical errors have occurred. Through the use of two-way mirrors, supervisory observation, and research protocols, the objective description of clinical errors can be a valuable tool of professional development (Coleman, 1985). To date, no such methods have been similarly applied in family mediation. They would be an important addition to current training methods.

Phase 5: Follow-Up

The final phase of TFM-based mediation is follow-up. This is restricted to clients who completed Positive Termination 1 and occurs 3 to 6 months after their "memorandum" has been signed. The goals, indications, and contraindications of follow-up are displayed in Table 7.2. Roughly 80% of

Table 7.2   Follow-Up

Timing

- 3 to 6 months after Positive Termination I

Goals

- Check compliance with agreement
- Check informal variation in agreement
- Negotiate any items in dispute
- Check positive changes in spousal relations:

    mutual listening

    conflict management

    flexibility

    affect frequency, intensity

- Check stress level
- Check changes in circumstances
- Check client satisfaction with process, outcomes
- Check progress in postdivorce parental adjustment
- Check progress in postdivorce child adjustment

Indications

- Good compliance

    Informal variation

    Spousal conflict low to moderate

    Stress management good

    Coping well with any changes

    High positive satisfaction

    Parent, child adjustment good

    Mediator congratulations

    Preempt: expect future problems, handle well

Contraindications

- Agreement not working

    Poor compliance

    Conflict high

    Stress high

    Parent and/or child adjustment poor

    Begin litigation

    Return to premediation

    Return to negotiation

the clients in question will comply with this request, although roughly 30% of them will cancel the follow-up on the grounds that things are working well and they see no reason for another session. Cost can also be a factor for refusing, as can simple fatigue with the process.

Goals

In essence, follow-up is designed as a checkup to determine the extent to which the clinical goals of TFM have been achieved and thus is a source of feedback on the design of our service delivery system. Mediation is intended to induce positive changes in parental relations, parent-child relations, individual postdivorce adjustment, and stress management. Given that the couples in question have achieved a comprehensive settlement, secondary goals include compliance, informal changes without the need for a return to mediation or litigation, and continued satisfaction both with the mediation process and its outcomes.

Indications

Probably the best indication that these goals have been achieved involves the quality of relations between former spouses. Evidence of mutual respect, attention, empathy, and support suggests that at least with respect to mutual parenting, mediation has had a positive effect. Equally important are indications that stress levels, once very high, have now become manageable, and the couple has demonstrated sufficient flexibility that they are able to adapt well to changing life circumstances. Next, evidence that changes to the agreement have been made informally and without undue conflict is an important marker that key mediation goals have been achieved. Finally, we routinely inquire into child adjustment and the extent to which the clients remain satisfied with the mediation experience and perceive that there was a causal relationship between current life changes and the mediation process.

Given evidence in support of TFM goals, the mediator reaffirms his or her earlier congratulatory comments and ends the session with the pre-empting maneuver, to the effect that future challenges can be expected and that the clients will continue to handle them well. In effect, good agreements are those that become integrated into the lives of the clients. The written document is quickly forgotten, useful only as a symbol of their new life together and apart.

Contraindications

Although successful outcomes will be true of most client couples, a minority will paint a much more negative picture. These couples will display little or limited change in conflict or stress management skills. One or both will complain of noncompliance on the part of the other parent and with varying degrees of difficulty coping with various life changes. They may complain also of poor adjustment, either on their own part or on the part of one or more children. In short, these couples were effective while in the presence of the mediator but unable to generalize from this experience. In some cases, this is plainly signaled by their return to litigation (despite having agreed to try mediation first). Perhaps most important, these couples often express some dissatisfaction with mediation, either with the process or with the mediator. Typical complaints include the following:

- Failure of timing: The mediator's pace was wrong, either too fast or too slow.
- Failure of connection: Clients did not feel that the mediator understood or supported them; the mediator did not listen to their concerns.
- Failure of impartiality: The mediator was perceived to have taken sides.
- Failure of control: The mediator was unable to give each client equal time to have his or her say.

Depending on the severity of their difficulties, these couples may be invited to reenter mediation either at the premediation or negotiation phase. However, given their dissatisfaction with the process and/or the mediator, many will refuse the invitation, having decided to "tough it out" on their own or turn either to another mediator (hoping for a better fit) or to litigation and an imposed settlement.

Discussion

TFM advances a model of family mediation based on twin premises—namely, that most postdivorce conflict is relational rather than substantive in character, and addressing these underlying relationship issues will dramatically increase the likelihood of resolving the issues, achieve a lasting settlement, and afford clients the opportunity for individual transformation.

The result is a therapeutic model that is both multiphasic and iterative, with each phase linked to all others via multiple feedback loops. Practitioners rely on a combination of clinical and negotiation skills designed to effect limited therapeutic change while facilitating cooperative problem solving, constructive negotiation, and future-oriented planning. Moreover, the model places a heavy emphasis on interactive processes that are co-constructed within the context of what we have called the mediatable frame. On the one hand, this approach screens out between 5% and 10% of clients as not amenable to mediation at that time. On the other hand, although it recognizes four possible outcomes, the majority of clients will achieve a comprehensive settlement. Most of those who settle will display positive adjustment at 3- to 6-month follow-up.

In short, TFM is a mediation model that is demanding of both its practitioners and its clients but yields positive results much of the time, especially as regards long-term durability and adjustment.

References

Acland, A. (1990). *A sudden outbreak of common sense: Managing conflict through mediation.* London: Hutchinson.

Allen, E. L., & Mohr, D. D. (1998). *Affordable justice: How to settle any dispute, including divorce, out of court* (2nd ed.). Encinitas, CA: West Coast Press.

Beer, J. E. (with E. Stief). (1997). *The mediator's handbook* (3rd ed.). Gabriola Island, BC: New Society.

Benjamin, M., & Bross, A. (1982). Family therapy: A typology of therapist error. In A. Bross (Ed.), *Family therapy: A recursive model of strategic practice* (pp. 90-113). Toronto: Methuen.

Boulle, L., & Kelly, K. J. (1998). *Mediation: Principles, process, practice* (Canadian ed.). Toronto: Butterworths.

Chornenki, G. A., & Hart, C. E. (1996). *Bypass court: A dispute resolution handbook.* Toronto: Butterworths.

Coleman, S. B. (Ed.). (1985). *Failures in family therapy.* New York: Guilford.

Fisher, R., Ury, W., & Patton, B. (1997). *Getting to yes: Negotiating agreement without giving in* (3rd ed.). New York: Penguin.

Goldberg, S., Sander, F., & Rogers, N. (1992). *Dispute resolution: Negotiation, mediation & other processes* (2nd ed.). Boston: Little, Brown.

James, P. (1997). *The divorce mediation handbook: Everything you need to know.* San Francisco: Jossey-Bass.

Lang, M. D., & Taylor, A. (2000). *The making of a mediator: Developing artistry in practice.* San Francisco: Jossey-Bass.

Leviton, S. C., & Greenstone, J. L. (1997). *Elements of mediation.* Pacific Grove, CA: Brooks/Cole.

MacFarlane, J. (1999). *Dispute resolution: Readings and cases.* Toronto: Edmund Montgomery.

Slaikeu, K. (1995). *When push comes to shove: A practical guide to mediating disputes.* San Francisco: Jossey-Bass.

Weeks, D. (1992). *The eight essential steps to conflict resolution.* New York: Putnam.

8

Full-Length
Case Study

Students and experienced practitioners come to mediation texts, such as this one, on very different terms. Experienced practitioners come with an organized body of knowledge, partly didactic, partly experiential. That body of knowledge allows them to incorporate new information easily and then readily translate that information into practice. Accordingly, for them, the wealth of information provided in the preceding chapters in this section will suffice in introducing therapeutic family mediation (TFM). Such is likely *not* the case for students who, by definition, are in the process of creating their own body of mediation knowledge. The absence of such knowledge typically means that the preceding treatment of TFM will still be inadequate and far too abstract. Students benefit significantly from hands-on, direct experience. Here, the best we can hope to do is to integrate the preceding material in the form of a *full-length case history*. In doing so, we happily join a tradition in both family mediation (Haynes & Haynes, 1989) and family therapy (Gurman, 1985) of using case histories for teaching purposes.

John and Maria Smith

Background

The Smiths were referred to family mediation from marital therapy. Telephone conversation between the mediator and the therapist yielded the following account of the clients' family background.

The Smith family consisted of John, age 34; his wife, Maria, age 31; and their two daughters, Rose, age 10, and Maggie, just turned 6. Theirs was an interfaith marriage; John came from an English Protestant background, and Maria came from an Italian Roman Catholic background. At the time of their separation 8 months previously, the Smiths were in an enviable financial position, being virtually debt free. Both had worked at their present employment for the past 10 years—John as a software developer for a large computer corporation and Maria as a social worker in a hospital. Both had incomes in the middle range. Consequently, they owned their own home outright, and they could each afford to buy a new car every 3 years or so.

John and Maria's relationship had begun in high school. It was the first romantic relationship for each of them, and both were very excited by it. After about a year together, they became intimate. When Maria became pregnant with Rose, Maria's parents insisted that they must marry ("They said it was the only decent thing to do."). The wedding itself was exciting, but Maria quickly became disillusioned. As a boyfriend, John had been funny, sweet, and attentive. As a husband, he was often taciturn, irritable, and distant. Closeness and intimacy between them were fleeting and infrequent. John immersed himself in work and was often gone for long periods. When not working, he was out with his friends and deaf to Maria's growing complaints of neglect and loneliness. Despite her growing dissatisfaction, their occasional intimacy resulted in a second child, Maggie. Eventually, however, Maria turned away from John and devoted herself instead to the children and her relationship with her parents and her sisters. John's involvement with the children grew increasingly peripheral.

At some point, Maria drifted into a relationship with Tony, an Italian friend of her parents' family. At first, these visits were strictly social. But they served to highlight her loneliness and the sharp difference between Tony's attentiveness and John's indifference. With her father's secret approval, her relationship with this "nice Italian man" became increasingly intimate. Even her mother's objections dissipated after a visit to her parish priest, who assured her that, given the circumstances of Maria's marriage, there would likely be little difficulty in having her marriage annulled. With her commitment to Tony now public, Maria told John of her decision to separate and asked him to leave the house.

Maria's bold announcement put John into crisis. First, he pleaded with Maria for a second chance, asked her to think about what this would do to the children, and insisted that all of this was the result of interference by her parents. When she would not relent, he became belligerent and accused her of being selfish and irresponsible, questioned her sanity, threatened to harm her lover, and thought aloud of "taking the children away from her." But all to no avail; Maria was adamant that it was all over between them.

Brief entry into marital therapy proved fruitless. By the end of the second marital counseling session, two things had become clear—namely, that there was no hope of reconciliation, and referral for family mediation was the couple's best alternative. However, to complicate matters, John's lawyer had recently advised him to remain in the matrimonial home because in the absence of a parenting plan, his departure could be construed by the court as child abandonment. Instead, John moved into the basement of their split-level home, a move that only reinforced John's continued hope that somehow his relationship with Maria might be saved.

Family Mediation

In his initial contact with John and Maria on the telephone, the mediator suggested that they begin with individual sessions aimed at giving him a better understanding of the issues in dispute. Both spouses agreed—John recognized his need for support in coping with the demands now being placed on him, and Maria hoped that such contact would help John deal with the situation "more realistically." She denied needing any support herself and was impatient to "get on with it."

Phase 1: Intake/Assessment. The assessment phase involved 2-hour interviews with each spouse. In addition to the marital history, reported above, these data supported seven interrelated observations concerning the pattern of relations between these spouses and their extended families. First, it was clear from the start that this was a couple with an extremely limited interactional repertoire. They dealt with conflict through avoidance, and occasional conflictual exchanges were invariably brief and characteristically muted, both in level and intensity.

Next, the spouses were strikingly unequal in their communication styles and skills. John had obvious difficulties formulating and articulating his thoughts. He was often hesitant, and the final production was often brief but not always clear. He was far more comfortable expressing his thoughts in actions than words. By contrast, Maria was extremely verbal, almost overwhelmingly so. Despite her verbosity, her verbal expressions were clear, well organized, and often forceful and dramatic. For much of their marriage, Maria had been extremely frustrated and often impatient with John's lack of verbal dexterity. Watching them interact was not unlike relations between the tortoise and the hare and equally ineffective.

Third, both John and Maria shared the same work ethic, which valued hard work, competence, and the accumulation of wealth. Their values also coincided as regards the importance of their children's well-being. However, their experience of child care differed sharply. John was the only child of parents who had little to say to each other and for whom child care was strictly a maternal role. John saw little of his father and generally spent much of his time alone, playing by himself; he had few friends. In contrast, Maria grew up in a large, boisterous family that socialized often. Maria was close to many people and quickly developed the skills that allowed her to get along with all of them. Moreover, as she was the middle child, she had been caring for younger children most of her life. In short, although both came by their particular set of attributes honestly, it made it difficult for each to fully understand the other. Maria was particularly puzzled by

John's diffident approach to his own children, and John secretly envied Maria's easy way with people.

Fourth, of the two spouses, John appeared to be coping least well with their marital separation. It became readily apparent that Maria was far better prepared for their separation than John. That was easily explained, as she had been planning something like for at least 6 months, if not more, before she announced it to John. Although she "hinted" about this possibility to John on several occasions, he was clearly unwilling to "hear" what she had to say. Little wonder, then, that Maria's dramatic announcement hit John "like a ton of bricks." This difference between them suggested two conclusions. The first and most obvious was that John would have to undergo much more change than Maria if the two of them were to begin negotiations on a level playing field. In particular, he would need to give up his lingering attachment before he would be able to move on with his life. For her part, Maria would need to let go of much of her anger, for it left her inflexible and prevented her from fully considering the best interests of the children. Less obvious but equally important was the extent to which John had been dependent on Maria for a social life. Although Maria knew many people, John knew few and fairly superficially. His drinking buddies, for example, were just that—men with whom he occasionally shared a beer but not with whom he could ever confide. His separation from Maria thus left him alone in his own house and feeling lonely and isolated.

Fifth, both spouses showed evidence of having identity problems, though for quite different reasons. With regard to John, in day-to-day terms, his relationship with Maria had ended some months before Maria's announcement. They spent little time together, had not made love in over a year, rarely talked about anything other than the minutiae of daily living, and did not feel close to each other. That John continued to think of himself as Maria's husband was patently inappropriate, yet it was the only identity John knew. Without it, it was not clear who he was, hence his tenacious hold on this unreality. This would need to change if John was to advance clear proposals. As for Maria, her identity was in transition. Although she was clearly no longer John's wife, her status with Tony was unclear, both in her own eyes as well as in the eyes of her community, especially her parents and the church. The only constant was that she was the mother of her beloved children. To move forward in mediation, she would need to clarify the former and build on the latter.

Sixth, there were various indications that the involvement of Maria's parents, especially her mother, might be an important factor in the case. Overinvolvement between mother and daughter might block negotiation and raised the possibility of the need for intervention should that prove true.

Finally, in co-constructing this account with the spouses, the mediator introduced the mediatable frame, with its emphasis on shared responsibility, mutual problem solving, and the importance of a long-term perspective on parenting. That frame was not inconsistent with the elements noted above and was well received by both John and Maria.

With these processes in mind, the goals of premediation were the following:

- help John restructure his relationship with Maria and the children so that he could accept the reality of their impending divorce and retain a positive and more involved relationship with his children,

- encourage Maria to plan for the future in keeping with the children's best interests while continuing to see John as their father,

- reconcile their divergent communication skills to allow them to engage effectively in mutual problem solving,

- build on their mutual love of the children and their interest in preserving and protecting the children's well-being within the context of the mediatable frame, and

- reduce the hostility and increase the extent of trust between them so that their efforts at negotiation would be productive.

Phase 2: Premediation

Given the different degrees of readiness of these spouses, premediation involved three individual sessions with John, two with Maria, and one conjoint session.

John. The first session with John had twin objectives—namely, to affirm John as a person separate from Maria and to begin to normalize his responses to the separation by reducing his continued attachment to her. Secondarily, we sought to emphasize the mediatable frame and establish a relationship of trust between him and the mediator.

To these ends, we began with a narrative approach by asking John to speak about the apparent loss of his family and to explore the sort of relationship he had and would like to have with his children. In particular, we asked John to bring the children into the session in symbolic form by describing what they looked like, indicating how they were doing in school, elaborating on how he felt about them, and so on.

Initially, John did not speak about the children and instead displayed a preoccupation with Maria. He went on at length to list her various negative attributes and behaviors, especially her most recent betrayal of their marriage vows. Haltingly, he spoke of his frustration, anxiety, and anger but especially about his sense of helplessness and powerlessness. To shift his interpretative frame from negative to positive, we made clear that his responses were perfectly normal under the circumstances but also narrowly conceived because they focused only on his relationship with Maria.

Shifting to a solution-oriented perspective, we then asked the "exception" question, that is, those instances in his dealings with the children when he was neither helpless nor powerless. John confirmed that this was so and that he wanted very much to be a "good father," one who protected the children, cared for them, and gave them love and attention. In his recent preoccupation with work, he conceded that he had not been as attentive as he might have been and, under pressure from the mediator, also admitted that Maria was and continued to be a "good mother" to them.

To build on the theme of "being a good father," we asked John how he proposed to continue to be a good father when, in all likelihood, the children would not be living with him on a full-time basis. Although reaffirming his good intentions, John was very light on details and clearly had not thought this issue through to completion. Indeed, it was major source of apprehension and concern, including the possibility that he would be supplanted altogether by the new man in Maria's life. Again, the mediator affirmed his concerns as "natural" among men in his situation while reframing his concerns as further evidence of his being a "good father." What, then, the mediator asked, could John *do* that would allow him to continue to be the good father that he wanted to be? Using specific questions, the mediator reintroduced the mediatable frame. Exactly how should he and Maria arrange it so that the children spent time with both parents? How would they share decision making about the children, to ensure that their best interests were always foremost in their thoughts? How would these changes be affected given that both he and Maria had demanding professional careers? And how was all this possible while he remained sad and depressed about his impending divorce?

As expected, John could not provide specific answers to any of these questions. However, he was clear about one thing: He could not see himself living without the children. This powerful statement was reframed in two ways. First, we emphasized that what he needed was important but not as important as what the children needed—namely, his continued involvement in their lives. Next, we suggested that perhaps there was a positive aspect of his separation that he had overlooked. That is, on his time off, he would have the time and energy to spend time with the children *by himself*, just as Maria would on her time off. From this novel perspective, his desire to be a good father would be that much closer to realization *the more he helped Maria be a good mother*. For the first time, he began to appreciate that it was both possible and desirable to separate marital and parental roles. Indeed, the two processes could now be seen as complementary. The more he accepted the end of his marital relationship with Maria, the easier it would be for both of them to begin to work together as good parents. Although he might eventually enter a new and more satisfying romantic relationship, this was an issue of little importance at the moment. For now, his relationship with his children mattered most, with a cooperative *parenting* relationship with Maria the primary means to that end.

As this session drew to a close, the mediator reaffirmed the elements of the mediatable frame—that is, the importance of shifting his priorities, spending less time concerned with reconciliation and more time thinking about good parenting. In particular, given their shared responsibility for the children, he needed to give serious thought to how he and Maria, working together, would make this happen for the children. As the session ended, John was visibly less anxious, made occasional eye contact, and even spoke more fluently.

The next session continued in the same vein. Although John was much clearer about his future involvement with the children, he continued to be preoccupied about the trauma of Maria's rejection and infidelity. The mediator's central strategy was to diminish the trauma while enlarging on John's role as a parent. The trauma was repeatedly framed as an aspect of the past that could not be changed and was fast receding. In continuing to relive these events and the feelings attached to them, John was allowing himself to be controlled by them and, indirectly, by Maria. In turn, although under the sway of those feelings, he was less effective as a father. In short, we juxtaposed his strong desire to be a good father against the strong negative feelings about Maria. The more he held on to the latter, which represented the past, the less likely he was to achieve the former, which represented the future. John's challenge was to regain control of his life and accept personal responsibility for shaping the future he longed for. What, for example, was he planning to do *now* that would lead to a more satisfying future for his children? As this session ended, that question became a homework task that would be returned to in the next session. At that time, he and the mediator would work together to formulate a concrete plan to ensure that future.

By the third session, the change in John was apparent. He was slowly coming to the painful realization that all he could ultimately do was gain better control over *his* choices. There was nothing he could do about the past and little to be gained by going over and over it in his mind. Rather, his children needed him to let those feelings gradually recede and focus instead on finding constructive ways of dealing with the present situation.

Accordingly, much of the session was concerned with consolidating these gains by having John consider *in detail* what might be involved on a day-to-day basis in caring for two active, growing children. What kind of accommodation would he need? Should he move into a house or an apartment? What could he afford? What sort of food, clothing, furniture, and so forth would the girls need? Should he buy it himself, or should the girls be involved in the selection? How often would he expect to see the children? For how long on each occasion?

The session ended on a positive note, as the mediator supported John by noting how hard he had worked and, in a final reframing, how lucky the girls were to have a father who cared as much as John obviously did. By that point, John's anger and preoccupation with marital issues had dissipated almost entirely. His attention had shifted from the past to the present and especially the future. The intensity of feelings had also lessened, and he was much more able to think rationally and in detail about all the elements of a parenting plan, typically the first set of issues that are addressed in the negotiation phase.

Maria. Like John, Maria was still very angry at her spouse. Unlike him, however, she had had a good deal of time to think through what her impending divorce would mean in practical terms. As a result, her thinking was less distorted by her feelings about John and was already oriented more toward the present and the future than the past. As she noted repeatedly, she was impatient to "get on with it."

Assessment had revealed that the major sticking point for negotiation concerned her vision of John's involvement with the children. Her anger and resentment toward him as a spouse, combined with his relatively peripheral role as a parent, meant that she fantasized Tony in his place in the future. This image was muddled in several respects, given that their future together was hardly a foregone conclusion. Given that Tony had virtually no parenting experience, his parenting skills were an unknown quantity. In addition, Maria had completely ignored the children's feelings for John. In this context, the goals of premediation were to defuse her anger toward John and to encourage her to see him less and less as a failed husband and more and more as the children's father.

Defusing her anger toward John primarily relied on joining and other supportive maneuvers. In many ways, her concerns about John's previous behavior—his long absences, his lack of support or understanding, his coldness and rejection—were not unreasonable, so it was easy for the mediator to be sympathetic with her complaints.

In contrast, efforts to shift her perspective of John met with initial resistance. She reasoned that because he had not been a good husband and had been a distant father in the past, he would likely be a poor father in the future. This appropriate concern with good parenting became the key lever for change. Her uncertainty regarding John's parenting adequacy was reframed in terms of the children's obvious love and concern for him. To prohibit father-child contact could undermine the children's healthy development and was therefore not in their best interests. Moreover, just because he had not been an adequate husband did not mean that he could not *become* an adequate father. Indeed, further probing using the "exception" question revealed several instances in which John had been good with the children. However, to ensure that he became the good father he could become would obviously require her help. Would she be willing to provide it *for the children's sake*? Framed this way, it was hard for Maria to refuse.

Over two premediation sessions, Maria's thinking underwent a significant shift. She began to let go of her anger toward John as a poor husband and instead focused on what her children needed to ensure their healthy development and a secure future. Although she remained leery of John as a father, she grudgingly acknowledged that the children loved him and would be very unhappy were he to disappear from their lives. She was therefore willing to consider some sort of arrangement that would preserve their relationship with him.

Conjoint Session. Premediation ended with a final conjoint session. There, the mediator explained that both were now ready to begin to negotiate the various issues in dispute between them. In mediation, he explained, the power and responsibility to make decisions about their future and that of their children rested with them—and them alone—and not an anonymous judge. Their control of the issues in mediation would be balanced by the mediator's control over the process. That control meant that both spouses would be expected to behave in accordance with the rules, and both would have ample time to express their views on the many issues to be discussed. The mediator's role was to facilitate this sharing of views, rather than judge or evaluate their views. Although impartial, the spouses were warned that the mediator was clearly biased in favor of the children and could be expected to speak up if the spouses contemplated arrangements that were inconsistent with their developmental needs. Finally, he recommended a mediation process that would be closed and confidential and encouraged them to see their lawyers so that both would be aware of their legal rights before signing the mediation contract.

Both lawyers supported the use of family mediation as the best way of resolving the issues in dispute. On the telephone with the lawyers, the mediator explained the goals and objectives of mediation with the Smiths and encouraged them to support the process. The mediator noted also that John and Maria would be sent back to their lawyers should the couple encounter any complicated issues that would benefit from their specialized expertise, and the lawyers would be expected to review and finalize any "memorandum" to emerge from the process.

Phase 3: Negotiation

The negotiation process began with individual sessions with each spouse. Such sessions are a bit unusual. However, in their case, the need to address clinical issues first had left the exact nature of the issue in dispute somewhat unclear. These sessions, then, were intended to list and clarify the issues, identify areas of dispute, deal with any lingering emotional concerns, uncover any hidden agendas, and allow each of them to talk frankly about their vision of the future without fear of contradiction or interruption.

Throughout these sessions, the mediator alternated between giving support and keeping them focused both on the issues at hand and on their feelings and concerns—and *not* those of the other spouse. The mediator's concern was that each spouse be as clear as possible on a range of issues, with each of them thinking through these issues in terms of their potential consequences.

Furthermore, because premediation efforts had focused so heavily on parenting, there had been little opportunity to consider any financial issues. These sessions had them begin to consider how they would prefer to divide the property they had accumulated during their marriage. The mediator also discussed how they could ensure their children's financial security and whether they thought alimony (spousal support) was in order and, if so, how they might begin to derive an amount that was fair under the circumstances.

Not surprisingly, what emerged from these sessions was that parenting was the single major issue for both of them, with each claiming custody for themselves. What was surprising was the toughness of their mutual positions and thus the distance between them.

John, for example, was adamant. He needed the children, and they needed him. Fearful that he would lose the children altogether to Maria's lover, he responded by trying to take control of the children away from her. This simultaneously allowed him to control his self-identity as a "father." In part, this was a positive move. The divorce had shocked him into realizing that he had become a peripheral father and that he needed to *do* something if he was to be involved with them in any meaningful sense. In part, this move was both unrealistic and irrational. It was unrealistic because his peripheral status made for a weak position in any litigation. It was irrational because of the hidden agenda it revealed—namely, to punish his wife in a way he knew would hurt and threaten her most.

As for Maria, she not only wanted custody of the children but also sought to deny John access. This was puzzling, for in premediation she had been willing to give John reasonable access. Why had her position hardened in the interval? Further probing revealed that her willingness to compromise had been unacceptable to her parents, especially her mother. They, and now she, wanted John out of the children's lives completely. The mediator's hypothesis that Maria's parents would play an important role in the negotiation process was confirmed.

In an effort to preempt future conflict, both parents were reminded that the events of the recent past had not only been traumatic for them but were at least equally so for their children. As they began the negotiation proper, in the next conjoint session, they were asked to keep the best interests of the children uppermost in their minds.

At that session, the mediator began by congratulating the couple on their decision to resolve their differences cooperatively and affirmed them as responsible adults capable of reaching agreements that would protect the best interests of their children. After reminding them of the rules, especially the need for mutual respect, the mediator asked each of them to state publicly what they thought were the "real" issues and what they saw as reasonable solutions.

Negotiation did not begin well. Playing the role of martyr, John said that he had no interest in the money and was prepared to be very generous on the property issues. He only wanted custody of the children because he knew how much they needed him. Angrily, Maria interrupted, accusing John of having shown little interest in the children in the past, disqualifying his speculation about what the children needed, and making clear that any arrangements involving John and the children were unacceptable to her and her parents.

To avoid an impasse, the mediator appealed to the one thing both said they had in common—namely, their love of and attachment to the children. Their mutual claims for custody were reframed as evidence of their mutual concern for the children's welfare. The question was not whether either was better suited to meet their needs but rather how each could contribute toward this mutually acceptable goal. On one hand, such involvement offered clear advantages. Maria's concern over the loss of time with the children was reframed as an opportunity to spend more time pursuing her many interests in life. Similarly, her concern over John's lack of parenting skills was reframed as a second chance for John to become involved with the children, something from which both John and the children would benefit. On the other hand, John's interest in greater involvement, although commendable, needed to be balanced against the demands of a challenging professional career. Similarly, parenting skills do not come naturally but need to be learned. Just as he had learned about computers by taking courses in the matter, so John might consider taking a parenting course, as part of his determined effort to become a good father. Thus, ongoing conflict between them had obfuscated what their discussion was now making increasingly clear—namely, that both parents wanted to be good parents and were prepared to do anything necessary to achieve that goal, and their children would benefit if they could find a way to work together rather than at cross-purposes. A shared parenting arrangement *of some sort* would appear to serve their purposes well and would benefit the children by ensuring their continued contact with *both* parents. As a major concession, John indicated that he was willing to consider shared parenting, provided it gave him a reasonable amount of time with the children. Maria continued to resist the idea on the grounds that it would put the children in the care of a man who was not competent to care for them.

Rather than force the issue, the couple was asked to "sleep on it," as good agreements take time to evolve. While that was happening, they would move on to other issues. In closing, then, they were asked to list other issues they would like to address. Both listed a series of financial issues, chief among them child support. These issues would be added to the agenda for the next sessions. Both were asked to come prepared to discuss these issues in detail.

At the next sessions, discussion began with a series of low-priority items, with the intention of giving them some experience of success. The issue of spousal support, for example, proved unproblematic, given that both had secure jobs for which they were well paid, with neither expecting to receive any monetary support from the other.

The division of property was also settled easily. The mediator would contact two real estate appraisers, each of whom would give them a written estimate of the value of their home. John and Maria agreed to accept the average of the two appraisals. They further agreed that Maria would buy out John's share of the property and register the property in her own name. This would occur within 30 days of the signing of any mediated agreement between them. In turn, John agreed to move out of the home on or about the day the house became Maria's. Furthermore, each would keep the car they were presently driving, and each would pick the items of furniture and household effects they preferred by the method of alternate choice. The balance of their joint bank account would immediately be divided equally. Adjustments as regards their pension plans would be left to an actuary.

Turning to child support, the mediator cautioned that the issues of child support and child custody would be treated separately. With that in mind, John and Maria agreed to contribute to the costs of child care in proportion to their income, until both children reached their 21st birthday or completed their university education. The health, life, and dental insurance premiums then in place would be considered part of the child care costs. Both agreed to continue to finance the children's extracurricular activities.

The mediator advised the Smiths to consult with their lawyers as regards the division of property, the child support arrangements, and the tax implications of either. He also noted that their child support agreement was necessarily provisional because the child support guidelines in their state were tied to their later decisions concerning how they would share the children's time and make decisions about them. In congratulating them on the fine work they had just completed, the mediator gave them a homework assignment in the form of two questions they were to think about in preparation for the next session:

- When all grown up, how would they want their children to remember them when looking back on this time in their history?
- What parenting decisions would they need to cooperate on to achieve these memories?

Finally, looking back on the first two conjoint sessions, it had become increasingly apparent that some sort of intervention would be essential if this couple was to avoid an impasse over the questions of time sharing and decision making around the children. Available evidence suggested that the involvement of Maria's parents was central to her inflexible position. What intervention could be used to encourage them to back off on these issues and allow Maria to compromise, as the mediator suspected she was inclined to do? Given their closeness to their grandchildren, one possibility was to invite the children to join a session. If, in front of Maria and her parents, the children indicated clearly that they wished to continue to have their father involved in their care, they might be persuaded to adopt a more flexible position. Although the mediator might suggest such a session, he suspected that it would be far more effective if the suggestion came from the parents themselves. Accordingly, he implemented a paradoxical strategy. Rather than encouraging them to continue, he canceled the homework and, looking dejected, suggested instead that they admit defeat. As both spouses were adamant about child care, an impasse seemed unavoidable. True, given all that they had accomplished, failure at this point was most unfortunate and would probably be a painful blow to the couple as well as *the children and the grandparents*. But there seemed no alternative *unless John and Maria had something new to suggest that the mediator hadn't thought of*. After planting the hint by verbal emphasis alone, he waited to see if they had "heard" him. They had. Shocked by the mediator's sudden and unexpected about-face, the couple vigorously rejected the mediator's suggestion that they terminate the mediation. Following much heated discussion, during which the mediator emphasized the hopelessness of the situation, it was Maria who eventually suggested a session in which the grandparents and the children be asked to attend. To bolster their commitment to the idea, the mediator was initially reluctant to accept their suggestion and raised several objections but finally allowed himself to be convinced that it was the only reasonable alternative left.

Events during the third conjoint session were to prove pivotal to the successful resolution of the child care issue. Interviews with children in mediation are typically confidential and in the absence of parents, with the mediator then acting as the children's mouthpiece. But this was a very special circumstance in which it was important that the parents and the grandparents witness what was said. This strategy involved considerable risk. Children's behavior in this situation is unpredictable under the best of circumstances. Under these conditions, the children might freeze up and say nothing or burst into tears under pressure. In fact, they said exactly what the mediator hoped they would—namely, that both wanted very much to spend time with their dad. Following this disclosure, it appeared that Maria came prepared to give John limited access to the children. Her mother was made of sterner stuff; she was adamant that it was best for the children to remain with their mother and, by implication, their grandparents. Every time John tried to express a contrary opinion, Maria's mother would interrupt by talking loudly to Maria in Italian.

The potency of the coalition between mother and daughter was palpable and a major impediment to the resolution of the issue in question. The mediator immediately dismissed any effort at direct confrontation as futile and likely to be destructive. Instead, he decided to go around the blockage in two ways. First, he reframed both the grandmother's concern for the children's welfare and John's recent interest in becoming an active parent. The mediator commended the grandmother's loving concern for the children but expanded it to include the beneficial effects of having *both* parents active in their children's lives. Similarly, the mediator openly commended John for *his* loving concern for the children but expanded it to include both direct physical involvement and having a say in planning for their future.

Second, the mediator acknowledged the grandmother's wisdom and power in the family but noted that she was not *merely* the children's grandmother. She was also Maria's mother and, as such, would be expected to come to her assistance in times of need. This was such a time. Would she be willing to "lend" some of her power and wisdom to Maria, confident that Maria would make whatever decisions she felt were "right" for the children? After a puzzled moment, the grandmother agreed. In so doing, this freed up Maria to follow her original inclination to give John access to the children while blocking any further interference from the grandmother.

The session ended with the mediator thanking the grandparents and the children for sharing their interest in the family's welfare and for playing an active part in it. He then reminded John and Maria of the two homework questions. He also asked them to prepare for the next session by thinking carefully about the sort of parenting arrangement that would be in the children's best interest. Finally, he expressed confidence in their ability to come up with a good plan because both really wanted the same thing for their children.

During the next conjoint session, John and Maria were less tense and anxious than in previous sessions and were less inclined toward conflict. John began with a major concession, relinquishing his claim for sole custody so long as he could spend a "reasonable" amount of time with the children and have an equal say in all major decisions concerning their welfare. John's cooperation around this sensitive issue was a great relief to Maria, who, in turn, agreed to explore the practical implications of a shared parenting arrangement.

The discussion that followed was marked by the mediator's efforts to apply the mediatable frame that called for John and Maria to think in terms of "two homes" for the children rather than "one home and one place to visit." In response, the parents agreed in principle to cooperate in establishing and maintaining mutually acceptable guidelines for their children's welfare and upbringing. To encourage them to become specific, the mediator introduced them to the "guidelines" of parenting in divorce (see Chapter 9, this volume) in which, among other things, the parents are regarded as the family "executives" responsible for decision making and agree to respect each other's "boundaries." These ideas made sense to the Smiths. They agreed to respect each other's ability and authority as parents. Both agreed to respect the other's parenting style, and neither would interfere with or disrupt the other's time with the children without advance notice. Minor day-to-day child-rearing decisions would be handled by the parent with whom the children were staying at the time, and any complaints the children might have would be dealt with by that parent and *not* carried forward to the other parent. Both agreed that each should have unlimited access to all official records about the children, and both were free to attend church ceremonies, sporting events, teacher conferences, and other events important in the lives of the children.

Discussion concerning the details of the children's living arrangements was extended and sometimes heated but was quite productive. To find a viable solution, Maria needed to acknowledge that the children would benefit from John's involvement with them, and John needed to acknowledge that there was much he needed to learn about parenting if he was to become the good father he wanted to be. In the end, on the basis of the mediator's suggestions, they developed an agreement in three parts. Part 1 involved an interim arrangement that would last 12 weeks. John agreed to enroll in an 8-week parenting course. As that was progressing, the children's time with him would gradually increase. Part 2 involved a permanent arrangement that would last about a year. During that time, the children would stay with John three weekends out of every four. He would pick up the children after school on Friday and return them to Maria by Sunday evening at 7 p.m. In addition, every week, he would pick up the children after school on Wednesday, keep them overnight, and return them to school the next day. Holidays would be divided equally. For the remainder of the time, the children would stay with Maria. If, for any reason, either parent needed to make changes in this schedule, neither would initiate the change unilaterally but rather would notify the other in advance and get their consent. Part 3 involved a commitment on the part of both parents to move toward equal sharing of the children. Accordingly, the parents agreed to review their parenting plan on an annual basis and move as quickly as seemed practical toward a full shared parenting arrangement.

This session was a particularly long and fruitful one. The mediator would prepare a written parenting plan containing all of the provisions they had agreed to. This document would be faxed to each parent between sessions. A final session was booked during which the parents would carefully review the plan and make any final changes to it. At that time, a clause was added that if they had any serious dispute, they would return to mediation before considering any legal action. Each parent would then take this document to a lawyer for legal review. Subsequent telephone contact with the lawyers showed them satisfied with the plan and ready to formalize it prior to it being signed by both parents.

In closing this final session, the mediator contracted with the Smiths for four follow-up sessions to be held at 3-month intervals, "just to see how things are going." These sessions would be used to monitor the parents' responses to the demands of shared parenting, help smooth out any practical problems they might have encountered, keep on eye on Maria's relationship with her mother to ensure the grandmother kept to her agreement, and give them support and encouragement in having made some wise but difficult choices in the best interests of their children.

Discussion

The case of the Smith family entailed a total of 13 sessions: 2 assessment/ intake sessions (1 with each spouse), 6 premediation sessions (3 with John, 2 with Maria, and 1 conjoint session), 4 negotiation sessions, and 1 review session. All but the final session lasted 2 hours; the review session only lasted 1 hour. In light of the outcome, this case would be classified as a complete success.

Although unusual in its complexity and duration, the case is otherwise representative of the TFM approach to family mediation and supplies the continuity missing from the walk-through chapters. Specifically, it contains several elements that capture the essence of the TFM model.

First, this case history makes clear that the mediator could not have proceeded with any hope of success *without attending to and intervening in the patterns that organized the relationship between John and Maria*. The nature of that relationship accounted for John's ambivalence toward Maria and his distant relationship with the children. Maria's ambivalent relationship with John, her growing relationship with Tony, and her close relationship with her mother accounted for the hard stand she took as regards child care. Although therapeutic methods were used to help both partners adopt more flexible and realistic perspectives, the goals of this effort were always limited to those processes directly relevant to productive negotiation. Indeed, failure to have attended to these processes would not only have yielded a couple at risk of impasse and/or dropout but would also have made John's postdivorce adjustment a great deal more difficult than it was.

Second, this case illustrates well the short-term, solution-oriented, and goal-directed character of the model. In it, the mediator is expected to be actively and continuously involved in shaping interaction, in keeping with the goals of mediation. This might involve giving support, encouragement, and praise; blocking dysfunctional interaction; or intervening to change perspectives, behaviors, or both. Furthermore, discussion is centered on the present and the future. Although past histories were explored, this was done briefly and with the aim of understanding current interaction. Otherwise, clients' preoccupation with past events was suppressed as unproductive and misleading. Although later sessions concentrated on the logical thinking associated with bargaining and negotiation, that did *not* mean that affective processes had been forgotten. On the contrary, discussion of their child-sharing schedule necessarily alternated between substantive and relational issues before agreement was possible.

Third, although agreement on the substantive issues in dispute is important, this case makes clear that agreement per se is *not* the only goal of the model. Substantive disputes are rooted in relational processes. For example, each spouse's relationship with his or her respective set of parents was directly related to the conflict over parenting and was indirectly related to the quality of the marital relationship. Such processes should neither be ignored nor blocked on principle. Rather, a successful outcome requires that they be engaged, worked through, or changed to ensure the durability of any settlement and thus client future satisfaction. Put differently, the terms of any agreement must "fit" the clients' new reality of their interaction as parents *only*. This "fit" ensures that parents either adhere to the terms of their agreement or change them informally out of genuine commitment rather than (judicial) coercion.

Fourth, intervention methods drew on the insights provided by a variety of family therapy models. Methods drawn from narrative, solution-oriented, and strategic family therapy models were all in evidence in this case. Reframing, for example, was used extensively. However, other, more generic methods were used as well, especially efforts at joining, support, and empathy. These methods help clients get through an emotionally demanding process, ensure that clients feel heard and understood, and give clients reason to trust the mediator's control over the process and have confidence in both the mediator's impartiality and wisdom and experience in the area of divorce. The use of praise and other statements that acknowledge and call on the clients' strengths is integral to the model.

Fifth, this case illustrates well a multilevel systemic model in action. Although in separation each partner has individual needs and concerns, the family system has *not* ceased to exist; it has merely changed form, with the children binding parents together in common cause. Although each parent must emerge from the process feeling that at least some of his or her individual objectives have been achieved, in pursuit of these objectives, it is all too easy for each parent to lose sight of what is in the best interests of the children. Such loss of perspective is commonplace under the tremendous stress of separation, let alone any individual trauma, and highlights the vital role the mediator can play in helping couples produce a balanced agreement. Client satisfaction, then, is important but not sufficient. Family system interests also require attention. Although children's healthy development does not rest solely on a cooperative coparental relationship, they invariably benefit enormously when it is present or can be brought into being through mediation. The value of this achievement should not be underestimated because regular interaction among these parents will need to continue for as long as their children are dependent on them. In this sense, conceptualizing clients in systemic terms—rather than in terms of their individual "needs" or "interests"—reflects both the daily dynamics of postdivorce binuclear family life and the theoretical underpinning of the model.

Finally, this case acknowledges the larger reality of extended kin and children. Although clients shape the relationships with these others, they are also shaped and influenced by them. After a certain age, children, for example, harbor certain goals and expectations and can and do behave in ways designed to achieve their ends. In practice, such influence means that children, grandparents, and others can save or sabotage the mediation process, whatever their stated intentions. In this context, the notion that parents' and children's interests *necessarily* coincide appears naive. Rather, on a case-by-case basis, their direct participation may make a significant contribution to the mediation process. The same is true of others, including grandparents. More generally, the hallmark of the TFM model is its flexibility, with the mediator ready to "fit" the process to the clients' requirements.

Discussion

TFM is *not* about magic, a single brilliant intervention that changes the face of a family and sets it right. Rather, it is a thoughtful approach to the dynamics underlying family systems in conflict. It can involve the creative use of a wide variety of interventions, custom-made to suit particular situations. When these are effective, as they were in the Smith case, the results can be truly dramatic. More often, successful outcomes result from simple hard work: keeping couples in conflict focused, blocking unproductive conduct, suggesting options and alternatives, clarifying the consequences of failure to agree, and using parents' love for their children as the lever for change and agreement. The salient features of the TFM model reviewed above and displayed in the case of the Smiths are intended to maximize the likelihood of a successful outcome with the widest possible array of divorcing families in dispute.

References

Gurman, A. S. (Ed.). (1985). *Casebook of marital therapy.* New York: Guilford.

Haynes, J. M., & Haynes, G. L. (1989). *Mediating divorce: Casebook of strategies for successful family negotiations.* San Francisco: Jossey-Bass.

PART 3

SUBSTANTIVE ISSUES

9

Parenting Plans

Part 1: Related Topics

Helping parents decide how they will share responsibility for their children has long been a staple feature of family mediation practice. This is so for two key reasons. One reason is that it reflects client demand. Roughly half of all divorcing couples in North America have one or more dependent children (Irving & Benjamin, 1995). Of these couples, sharing responsibility for their children is a universal issue and, among a minority, a hotly contested one (Ahrons & Rodgers, 1987; Saposnek, 1998). The rise of family mediation, coupled with efforts at court diversion, has meant that an increasing number of couples in dispute over child care issues have sought a mediated resolution.

The second reason for an emphasis on parenting in mediation is that such demand dovetails neatly with the character of the mediation community. Although the makeup of that community is in flux, as of this writing, the majority of practitioners enter the community with a mental health or social service background as opposed to legal training. Typically, such practitioners have considerable background training in family life and child development and relatively little, if any, training in finances and taxation (see Chapter 11, this volume). Consequently, the majority of family mediators specialize in parenting issues, referring these client couples back to their lawyers to deal with the financial issues; unfortunately, comprehensive family mediators continue to be in the minority.

In recent years, this emphasis on parenting issues has focused on the creation of *parenting plans* (Emery, 1994; Lyster, 1997; Ricci, 1997), that is, documents that set out a systematic and detailed account of how parents will share responsibility in keeping with the best interests of their children. Given this practice focus, it is curious that although contemporary mediation texts address parenting issues, with the exception of Emery (1994), none does so under the rubric of "parenting plans" (Haynes, 1994; James, 1997; Landau, Wolfson, Landau, Bartoletti, & Mesbur, 2000). Even more important, available treatments of this topic tend to be generic in character. Given our therapeutic perspective, we agree with Saposnek (1998) when he argues that generic skills may not be adequate to the complexity of the task:

> Some generic mediators . . . believe that the skills they utilize in their work are sufficient for child custody mediation. While it may be true that such general mediation skills are necessary for child custody mediation work, they are not sufficient. Child custody mediation is a very special type of mediation. The mediator must be competent to give valid, current, and helpful information about child development, about children's typical and atypical responses to family conflict, about family members' needs and feelings, about family dynamics, about the divorce process (emotionally, structurally, and legally), and about the likely future outcomes for children and parents of a variety of different postdivorce family structures. The mediator should be knowledgeable about individual psychodynamics, interactional dynamics, family systems, and behavior change and should have a broad general knowledge of psychological functioning of both adults and children of various ages. Child custody mediators who are not specifically training in these areas may seriously compromise the benefits of child custody mediation. (p. 48)

With these sentiments in mind and given the range of topics to be addressed, treatment of parenting plans will be divided into two chapters. This chapter will focus on seven background topics that warrant our attention:

- The conceptual significance of the "parenting plan"
- The link between child development and divorce
- The parental strategies mediators encounter
- Advocacy in mediation
- The decision to include children in mediation
- First principles in the construction of parenting plans
- Practical guidelines in enacting parenting plans

For convenience, all references cited in this chapter and the next will be found at the end of Chapter 10.

Parenting Plans:
A New Conceptual Approach

In what has become a classic text, Ricci (1997, pp. 38-42) argues, and we agree, that mediators ought to pay close attention to the language parents use with each other because their language both reveals and shapes how they conceptualize and enact their relationship. The practice implication of this insight is clear: Change the language in use, and you have an important lever for changing how parents think about and deal with each other. But this important concern with language extends well beyond any given relationship to affect the larger field of divorce itself.

Historically, family law statutes have been centered on a concern with the individual rights of adult parents; children, if they were seen at all, were treated as chattel. Thus, the language of the law and inevitably of its practitioners was the language of ownership and possession. Concerns about "winning" or "losing" custody had and have little to do with children and much to do with an adult struggle over power and control over property (McWhinney, 1995). Now, it may seem ludicrous to speak about "visiting" one's own children (Everett, 1984), but that was not always true. Indeed, the language of primary parenting remains commonplace in the literature, as in a recent family law text: "Children benefit from any custody and access arrangement that provides them with warm and responsive parenting by *a psychologically healthy parent*, in a stable or predictable environment with support from extended family members and other loving adults" (McCarthy, 1997, p. 34, emphasis added).

However, during the past 15 years or so, such language has increasingly become obsolete. We speculate that this is so for several reasons:

- increasing awareness of the reciprocal character of relations between parents and children (Ambert, 1992, 1997);
- recognition of the important role fathers play in the development of their children, both male and female (Lamb, 1997, 1999);
- increasing sensitivity to issues of equality, one of the many consequences of the contemporary feminist movement (Benjamin & Irving, 1992);
- the extraordinary influx of women into the workforce (Duffy & Pupo, 1992), with consequences in the organization of family systems (Mandell & Duffy, 1995; Veevers, 1991);
- the rapid and sustained rise in the proportion of families with "joint" or "shared" parenting arrangements (Ehrenberg, 1996; Joint Committee on Child Custody and Access, 1998; Saposnek, 1998); and
- recognition of the negative impact on children of ongoing parental conflict (Irving & Benjamin, 1995), including litigation about control of the children and subsequent variations (Ahrons, 1994; Braver, 1998; Chambers, 1984; Dillon & Emery, 1996; Kruk, 1993; Maccoby & Mnookin, 1992).

The upshot of these various processes has been statutory changes, or recommendations for change, that emphasize the central importance of parenting plans and, with them, the concomitant shift in language from *child custody* to *shared responsibility* and the preferred use of family mediation (McIsaac, 1998). In the United States, for example, states such as Colorado,

Florida, Maine, Michigan, Oregon, and Washington have recently enacted legislation that formalizes all three changes. Similar changes have also occurred in Australia, New Zealand, and the United Kingdom. In Canada, such changes have recently been proposed by a Joint Committee of the House of Commons and the Senate (Joint Committee on Child Custody and Access, 1998; see Irving & Benjamin, 1999).

Although belated—such changes have been proposed for some time (Irving, 1980; Irving & Benjamin, 1987; Roman & Haddad, 1978)—the salience of these changes cannot be overstated. On one hand, they speak to a perspective on postdivorce parenting that shifts the emphasis from adult rights to parenting responsibilities and from adult interests to the best interests of the children (Kelly, 1997). On the other hand, they make plain that the primary focus of *both* family litigation and family mediation is the construction of detailed parenting plans.

The Links Between Child Development and Divorce

Given the child-centered character of parenting plans, their construction is a complex undertaking. Enacted by the parents, such plans must obviously be sensitive to the different needs, concerns, and circumstances of each parent. At the same time, they must place the best interests of the children paramount. In turn, determining the latter will involve the confluence of two separate but related concerns, namely, the following:

- the normal developmental trajectory of children, based on their age and gender (Bornstein & Lamb, 1999; Craig, 1976; Wallerstein & Kelly, 1980);
- the various ways in which the divorce process can affect children (Emery, 1999; Irving & Benjamin, 1995; Kelly, in press; Kelly & Lamb, 2000), especially the impact of interparental conflict (Ayoub, Deutsch, & Maraganore, 1999; Garrity & Baris, 1994; Ricci, 1997, p. 149).

Clearly, it would be of value to practitioners to have available a full integration of these disparate data sets. To date, only partial integrations are available. Garon, Donner, and Peacock (2000), for example, call for a developmental approach to parenting plans. Menin (2000) has sought to integrate developmental and impact data, and Garrity and Baris (1994) have sought to integrate impact and conflict data. Table 9.1 integrates these various sources to provide a general overview of children's responses to divorce.

Following Ricci (1997, p. 150), children's responses to negative parental intimacy and conflict in divorce can represent danger signals indicating that the child or children need help. This is a message mediators should routinely give clients, along with referral information should they detect evidence of such dysfunction in a particular case.

To concerns raised by Table 9.1, mediators should attend to two additional factors. The first factor concerns individual differences, or what Ricci (1997, p. 135) has called the child's "unique TLC," that is, temperament, level of development, and constitutional sturdiness. Some of these differences are inherited, as in differences in temperament (Chess & Thomas, 1984, 1986). Other differences are learned, as in differences in attachment (Bartholomew & Horowitz, 1991; Bowlby, 1988), differential family experience (Bussell & Reiss, 1993; Dunn & Plomin, 1990), and differences in the capacity to manage stress, a key component of "social intelligence" (Goleman, 1998). A further source of variation, differences associated with gender, appears to be partly inherited and partly learned (Gilligan, 1982; Goldberger, 1996; Maccoby & Jacklin, 1974). Taken together, these different sources of variation mean that some children will be much better able than others to withstand the emotional rigors of their parents' divorce, with "sensitive" children especially vulnerable to psychological harm.

The second factor concerns the role of adults and their interpretation of children's behavior. Many adults persist in regarding children as miniature adults and thus explain children's behavior in terms of adult motives and reasoning. Such explanations are invariably in error, suggesting a sharp and persistent discrepancy between the motives underlying children's conduct and their parents' adult interpretation of the same. Saposnek (1998) highlights such differences as contributing to parental conflict over child care in divorce. For example, although the real intention of the child's conduct is to protect parents' self-esteem, both parents will tend to interpret such behavior as indicating that "the child wants to live at [their] house and is afraid to tell [the other parent]" (p. 166). Similarly, when the real intention of the child's conduct is to test the love of a parent, mothers will tend to interpret this behavior as indicating that "[the] child desperately wants to live with mother [and] is probably afraid of his father or is not being nurtured enough by the man; custody should be changed to mother" (pp. 162-163). In contrast, the same conduct will tend to be interpreted by fathers as indicating that "[the] child is just trying to make mother feel better because mother has been complaining to the child about how unhappy she is. . . . Contact between child and mother should be restricted until she stops burdening the child with her own problems" (p. 163).

These data support several conclusions relevant to the mediation of parenting plans:

- Parenting plans should be sensitive to the children's age, gender, and developmental level.
- The normal developmental trajectory of children can be seriously disrupted in the face of ongoing marital conflict, especially when it is coupled with the major reorganization arising from divorce.

Table 9.1   Child Responses to Positive and Negative Parental Intimacy (divorce) by Child Age

	Parental Relations	
Child Age	**Positive Intimacy**	**Negative Intimacy (Divorce)**
	• Acceptance, trust, support, healthy interdependence; closure of issues in dispute	• Rejection, lack of trust, competitiveness, unhealthy dependence; no closure of issues in dispute • Mild to moderate conflict: frequent, raised voices, threats, accusations, negative attributions; may involve efforts by parent to form coalition with children against other parent
0 to 3 years	• Development of social and emotional attachment. Totally dependent on parents. Develop a core sense of trust. Very limited concept of time. Beginning use of language for communication.	
3 to 5 years	• Develop cognitive concepts of time and space. Awareness of the impact of external events. Learn to tolerate separation from caregivers and experience fear and anxiety at separation. Less time distortion than infants but still significant. Striking increase in language skills. Often fantasize what they do not understand and are likely to make things up from elements of their own experiences. Can perceive parental conflict as criticism of self.	• Divorce process may undermine child's struggle for personal autonomy. Regressive behavior commonplace, including lapses in toilet training, disruption of sleep patterns, increased aggression toward siblings and authority figures, and deterioration of language skills. Shock or depression common. Child able to tolerate separation from the other parent for 2 to 3 days.

Parental Relations

Child Age	Positive Intimacy	Negative Intimacy (Divorce)
6 to 12 years	• Greater understanding of social relationships. Evolution of self-discipline. Increased independence, flexibility and reasonableness. Can talk about their own feelings but have difficulty expressing their concerns and fears. Attachment to peers.	• Intense emotional responses common, including sadness, crying, and longing for the absent parent. Excessive loyalty to missing parent coupled with anger toward primary caregiver. Loyalty conflicts common, coupled with an intense wish to restore their parent's relationship. Anxiety may manifest as somatic symptoms (headache, stomachache). May assume responsibility for the separation. Extreme responses, with things being "really good" or "really bad." May be distracted in class, lost in pervasive concerns about family events. Children able to tolerate separation from the other parent for 5 to 7 days.
13 to 18 years	• Time of great physical, emotional, and sexual changes. Relationships viewed contextually and as a process. Greater insight into the connection between emotions and behavior. Strong emphasis on independence and relations with peers.	• May notice changes in their financial stability that reflect the divorce. Sexual confusion coupled with anger at and rejection of resident parent. Confusing feelings over parent's reentry into the world of "dating." Anxiety and distress over continued parental conflict. Related school problems common.

215

- Individual differences may mean that parenting arrangements that are suitable for one child may not be suitable for another; suitability, then, is an empirical rather than a theoretical issue, with trial periods and interim arrangements useful tools.
- Adults and children respond to divorce in very different ways, with neither understanding the other; adult efforts to help and protect their children, based on adult "commonsense" reasoning, often misinterpret children's intentions and can make matters worse, rather than better.
- As experts in child development, mediators can educate parents as to the potential consequences of their current conduct for their children's long-term development, including appropriate interpretations of the children's conduct; they can also help parents clearly differentiate between issues that are essentially marital in character and those that genuinely concern parenting.
- Finally, in the absence of detailed knowledge about the children, mediators should intervene cautiously, lest they, like the parents themselves, inadvertently do more harm than good.

Parental Strategies in Divorce _____

Parents, like children, vary in their responses to divorce. It is possible for parents to have a "good" divorce (Ahrons, 1994), in which they are trusting, affectionate, and mutually supportive. Although such divorces do occur, they will not be common in family mediation. Rather, four parental responses will be more typical—namely, conflict, negative feelings, mistrust, and the absence of ongoing dialogue (communication breakdown). In our experience, such responses vary in intensity, with couples who have been through litigation more likely than those who have not at the extreme end of each dimension.

In this context, Saposnek (1998, pp. 172-192) lists eight common strategies that operate as hidden agendas reflecting parents' underlying motives. Moreover, these are motives that parents typically deny, preferring the more altruistic rhetoric of children's best interests. Indeed, in our experience, parents vary widely in the extent to which they are consciously aware of such motives, with premediation efforts often directed at bringing them to light, thus making them subject to discussion, negotiation, and intervention.

In listing these strategies, little would be served by reproducing Saposnek's (1998) insightful discussion. Instead, our aim is to supplement that discussion while alerting mediators to the sorts of conduct they will likely encounter in their efforts to help couples negotiate productively.

Reuniting Strategies. In the majority of cases, the divorce is initiated by one spouse (more often the wife) against the will of the other spouse

(Irving & Benjamin, 1995). The spouse who was left may accept the situation, or he or she may engage in a number of responsive strategies. The reuniting strategy is a responsive strategy that involves several variations, three of which are common in mediation. The first variation involves the "yes man" approach, that is, the parent who will agree to virtually any suggestion by the other, however extreme or outlandish. This approach carefully avoids all conflict and presents the party as cooperative and agreeable, in effect, bowing to the other parent's superior knowledge and insight. Of course, the underlying hope is that by presenting in this way, the other parent will realize that the divorce was a mistake, and the two can be reunited. This strategy is problematic for the mediator in two ways. First, it may yield plans that are not in keeping with the children's best interests because the underlying motive has to do with marriage rather than parenting. Second, the reuniting motive is often built on a fantasy that is wildly out of keeping with the other parent's sentiments. Challenging that fantasy may mean that one or both parents may drop out of mediation.

The second variation involves getting as close to the other spouse as circumstances will allow, thus opting either for shared parenting or sole custody *with the other spouse,* coupled with generous access. Here, the spouse seeking reunion presents as eminently reasonable and highly flexible. Furthermore, interest in and involvement with parenting, which may have been minimal previously, are now high. The spouse may be willing to attend classes (on cooking, parenting, etc.), volunteer to become involved in taking the children places, spend time with the children to give the other spouse a break, and so on. Such heightened parental involvement may provide some immediate benefit to the children. It may also provide the spouse with the opportunity of genuine transformation, as he or she "falls in love" with the children. Conversely, there is a danger that such involvement may be ephemeral and remain in place only so long as the hope of reunion is alive; once that hope fades, the threat of parental withdrawal may become real.

The third variation involves playing "hard to get," in which one spouse may threaten to take the children away unless the other spouse returns to the fold. Such spouses present as angry and bitter and come prepared with a wealth of anecdotes "proving" that the other spouse is incompetent, emotionally unstable, irresponsible, and self-centered. By contrast, these spouses present themselves as competent, caring, diligent, conscientious, and, above all, stable, fair, and even-handed. In this context, they suggest, the courts would have little choice but to give the children to them. Although the outcome of such a battle would be a certain win for the spouse, so the argument goes, such a battle can be avoided altogether if only the other spouse would be reasonable in reunion. This variation is a prime candidate for premediation because the position of the spouse is built on even parts of fantasy, denial, and fear. It is also a process that can be very difficult for the children because it is often accompanied by parental conflict at transition points.

Emotionally Disengaging Strategies. If the spouse who was left is prone to reuniting strategies, the spouse who initiated the divorce, the leaver, is equally prone to disengaging strategies. We note three variations here, all of which can be quite destructive of the children.

The first variation involves controlling or limiting the other parent's access to the children. In extreme cases, the parent may repeatedly defy court-ordered access by the other parent. More typically, such access is simply difficult to get for a variety of seemingly plausible reasons: The children are ill, the parent is ill, the children are with their grandparents, and so on. Alternately, the timing of transitions may continuously vary, always at a time difficult or inconvenient for the other spouse. Still another variation involves marital conflict at transition points, or the imposition of arbitrary restrictions concerning the food the children may consume or the activities they may engage in when with the other spouse, how far away from the house the car must be parked at transition, whether or not the parent may enter the house on transition, and so on. In short, access to the children becomes a virtual obstacle course that is intended to become so aversive that they will withdraw altogether.

The second variation involves overt efforts at child alienation. Here, in talking to the children, the resident parent vilifies the other parent. Such efforts cast aspersion on the other parent's motives, conduct, relations with the children, and relations with the parent and, above all, highlight the "injury" done to *both* resident parent and children when the other parent "abandoned" them. In this context, the other parent is caught in a double bind, for everything he or she does is interpreted negatively. Should they fail to visit, they are characterized as "uncaring," whereas if they do visit, they are seen as "fraudulent" or "manipulative." Similarly, the children are caught in a loyalty bind and forced to choose "the parent who loves them the most." At great cost to themselves, they may refuse to see the other parent, thus giving the resident spouse the support the children think they need. At the same time, they may confide in the mediator that they sorely miss the other parent but cannot admit or even hint at this lest they cause pain to the parent with whom they live.

The third variation is one of parental abandonment in which the other parent refuses contact with the children and moves on to start a new family (Irving & Benjamin, 1995; Kruk, 1993). We list this variation here for the sake of completeness because such cases do not enter mediation.

Emotional Survival Strategies. Next to the death of a family member, divorce is the most stressful event that can occur in a family. Some spouses cope well, others much less so, and still others go into what Saposnek (1998) describes as "survival" mode. The two variations we note here are both characterized by extreme behavior that is out of character for the individual and involves efforts at feeling safe by overcontrolling the other parent.

One variation involves an adamant demand for sole custody, with limited or no access by the other parent. Parents advance a variety of reasons for restricting or denying access and have learned the value of often repeating the phrase "the best interests of the children." They may even accept that it is good for the children to have access to both parents but insist that that is not appropriate "right now." The latter phrase is an important clue that the resident parent is in survival mode; that is, these parents need their children around them right now because without them they will die (of loneliness, of a broken heart, etc.). Such cases are a good example of arrangements that are not mediatable at that time but may become so some time in the future. The impact of such arrangements, however temporary, on the children are not known.

The second variation involves a breach of boundaries. Under normal circumstances, in divorce, the parents establish two separate households in which they live independent lifestyles, free of intrusion by the other spouse. In this variation, one or both parents refuse to recognize these new boundaries. One or both may claim the right to show up at any time of the day or night "to see the children." If the locks on the matrimonial home have not been changed, they may enter the home and roam around unannounced (e.g., one parent may report finding the other parent in the bedroom at midnight). They may prolong the transition or pointedly inquire about the goings-on in the household of the children or may audiotape telephone conversations between the children and the other parent. In part, these strategies may be in response to the demands of litigation. In large part, however, they reflect a form of denial, that is, feeling safe by pretending that the divorce never really happened and that the children are not really moving back and forth between two households.

More generally, parents in survival mode are highly unpredictable because their conduct is not entirely under conscious control. They may be optimistic and affectionate in one session, bitter and enraged the next, and depressed and teary eyed the next. Such lability may similarly be evident within sessions and can make for mediation efforts that are extremely taxing for the mediator. This is especially true as regards last-minute impasses that may temporarily or permanently disrupt weeks or even months of productive negotiation. Under these circumstances, when all impasse-breaking techniques have failed, one can only acknowledge that this is what is right for this parent at this time while leaving the door open to mediation in the future.

Financial Survival Strategies. In a later chapter (Chapter 12), we discuss relational processes likely to arise when couples seek to mediate financial matters. Accordingly, we have nothing to add here beyond Saposnek's (1998) acute observations.

Power Assertion Strategies. Parental relations in mediation either may be an extension of relations during the marriage or may signal an important change. Either the more powerful parent seeks to maintain control, or the less powerful one seeks to assert a newfound independence.

In the former instance, a powerful parent may seek to take over the mediation process. He or she typically attempts this by usurping the mediator's agenda-setting function by advancing a detailed plan. Subsequent discussion then focuses on reacting to the plan. Such plans tend to be lengthy and highly detailed, with the parent having thought to foresee every conceivable contingency and with meticulous attention to an *exact* time-sharing schedule. Reference to existing statutes may also be included, suggesting previous consultation with the parent's lawyer. In reaction, the other parent typically feels overwhelmed and manipulated, often noting that such behavior was typical of the parent during their marriage. It is imperative that the mediator maintain control of the process, putting aside the parent's plan as "a very useful contribution" while walking the parents through the plan elements (see Chapter 10, this volume) to ensure that "each of you has an equal opportunity to say your piece."

In the latter instance, the weaker spouse asserts authority by ensuring that he or she has the last word on any issue. This renders interaction highly conflictual because no detail is too small to warrant extended and rigorous scrutiny. For example, if the other parent suggests a pickup time of 5:30 p.m. to coincide with his or her work schedule, the resident parent will advance six reasons why the best time *for the children* is 5:10 p.m. Using the rhetoric of the children provides a convenient rationale for demanding changes while allowing one parent to blandly suggest arrangements that just happen to restrict access or at least make it very difficult for the other parent. A similarly litigious attitude is evident with regard to such issues as the number and duration of telephone calls, food appropriate for children's healthy snacks, children's bedtimes, appropriate activities, the management of transitions, vacation times, and so on. Such cases are best dealt with in premediation, where the issue of power in mediation can be addressed directly. Unfortunately, such couples will often need to get to premediation by first attempting negotiation because such litigiousness is only evident once negotiation has begun. In assessment, weaker parents appear earnest, motivated, and flexible and may even express some concern about being intimidated by the other parent.

Retaliation Strategies. It is commonplace for parents to emerge from a marriage feeling betrayed, hard done by, humiliated, and used by the other parent. Mediation is one forum in which they can get back at the other parent, using the children to achieve this end. They are convenient to this purpose not only because they represent something of value to the other parent but also because such valuation only arose *after* the divorce and so can be interpreted as superficial or false and manipulative.

In this context, the classic retaliatory move is to seek exclusive control over the children while drastically limiting or denying access to the other parent (child alienation syndrome) (Gardner, 1992; Garrity & Baris, 1994). That this is identical to the move in power strategies should come as little surprise because the two motives are closely allied. One variation involves the primary parent, typically the mother, demanding exclusive control of the children on the grounds that because the husband had had little or no contact with the children while they were married, he has lost the right to such contact now. The wife will typically tell of having begged her husband to pay more attention to the children, all to no effect. Consequently, she is outraged and highly suspicious when the husband discovers an interest in the children only after she has left. Depriving the husband of the children is "only what he deserves" for what he has put her through. Here, the mediator can use his or her own logic to suggest a softer stance. If the husband's involvement was good for the children then, surely it is still good for them now, despite the lost time. Depriving *the children* of their father is a marital issue that has little or nothing to do either with parenting or the best interests of the children.

The related variation involves the husband's demand that the children come stay with him. His rationale is that in leaving him, his wife has "obviously" gone crazy and has thus become unfit to care for the children. The clue that this is about revenge and *not* parenting is that the idea is poorly thought through and patently impractical. It may be impossible in light of the husband's work schedule, his complete lack knowledge about child care, or his failure to consider how the children would feel without their mother. Rather, the demand reflects the husband's combined sense of outrage, humiliation, anger, and fear his wife has left him. Taking the children away from her is the most obvious way in which he can get back at her. That a good father, who loves his children, would never deliberately harm them becomes the basis for suggesting that he take a softer stand *in the best interests of the children.*

The third variation, and perhaps the most difficult of the three, involves a parent who has decided—sometimes consciously, sometimes not—to make life miserable for the other parent as revenge for real or imagined hurts. This strategy can take a variety of forms: restricting access, withholding child support, making every issue (no matter how tiny) contentious, demanding shared parenting (thus ensuring frequent aversive contact), and repeatedly seeking variation in the court (thus depleting the other parent's resources). In more extreme cases, revenge may involve stalking, harassment (at home and/or at work), breaking and entering, destroying property, issuing threats, and, in rare cases, first-time violence and even murder. The good news is that the intensity of anger leading to revenge should be obvious on assessment and may either be referred elsewhere (for litigation, counseling, or both) or may enter mediation via premediation.

Pushing to Lose Strategies. These strategies emerge when, pushed by family and friends, parents may push for a custody arrangement about which they feel highly ambivalent. Consequently, they use strategies that almost certainly ensure failure. Such strategies are rare in mediation and have been well addressed by Saposnek (1998). We would only add that pressure from relatives is not the only basis on which these strategies may be enacted. Society assumes that mothers who love their children would automatically want to be with them. In fact, a small proportion may have found parenting unrewarding and exhausting and may welcome the opportunity in divorce to give the children to the other parent. However, for fear of public condemnation, they may be loath to advance such a position openly. Instead, they mouth platitudes about a mother's love while adopting "pushing to lose" strategies. This allows mothers to achieve their hidden objective while saving face in doing so.

Strategies for Appeasing a New Partner. Finally, these strategies have much in common with "pushing to lose" strategies because in both cases, the parent—in this case, more often the father than the mother—has no real commitment to the children and is only going through the motions for the sake of a new partner. Because such a motive would attract public condemnation, other rationalizations are advanced, either for taking the children away from the other parent or for abandoning the children altogether. We know from the divorce literature that such cases are all too common in life (Irving & Benjamin, 1995), although they are relatively rare in mediation. They speak of a family tragedy in which the children are the victims and about which mediators can do little save tidy up the details.

These eight strategies, with their variants and combinations, still do not exhaust the variety of possibilities in mediation. They do, however, represent much of what mediators must contend with on a day-to-day basis, and they are perhaps the best argument for the advantages of a therapeutic approach in general and the therapeutic family mediation (TFM) model in particular. This is especially true of the premediation phase because many of the strategies listed above are inimical of productive negotiation. Accordingly, they are best dealt with prior to negotiation, when frankly therapeutic methods can be brought to bear to good effect in the majority of cases.

Advocacy in Family Mediation: Practice Rationale and Public Accountability[1]

On entering mediation, clients typically assume that, like doctors or lawyers, mediators share universal standards of practice. At once, this assumption is both true and false. It is true in the sense that mediators universally subscribe to impartiality and self-determination as practice principles (Kandel, 1998; Taylor, 1997). The notion of self-determination holds that clients should construct their agreements based on their own sense of their needs and interests and free from outside constraint or direction. The notion of impartiality holds that mediators should be free of bias toward either party, refrain from imposing their own subjective opinions, and be "equidistant" from them, temporarily aligning with each party to encourage disclosure and build trust and confidence (Rifkin, Millen, & Cobb, 1991).

Although all mediators intervene to control process (so-called "agenda management"), as regards content, some mediators prefer a practice style strictly in keeping with these principles (Bush & Folger, 1994; Grillo, 1996). Most others (Kruk, 1998; Waldman, 1997), ourselves included (Irving & Benjamin, 1995), openly demonstrate a "willingness to shape and direct parties' thinking in order to move them toward outcomes that best meet the mediator's sense of what will best solve the problem and meet the parties' needs" (Bush & Folger, 1994, p. 39).

More generally, mediation practice varies across two continua (Kressel, Butler-DeFreitas, Forlenza, & Wilcox, 1994; Riskin, 1996). One continuum, concerning problem definition, is "narrow" at one end and broad at the other. The narrow approach is restricted to legally relevant issues and is preferred by mediators with legal training. In contrast, the broad approach includes concerns related to relational, professional, and/or community interests and is preferred by mediators with a mental health background. As noted in a previous chapter (see Chapter 2), we adopt a constructivist approach in which problem definition emerges from interaction between the mediator and the couple. The second continuum concerns practice style, with a facilitative approach at one end and an evaluative approach at the other. On the assumption that the parties know best, the facilitative approach focuses on enhancing communication and encouraging disclosure. In contrast, on the assumption that the parties need and desire guidance, the evaluative approach is explicitly directive, at least as required in context.

Directive interventions vary widely. One class of such interventions involves recommendations favoring one or another settlement option ("I would (not) recommend. . . .") (Alfini, 1991). Greatbatch and Dingwall (1989, p. 636) identify a second class of intervention as "selective facilitation" in which mediators pressure clients to prefer one option by "differentially creating opportunities to talk through the favoured option" (see Berlin, 1998). Kandel (1998) identifies a third class as "implicit communication," which refers to the timing of the mediator's head nods, "un-huh," and questioning, because this sends a powerful, if subtle, message to the clients. In a previous chapter (see Chapter 3), we listed a fourth class of such interventions whose objective is frankly therapeutic and includes "time-outs," the use of caucusing, informing the parties, and explicit efforts at client education. Finally, Golann and Aaron (1997) go further by arguing that substantive influence inheres in the mediation process itself, as a by-product of the necessary authority of the mediator. In a study of civil mediation, they found that as mediators became familiar with the details of a given case, they began to form judgments as regards available options. Despite the mediators' best efforts to the contrary, this judgment-forming process "leaked out" and influenced clients who were sensitively attuned to any such cues, however subtle.

That said, interventions designed to shape both content and outcome raise obvious ethical concerns. On one hand, the range of intervention discussed above raises grave concerns about the utility of traditional notions of mediator neutrality (Balto, 1990; Cobb & Rifkin, 1991; Cohen, Dattner & Luxenburg, 1999; Cooks & Hale, 1994; Kolb & Kressel, 1994; McCormick, 1997; Smoron, 1998). On the other hand, such interventions may undermine client self-determination, ignore client consent, and yield agreements that reflect only the subjective concerns of the mediator but not the interests of the parties. Such practices may also blur the distinction between mediation and other forms of alternative dispute resolution and, in extreme form, may be frankly coercive (Taylor, 1997) and involve an abuse of power.

In light of these important concerns, on what grounds can such practices be rationalized, and what criteria should be in place that would render such conduct publicly accountable?

There are, in fact, a number of good reasons for the use of directive interventions:

- Mediators have considerably more experience in divorce settlement than most clients. Giving clients access to that experience assists them in making informed choices.
- Mediators have a social responsibility to avoid agreements that they judge are unlikely to hold up through time or that they perceive as unconscionable, as in the exploitation of a weaker party by a stronger one (McCormick, 1997).
- Mediators have a social responsibility to protect the interests of third parties who are not at the table but who will suffer the consequences of terms of settlement, whether based on malice, ignorance, or the desire for control. Children are the obvious case in point (Menin, 2000). For example, an agreement that proposes to give unlimited access to a parent with a history of child abuse would not be in the children's best interests (for other examples, see Saposnek, 1998). In addition to children, a similar case might be made for grandparents.
- Finally, different classes or categories of clients would simply be unable to participate meaningfully in mediation in the absence of direct intervention. High-conflict couples (Johnston & Campbell, 1988) and "undifferentiated spouses" (Mathis, 1998) are representative examples.

The utility of such interventions, however, fails to address the issue of making the mediators who use them publicly accountable. As Greatbatch and Dingwall (1989) observed, directive interventions become problematic only when "formal and substantive neutrality are confused so that the pressure [to select a preferred option] becomes invisible or when the choice of goals remains a purely personal matter rather than one for which the practitioner may be socially accountable" (p. 639). In this context, Kandel (1998) advises, and we agree, that "mediation guidelines should recognize the inevitability of substantive intervention and encourage mediators to make such interventions better" (p. 312). One way to improve the use of such interventions is by establishing public criteria for their legitimate use, such as the following:

- *Transparent practice model.* On entry into mediation, clients should be routinely introduced to the practice model in use, including those assumptions, values, and beliefs that shape the mediator's conduct. With that introduction in place, clients who sign the mediation contract give explicit consent to the use of that model, including the range of interventions associated with it.

- *Transparent bias regarding "best interests."* We routinely make statements to the effect that, although impartial, we are clearly biased in favor of children's "best interests" and will comment accordingly on any client parenting proposals that, in our judgment, are likely to place the children at risk.

- *Transparent "voluntariness."* Both clients and mediators join together on a purely voluntary basis. The mediation contract should specify that both are free to withdraw at any time and that clients are free to refuse the mediator's advice or recommendations (Taylor, 1997).

- *Congruence of "advice" and professional background.* Mediators' credibility rests on the assumption of congruence between the suggestions they make and their professional background and knowledge. Mediators with a mental health background may reasonably claim expertise in child development and so may be free to tender advice in that area. Mediators with a legal background may reasonably claim expertise in matters concerning finances and taxation and so may be free to tender advice in that area. The ability of mediators to tender advice in areas inconsistent with their professional background will depend on specialized supplementary training.

- *Reliance on empirical research.* Mediators who intervene in areas covered by available research should be able to point to such research as the basis for their efforts to inform or educate (Freeman, 1998). That said, two qualifications are in order. First, not all areas of intervention will be covered by research. On those occasions, the mediators' credibility will rest instead on their knowledge, experience, and the relationship of trust they have developed with their clients. Second, as part of the self-reflexivity required of all TFM mediators, the mediators should be critical consumers of research data. Much research reflects fine work, but not all. Mediators should rely only on work they themselves know and respect.

- *Intervention and social norms.* We have argued elsewhere (Benjamin & Irving, 1992) that intervention should *not* be automatic but rather tied to the needs of the client and the requirements of the process. In some cases, intervention will not be required at all, such that mediation may proceed strictly on the basis of mediator impartiality and client self-determination. In other cases, intervention may be limited to information and/or education. In still other cases, especially when children's best interests are called in question, advocacy may be required. These different levels of intervention correspond exactly to Waldman's (1997) distinction between norm-generating, norm-educating, and norm-advocating types of intervention. When client proposals contravene no existing social norms, clients should be free to construct their own agreement; that is, they should be free to generate their own rules or norms. When their proposals violate norms of lesser importance and do not put the children or others at risk, intervention may be limited to educating the clients about prevailing norms and then allowing them to decide whether to abide by them. However, when their proposals violate serious norms—for example, as regards the safety or security of one of the parties and/or of third parties, such as the children—then they cannot be allowed to stand, and the mediator should be free to advocate for alternate proposals or, in extreme cases, terminate the mediation.

- *Intervention and the mediation process.* Reasonable outcomes not only assume that the interests of various parties are protected but that the parties themselves have an equal opportunity to pursue those interests in mediation. In accordance with a feminist-informed perspective (Irving & Benjamin, 1995), this can only happen when both parties have an equal opportunity to advance their proposals, without hindrance or intimidation. When such processes are not in evidence, the mediator is obliged to intervene to produce a more balanced process (Kelly, 1995). The range of possible interventions is wide and limited only by the mediator's imagination and the constraints of the context. Such efforts are typically successful, and the process should be allowed to continue. Failing that, however, the mediator would have no choice but to end the process and refer the parties elsewhere.

Inclusion of these criteria in existing standards or guidelines would recognize the modern reality of family mediation, optimize mediator intervention options, and safeguard the rights of clients and third parties to impartiality and self-determination.

Including the Children

In assisting parents to construct a parenting plan, the mediator has the option of inviting the children to attend one or more sessions. There is some reason to think that including the children on a routine basis might be helpful. In a small Australian study, McIntosh (2000) found that gathering information from the children by a professional not involved in the mediation aided the mediation process by reducing conflict between the parents and changed the parent-child relationship. Alternately, as seen in our discussion of advocacy (above), most mediators, ourselves included, are selective in including the children.

The positive factors we consider for including the children are as follows:

- Both parents consent to child inclusion.
- The children have asked to be part of the process.
- The children may themselves benefit from their participation.
- The parents are at an impasse regarding one or more parenting issues.
- One parent is unable or unwilling to "hear" the other parent as regards some aspect of the first parent's relationship with the children.
- Including the children will likely assist in moving the process along.

The negative factors we consider for excluding the children are as follows:

- One parent refuses to consider inclusion of the children.
- There is some reason to think that the children have recently been exposed to some form of trauma in this family.
- The children are under 2 years of age and thus too young to participate in any meaningful way.
- There is some reason to think that there is a coalition between one parent and the children.

The last issue of a parent-child coalition warrants special mention because such evidence can be seen in two ways. On one hand, children in such an arrangement may have little to contribute because one would expect them to have been coached to parrot the resident parent's party line. On the other hand, it may be important to include such children in the hope that they can be persuaded to speak their own minds and thus deviate from the party line. For example, after repeatedly and categorically refusing to see his father, a child confided in strict confidence to the mediator that he missed seeing his dad terribly, but he was sure his dad understood that he could not see him right now because to do so would hurt his mom. In fact, the father was deeply hurt by his son's apparent defection, and the mediator was dismayed at the damage that had been done to this child. Yet the son's information was vital in confirming child alienation and in indicating that there was no way around the impasse in this case. Mediation was subsequently terminated and the case returned to the court.

Even when the mediator has decided *not* to include the children, there is another option—namely, including them symbolically. Children can be brought into the session by a particular questioning technique. For example, each parent separately may be asked by the mediator to "describe the children to me." Subsequent questions may make that description as detailed as the mediator thinks necessary ("Do they look more like you or the other parent?

What is their personality like?"). Supplementary questions can also invoke the children's presence in session ("How would you like your children to speak about you [or the other parent] when looking back on this time 10 years from now [or when they turn 18, or as an adult]?").

Finally, when children are included in mediation, taking greatest advantage of their participation involves specialized skills and resources. Techniques vary as a function of the children's age. Children 6 years of age or older can be interviewed. Questions should be short, simple, and clear, with appropriate vocabulary. Questions should be descriptive and comparative but with great care taken *not* to put the children in any kind of "bind" ("Who do you love better, your mother or your father?"). However, handled appropriately, even young children may have much to contribute ("I wonder what it would be like if . . ."). Such interviews should be timed to accord with the children's attention span, and the mediator should be sensitive to any signs of distress, discomfort, fear, or anxiety. With these concerns in mind, the mediator may prefer to interview children one at a time or with all the siblings together. In addition, with children 5 years of age and younger, the mediator is likely to have better results using dolls, toys, and crayons than by relying exclusively on talk. In turn, mediators who see children on a regular basis should have these materials at hand.

Even so, across the age spectrum, children's behavior is unpredictable. Many children, despite their immaturity, are acute observers of family life and can provide a great deal of material that will be useful in facilitating the mediation process. Other children may refuse to talk, freeze up, cry, act out, prove distractable and impulsive, or simply insist on talking about matters that are irrelevant to the mediation. In short, child inclusion is a judgment call made on a case-by-case basis and carefully mindful of the selection criteria listed above.

First Principles in the Construction of Parenting Plans

The movement from traditional custody orders to modern parenting plans was very much a hit-and-miss affair, based on equal parts theory, common sense, and experience. What has evolved is a child-centered approach to parenting in divorce, based on a handful of basic principles whose brief review below has relied on Ricci (1997, pp. 7, 11, 17).

1.   The children are the primary owners of the relationship with their parents. Traditional discussions of child custody and access have focused heavily on the individual rights of parents. Such rights may or may not coincide with the best interests of the children. With parenting plans intended to make those interests paramount, this principle highlights the child-centered character of parenting plans.

2. Children and their parents have certain rights in divorce:

(a) Each child has the right to have two homes where he or she is cherished and given the opportunity to develop normally.

(b) Each child has a right to a meaningful, nurturing relationship with each parent.

(c) Each parent and child has the right to call themselves a family, regardless of how the children's time is divided.

(d) Each parent has the responsibility and the right to share in raising his or her children.

(e) Each child has the right to have competent parents and to be free from hearing, observing, or being caught up in their parents' arguments or problems with one another.

(f) Each parent has the right to his or her own private life and territory—the new family boundary—and to raise the children without unreasonable interference from the other parent.

These rights serve to give substance to the central notion that, regardless of their particular arrangement, in principle both parents share in the responsibility of caring for their children. This is so *not* because they have a right to do so but because their mutual involvement is in keeping with children's healthy development. That principle, however, comes with an important qualification—namely, that such involvement serves the needs of children only so long as it keeps them separate and apart from their parents' marital difficulties. Finally, these rights recognize that divorce does *not* mean the end of the family system but rather its reorganization into two subsystems, each with its own separate boundary. So long as parenting within each subsystem does not place the children at risk, it should be allowed to continue without interference by the other parent.

3. Each child is unique. Although children have needs in common, each is in some ways unique, an individual blend of strengths and weaknesses—some constitutional, others environmental. This principle recognizes that a parenting arrangement that works well for one child may be harmful to another. It is the responsibility of parents in divorce to construct parenting plans that recognize and acknowledge such differences in their children.

4. A good legal agreement cannot guarantee a good result. Parenting agreements arrived at through litigation vary widely. Some are good agreements that are fair and sensitive to the needs of the children, but others are bad agreements that are neither fair nor sensitive to the children. However, irrespective of their quality, such agreements cannot and do not teach parents how to get along in a positive and constructive way, nor do they tell parents how to maintain a supportive and loving relationship with their children. Such agreements, then, are important in formalizing parenting arrangements after divorce but are insufficient in and of themselves to ensure that children will be protected and allowed to develop normally.

5.   How parents relate to one another after separation is crucial. One of the most potent predictors of child development after divorce is the way in which parents relate to each other in front of the children (Irving & Benjamin, 1995). Parents who allow the children to have a loving and supportive relationship with each parent and who systematically exclude the children from adult affairs, including conflict, ensure that their children will be least affected by their parents' divorce. Those who compete for their children's affection, engage in destructive conflict in front of the children, and/or encourage the children to take "sides" in the conflict ensure that their children's development will be impaired, perhaps permanently (Wallerstein, Lewis, & Blakeslee, 2000).

6.   As the "executives" in their family, only adults make final decisions. Healthy families are organized hierarchically, with a clear separation between the roles played by parents and children. Executive functions—that is, adult issues and final decisions regarding parenting—are the parents' sole responsibility. Although children can and should be encouraged to have a say in decisions affecting them, final decisions always rest with their parents. Children's responsibilities increase with age and involve the range of issues associated with normal growth and development, including social relations with family members, peers, and others, and the work and play associated with curricular and extracurricular activities.

7.   Divorce precipitates a confrontation with many traditional values and beliefs. The divorce rate in North America has ensured the destruction of the negative stereotypes previously associated with divorce. Even so, on an individual basis, parents may still emerge from divorce feeling that they have failed at two of life's primary adult tasks—namely, marriage and parenting. As part of their education in parenting in divorce, parents must come to realize that although their marriage has ended, their family continues to survive in a different form. They must also accept that they have an ongoing responsibility to be good parents to their children, even if that means disposing of traditional notions of parenting. That is, both parents can continue to parent well despite the fact that they live in different households, may need to learn to relate to the other parent in new ways, and may even have new partners.

8.   There is such a thing as a "sensible" divorce, and it is worth the effort it takes to get it. A "sensible" divorce is a shorthand way of speaking about a structural model of a healthy family in divorce. That model encompasses four primary features:

- adult issues and parenting decisions solely in the hands of the parents as family "executives," with the children excluded from such affairs and from anything to do with parenting conflict and hostility;
- separate bounded households involving each parent and the children, each free to carry on with normal parenting, with the flexible support of the other parent;

- parents who develop a positive, constructive, and business-like relationship characterized by cooperation, mutual respect, negotiation, and effective problem solving; and
- children who are encouraged to have a loving and supportive relationship with each parent, with the approval and support of the other parent.

Practical Guidelines in Enacting Parenting Plans

Taken together, the above principles set out the goals and objectives of healthy parenting in divorce. For many parents in divorce, especially those now caught up in a cycle of destructive conflict and hostility, these principles are inadequate because they fail to specify *how* these goals are to be achieved. For advice in enacting these principles, we turn to the following practical guidelines, based on our own experience and the accumulated wisdom of Ricci (1997) and centered mostly on the coparental relationship and the relationship between parents and children in divorce. These are offered as "guidelines" only—parents in divorce may have other ways to achieve desirable outcomes for themselves and their children—that mediators can pass on to their clients and that we routinely include as an appendix to their "Memorandum of Understanding."

1. Parents should strive for a decent, business-like, working relationship with one another that meets the needs of their children (Ricci, 1997, pp. 51, 83, 89-92):

    (a) Watch your language; be courteous and mutually respectful.
    (b) Keep your feelings in check.
    (c) Respect the other parent's privacy and expect the same in return.
    (d) Act like a guest in the other parent's home.
    (e) Don't expect appreciation or praise from the other parent, but do acknowledge when your partner shows understanding, sensitivity, compromises, or flexibility and support, and expect the same in return.
    (f) Keep a positive but realistic attitude.
    (g) Keep your sense of humor and encourage it in the other parent.
    (h) Be reliable; do what you say you're going to do, and expect the same from the other parent.
    (i) Be flexible and supportive of the other parent and expect the same in return.
    (j) Be patient; Rome wasn't built in a day.

    (k) Expect to feel strange about this new relationship at first; give yourself time to adjust.

    (l) Though it may be difficult at first, don't give up; the effort is worth it.

For parents in divorce to develop and maintain a positive, constructive, and cooperative relationship, they must begin behaving like colleagues or business associates. That is, they must be moderate in their language and conduct, be positive in outlook and expectations, focus on a series of shared projects or tasks, and work as a team toward shared goals and objectives. Furthermore, such relationships take time to "gel" and so may feel odd or awkward at first, feelings that gradually fade with experience. As important, such efforts, because of inevitable start-up problems, require patience and perseverance because the stakes in this case are very high indeed—namely, the present and future well-being of their children. Succeed, as many can and will do, and that future is as assured as any set of loving parents can make it. Fail, while continuing to be caught up in a cycle of negative intimacy, and that future may very likely be compromised in many ways.

    2. In all interactions between parents, use good communication practices (Ricci, 1997, pp. 91, 95, 104, 108):

    (a) Be explicit with the other parent.

    (b) Direct communication between parents should be preferred at all times; never use the children to send messages to the other parent.

    (c) Say what you mean and mean what you say; make no assumptions.

    (d) Double-check your verbal understandings; to build trust, don't take the other parent for granted.

    (e) Demonstrate you understand what the other parent is saying.

    (f) Try to ensure that verbal and nonverbal "messages" are the same and not in conflict.

    (g) Know the things that trigger conflict between parents and avoid them.

    (h) Confront only with great care.

    (i) Keep the other parent a person in your mind; don't make him or her into a "monster."

One of the key aspects of any business-like relationship is how effectively the parties communicate with one another. This goes much beyond the matter of trading insults or engaging in shouting matches. Rather, it is centered on the extent to which the parties have learned good communication practices. Such practices assume that, unlike friends or lovers, who know each other well, business colleagues know each other superficially and so must work hard to ensure that they consistently communicate clearly. Among other things, this means that communication—both verbal and nonverbal messages—is direct (excluding third parties), explicit, and congruent; avoids forms of communication (such as sarcasm or irony) that might obscure meaning; is checked to ensure that the right message has been received by the other; and acknowledges receipt of the message from the other. Furthermore, effective communication does *not* routinely involve confrontation or conflict but restricts such efforts to high-priority issues and proceeds cautiously, mindful of the need for periodic relationship repair. Such repair includes a mental portrait of the other as a person, like the self, doing his or her best under conditions that are stressful and often very trying.

3. Parents should work to maintain a healthy, positive parenting pattern (Ricci, 1997, pp. 90, 95, 117):

    (a) Time with the children is time together, not baby-sitting.
    (b) Make your children's needs more important than your territorial rights or your independence; always, children before rules or procedures.
    (c) Respect the other parent's time with the children.
    (d) Respect the other parent's parenting style.
    (e) Interfere with the other parent's effort *only* if your children need your protection.
    (f) Share information about the children frequently with the other parent; parenting continuity is important as the children move between households.
    (g) Parents should compare notes on the other adults in your children's lives, including teachers, coaches, medical and dental professionals, and others.
    (h) Each parent should be supportive of the other parent's relationship with the children.
    (i) Don't use the children to carry messages to the other parent.

These efforts to establish and maintain a business-like relationship are directed toward good, competent, or healthy parenting. Following the principles, parenting patterns or practices are deemed healthy to the extent that they encourage, promote, approve, and support a loving, affectionate, and ongoing relationship between each parent and each of the children and consistently keep parenting functions separate from adult affairs. Pursuant to these goals, parents should go beyond grudging acceptance or guarded tolerance of the other parent's involvement with the children to encourage and promote such relations because they are good for their children. Such support includes respecting boundaries and accepting the other parent's parenting style, even if one parent does things with the children that the other parent might not do. It means opening and maintaining a one-on-one dialogue that enables both parents to share information with one another, so that both are equally up to date on what is happening with and to their children. It may mean sacrificing one's territorial and other rights or compromising on issues about which one parent knows that he or she is "right" because the resulting conflict about these issues is not good for the children.

4. Parents should work to develop and maintain a healthy, positive relationship with their children (Ricci, 1997, pp. 125-130, 142-153):

   (a) Let your children know you are thinking about them and expect them to keep in touch with you.
   (b) Make regular contact with the other adults in your children's lives, including teachers, coaches, medical and dental professionals, and others.
   (c) Talk to your children regularly; young children especially need to understand the changes in their lives in ways that are seeable, touchable, and concrete.
   (d) Give children a say in the decisions that affect their lives based on their TLC; ensure that they feel heard, even though adults make all final decisions.
   (e) Don't "bad-mouth" the other parent in the presence of the children.
   (f) Do not participate in the children's angry feelings about the other parent.
   (g) Encourage the children to speak about any difficulties they are having with the other parent, but do not pursue it at length; suggest other adults in whom the child might wish to confide.
   (h) Do not ask the children about the other parent's life or circumstances; respect the other parent's privacy and give his or her motives the benefit of any doubt.
   (i) Do not tell the children to keep secrets about you from the other parent.
   (j) Be the grown-up; avoid leaning on the children to satisfy your need for support, encouragement, and/or care.
   (k) Keep changes to a minimum during the first few years, especially in regard to young children.
   (l) Never threaten to abandon your children.
   (m) Know and respond to danger signals in your children and get help as required.
   (n) Provide your children with structure and predictability.
   (o) Don't lead your children to believe that you may reconcile with the other parent.

(p) Calm your children's fears and help rebuild trust and security.

(q) Frequently reassure the children of your love and that you will always be there to care for them and look after their needs.

A healthy parenting pattern is about the means by which parents learn to get along. It is also about the ways loving parents relate to each of their children. Above all else, healthy parenting involves regular and predictable contact and ongoing dialogue between parents and children. The process of divorce is not only hard on the adults; it is just as hard or harder on the children. Their healthy development depends on knowing that their parents will always be there for them, that their needs will be met, and that they will continue to be loved and cherished by *both* parents. It depends also on knowing that *both* parents will continue to function as *parents*; that is, that they will behave like adults, speak honestly about the divorce, address children's fears and concerns, and maintain those family rules and routines that have given the children's lives order, structure, and meaning. Furthermore, healthy parenting involves respect for boundaries and for the relationship each child has with the other parent. Parents demonstrate such respect by speaking well of the other parent in front of the children and in *not* inquiring too closely of the children about the other parent's lifestyle, habits, and circumstances. Similarly, the children should not be burdened with keeping secrets from the other parent because this involves them in adults' affairs, nor should they be expected to care for their parents. Although parents should allow the children to speak of any difficulties they may be having with the other parent, any solutions to these difficulties should be the other parent's responsibility. Finally, as parents know well, each child is unique and may respond to the demands of the divorcing process quite differently than his or her brothers or sisters, even though they may be quite close in age. It is the responsibility of both parents to be sensitive to any danger signals indicating a child in distress and to get that child whatever help is needed.

5. To make wise, informed decisions, parents should be informed of advances in research concerning parenting in divorce.

Parenting in divorce is an emotionally charged area of experience. Consequently, it acts as a magnet for divergent opinions, positions, and advice. This state of affairs makes it possible for parents to attend selectively to those views consistent with their own while ignoring any advice with which they do not agree. Because this practice is available to both parents, it is not uncommon for parents to advance diametrically opposed views, both of which are supported by opinions cited in the scientific literature. The counterweight to contesting by opinion is to give extra weight to opinions based on empirical research, often presented in review articles. Recent reviews offer a case in point:

- Lamb, Sternberg, and Thompson (1997), for example, show that on consent, various parenting arrangements can be effective in divorce, with shared parenting offering the best opportunity for children to have a meaningful relationship with both parents.
- Kelly and Lamb (2000) show that children's requirements for a healthy attachment to their parents change with age, with frequent movements between parents with children younger than age 6 and less frequent movements with children older than 6. The authors also affirm that there is no evidence of harm in overnight visits, even with very young children.
- Warshak (2000) shows that the view that overnight visits with more than one parent is bad for children is an opinion based on no evidence whatsoever. Available evidence, much of it indirect, suggests that even in very young children, such visits promote a healthy relationship between children and both their parents.

Discussion

The idea of parenting plans involves a radical shift away from traditional views of parenting in divorce. Whereas traditional views saw divorce in terms of parental rights and the children as chattel, parenting plans are now child centered and focus on the need for children to have a loving and supportive relationship with both parents. Such plans, then, involve shifts in thought and language and require us, as family mediators, to be sensitive to a range of related issues, including child development and divorce, adult-centered parental strategies in divorce, advocacy in mediation, the decision to include or exclude children from the mediation process, first principles underpinning parenting plans, and a range of derivative practice guidelines. Taken together, consideration of these various issues is intended to highlight the twin purpose of such plans—namely, to protect the welfare of dependent children in divorce and to ensure that each and every child is accorded the maximum opportunity for healthy growth and development.

Note

1. We wish to acknowledge the contribution of Henry White (1999), a law and social work student whose unpublished paper, "Substantive Influence in Family Mediation: A Discussion of Its Normative Role," has been most helpful in the preparation of this section.

10

Parenting Plans

*Part 2: Basic Elements
and Special Circumstances*

Basic elements are those that appear in some form in *all* parenting plans, including where the children will live, how they will share time with each parent, how major decisions will be made about their care, how parents will deal with changes in circumstances, and how they will deal with future impasses. At present, several variations on such elements are available in the literature (Emery, 1994; Lyster, 1997; Ricci, 1997). The basic parenting plan advanced by the therapeutic family mediation (TFM) model encompasses eight elements, which we list in a form (see Appendix 10.1) and routinely hand out to clients. Below, we explore these elements in some detail, followed by a brief review of supplementary elements that crop up from time to time. Where applicable, additional practical guidelines will be noted. A sample parenting plan, taken from a real case, is appended to Chapter 6.

Parenting Plans: Basic Elements

Time Sharing: Routine or Daily Schedule

All plans must specify how the children will spend time with each of their parents. In the interests of clarity, we will distinguish between routine or daily schedules and holiday schedules, deferring discussion of the latter to the next section. Although preferred arrangements will certainly vary across North American jurisdictions, the five daily schedules that are the most common in our experience are the following.

3/2/2 Rotating Schedule. This schedule is organized over a 2-week interval. In Week 1, the children spend 3 days with the mother, 2 with the father, then 2 with the mother. In Week 2, the schedule rotates, beginning with 3 days with the father, 2 with the mother, and 2 with the father. Thus, the children spend equal amounts of time with each parent but with frequent shifts between them. Such shifts are designed to accommodate the urgent need of small children to spend time with both parents while having a limited ability to be apart from either parent. In such children, longer intervals apart would put these children into distress, such that the 3/2/2 schedule, although logistically demanding, is nevertheless in the children's best interest.

3/4 Rotating Schedule. This schedule is similarly organized over a 2-week interval. Here, in Week 1, the children spend 3 days with one parent and then 4 days with the other parent. In Week 2, this arrangement is reversed. This ensures that the children spend equal time with each parent. The relatively quick turnover makes this schedule particularly suitable for young children (younger than 5 years of age) who typically become distressed if they are away from either parent for more than a few days at a time. Indeed, for very young children (2 years of age or younger), intervals of only a day or two would be preferred. However, parents should be cautioned that this is a logistically demanding schedule and will require considerable flexibility on their part, especially if both parents work and so have complex schedules of their own.

5/2 Rotating Schedule. This is a less demanding schedule, and several variations are possible. In one variation, the children spend 5 days with one parent and the weekend with the other during Week 1. This reverses in Week 2, thus ensuring that the children spend equal time with each parent. In a second variation, the children spend Monday to Friday *every* week with one parent and three out of four weekends per month with the other parent. Because the 5 days correspond to the school week, this schedule is particularly appropriate for school-age children (6-9 years of age) who adapt comfortably to the longer interval away from one parent. It is also attractive to parents who work because the schedule allows each of them quality time with the children on weekends while giving each of them a break from child care and thus the opportunity for some sort of social life. In addition, the parties may choose to define "the weekend" in various ways, from Friday after school to Monday before school, from Friday after school to Sunday evening, from Saturday morning to Sunday evening, or any other variation of these days.

7/7 Alternating Schedule. In this arrangement, the children spend 7 consecutive days with one parent, followed by 7 consecutive days with the other parent. The 7-day interval may correspond to a regular school or work week, with Sunday or Monday as the transition point, or it may cross weekends, with a midweek day as the transition point. Some parents also insert a midweek break, such as an evening or an overnight with the other parent. The relatively long interval away from one parent makes this schedule suitable for older children (10 years of age or older). Of the four schedules listed thus far, this schedule is the least demanding logistically.

2/14 Alternating Schedule. In this arrangement, the children spend most of their time with one parent (the primary parent) and every second weekend with the other parent. As noted above, "weekend" time with the children may involve several variations. This is a conventional schedule often imposed by court order. Under some circumstances, weekend parenting is quite appropriate, as in cases in which peripheral fathers are content to remain so and mothers accept the burden of being the children's primary parent. However, assuming the importance of the children having a meaningful relationship with both parents (see Chapter 9, "First Principles"), this arrangement is *not* recommended because it ensures that the children are deprived of any meaningful relationship with one parent, typically their father.

Other Considerations. All parenting plans also include five additional concerns.

* *Residence.* The first concern is *where* the children will live. The usual arrangement is one in which each parent has separate accommodations, such that the children move back and forth between homes. Under special circumstances, however, parents have been known to prefer a "bird's nest" arrangement, in which the children remain in the matrimonial home and the parents move in and out for specified intervals. For this to work, both parents must have separate accommodations when they are not with the children, typically with parents or friends. This choice is usually a transitional one, for example, while one or both parents search for new accommodations as the matrimonial home is being sold. Still another variation is one in which all family members remain in the matrimonial home, with each parent "living" on different floors. This temporary variation typically remains in place while a parenting plan is being negotiated and ensures that the parent who then leaves the matrimonial home and establishes a new household is *not* seen by the courts as having "abandoned" the children.

* *Transportation.* The second concern relates to the transition process, that is, *who* is responsible for transporting the children from one parent to the other. One variation involves travel by both parents, with the resident parent responsible for transporting the children to the home of the nonresident parent. A second variation involves the use of third parties, such as teachers, day care providers, or baby-sitters from whom a parent can pick up the children or who may volunteer to transport the children to a parent. When both parents work, as is often the case, transfer can be

between third parties, for example, from a day care provider to a baby-sitter who cares for the children until a parent gets home from work. A third variation is one in which one parent is responsible for all transportation between homes. In some cases, this variation reflects the fact that only one parent has access to a vehicle and/or that the other parent has certain driving preferences, such as avoiding any nighttime travel. More often, this variation reflects an unequal relationship between the parents.

- *Timing.* The third concern relates to the timing of transition points, that is, *when* transitions are scheduled to occur. Most child-sharing schedules reflect parents' work schedules, the children's school schedule, or both. Consequently, pickup and drop-off times are typically before school, after work, or both. More variations can be found when transitions occur on the weekend. In all cases, transition points (a) usually refer to specific times, such as 8 a.m.; (b) include some definition of what *late* means, with *on time* often referring to a 10- to 15-minute interval (such as 8:00 to 8:15 a.m.) rather than a point in time, to take account of unexpected delays; (c) assume "due notice" when the parent doing the pickup or drop-off is going to be late; and (d) include some understanding about what is to happen at transition (e.g., that the children will be ready to go; that any conversation between the parents be of a limited duration, such as 5 or 10 minutes; and that such conversations be confined to matters concerning the children) (see below).

- *Conduct.* The fourth concern refers to the *conduct* of parents in interaction at transition points. Among parents in conflict, transitions in which parents meet each other face-to-face can be points of tension. That tension can be considerably reduced if both parents commit to conduct that is in keeping with parenting guidelines (see Chapter 9, this volume) and, as such, is mutually respectful and business-like. The focus of such transitions should be on child transfer rather than problem solving, conflict management, or the airing of grievances (see "Shared Decision Making," below). Consequently, transition points should deliberately be brief, with the pickup or drop-off parent on time and with the resident parent having the children ready to go and dressed in seasonally appropriate clothing.

- *Parenting continuity.* The final issue relates to the *content* of conversation during transition points and highlights the importance of *parenting continuity.* Parents in conflict have often broken off communication by the time they enter family mediation. Rather than parenting together, they are actually parenting in parallel. This is often dysfunctional and makes for very inefficient parenting. It is also very hard on the children because both parents must start over with the children, unaware of what has transpired in their absence. Children benefit from knowing their parents are talking about them and care enough to share information about them. To begin the arduous task of re-creating dialogue between parents, transition points can offer an ideal opportunity. Accordingly, at each transition, the resident parent may be required to list for the other parent, in summary form, the highlights of the children's time with him or her. These highlights can vary widely, concerning time at home, time at school, time with friends, time with relatives, health issues, and so on. The other parent is to receive this report *without comment*, save for any clarifying questions and a brief "thank you" for the information (see "Parental Communication," below).

Time Sharing: Holiday or Special Events Schedule

Family daily routine is broken up by holidays and various special events. Among school-age children, holidays include summer vacation and various statutory or religious holidays such as Christmas, Easter, and Thanksgiving. Special events may be tied to quasi-official events, such as Mother's/Father's Day and March break or Halloween, or may be family related, such as birthdays or anniversaries. Special events may also be tied to cultural norms and conventions (Benjamin, 1996). In divorce, families can vary widely as to which of these holidays and special events they choose to honor; however, it would be quite rare for families to honor none. Conversely, for many couples in mediation, the organization of these special times is often hotly contested. Indeed, it would not be uncommon, for example, for litigation to focus on child sharing during Christmas. Thus, holidays and special events are a standard feature of parenting plans, and four variations in sharing arrangements are commonplace.

Annual Rotation. One variation involves annual rotation. For example, in Year 1, the children may spend Christmas Eve with the mother, Christmas Day and Boxing Day with the father, and New Year's Day with the mother. In Year 2, the arrangement reverses, with the children spending Christmas Eve with the father and so on. In addition, holiday schedules come with an important proviso—namely, that for specified holidays or special events, the regular schedule is suspended. This is important because otherwise conflict can erupt because these special events fall on the mother's or father's "regular days." Because rotating schedules cross years, use of a 16-month calendar to mark off the days can avoid later confusion or conflict.

Annual Alteration. A second variation involves annual alteration. For example, in Year 1, the children will go out for Halloween with the mother. In Year 2, they will go out with the father. Alteration, then, is logistically less complex than rotation and requires less interaction between the parents. However, it also involves less contact between the children and each parent and is thus less desirable from a developmental perspective. In practical terms, the choice between rotation and alteration usually turns on the degree to which parents can tolerate interaction between each other.

Sequential Arrangements. A third variation involves sequential contact between the parents and the children, with or without rotation. For example, a given family may have a Christmas tradition of visiting with relatives. Because the children cannot be at two places at one time, a sequential arrangement may be created in which the children visit with the mother's relatives in the morning, perhaps staying for lunch, and then move on to the father's relatives in the afternoon, perhaps staying for supper. In a related example, the children may remain in one neighborhood for Halloween, with the mother walking with them from 6 to 7 p.m., at which time the father takes over and walks with them from 7 to 8 p.m. These sequential arrangement may remain fixed, year on year, or they may rotate. For example, in the case of Halloween, the sequence may remain fixed, but the neighborhoods may rotate annually—first the mother's, then the father's.

Combined Arrangements. Finally, couples may assign different priorities to different holidays or special events, resulting in a mixed set of arrangements. For example, it would not be uncommon to use a sequential arrangement for summer holidays (each parent entitled to 2 consecutive weeks with the children), a rotating arrangement for long holidays (such as Christmas), and an alternating arrangement for special events (such as Halloween). Although negotiating such mixed arrangements can be time-consuming and tedious for the mediator, it is nevertheless necessary, both as a way of showing respect for client priorities and as a way of reducing conflict on occasions that should be enjoyable for the entire family, especially the children.

Due Notice. Finally, some occasions will require advanced notice from one parent to the other. For example, the precise time at which each parent takes his or her summer vacation may vary year on year. To avoid confusion and possible overlap, each parent will be asked to notify the other of vacation plans 6 to 8 weeks in advance and often in writing. The same applies should such plans involve foreign travel. Here, notice should be accompanied by a written itinerary, including dates, places, and emergency telephone numbers. Such requests for information should not be seen as intrusive, only prudent in the case of unforeseen events. Furthermore, note that the parent doing the traveling will typically require a consent letter from the other parent to clear customs.

Shared Decision Making

On the assumption that both parents are competent, minor, daily decisions will be the responsibility of the resident parent alone, with no need to consult or inform the other parent. However, three areas of child care are generally held to involve major decisions that require the involvement of *both* parents: *education, health care,* and *religious instruction.*

- *Executive and routine decision making.* In two-parent families, the parents—*and only the parents*—are the executives charged with making decisions about all important matters affecting the children. Although parents can and should consult the children as to their wishes and opinions, as well as others (such as teachers, grandparents, and friends), the final decision is theirs and theirs alone. Furthermore, the process of arriving at such decisions should be held strictly in private and certainly out of the earshot of the children. Once such decisions have been arrived at, they will be conveyed to the children on the understanding that they are *no longer negotiable.* This approach to decision making recognizes that too often children become part of the power struggle between parents, and they are simply unequipped to avoid being caught in a loyalty bind. On one hand, parents are often unaware of such binds, simply blaming the other parent for their irresponsible behavior. On the other hand, such binds can be highly destructive of children. The rule of executive decision making is intended to remove the children from the loop. That said, child involvement in age- and gender-appropriate decisions facilitates their normal development. The notion of *routine* decisions attempts to capture this aspect of child rearing. Thus, although children would never be asked if they want a medical operation, they could be asked to choose between a teddy bear and a toy truck as the toy they want to take with them to the hospital. Similarly, they might be asked to choose between a red T-shirt and a green T-shirt when they are choosing their clothes for school the next day. Thus, parents set the limits, but the children are free to act within these limits. This arrangement makes for clear rules of authority within families of divorce, with parents alone responsible for major decisions and children responsible for those minor decision that affect them. Furthermore, children's routine decisions should become increasingly significant with advancing age and maturity. Among teenagers, for example, executive decision making will gradually shade into intergenerational negotiation. This is an entirely appropriate way to teach children about responsible decision making, such that they will be ready to take on this responsibility in adulthood.

- *Boundaries.* In moving to separate households, parents create boundaries around their new family system, that is, each parent together with the children. On the assumption that both parents are competent, they should then be free to run their household as they see fit, without interference or intrusion from the other parent. That freedom includes lifestyle choices, family values, and daily practices, such as the choice of meal plans, bedtimes, bathing frequency, and allowable times for television and homework. Moreover, differences on any of these matters, although they may be offensive to one or both parents, will *not* place the children at risk and are well within the normal range. Thus, however difficult it may appear at first, both parents must come to terms with these differences and must accord the other parent the freedom to parent as he or she wishes. The key proviso here is that any such arrangements do *not* place the children at risk. On evidence of the latter, the issue requires an executive decision, based on negotiation between the parents.

- *Education.* For clients with toddlers, educational concerns focus on day care and baby-sitting. With school-age children, the focus shifts to academic programs, remedial programs, academic achievement, relations with teachers and other school staff, and the choice of school catchment area. With adolescents, the focus shifts again to vocational concerns, college preparation, college funding, and the transition from one school system to another (see "Extracurricular Activities," below). Each of these issues involves shared responsibility, as well as the need for parental dialogue and negotiation, and thus is a potential site for conflict. For example, it is preferable that parents attend parent-teacher meetings together, though separate meetings can be arranged if need be. The consent of both parents will be required should the children require remedial help and/or testing. The same will be true for vocational or special programs, such as driver's education. It is important that children *not* be used as couriers between parents, such that each parent should make his or her own independent arrangements to get school notices, report cards, school records, and the like. Continuity is also to the children's advantage as regards homework and work on special assignments or projects. All of these issues *require* parental cooperation in the best interests of the children. Creating a parenting plan will involve walking parents through these and other, more specialized issues concerned with education.

- *Health care.* A second area of joint decision making concerns health care. Care of minor injuries or illnesses will be the responsibility of the resident parent alone. However, both parents should be informed of their children's medical records, medical and dental appointments, and medical and dental treatments, including drugs and antibiotics, orthodontic or endodontic care, specialized nutritional regimens, and the need for invasive treatments, such as surgery. As much as possible, both parents should be involved in medical decision making, although the resident parent should be invested with the authority to make emergency decisions regarding the children's health care. Furthermore, treatment regimens absolutely require parenting continuity and thus mutual cooperation. For example, a 10-day antibiotic regimen means that the medicine travels with the children from one household to the other. More generally, parents should apply the following guideline: *The children's best interest supersedes routine time-sharing arrangements; children who are ill should not be made to travel, and parents who are ill should not receive their children, whether or not it is "their" time with them.* In practice, this means that sick children do *not* transport well and should be left in the care of the resident parent, even if this disrupts the routine time-sharing arrangement temporarily. The same is true when parents are ill and may infect the children who are supposed to come into their care. In both cases, such unexpected changes typically do *not* involve makeup time because they can occur when the children are with either parent, although makeup time may be offered on consent.

• *Religious instruction.* Religious instruction is a third area where both parents should be involved in decision making. The gradual decline of religion across North America means that, in many cases, parental religious affiliation will be nominal. For these clients, religious instruction does not become a major issue in dispute, with both parents usually in agreement that both will be free to instruct the children in keeping with the religious affiliation in place prior to the separation. Similarly, among families that are more traditional, both parents can agree to carry on the religious tradition in place prior to the divorce. However, among the latter, and especially among those who are more devout, religious instruction can raise a series of hotly contested issues, including the regularity of attendance at religious services, the particular location of religious worship, and the identity of those providing religious instruction. One variation involves families marked by religious conversion (e.g., a Christian woman who converts to marry a Jewish man) or reversion to the person's original faith. Another variation involves devout parents who, on divorce, choose either a less religious form of worship within the same faith or reject the faith altogether. Such cases invariably prove difficult in mediation, given conflict rooted in values whose divergence resists normal compromises. This is true more generally, for it is difficult for parents to find a middle ground where value-based differences are concerned, whether the details refer to child-related education, health care, or religious instruction. In such cases, we have found it useful to contrast mediated as opposed to litigated outcomes. However difficult the necessary compromises and however important mutual respect for boundaries, at least in mediation parents have control over the outcome. By contrast, in litigation, they are rendered helpless, at the mercy of an adjudicator who may not share their values. Furthermore, such cases also illustrate instances in which consulting religious authorities can be worthwhile. In a recent case, a mother claimed that the complex set of restrictions she wished to impose on the father's time with the children was required by her religion. When this was denied by a religious authority she respected, she moderated her demands, and a compromise solution was negotiated that was acceptable to both parties.

Parental Communication

By the time they enter mediation, it is commonplace that parents have broken off communication altogether. They may have done so because, more and more, every effort at dialogue quickly transformed into destructive conflict and impasse. Such conflict is not only exhausting, depressing, and highly stressful but also very hard on the children. Parenting continuity goes by the wayside, parents are less emotionally available to the children than they were previously, and the children may be caught in a bind as each parent rails at the other in front of the children. Such problems are subject to several different solutions in mediation.

• *Parental conduct.* The key reason clients enter mediation is because they are unable to resolve matters informally between them. This is typically so insofar as all such efforts quickly dissolve into uncontrolled conflict, with little or nothing accomplished. Such lack of control is characterized by the use of extreme language, the use of threats ("comply with my wishes or I'm going to court"), cross-talk (both parties talking at the same time), and "bad-faith" bargaining on the assumption that neither party's word can be trusted. Teaching the clients the guidelines reviewed above (see Chapter 9, "Practical Guidelines") and enforcing their use in mediation immediately reduce conflict in session and, more important, give the clients an opportunity to talk informally between sessions. In one case, the parties readily admitted that they were unable to talk together, either on the telephone or in person, without shouting, swearing, and causing much distress. By the third joint session, with the guidelines in place throughout, they reported their first "civil" conversation over the telephone in more than a year. Praise for this important accomplishment was lavish and doubly preempted; that is, they were warned that episodes of negative affect should be expected in the future while the parties were simultaneously characterized as "different people now than when you entered mediation" such that they would be able to approach conflict in a constructive manner, without taking it personally or resorting to attack, threats, or shouting, as they had routinely done in the past.

• *Marital versus parenting issues.* Despite the use of child-related rhetoric, struggles between parents often have little to do with parenting per se and much to do with a marital struggle for control that often predates the divorce. The divorce has merely served to heighten the struggle and increased the stakes, thus encouraging extreme conduct on both sides. Citing the guidelines concerning language and mutual respect and providing illustrative examples from their own struggle can often, and for the first time, place the ongoing conflict between them in perspective for parents, especially as regards its destructive impact on the children. Helping parents reaffirm their desire to love and protect their children—and the guilt they feel at having failed to do so—can be a powerful lever for change, with the guidelines offering them an alternative approach to various parenting issues.

• *Plan revision.* The parenting plan is one way parents attempt to respond to the individual needs of their children. With growing children, such needs change year on year, often with dramatic differences across children through time. A 4-year-old is a very different person from a 2-year-old. Charting these differences and having them reflected in a changing parenting plan necessitates ongoing dialogue between the parents. In the absence of such dialogue, rigid adherence to a plan will eventually render that plan actively destructive of their children. This reasoning has twin implications for parental dialogue: It must occur on some regular basis, and it must cover the spectrum of child care issues, *not* only those that are currently proving problematic.

- *Regulating contact.* In light of the guidelines, parents are asked to specify the frequency and method of parental dialogue. For example, parents may agree to meet on a face-to-face basis once per month to review the plan and negotiate any changes that seem to them to be warranted. Such meeting would be bolstered by brief chats at each transition point and by an annual meeting used to review the plan in detail. Telephone contact may also be used to deal with unexpected events as well as changes to planned events occasioned by work, illness, weather, and family. In short, regulating parental contact is one way of acknowledging that sharing parenting arrangements involves hard work, cooperation, understanding, flexibility, and thus relatively frequent parental dialogue. The irony of this statement is not lost on many divorced parents, who may find themselves interacting more often in divorce than they did while they were still married!

- *Communication book.* For parents who are simply unable to tolerate direct interaction or who find such interaction problematic, a communication book can be very useful. Roughly the shape of a "steno pad," such books can be used to contain all manner of information about the children, from their immunization record to the names and telephone numbers of their friends. However, its primary purpose is to provide a means of communication between parents. Here, they can list upcoming events in the children's lives (from school plays to soccer games to academic test grades), the highlights of their time with the resident parent, and important family occasions (such as birthdays, anniversaries, family visits, family outings, etc.). In other words, the communication book can be used either *in place* of direct communication between parents or as an adjunct to such communication.

- *Parent-child communication.* Irrespective of the time-sharing schedule, children should be accorded the opportunity to communicate with the other parent while they are staying with the resident parent. They may do so on the telephone, by fax, and/or by e-mail. Depending on the children's age, such access may be unlimited (on demand) or scheduled for specific days and times. In either case, communication schedules should be mindful of household routines around mealtimes, bedtimes, bathing, homework, playtime, and so on. It may be initiated by the other parent or left to the children. That said, such communication may be problematic. Parents may label such efforts as "intrusive" and attempt to dramatically restrict any such contact. One parent may attempt to bypass the other parent by "generously" offering to install a private telephone line directly into the children's bedroom. Others may attempt to secretly or openly tape-record conversations between the children and the other parents for later use in court, despite the fact that it is illegal to do so in many jurisdictions. Any such efforts have little to do with parenting and much to do with a marital struggle for control over the children. The mediator should label these efforts appropriately and can confront them on the basis of several guidelines listed in Chapter 9. Most important, such efforts, witting or unwitting, inevitably suck the children into the marital struggle and are thus highly destructive of their psychological well-being.

Extracurricular Events and Activities

Extracurricular events and activities are a regular feature of the lives of many children. However, in families in which parents live apart, such activities can pose logistical and monetary challenges. In turn, such activities can constitute a fertile breeding ground for conflict between parents. To avoid such conflict requires careful planning, good communication, and clear rules of engagement.

Week-Over-Week Arrangements and Mutual Consent. Family boundaries mean that both parents should be able to raise their children as they see fit *on their own time,* free of interference from the other parent. In the area of extracurricular activities, this reasoning suggests the following guideline—namely, that *neither parent may commit to week-over-week activities for the children except on mutual consent.* Thus, each parent should be free to enroll the children in any *one* activity without the other parent's consent, providing (a) the children are willing to become involved, (b) it does not place the children at physical or emotional risk (i.e., it is appropriate to the children's age and ability level), and (c) the activity is confined to that parent's time with the children. To do otherwise would be to violate the guideline concerning respect for boundaries. Moreover, each parent's choice is limited to one activity to avoid inadvertently overburdening the children. However, this clearly limits the activities in which the children may become involved. Many activities, such as sports or dance or music, for example, require weekly attendance and thus cross week-over-week boundaries. To proceed, such activities require *mutual consent* that can only arise out of mutual dialogue.

Scheduling. Dialogue must not only ensure mutual commitment to the activity but also establish a clear and specific schedule of mutual involvement. For example, each parent may agree to take the children to the activity while he or she is the resident parent, leaving the other parent to attend on a purely voluntary basis. Similarly, the resident parent may also be obliged to obtain information about activity schedules or participate in car pooling activities, and the names and telephone numbers of coaches, instructors, and other parents will be needed for this parent's own use, with no obligation to pass such information on to the other parent.

- *Executive decision making.* Parents often have strong feelings about the activities that are or are not good for their children. One parent may stress the importance of artistic expression and therefore prefer ballet or music lessons. Another parent may highlight the importance of teamwork and cooperation and thus prefer team sports. Both preferences are entirely legitimate and should be the subject of negotiation between them. Such negotiation may *not* be problematic, as different children may themselves have different tastes, preferences, and/or abilities. The cost of these activities may also limit the parent's choices. So as not to overburden the children, activities may be selected on an annual rotation basis—an artistic activity in one year, a sporting activity in another, and so on. Furthermore, the children and others (such as coaches or teachers) may be consulted ahead of time as to their preferences and the children's abilities. Thus, while children can and should be consulted as to their preferences, it will be important that the final decision be confined to discussion among the parents. Once the decision is made, it can then be conveyed to the children as a nonnegotiable choice, as in "Mommy and Daddy have talked together and have decided. . . ." Unfortunately, in an attempt to gain leverage for their preference, parents may involve the children in such decisions. For example, one parent, having persuaded the children to his or her preference, can then form an alliance with the children against the other parent and without his or her knowledge. The other parent is thus set up to become the "bad parent" unless he or she complies with the other parent's wishes, for to do otherwise would be to disappoint the children. In another variation, the parent may actually enroll the children in his or her preferred activity and then present it as a *fait accompli* to the other parent. In rationalizing these actions, parents invariably use the rhetoric of children's best interest. However, to the extent that their actions promote conflict between parents and between the other parent and the children, the underlying motive has little to do with parenting but much to do with a struggle for control in the marital relationship. Placing the children at the center of this struggle puts them at risk and is thus manifestly destructive of their psychological well-being. Teaching parents the applicable guidelines is the mediator's way of naming the underlying dynamic and of organizing their relationship in ways that will protect the children and minimize conflict between the parents.

Unexpected Events

Despite carefully laid plans for sharing the children, life sometimes intervenes. Business trips may arise unexpectedly, baby-sitters or day care providers are unavailable, severe weather or labor disruptions block scheduled vacations, and so on. Although parenting plans cannot anticipate every conceivable event, they can be used to set out guidelines and procedures that *anticipate* this class of event, thus reducing conflict when they inevitably occur.

- *Parents as preferred caregivers.* Parents often lead complex lives, such that other caregivers may need to be called in, either routinely or on an occasional basis. Sometimes, these caregivers may be family members, especially grandparents or aunt and uncles. Other times, they may take the form of day care providers or baby-sitters. There is no question that in most cases, they provide perfectly adequate care. However, their choice may be problematic when it is made merely to fulfill the obligations of the resident parent, while the other parent is ready and willing to take up the responsibility, despite the fact that he or she is *not* obliged to do so. Thus, the choice of caregiver does *not* turn on the quality of care but rather on the quality of the parent-child relationship. Maintaining or enhancing that relationship will be to the children's developmental advantage. It follows that when a choice is available *on a purely voluntary basis*, parents should be preferred over other caregivers. However, we should stress that that preference is not an obligation. One of the key advantages of a shared parenting arrangement is that each parent has some time away from the children. Furthermore, it is increasingly the case that both parents work, often making the need for third-party caregivers unavoidable. Even when the other parent is available to take the children, he or she may not wish to do so. Under these conditions, a third-party caregiver is the obvious choice. However, when the other parent is available during the parent's time with the children and would be willing to take the children, the other parent should be preferred as the children's caregiver.

- *"Right of first refusal."* Consider the case in which, for any number of reasons, the parent scheduled to receive the children is unable to do so. The resident parent who has them is then given the opportunity to keep them in the other parent's absence. This is known as the "right of first refusal." The parent who has the children can agree to continue to care for them or refuse to do so, having plans or obligations that would otherwise be disrupted. Should this parent refuse, the other parent is then obliged to make alternative care arrangements at his or her own expense, with no right to compensation or makeup time (although makeup time may nevertheless be offered). The same applies when the resident parent must cut short his or her time with the children, perhaps because of a family, social, or business obligation. The absence may be for an evening, a day or two, or even longer. This parent would then invoke the "right of first refusal," informing the other parent of the planned absence and offering him or her the opportunity to be with the children while this parent is gone. Generally, the right of first refusal does not apply for brief absences—the parent who will be 2 hours late from work—when baby-sitters are a legitimate source of alternate child care.

- *Due notice.* The parent who is making the unilateral change in the schedule is obliged to give the other parent as much notice of the change as possible, under the circumstances. He or she is also obliged to ensure that such "unexpected" changes occur rarely. So long as this is so, resident parents should be flexible and understanding, for life is just like that from time to time and will apply equally to both of them. However, should such changes become increasingly predictable, an executive decision should be made either to change the time-sharing schedule or have the other parent change the circumstances that would make such changes necessary. For example, it is unreasonable to have the resident parent take responsibility for the other parent's social life (see "Special Circumstances," below).

Moving Households

A common feature of parents' complex lives is the occasional need to move from one household to another. Understandably, long-distance moves can materially affect the time-sharing arrangement and thus can become the focus of intensive negotiation, if not heated dispute. Consequently, such moves have become the subject of much case law, under the rubric of "relocation" in the United States (Galper-Cohen, 1989; Rotman, Tomkins, & Schwartz, 2000; Saposnek, 1998, pp. 279-283; Schwartz & Kaslow, 1997) or "mobility" in Canada (Irving & Benjamin, 1996; Landau et al., 2000, pp. 125-128). Understandably, such cases can be highly contentious. That said, the frequency with which such enter mediation is likely to vary widely across jurisdictions. In our experience, such cases are unusual in mediation. Rather, the couples we encounter either have no intention of moving, or the residential moves involve short distances (less than 20 miles) and so pose no threat to their routine time-sharing arrangement. Consequently, moving tends to arise more as a hypothetical rather than a real issue and can be dealt with readily and in a straightforward manner.

• *Due notice.* Clients typically agree to provide each other with 90 days' written notice of their intention to move. This is usually a formality. In practice, most parents will know that the other parent intends to move long before it is due to occur and have already discussed its impact, if any, on their current plan to share the responsibility for the children. Given the relatively short distances involved, the impact of any such moves would, at most, add 15 or 20 minutes to the parents' travel time, as the children continue to move between their two households.

• *"Consult" versus "consent."* Given the hypothetical character of this issue for most parents, they have the option of different sorts of language in their plan. Their agreement to "consult" following news of a planned move is merely their way of acknowledging that each parent is free to move if he or she chooses to do so, and both parents will discuss any changes needed to their time-sharing arrangement. Alternately, they may both wish to ensure the continuity of their sharing arrangement by, in effect, giving each parent the right to "veto" any such move if one feels it will adversely affect the sharing arrangement. In that case, they will both agree that any proposed move can occur if and only if they receive the "consent" of the other parent. Still another alternative is to establish an arbitrary limit beyond which neither parent may move without the other parent's written consent, often within the 10- to 20-mile range.

• *Long-distance moves.* Occasionally, one or the other parent does contemplate a move that will materially affect the shared plan then in place. Such moves raise two sorts of issues for the mediator: Is it in the best interests of the children? Can some new time-sharing arrangement preserve the relationship between the children and both parents? Disruption of a close relationship between a parent and a child places that child at risk. Thus, long-distance moves raise a series of questions for the mediator: What is the quality of the relationship between the children and the parent who is moving? Will the move necessarily disrupt that parent's relationship with the children? Or will it disrupt the children's relationship with the other parent (the parent who is moving proposes to take the children with him or her)? Is there some way to preserve the children's relationship with both parents under some changed time-sharing schedule? If the answer is no, than the issue turns on the best interests of the children, for in our view moves that are likely to harm the children should be prohibited. If the answer is yes, then what sort of new arrangement would allow the move but protect the relationship between the children and both parents?

Impasse-Breaking Mechanism

Finally, impasses can arise in mediation in two different contexts. First, impasses can occur while mediation is ongoing. In addition to the techniques listed in Chapter 3, a series of guidelines can also assist in breaking impasses. Second, after leaving mediation with an agreement and having gotten on with their lives, parents may still be unable to agree and thus reach impasse. Whereas previously such an impasse would automatically have triggered a litigated solution, in mediation that solution is usually seen as a last resort. The objective of the mediator is to offer clients alternative options.

• *Children and lifestyle choices.* It is often the case that parents in conflict confuse children's best interest with differences in lifestyles. Among other things, children's best interest refers to risk or harm, either in the immediate present or over the long term. Abusive conduct by a parent creates that risk in the present. Putting a child in a loyalty bind creates that risk in the long run. If it can be shown that neither risk applies, then the conflict centers on a difference in lifestyle. How much television the children watch, how much "junk food" they consume, whether their clothes are color coordinated, and whether they go to bed at 7:30 p.m. as opposed to 9:00 p.m. are often interpreted by parents in dispute as crucial issues bearing on the children's best interests. In one case, for example, a father was adamant that the child should only receive "organic" milk; in another case, a mother was deeply upset that the father did not feed the children enough green vegetables. In fact, there is absolutely no evidence that variation across any of these issues involves any risk whatsoever. Rather, they reflect lifestyle choices that each parent should be free to make and that the other parent should respect, based on the new boundaries around their respective households. Invoking this guideline can offer the mediator some leverage in breaking impasses. In the cases noted above, the father grudgingly accepted that the child would receive "organic" milk only while the child was with him, and mother reluctantly acknowledged that missing some green vegetables would not result in the child's death or long-term disability.

- *Children's and adults' sense of fairness.* Impasses often arise based on parents' different interpretations of what is "fair" under the circumstances. "You had them last year, so I should have them this year," one parent will argue. "But you gave them up last year voluntarily and in contravention of the prevailing parenting plan. I should not be punished for being so accommodating," the other parent replies. "The children should come with me." Such disputes around what is "fair" are commonplace in mediation and provide reasonable bases for ongoing negotiation. However, as the conflict escalates and each side digs in its heels, with no decision forthcoming, the children can begin to suffer. The joyous Christmas they were looking forward to is put on hold or, worse, the children can be directly involved in the conflict, being asked to take one "side" or the other. Here, ordinarily useful notions of *fair* conflict with the best interests of the children. When that occurs, the best interests of the children should be seen as paramount, with one or both parents asked to "swallow" some form of agreement whose terms they perceive as unfair but in which the cessation of hostilities serves the best interests of the children.

- *Letting go of past hurts.* Despite our routine admonition to "leave the past in the past," it is commonplace for each parent to blame the other for some previous hurt, real or imagined. Such perceptions actively interfere with ongoing efforts at negotiation while driving conflict in the present, up to and including impasse. Given that such hurts are now a fixed feature of their shared past and that parents may be locked in conflict through their children for as much as 20 years, mutual forgiveness and healing are crucial to their long-term commitment to shared responsibility in parenting.

- *Family mediation.* Turning to hypothetical impasses in the future, one alternative is to have the couple return to family mediation. Here, parents agree to use the skills they have already learned in mediation to attempt to break the impasse themselves. Failing that, they agree to reenter family mediation, often (but not necessarily) with the same mediator who helped them create their original parenting plan. Once in mediation, all of the guidelines set out in Chapter 9 and this chapter would apply, as would the distinction between premediation and negotiation. That is, in accord with the principles underpinning the TFM model, the mediator would first address the relational or personal dynamics underpinning the conflict and only then turn to the substantive issues in dispute. Assessment in such cases typically reveals the operation of one of three processes: The mediator has made an error and failed to address some underlying process in the original mediation, the couple require further and perhaps more extensive training in effective communication and/or negotiation, or, in the fullness of time, some new, dysfunctional process has evolved in relations between the spouses. In any case, the likelihood of achieving an agreement with couples who have agreed previously is very high.

•   *Mediation/arbitration.* Although the odds are in the mediator's favor, it is still possible that the parents may fail to agree. To allow them to get on with their lives while preserving the gains made in the previous parenting plan, the couple may then opt to have the mediator act as an arbitrator. Arbitrators adjudicate binding decisions on specific issues. Here, based on the parents' faith and trust in the mediator, they agree to have him or her decide the issue after having given both parents the opportunity to fully explain their perspective on the issue, including their preferred solution(s). Having heard the adjudicator's decision and his or her underlying rationale, both parents agree to comply with it, with neither objection nor resentment, for the sake of the children. In many situations, such settlements, despite the fact that they are imposed, bring closure and allow both parents to move on with their respective lives.

•   *Litigation.* Finally, parents may refuse the arbitration option and instead insist that failure in mediation will lead to litigation. Given that parents who have previously been in litigation have invariably described the experience in traumatic terms, their decision to leave the option open speaks to the continued lack of trust between these parents. On one hand, an effective parenting plan will help these parents reestablish trust, based on repeated positive experience. In that light, parents will be free to amend their parenting plan informally and may in the future prefer mediation/arbitration to litigation. On the other hand, the utility of any parenting plan is necessarily limited to the parents' commitment to it. Thus, even among couples who opt for mediation/arbitration, the litigation option is never permanently closed. In the face of some untoward event or circumstances in their lives, the parent who insists on his or her day in court should have this opportunity, given that mediation is no longer appropriate. Although the mediator may regret that choice, his or her responsibility is to have done the very best by each client couple and to respect and support parental decisions.

Special Circumstances

Families entering mediation are alike in many respects, hence the list of standard elements discussed above. However, they are also different or unique in a variety of ways. These unique issues must also be reflected in their parenting plan. Bases of family variation in divorce are so wide that very large lists of such elements would be needed to cover them all. However, a handful of elements comes up with sufficient regularity that they deserve special mention here.

Graduated Schedules

Standard time-sharing schedules have been described above. Here, we will address a special type of schedule, the graduated schedule. In it, one parent, typically the father, spends increasing amounts of time with his children in accordance with a graduated schedule. Such schedules will typically apply in three contexts.

One context involves a parent's irresponsible behavior that has placed the children at risk in the past. The risk may be such that the court will permit that parent to reconnect with the children only under supervised access. In response to such cases, access centers have begun to spring up across North America (Pearson & Thoennes, 2000). Such families enter mediation to discuss what they would like to see happen after the period of supervised access is over. Here is where the graduated schedule applies. In a recent case, for example, the parents negotiated a 2-year schedule in which the father would gradually spend more and more time with his son, first in a public place and only later in a private setting, the father's own home. Concurrently, he agreed to complete an 8-week course in parenting and another in anger management. Only with this schedule and these courses in place would the mother consent to a time-sharing arrangement with father.

In another case, a mother admitted that she was an alcoholic who could not guarantee the children's safety when she was under the influence. Accordingly, a graduated schedule was developed that would see the mother have increasing contact with the children over a 12-month period. Concurrently, she agreed to enter an alcoholic treatment program, refrain from drinking within 48 hours of seeing the children, refrain from drinking while the children were with her, and submit to a urine test to prove her sobriety within 24 hours of seeing the children.

In both cases, the at-risk parent understood that a single instance of misconduct would terminate the parenting plan and, with it, any hope of further contact with their children.

Two additional contexts in which graduated schedules can be useful include parental incompetence and parenting mistrust. The former case involves parents who were uninvolved with parenting while the marriage was intact. In divorce, these parents now fear that they will completely lose contact with their children. However, their typical demands for shared parenting are problematic insofar as they lack competence in child care. The graduated schedule recognizes the benefits to the children's involvement with both parents while giving them time to acquire the requisite skills.

The latter case, parenting mistrust, involves couples in which the level of mistrust is such that they would ordinarily prefer a litigated solution. In mediation, one way to overcome their mutual mistrust is to give them sufficient time to see firsthand that their parenting plan can be effective. The graduated schedule is the means to that end.

Grandparents

There is increasing recognition that grandparents can play an important role in the lives of their grandchildren (Emery, 1994, pp. 56-57, 159-160). Indeed, in some cases, they may have been the primary caregiver. However, arranging for their involvement can be problematic; the split between the parents may effectively cut off one set of grandparents, with negative consequences for child development. In recent years, this issue has become less pressing with the increasing popularity of shared parenting arrangements. With both parents accepting responsibility for child care, the involvement of both sets of grandparents has been increasingly accepted. The problem centers on the extent to which grandparents are tarred with the same brush used to paint the other parent in negative terms. For example, mothers may charge fathers as having been too involved with their own parents, thus rendering the grandparents a "bad" influence on the children.

One solution is to invoke the boundary rule whereby each parent is free to raise the children as he or she sees fit, including the continued involvement of the grandparents *on that parent's time*. Another solution is to argue in favor of shared responsibility, with grandparents seen as adjunct parents. A third possibility involves distinguishing between best interests and lifestyle choices, such that benefits to the children of the involvement of their grandparents outweigh objections based on lifestyle differences. In general, then, grandparent involvement is in the children's long-term best interest. However, that said, application of this sentiment in specific families must be predicated on careful intake assessment because specific grandparents can indeed behave in ways that are destructive, rendering their involvement contraindicated (Johnston & Campbell, 1988).

New Partners

Among the issues in contention between divorcing parents, the involvement of a new partner can be especially contentious. This issue involves twin concerns—namely, the *means* by which these relationships arise and the *fears* that such relationships promote. That is, new partners may become involved in family affairs in one of three ways, each of which is associated with different fears.

The first and by far the most traumatic is as a partner to an affair that may have been one of the catalysts responsible for the breakdown of the marriage (Maslin, 1994; Spring, 1996). In such cases, the victimized parent is often intensely angry and hurt by the other parent's betrayal while suffering a deep sense of loss and sadness by the disruption of the relationship. In response, he or she may be unwilling even to consider having the new partner come anywhere near his or her children. There also may be some concerns about the other parent's conduct with the new partner, such as overt sexuality, which may be harmful if witnessed by the children.

As we saw in Chapter 8, another variation may crop up after the separation, when a stable arrangement is threatened by the new romantic involvement of one of the parents. In this context, the new romantic relationship reawakens feelings of attachment in the other parent, feelings that they themselves may not have been aware were there. Standard fears here include the possibility that the new partner will take the place of the corresponding parent in the eyes of the children. This fear is especially prominent in fathers whose former partners have new romantic attachments. The other common fear is that the children may have been exposed to the new partner too quickly, when the stability of the new relationship has not yet been established. In this situation, the children may be put at risk, becoming attached to the new partner only to lose that connection when the relationship breaks down. Such losses, coming on the heals of the divorce, can be destructive of children's long-term well-being (Wallerstein et al., 2000).

The third variation is one in which both parents may each develop a romantic relationship with a new partner. In one sense, this can be the least threatening of the three variations because it is bilateral and thus the most stable. In another sense, this variation can prove the most problematic, especially if both sets of parents have remarried or are living together. Such arrangements accord the new partner a new legitimacy as the children's new stepparent. As we have seen in Chapter 8, third parties can have considerable power to influence the conduct of the parents. In so doing, they may deliberately or unwittingly promote the aims of mediation or interfere with them.

These variations raise a complex set of issues for mediation and will require the full range of practice methods and techniques if they are to be dealt with effectively:

•   Trauma can be dealt with using a combination of diminishing and ordeal methods, and both parties will typically benefit from intensive support.

- Conflict can be reduced by expanding on the notion of boundaries. In this context, each parent has a right to a new partner and does not require the consent of the other parent. So long as the relationship between the parent and his or her new partner does *not* place the children at risk, that relationship can proceed as the participants see fit. Indeed, in many cases, the presence of a stepparent may offer good support for the children by complementing the practices of both parents.

- Conflict can be further reduced by referring to the notion of executive decision making. For example, any conduct on the part of the parent and the new partner that is seen as placing the children at risk requires an executive decision and thus dialogue and negotiation. Similarly, the time-sharing schedule is each parent's assurance that he or she will not be supplanted in the children's mind and heart.

- Reference to the children's developmental needs is relevant here. Children, although resilient, are not infinitely so. They need time to adjust to changes, especially one as important as a relationship with a new stepparent. Accordingly, introducing the children to a parent's new partner should follow twin guidelines—namely, go slow in making such changes, and only do so when there is good reason to think that the relationship with the new partner is serious and has the potential to become long term.

- Evidence of interference by the new partner would be a good reason for the mediator to invite the partner to join the mediation process. By doing so, the mediator may intend to recruit the new partner as an ally in the mediation process. Alternately, as in Chapter 8, this approach may be used to reaffirm the importance of the parental relationship, thus encouraging the new partner to defer to the parents in decision making about the children.

Safety Concerns

Three classes of conduct raise safety concerns in family mediation. The first involves violence and the use of threats and intimidation in relations between parents. The second concerns the use of violence or irresponsible conduct when a parent is under the influence of alcohol or drugs. Both place children in imminent danger. The third involves a range of parent behavior associated with their lifestyle that may expose the children to varying degrees of risk.

In Chapter 2 and elsewhere, we have discussed the various ways mediators have of ensuring the safety and security of clients. Earlier, in this chapter, we discussed the use of supervised access and graduated access schedules as ways of protecting children from imminent danger. Below, we address the various ways in which parents' lifestyle preferences can potentially place their children at risk and ways in which such risks can be mitigated or eliminated in parenting plans.

Given the wide range of behaviors in question, the following examples will suffice to illustrate the sorts of conduct addressed in mediation that raise safety concerns, together with appropriate responses that can be included in mediated parenting plans.

- *Guns.* Across North America, the distribution of handguns and rifles is very wide. These weapons may serve a variety of functions, including hunting, sport (e.g., target shooting), and self-protection. Unfortunately, every year, their unsafe storage, coupled with children's natural curiosity, results in many unnecessary deaths or serious injuries. Safe storage includes the use of trigger locks, gun safes, and the secure and separate storage of ammunition. Such precautions are essential to ensure child safety with guns in the house.

- *Recreational vehicles.* ATVs, skidoos, and seadoos are examples of a class of recreational vehicle that is intended for use by adults. Allowing their use by children exposes the children to unnecessary risk, with many fatalities and serious injuries reported as a result. At minimum, children should be allowed on such vehicles only when accompanied by an adult, and they should only be allowed to drive them alone when they are licensed to drive the family car.

- *Motorcycles.* Similarly, motorcycles are intended for adult use. That being so, it is impossible to secure crash helmets suitable for children. In addition, smaller children may not be strong enough to hold on properly, even when there is an adult driver. Children should not be allowed on such vehicles until they are at least 12 years of age, and they should not be allowed to drive them until they are licensed to do so.

- *Cigarette smoke.* There is now good evidence that long-term exposure to second-hand cigarette smoke poses a serious health risk. When both parents are smokers, neither may raise this issue in mediation, leaving it to the mediator to do so and advocate against it if necessary. When one parent smokes and the other parent does not, the nonsmoker can usually be relied on to raise the issue. The best solution is for smokers to agree to stop smoking, in the best interests of their children. Failing that, they should be asked to smoke outdoors and agree to install appropriate filtration equipment in the home so as to bring to an absolute minimum the amount of smoke to which the children are exposed.

Related examples include the use of hot tubs, the amount of time children should be alone (even with an adult nearby), and the sorts of films and videos to which children should routinely be exposed. In any given parenting plan, mediators can anticipate that some combination of these issues will come up from time to time.

Discussion

Parenting plans have become a routine facet of parenting in divorce. This is especially true in family mediation, with its special attention to detail. In TFM, constructing such plans involves routine elements, special circumstances, and (as seen in this and the preceding chapter) a number of principles and guidelines regarding parenting in divorce. This combination is intended to minimize conflict between parents, promote agreement and cooperation between them, and provide them with the relational tools they will need to continue to parent effectively long after mediation is concluded. Even so, the door to mediation is always open to them should they encounter problems in the future and seek to preserve and protect their children's best interests.

Appendix 10.1

Basic and Supplementary Elements of Parenting Plans

Parenting Plan	Financial Plan
1. Shared decision making	1. Child support
A. Health care	A. Basic expenses (guidelines)
B. Education	B. Extraordinary expenses (proportional)
C. Religious instruction	
2. Time-sharing schedule	2. Spousal support/alimony
A. Routine/daily schedule	• Self-sufficiency
B. Holiday schedule (including travel)	• Financial hardship
C. Transitions	• Short versus long marriage
D. Children's clothing, belongings	• Lump sum versus periodic payment
• Due notice	
3. Communication	3. Property division
A. Parental communication	A. Assets at separation
B. Parent-child communication	B. Debts at separation
C. Parental communication with the children present	• Separate versus marital property
4. Extracurricular events and activities	• Local statutory regime

5. Unexpected events

   A. Changing the schedule

      - Due notice
      - Right of first refusal

6. Moving households
   (relocation)

      - Due notice

7. Annual review

8. Dispute resolution mechanism

9. Supplementary issues (if applicable)

References

Ahrons, C. R. (1994). *The good divorce: Keeping your family together when your marriage comes apart.* New York: HarperCollins.

Ahrons, C. R., & Rodgers, R. H. (1987). *Divorced families: A multidisciplinary developmental view.* New York: Norton.

Alfini, J. (1991). Trashing, bashing, and hashing it out: Is this the end of "good mediation"? *Florida State University Law Review, 19*(1), 47-93.

Ambert, A.-M. (1992). *The effects of children on parents.* New York: Haworth.

Ambert, A.-M. (1997). *Parents, children, and adolescents: Interactive relationships and development in context.* New York: Haworth.

Ayoub, C. C., Deutsch, R. M., & Maraganore, A. (1999). Emotional impact in children of high conflict divorce: The impact of marital conflict and violence. *Family & Conciliation Courts Review, 37*(3), 297-314.

Balto, B. (1990). Mediator directiveness in child custody mediation: An exploration of alternatives and decision making. *Mediation Quarterly, 7*(3), 215-227.

Bartholomew, K., & Horowitz, L. (1991). Attachment styles among young adults. *Journal of Personality & Social Psychology, 61,* 226-244.

Benjamin, M. (1996). *Cultural diversity, educational equity and the transformation of higher education: Group profiles as a guide to policy and programming.* Westport, CT: Praeger.

Benjamin, M., & Irving, H. H. (1992). Toward a feminist-informed model of therapeutic family mediation. *Mediation Quarterly, 10*(2), 129-153.

Berlin, R. (1998). Mediation: Sharing vs. instructing. *Dispute Resolution Journal, 53,* 48-49.

Bornstein, M. H., & Lamb, M. E. (Eds.). (1999). *Developmental psychology: An advanced textbook* (4th ed.). Mahwah, NJ: Lawrence Erlbaum.

Bowlby, J. (1988). *A secure base.* New York: Basic Books.

Braver, S. L. (with D. O'Connell). (1998). *Divorced dads: Shattering the myths.* New York: Tarcher/Putnam.

Bush, R., & Folger, J. (1994). *The promise of mediation: Responding to conflict through empowerment and recognition.* San Francisco: Jossey-Bass.

Bussell, D. A., & Reiss, D. (1993). Genetic influences on family process: The emergence of a new framework for family research. In F. Walsh (Ed.), *Normal family processes* (2nd ed., pp. 161-181). New York: Guilford.

Chambers, D. L. (1984). Rethinking the substantive rules for custody disputes in divorce. *Michigan Law Review, 83,* 477-569.

Chess, S., & Thomas, A. (1984). *Origins and evolution of behavior disorders: From infancy to early adulthood.* New York: Brunner/Mazel.

Chess, S., & Thomas, A. (1986). *Temperament in clinical practice.* New York: Guilford.

Cobb, S., & Rifkin, J. (1991). Practice and paradox: Deconstructing neutrality in mediation. *Law & Society, 16*(1), 201-227.

Cohen, O., Dattner, N., & Luxenburg, A. (1999). The limits of the mediator's neutrality. *Mediation Quarterly, 16*(4), 341-348.

Cooks, L. M., & Hale, C. L. (1994). The construction of ethics in mediation. *Mediation Quarterly, 12*(1), 55-76.

Craig, G. J. (1976). *Human development.* Englewood Cliffs, NJ: Prentice Hall.

Dillon, P., & Emery, R. (1996). Divorce mediation and resolution of child custody disputes: Long-term effects. *American Journal of Orthopsychiatry, 66*(1), 131-140.

Duffy, A., & Pupo, M. (1992). *Part-time paradox: Connecting gender, work, and family.* Toronto: McClelland & Stewart.

Dunn, J., & Plomin, R. (1990). *Separate lives: Why are siblings so different?* New York: Basic Books.

Ehrenberg, M. F. (1996). Cooperative parenting arrangements after marital separation: Former couples who make it work. *Journal of Divorce & Remarriage, 26*(1-2), 93-115.

Emery, R. E. (1994). *Renegotiating family relationships: Divorce, child custody, and mediation.* New York: Guilford.

Emery, R. E. (1999). *Marriage, divorce, and the children's adjustment* (2nd ed.). Thousand Oaks, CA: Sage.

Everett, W. J. (1984). Shared parenthood in divorce: The parental covenant and custody law. *Journal of Law & Religion, 2,* 85-99.

Freeman, R. (1998). Parenting after divorce: Using research to inform decision-making about children. *Canadian Journal of Family Law, 15*(1), 79-123.

Galper-Cohen, M. (1989). *Long-distance parenting: A guide for divorced parents.* New York: Signet.

Gardner, R. (1992). *The parental alienation syndrome.* Creskill, NJ: Creative Therapeutics.

Garon, R. J., Donner, D. S., & Peacock, K. (2000). From infants to adolescents: A developmental approach to parenting plans. *Family & Conciliation Courts Review, 38*(2), 168-191.

Garrity, C. B., & Baris, M. A. (1994). *Caught in the middle: Protecting the children of high-conflict divorce.* San Francisco: Jossey-Bass.

Gilligan, C. (1982). *In a different voice: Psychological theory and women's development.* Cambridge, MA: Harvard University Press.

Golann, D., & Aaron, M. (1997). Using evaluation in mediation. *Dispute Resolution Journal, 52*(2), 26-33.

Goldberger, N. R. (1996). Looking forward, looking back. In N. R. Goldberger, J. M. Tarule, B. M. Clinchy, & M. F. Belenky (Eds.), *Knowledge, difference, and power: Essays inspired by women's ways of knowing* (pp. 1-21). New York: Basic Books.

Goleman, D. (1998). *Working with emotional intelligence.* New York: Bantam Books.

Greatbatch, D., & Dingwall, R. (1989). Selective facilitation: Some preliminary observations on a strategy used by divorce mediators. *Law & Society Review, 23*(4), 613.

Grillo, T. (1996). Respecting the struggle: Following the parties' lead. *Mediation Quarterly, 13*(3), 279-286.

Haynes, J. M. (1994). *The fundamentals of family mediation.* Albany: University of New York Press.

Irving, H. H. (1980). *Divorce mediation: The rational alternative.* Toronto: Personal Library.

Irving, H. H., & Benjamin, M. (1987). *Family mediation: Theory and practice of dispute resolution.* Toronto: Carswell.

Irving, H. H., & Benjamin, M. (1995). *Family mediation: Contemporary issues.* Thousand Oaks, CA: Sage.

Irving, H. H., & Benjamin, M. (1996). Mobility rights and children's best interests: Empirically-based first principles as a guide to effective parenting plans. *Canadian Family Law, 3,* 249-260.

Irving, H. H., & Benjamin, M. (1999). Child custody disputes, family mediation, and proposed reform of the Divorce Act. *Canadian Family Law Quarterly, 16,* 413-421.

James, P. (1997). *The divorce mediation handbook: Everything you need to know.* San Francisco: Jossey-Bass.

Johnston, J. R., & Campbell, L. E. (1988). *Impasses of divorce: The dynamics and resolution of family conflict.* New York: Free Press.

Joint Committee on Child Custody and Access. (1998). *For the sake of the children: Report of the Special Joint Committee on Child Custody and Access.* Ottawa: Public Works & Government Services.

Kandel, R. (1998). Situated substantive expertise: An ethnographic illustration and a proposed standard of practice for mediators. *Mediation Quarterly, 15*(4), 303-318.

Kelly, J. B. (1995). Power imbalance in divorce and interpersonal mediation: Assessment and intervention. *Mediation Quarterly, 13*(2), 85-98.

Kelly, J. B. (1997). The best interests of the child: A concept in search of meaning. *Family & Conciliation Courts Review, 35*(4), 377-387.

Kelly, J. B. (in press). Children's adjustment in conflicted marriage and divorce: A decade review of research. *Journal of Child & Adolescent Psychiatry.*

Kelly, J. B., & Lamb, M. E. (2000). Using child development research to make appropriate custody and access decisions for young children. *Family & Conciliation Courts Review, 38*(3), 297-311.

Kolb, D. M., & Kressel, K. (1994). Practical realities in making talk work. In D. M. Kolb (Ed.), *When talk works: Profiles of working mediators.* San Francisco: Jossey-Bass.

Kressel, K., Butler-DeFreitas, F., Forlenza, S. G., & Wilcox, C. (1994). The settlement-orientation vs. the problem-solving style in custody mediation. *Journal of Social Issues, 50*(1), 67-83.

Kruk, E. (1993). *Divorce and disengagement: Patterns of fatherhood within and beyond marriage.* Halifax, NS: Fernwood.

Kruk, K. (1998). Practice issues, strategies, and models: The current state of the art of family mediation. *Family & Conciliation Courts Review, 36*(2), 195-215.

Lamb, M. E. (1997). *The role of the father in child development* (3rd ed.). New York: John Wiley.

Lamb, M. E. (1999). Non-custodial fathers and their impact on the children of divorce. In R. A. Thompson & P. Amato (Eds.), *The post-divorce family: Research and policy issues* (pp. 105-125). Thousand Oaks, CA: Sage.

Lamb, M. E., Sternberg, K. J., & Thompson, R. A. (1997). The effects of divorce and custody arrangements on children's behavior, and adjustment. *Family & Conciliation Courts Review, 35*(4), 393-404.

Landau, B., Wolfson, L., Landau, N., Bartoletti, M., & Mesbur, R. (2000). *Family mediation handbook* (3rd ed.). Toronto: Butterworths.

Lyster, M. E. (1997). *Child custody: Building parenting agreements that work* (2nd ed.). Berkeley, CA: Nolo.

Maccoby, E., & Jacklin, C. N. (1974). *The psychology of sex differences.* Palo Alto, CA: Stanford University Press.

Maccoby, E., & Mnookin, R. (with C. E. Depner & H. E. Peters). (1992). *Dividing the child: Social and legal dilemmas of custody.* Cambridge, MA: Harvard University Press.

Mandell, N., & Duffy, A. (1995). *Canadian families: Diversity, conflict and change.* Toronto: Harcourt Brace.

Maslin, B. (1994). *The angry marriage: Overcoming the rage, reclaiming the love.* New York: Hyperion.

Mathis, R. D. (1998). Couples from hell: Undifferentiated spouses in divorce mediation. *Mediation Quarterly, 16*(1), 37-49.

McCarthy, M. A. (1997). *Family law for every Canadian.* Toronto: Prentice Hall.

McCormick, M. (1997). Confronting social injustice as a mediator. *Mediation Quarterly, 14*(4), 293-307.

McIntosh, J. (2000). Child-inclusive divorce mediation: Report on a qualitative study. *Mediation Quarterly, 18*(1), 55-69.

McIsaac, H. (1998). Changing the paradigm: The effect of recent family law legislation in England, Australia, and the United States. *Mediation Quarterly, 16*(2), 163-183.

McWhinney, R. (1995). The "winner-loser syndrome": Changing fashions in determination of child custody. *Family & Conciliation Courts Review, 33*(3), 298-307.

Menin, B. (2000). The party of the last part: Ethical and process implications for children in divorce mediation. *Mediation Quarterly, 17*(3), 281-293.

Pearson, J., & Thoennes, N. (2000). Supervised visitation: The families and their experiences. *Family & Conciliation Courts Review, 38*(1), 123-142.

Ricci, I. (1997). *Mom's house, Dad's house: Making two homes for your child* (2nd ed.). New York: Simon & Schuster.

Rifkin, J., Millen, J., & Cobb, S. (1991). Toward a new discourse for mediation: A critique of neutrality. *Mediation Quarterly, 9*(2), 151-164.

Riskin, L. (1996). Understanding mediator's orientations, strategies and techniques: A grid for the perplexed. *Harvard Negotiation Law Review, 1*, 7-40.

Roman, M., & Haddad, W. (1978). *The disposable parent: The case for joint custody*. New York: Holt, Rinehart & Winston.

Rotman, A. S., Tomkins, R., & Schwartz, M. D. (2000). Reconciling parents' and children's interests in relocation: In whose best interests? *Family & Conciliation Courts Review, 38*(3), 341-367.

Saposnek, D. T. (1998). *Mediating child custody disputes: A strategic approach* (Rev. ed.). San Francisco: Jossey-Bass.

Schwartz, L. L., & Kaslow, F. W. (1997). *Painful partings: Divorce and its aftermath*. New York: John Wiley.

Smoron, K. A. (1998). Conflicting roles in child custody mediation: Impartiality/ neutrality and the best interests of the child. *Family & Conciliation Courts Review, 36*(2), 258-280.

Spring, J. A. (1996). *After the affair: Healing the pain and rebuilding trust when a partner has been unfaithful*. New York: HarperPerennial.

Taylor, A. (1997). Concepts of neutrality in family mediation: Contexts, ethics, influence, and transformative process. *Mediation Quarterly, 14*(3), 215-236.

Veevers, J. E. (1991). *Continuity and change in marriage and family*. Toronto: Holt, Rinehart & Winston.

Waldman, E. (1997). Identifying the role of social norms in mediation: A multiple model approach. *Hastings Law Journal, 48*, 703-769.

Wallerstein, J. S., & Kelly, J. B. (1980). *Surviving the breakup: How children and parents cope with divorce*. New York: Basic Books.

Wallerstein, J. S., Lewis, J. M., & Blakeslee, S. (2000). *The unexpected legacy of divorce: A 25 year landmark study.* New York: Hyperion.

Warshak, R. A. (2000). Overnight contact between parents and young children. *Family & Conciliation Courts Review, 38*(4), 422-445.

White, H. (1999). *Substantive influence in mediation: A discussion of its normative role.* Unpublished manuscript, University of Toronto.

11

Financial Plans

Part 1: Technical Matters

Money is integral to the marital relationship. As such, conflict over its acquisition, accumulation, distribution, and expenditure is commonplace if not universal (Millman, 1991). Indeed, Betcher and Macauley (1990) regard money as one of "the seven basic quarrels of marriage." Across couples, such conflict varies widely in both frequency and severity. At one extreme, conflict about money may be routine but mild and infrequent and thus integral to the ongoing marital relationship (Gottman & Silver, 1999). At the other extreme, it may be frequent and bitter, prompting couples to seek help (Carter & Peters, 1996) or becoming a key reason for divorce (Gigy & Kelly, 1992). That being the case, it will come as little surprise that among couples undergoing divorce, money (assets) and its division can be a major source of conflict in family mediation. We take this last statement as self-evident, yet with few exceptions one would be hard-pressed to go much beyond this statement, either in the mediation literature or in other, related literatures.

Literature Review

Given a heavy emphasis in the mediation literature on parenting issues, money is either omitted entirely (Bush & Folger, 1996; Emery, 1994; Erickson & Erickson, 1988) or noted very much in passing (Folberg & Taylor, 1984; Haynes, 1981; Haynes & Haynes, 1989; Moore, 1986). Although a few mediation texts actually devote a chapter or more to property division (Irving & Benjamin, 1987; James, 1997; Landau, Wolfson, Landau, Bartoletti, & Mesbur, 2000), these are invariably complex, technical treatises that deal more with family and tax laws than with spousal relations. To be fair, Irving and Benjamin (1987) devote a chapter to various interventions, and James (1997) devotes a chapter to sources of emotional blockage. The problem is that neither source linked such clinical material to their subsequent discussions of financial mediation.

Thus, bewildered by the intensity of spousal conflict around money matters, students or novice mediators who turn to the mediation literature for guidance will likely be sorely disappointed. At worst, they will either be confronted by total silence or advised to refer such cases to others (such as lawyers) with the requisite technical expertise. At best, and by implication more than explicit advice, practitioners are asked to have patience with clients' distress around money and, by focusing on the issues, avoiding the conflict, and rephrasing clients' more incendiary statements, persuade them to behave rationally. In the end, mediator conduct will likely reflect their preferred practice model. Those favoring structural models (Fisher, Ury, & Patton, 1991) will rely on generic techniques that aim to block or go around conflict, whereas those favoring therapeutic models, including therapeutic family mediation (TFM) (Irving & Benjamin, 1995), will rely on intervention techniques primarily drawn from family therapy. Although these various approaches may all be quite useful, their selection and implementation will derive from *no systematic formulation* that links money, conflict, and intervention, for in that regard the mediation literature is presently bereft.

Those frustrated by this state of affairs may be tempted to look beyond family mediation to other literatures. Doing so, however, would only get one slightly ahead. For example, the stress literature recognizes that the lack of money (poverty) is a primary source of stress, whereas having plenty of money (affluence) can buffer against stress (Patterson, 1989). Alone, this important insight is of limited utility to the mediation practitioner. Much the same is true of the family therapy literature. Carter and Peters (1996, p. 4), for example, argue that much of this literature treats money as taboo, such that marital conflict around money *must* originate in some underlying dysfunction. Betcher and Macauley (1990) agree, noting that the available literature is "small and sketchy" and suggesting that "the privacy taboo about money affects even psychotherapists" (p. 95). For example, Karpel (1986) devoted an entire volume to "family resources" in which money is scarcely mentioned. Carter and Peters (1996), their colleagues (Walters, Carter, Papp, & Silverstein, 1988), and others (Betcher & Macauley, 1990; Millman, 1991) are rare exceptions. These authors treat money as a central marital issue based on a struggle for control and reflecting the "golden rule: whoever has the gold makes the rules" (Carter & Peters, 1996, p. 9). Indeed, Carter and Peters advance a series of typologies based on how couples deal with this issue. Unfortunately, and mysteriously, these typologies do not carry over to their discussion of divorce. Although this material confirms what mediators routinely observe—that money can be an extremely divisive issue—and goes further to explain why this is so, it offers little by way of practical advice as to what mediators can do to be helpful in the midst of such conflict.

This review makes plain that competence in the mediation of financial issues involves *two* separate but related areas of expertise. *Technical expertise* involves knowledge of and experience with the statutory and taxation regimes that apply in each local jurisdiction. Both in the United States (James, 1997) and Canada (Landau et al., 2000), these regimes vary widely. Happily, texts that address such variation are freely available. In regard to American jurisdictions, we have relied on several sources (Friedman, 1999; Johnson & Benesek, 1997; McKay, Rogers, Blades, & Gosse, 1999; Mercer & Pruett, 2001; Woodhouse & Fetherling, 2000; for a summary of the property laws of each state, see Sitarz, 1999 or the Internet site of Cornell University at www.secure.law.cornell.edu/topics/Table_Divorce.htm). In regard to Canadian jurisdictions, we have relied on Kronby (2001; for a summary of the property laws of each province, see Appendix F). Unfortunately, none of these texts were written by a family mediator or for the mediation of financial matters in divorce. Given that it is the mediation practitioners' obligation to be both knowledgeable and current as to applicable laws, rules, and procedures, this chapter will attempt to fill that gap in the mediation literature.

As will shortly become evident, in our view, such knowledge is well within the grasp of all otherwise competent family mediators. For mediators who prefer to allow others to deal with financial matters, this chapter will serve as useful background in helping make clear to clients how parental and financial plans may impinge on each other. For those who prefer to deal with such matters themselves but only in comediation with a financial expert (lawyer, accountant, or financial planner), this chapter will help them to ensure that their clients participate in the mediation process in a meaningful and informed manner. For those who prefer to do comprehensive family mediation themselves, this chapter will walk them through all the technical issues likely to arise in a majority of cases while alerting them to issues likely to require the inclusion of specialized consultants.

However they choose to handle the financial issues, within the context of the TFM practice model, it should now be clear that mediation competence requires more than merely technical expertise. As with conflict around parenting issues, conflict around money is necessarily and often primarily about a range of relational issues. Mediation competence, then, will require mastery of a range of *clinical skills* (see Chapter 2, this volume). Patterns of conflict around financial matters are such that the mediation of financial matters can be relatively simple and straightforward or complex and prolonged. In either case, what has been missing in the literature is a *systematic formulation* linking money, conflict, and intervention. In Chapter 12, we will seek to fill that gap by systematically describing five patterns of conflict around money. For convenience, all references cited in this chapter and the next will be found at the end of Chapter 12. Before proceeding, two preliminary comments are in order as regards comprehensive family mediation and clarifying issues, respectively.

Comprehensive Family Mediation: Pros and Cons

The TFM model is designed with comprehensive family mediation as the option of choice. This is so because the advantages of the comprehensive approach outweigh the disadvantages. Advantages include the following:

• Relational gains achieved in mediating the parenting plan carry over into subsequent efforts to mediate the financial plan. Having each part of the overall plan dealt with by different processes and different practitioners means that such gains may be lost. The obvious example is one in which the parenting plan is dealt with through TFM, whereas the financial plan is dealt with through litigation. One possible outcome is that conflict exacerbated by the adversarial system may back up to undermine the gains made in mediating the parenting plan.

• Parenting and financial issues are inextricably linked, with decisions in one necessarily affecting decisions in the other. The comprehensive approach merely recognizes the integrative character of these two sets of issues. For example, parenting involves decisions not only about time sharing and decision making but also about child care costs, future plans, and how these costs will be shared.

• The integrative character of these issues presents the obvious possibility of integrative bargaining, that is, trading off in an effort to create a comprehensive settlement. In this context, the more potential solutions on the table, the greater the likelihood one or some combination of solutions will be attractive to any given couple. This arrangement also encourages both creativity and flexibility among mediators and clients, thus maximizing the likelihood of both agreement and durability.

• Finally, the comprehensive approach maximizes client self-determination. As we explain to clients as regards parenting, "No one knows your children better than you do. You should be the ones who decide what is best for them." The same is true as regards their finances and the necessary financial decisions that arise from divorce. This is especially so given that most divorcing couples report rather modest assets (Irving & Benjamin, 1995). Indeed, a fair minority confront the twin disasters of divorce coupled with significant debt and thus no assets whatever. Moreover, any fears clients may have about being taken advantage of by the other spouse may be allayed, first by the mediator's financial expertise and, second, by the fact that any agreement will necessarily be reviewed by lawyers before it becomes legally binding.

These advantages of comprehensive mediation are partially offset by several noteworthy disadvantages:

• Comprehensive mediation obviously takes longer and is thus more costly than focusing on parenting alone. The strength of this argument, however, is doubly mitigated: Divorcing couples *must* address various financial concerns in some forum, and the legal process is typically more expensive than mediation. In the long run, we would suggest that mediating the financial plan is likely to save most couples time, money, and effort.

• When spouses are very unequal in their knowledge of finances, efforts at mediation may yield agreements that are unconscionable, that is, clearly favoring one spouse over the other. This argument has merit in the sense that one spouse may be so intimidated by the prospect of negotiating a financial plan that he or she would prefer to hand the matter over to his or her lawyer(s). The same argument lacks merit in two other respects. First, we have repeatedly noted the educative role of the TFM-based mediator. A spouse's lack of knowledge is remediable and in a relatively short time. As noted above, the financial issues in question are typically neither arcane nor complex. Second, the unequal position of one spouse often reflects a tacit agreement between the spouses that one of them, the other spouse, will take responsibility for the family's finances. In this sense, mediating a financial plan can be both empowering and liberating for the less knowledgeable spouse, providing the basis to chart a future course for himself or herself and the children.

• Finding a qualified mediator can be problematic. Given the taboo against dealing with money among those with a mental health background, most mediators with that background restrict their involvement to the construction of parenting plans; those who do comprehensive mediation continue to be in the minority. Furthermore, in the United States and Canada, mandatory standards of competence do not apply. Rather, in joining various professional associations, members voluntarily agree to meet specific standards of competence. However, such membership is not a requisite of practice, at least not as of this writing. Consequently, across the existing population of practicing mediators, competence standards as regards the mediation of financial plans are likely to vary, with the onus on the consumer. In practice, the client's route to the mediator is either through an organization of family mediators (in the United States, an example would be the Academy of Family Mediators [781-674-2663]; in Canada, an example would be Family Mediation Canada [519-585-3118]) or through a lawyer, both of which can usually vouch for the mediator's competence.

Thus, although the search for a competent TFM-based mediator may be complex, the occasions on which clients are unable to locate such a professional or do locate one who is incompetent are likely to be rare.

In short, despite their discomfort over money, there are some compelling reasons why mediators with a mental health background *should* seriously consider becoming qualified as comprehensive family mediators, especially those attracted to the TFM model.

Clarifying the Issues

Parenting and money involve different orders of experience. Parenting tends to be immediate, visceral, and emotionally charged. Money tends to be removed, factual, and heavily symbolic, as in lines of credit, secured liabilities, and interest-bearing investments. It also can be an emotionally charged topic, but that will depend on a variety of factors; it is certainly not the case automatically.

These various considerations have two immediate consequences for mediation. First, the mediator cannot act without first having a clear picture of the client's financial situation. That situation is heavily fact dependent, such that someone must be able to lay out all pertinent facts on the table. Second, the commonsense assumption that for every couple such facts are readily available is often *false*. Rather, clients tend to vary on a continuum. At one end are couples who come to mediation completely prepared, with all pertinent facts available and verifiable. At the other end are couples who are completely unprepared, with facts that are neither available nor verifiable. The combination of a number of factors determines where on this continuum any given couple is likely to fall.

• As noted above, spouses vary tremendously in the extent, level, and sophistication of their financial knowledge. This is especially true in "traditional" relationships in which there is a clear separation of roles, with the mother responsible for parenting and household management and the father responsible for income and money management. Indeed, in some cases, the struggle to realign relationships after the last child has left home precipitates the divorce. In such cases, women may be systematically uninformed about family finances and may even be unaware of what their husbands earn. Although such relationships are still commonplace, their numbers are dwindling with the massive influx of women into the workforce. In our experience, couples in which both spouses work tend to be more equal as regards financial knowledge.

• Spouses vary in their ability to articulate the issues in dispute and/or define and defend a given point of view. In such cases, it is not so much that the facts are concealed as that clients tend to present such facts in a manner that is muddled and confused.

- Spouses vary in the extent to which factual and emotional issues overlap or intermingle. For example, so urgent may be a client's need to describe his or her sense of deprivation and mistreatment that the facts are either submerged or heavily distorted. Given that mothers bear the heaviest burden of child care, fathers may have no realistic sense of the cost of child care. Similarly, mothers may have no realistic sense of the cost of their lifestyle, including the continuing costs of the matrimonial home and its attendant upkeep and maintenance. Consequently, fathers may come to the mediation with unreasonably low estimates of child support, whereas mothers may have unreasonably high estimates of spousal maintenance (alimony) and/or property division. In both cases, the problem has the same origin—namely, that both estimates are rooted in spouses' feelings rather than a factual portrait of their financial situation.

- Finally, in a small minority of cases, the mediator's difficulty in developing a clear picture of the couple's financial situation results from systematic efforts on the part of one or both spouses to conceal relevant facts. In one case, a self-employed businessman had routed most personal expenses through the business, thus defrauding the tax department. He was loath to disclose such information in fear that he would be reported. In another case, a wife, who controlled the family's financial affairs, planned the divorce 2 years in advance. During that time, she transferred a substantial amount of money into a foreign account of which her husband had no knowledge. Although these cases may be rare, they pose particular problems for the mediator, who has no means to detect subterfuge among clients who enter mediation on a voluntary basis. Although pertinent experts (such as forensic accounts) may be added to the process where the need is suspected, their presence suggests a degree of distrust between the parties such that mediation may *not* be the best way to resolve their disputes. Conversely, lawyers may take much of the responsibility for ensuring that relevant financial facts are both correct and available and in that sense can provide both their clients and the mediator with an invaluable service.

In general, then, even at the outset, financial mediation will require *both* clinical and technical skill sets. The particular balance between the two will vary as each case unfolds. However, it has been our experience that clinical skills are especially critical in the beginning phases, and technical skills become increasingly important toward the middle and end phases. Finally, such cases vary widely in terms of complexity, with the majority of cases involving a relatively simple set of facts that reflect the modest holdings of most divorcing families.

Part 1: Technical Matters

Financial mediation centers on three subject areas: child support, alimony (spousal maintenance), and property division, with tax implications an ancillary concern throughout. Before proceeding, two important qualifications are in order. First, we cannot stress sufficiently that in creating a financial plan, we regard the clients' lawyers as members of the mediation team because they will be the ultimate arbiters of the fairness and the reasonableness of any "memorandum" that will emerge from the mediation process.

Second, the United States and Canada are separate nations, with different legal histories, including their treatment of the three financial issues in question. Accordingly, throughout the following, we will be at some pains to highlight areas of commonality as well as difference.

Child Support

In both the United States and Canada, the assumption of shared responsibility for child care extends to sharing the burden of its costs. Furthermore, this responsibility is tied to the presence of one or more dependent children and thus is independent of the couple's marital status; child support obligations apply whether the couple is legally married or not.

Similarly, in both countries, three concerns need to be addressed:

- who pays child support,
- how much should be paid, and
- how long this obligation should be in force.

How these issues are addressed is somewhat different in each nation.

Who Pays

In both the United States and Canada, both parents are responsible for paying the costs associated with raising their children. However, they differ in their respective means of identifying who pays child support (the payer).

United States. In each state, child support is determined by law, based on need and the ability to pay. Need refers to basic and extraordinary child care expenses. Basic expenses typically refer to the costs of food, shelter, and clothing. In some states, they may also include other routine expenses, such as telephone and cable television charges, transportation costs (such as school busing), school supplies, and/or health insurance. Extraordinary expenses refer to other expenses, such as nutritional, medical, education, and travel expenses (pursuant to access). In some states, they may also include one-time costs, such as children's summer camp; seasonal costs, such as the cost of snowsuits; and/or other expenses, such as child day care costs.

As for ability to pay, this refers to each parent's *net* income, after deductions for taxes and, in some cases, other child-related expenses. Income refers to any monies received by each parent on a periodic basis, even if these monies are not part of their daily budget (such as in dividend reinvestment plans) or their receipt may be delayed (as in bonuses paid at the end of the year). Depending on the state, Social Security payments may also be included in calculating income. More generally, then, for purposes of child support, income refers to earning capacity rather than actual income, as reflected in each parent's stable income history.

Identifying the person who will pay child support, the payer, will depend on balancing need against ability to pay. The parent who spends the most time with the children will typically display the greater need, such that the other parent will be expected to pay support. When both parents spend the same amount of time with the children, their respective ability to pay will determine who pays support, including the possibility that no support will be paid, with each shouldering an equal share of the child care costs.

Canada. In Canada, child support is subject to the federal Child Support Guidelines (1997), based on the "40% rule," a measure of the time the children spend with each parent. In the typical instance in which the children spend more than 40% of their time with one parent (often their mother) and less than 40% of their time with the other parent (often their father), the father would be expected to pay child support. That is, by virtue of the time they spend with her, the mother pays most of the costs associated with child care. However, given their shared responsibility for the children, it is only reasonable that the father pay a portion of these expenditures by his child support contributions.

In such instances, the application of the guidelines is mandatory and, unlike the United States, excludes concerns about ability to pay. The exception involves instances when the children spend roughly equal time with each parent. In that case, parents may opt into the guidelines or opt out of them, thus raising the possibility that none will be paid, with each parent shouldering an equal share of the child care costs.

How Much

The United States and Canada have different, albeit similar, methods for determining or calculating the amount to be paid monthly.

United States. Each state maintains guidelines designed to even out the incomes of each parent. In some states, determining the actual amount is based on complicated calculations concerning the percentage of time the children spend with each parent. Other states treat each parent separately, based on their respective financial circumstances. In either case, the state guidelines indicate the approximate amount each parent is expected to pay. For example, in 2000, parents in Connecticut with one child were expected to pay 21% of their net income in support. As noted above, in considering the facts concerning respective need and ability to pay, specific payment schedules may deviate from the state guideline.

Canada. For most parents subject to the guidelines, determining the specific amount of child support involves a two-step process. First, the basic amount is determined by looking up the "table" amount. That is, each province has its own child support table, organized by gross annual income (from $6,700 to $150,000, in $100 increments) and number of dependent children (between one and four). The intersection between the two yields a specific amount to be paid monthly by the payer. For example, a parent living in Ontario with a gross annual income of $60,000 and two children would be expected to pay $823.00 per month. Special calculations are needed to determine the amount if the payer reports income in excess of $150,000 and/or has more than four children. In a recent case, a parent who reported annual income in excess of $900,000 was expected to pay slightly more than $10,000 a month in child support.

The table amount is intended to cover basic expenses. The next step involves determining each parent's proportional share of extraordinary or "add-on" expenses. Such expenses take account of the facts in each case, including a real-time child care budget. In calculating their proportion of these expenses, mediators begin by first subtracting a fixed amount for basic living expenses, such as $20,000. Given parents who earn $70,000 and $40,000, respectively, subtracting the base amount leaves $50,000 and $20,000, respectively, or 71% and 29% as their respective proportion of family income. Assuming total monthly child care costs of $1,000, the parents should pay $710 and $290, respectively. To equalize these costs, one parent would pay the other *half the difference* in his or her respective contributions, or $210 per month, thus allowing each parent $500 per month to cover child care cost. Further adjustments would be required if the parents differed as regards *both* time sharing *and* income (e.g., the mother has the children 60% of time but with only 30% of father's income).

Thus, the final child support amount combines basic and extraordinary costs, paid monthly. Following the above example and assuming that the payer earned $70,000 annually and had two children in Ontario, the payer would be expected to pay $927 in basic expenses and $210 in extraordinary expenses, for a monthly child support total of $1,137.

Finally, two exceptions are noteworthy. The first exception concerns instances in which couples are free to "opt in" or "opt out" of the guidelines. Those who "opt in" use the annual income of each spouse to calculate his or her respective "table" amounts, with half of any difference between them the amount the higher paid parent would pay in support to the other parent. Extraordinary expenses are then added on a proportional basis. Those who "opt out" use a child care budget to determine real costs that are then shared on a proportional basis (also known as the "Paris formula"), including both basic and extraordinary expenses. From a mediation perspective, creating such budgets can be a useful experience in reality testing. Whenever one parent does the cooking, grocery shopping, and clothes buying for the children, that parent has a thorough understanding of the real costs of raising children. This may and often does come as something of a surprise to the other parent, who did not realize just how expensive such costs could be. Indeed, in very affluent families, neither parent may appreciate such costs because one or both parents may be accustomed to buying whatever they need, without regard to cost.

The second exception concerns payer parents who request a reduction in the table amount due to hardship. The onus is on these parents to prove hardship, based on stringent criteria. It follows that variation based on hardship would be unusual and tied to circumstances that may or may not be time limited. Indeed, in some cases, parents may agree to a reduced amount but only on the proviso that the payer accumulate a debt that must be repaid when his or her financial circumstances improve. Furthermore, because child support is regarded as a basic parental obligation, it may not be waived, even if the payer declares bankruptcy.

The unfortunate consequence of this approach to determining the child support amount is that the "guidelines" themselves create a financial incentive for payers to push for more time with the children. If they are able to meet the "40% rule," they may opt out of the guidelines in an effort to relieve or reduce the financial burden associated with child support. From the perspective of family mediation, this is decidedly the wrong reason to negotiate how much or how little time one or the other parent spends with the children.

Other Issues

Eight additional sources of variation in child support concern (a) the age of the children, (b) the basis of annual variation in such amounts, (c) third-party payments, (d) the duration of such payments, (e) payment of monies intended for purposes other than immediate child care costs, (f) nonpayment or arrears, (g) financial planning, and (h) taxation. These issues apply equally in the United States and Canada and are dealt with similarly.

Child Age. In both the United States and Canada, child support is intended to cover the child care costs of *dependent* children, that is, children younger than 19 years of age. However, application of this expectation varies by jurisdiction. In the majority of states (including California), the legal obligation to pay support ends when the child turns 18 years of age (Wallerstein, Lewis, & Blakeslee, 2000, pp. 248-251). What that means in practice is that many children of divorce are denied a college education because one or both of their parents refuse to cover these costs. In a handful of states (such as Hawaii, Massachusetts, New Hampshire, New Jersey, New York, Oregon, and Washington), support may be extended to cover college attendance or until the child turns 21 years of age.

In contrast, in Canada, there is no age limit on support obligations. So long as older children remain financially dependent—by virtue of illness, disability, and/or ongoing education—they too may be included within parental support obligations and need to be factored into the real-time budget. In one instance, parents had a son in university. They agreed that he was responsible for paying his own tuition through part-time work, and they agreed to split the estimated costs of his books and living expenses. They did so because ensuring that their son completed his university education was an important goal they both shared, despite their many other differences.

Annual Variation. The basis for annual variation in child support will depend on the method used to calculate the amount in question. The majority of parents who rely on state or federal "guideline" amounts must await annual variation in the appropriate tables, together with any changes in either child care costs and/or each parent's annual income. Should either of these change substantially, either up or down, appropriate changes would need to be made in the child support amount, whether this was calculated using guidelines and/or by proportional sharing of child care costs. It is therefore incumbent on each parent to keep the other parent informed of any such changes.

Third-Party or "In-Kind" Payments. Depending on their circumstances, there may be some advantage to considering third-party or "in-kind" payments. These are payments from one parent to a third party in regard to goods and/or services for the children. For example, rather than have a father pay the mother a fixed amount to cover the children's winter coats, he may volunteer to take them to a nearby mall and buy the coats directly. Other common examples include health care (dental, medical, and prescription drugs), electronic equipment, cellular telephones or pagers, car leases, tutorial services, transportation costs, private school tuition, and/or child day care costs. When relations between parents are cordial, such payments can offer the payee spouse tax advantages, be convenient, and provide a basis for encouraging interaction between the payer and the children. When relations between parents are conflictual, such payments may be refused because they may cede some measure of control to the payer and may promote conflict by encouraging parental interaction.

Duration. As noted above, the duration of child support turns on the children's dependent status and age, the income of both parents, and applicable statutes in the local jurisdiction. As the children successively reach the age of majority and thus become independent, support obligations may no longer apply. Similarly, the changing financial obligations of either parent may affect child support. For example, as one or both parents remarry and have subsequent children, their respective ability to meet their obligation to existing dependents will vary or be mitigated. Early on in the process, when money intended for one household must now stretch to cover two, child support payments may make the difference between financial stability and social assistance. Later, as both parents adjust to their new situation, the need for those payments may become more or less urgent. As one parent remarries and perhaps begins a new family, this may result in resources that are more abundant (if his or her spouse works) or more scare (if his or her spouse does not). Thus, although the financial requirements of the children gradually increase through time until independence, the ability of fathers and mothers to meet those obligations will vary on several dimensions.

Nonpayment. Such variation notwithstanding, as of this writing, the amount of child support in arrears across North America stands in the *billions.* So serious is this matter that many jurisdictions have transferred the onus of collection from parents to the state itself, which has the power to garnishee wages, withhold driver's license renewal, and, in extreme cases, inprison those who have accumulated substantial arrears.

From the perspective of mediation, such cases fall into three categories. The first group of parents, mostly fathers, are those who simply cannot pay. In some cases, child support awards by the courts were inappropriately high in relation to real income. In other cases, the award was appropriate at the time, but a change in circumstances (especially unemployment, illness, or disability) has not yet caught up to the undermanned bureaucracy enforcing the old order. In either case, husbands fail to pay the specified amount, *not* because they do not want to but because their income is inadequate. In such cases, husbands typically pay what they can afford, even though it falls short of the official order.

The second group of parents, mostly fathers, reflects those who can pay but refuse to do so because they perceive that the mothers are blocking access. In other words, nonpayment reflects an ongoing marital dispute that typically has nothing to do with parenting. In rare cases, some mothers have been jailed for their refusal to allow access despite a court order to do so. Similarly, some fathers have been jailed for accruing substantial arrears. Although such extreme actions may be warranted, mediation is the better alternative, especially TFM, whose practitioners are trained to address just such marital dynamics.

The third and largest group are those parents, mostly fathers, whose refusal to pay support is indicative of their having abandoned the children along with the former spouse. Of the three reasons for nonpayment, this is the most tragic and the most intractable because few such cases would be amenable to mediation. On one hand, evidence of their ability to pay is often apparent because all their resources are going to support new families, often with one or more new children. On the other hand, the damage such parents exact on the children left behind is incalculable and often long-lasting (Wallerstein et al., 2000).

Financial Planning. Finally, although child support covers the children's immediate expenses, other financial issues require a long-term perspective and are intended to secure the children's financial future. Although efforts can encompass a wide range of financial planning measures, three are frequently negotiated in mediation. The first involves life insurance. When the father is the breadwinner, only he is typically insured. In divorce, such insurance should apply to both parents. Next, with the rapidly rising cost of higher education, many parents may wish to establish an education fund to which both parents may contribute in proportion to their income (but see "Child Age," above). Finally, in divorce, both parents should create a will to indicate how their assets should be disposed of on their death and who will act as their executor. This is important, because in divorce, the automatic assumption that assets will flow to the other parent, who will also act as the executor, will no longer apply. Only a will can serve to ensure an orderly disposition of assets to the selected beneficiaries (such as the children) and with a selected executor (such as a family member or a lawyer).

Taxation. Mediated financial settlements may have no or minor tax consequences, or taxation may affect the final outcome dramatically. It follows that mediators should routinely examine the tax consequences of *all* mediated financial agreements and help clients understand the tax consequences of various options, so that they are in a position to make informed choices.

In terms of child support, in both the United States and Canada, child support is *not* taxable; that is, payers may not claim such payments as a tax deduction, and recipients (payees) do not treat such payments as a taxable benefit. However, in the United States, divorced parents do have the option of either characterizing such payments as "child support" or as "unallocated child support and alimony." In the latter case, payments would be deductible to the payer and a taxable benefit to the recipient. Such a characterization would typically apply when the payer's income is much higher than that of the recipient's. Family support allows the higher-income spouse to benefit from the deduction, and the lower-income spouse would benefit from taxation at a lower marginal rate.

Four additional tax provisions apply in the United States (Mercer & Pruett, 2001, p. 114):

- By law, the children's dependency exemption goes to the primary parent. However, parents can use IRS Form 8332 to transfer the exemption to the other parent.
- The primary parent would typically file as the head of the household. However, in the case of shared parenting, both may do so.
- The primary parent may be entitled to receive the child care credit.
- Either parent may claim medical and/or dental expenses that exceed the designated percentage of their adjusted gross annual income.

Alimony/Spousal Support

The next major component for negotiation in mediation concerns *alimony*, also known as spousal maintenance or spousal support. These are monies paid by one spouse to the other following divorce. Although such payments are usually from husband to wife, alimony is not gender specific and may be paid by either spouse. Its treatment is similar, but not identical, in the United States and Canada.

United States. In the United States, alimony serves the general function of income maintenance, particularly in situations in which the spouses have unequal earning capacity. Unlike child custody, which is determined by law, alimony is completely negotiable. That said, states vary widely in their perspective on alimony. Some states do not favor alimony, making other provisions associated with property division to ensure equity in the financial situations of the spouses. Some states support alimony but are reluctant to grant it to spouses who have been married less than 5 years or who are able-bodied, despite having been married more than 5 years but less than 10. In all states favoring alimony, couples involved in long-term marriages of 25 years or more are most likely to be awarded alimony.

Apart from marital duration, states consider a wide range of factors in determining if alimony is warranted, including age, health (both mental and physical), education, income, future prospects, the availability of separate property (see below) that may be used for support purposes, the presence of small children (making it desirable for one parent to stay at home), the reasons for the breakdown of the marital relationship, and each spouse's relative contribution to the household (both monetary and nonmonetary).

Unlike child support, where state guidelines determine the amount to be paid, alimony awards are determined on a case-by-case basis, in an effort to balance need against ability to pay. In turn, this is related to the duration of the award. A common formula is that alimony is awarded for half the duration of the marriage, with awards to spouses involved in long-term marriages typically for life. Recently, "rehabilitative" alimony has become increasingly common, that is, a short-term award intended to promote self-sufficiency in the recipient. Such awards may involve a fixed amount paid monthly or an amount that decreases through time. In addition to time-limited payment periods, alimony generally terminates on the death of either spouse or when the recipient remarries or lives with a partner (cohabits) in a relationship equivalent to marriage.

Finally, spouses must consider whether an alimony award can be modified. Some awards indicate that they may not be modified under any circumstances. Others indicate that the award may be modified if there is *any* change in circumstances, and still others may be modified *only* under predetermined changes in circumstance, such as physical or mental disability or an increase in the recipient's income beyond a certain amount. Yet another possibility involves no alimony award at divorce but indicates that the issue may be reopened should circumstances change in the future.

Canada. The legal regime rationalizing spousal support in Canada has changed dramatically over the past 40 years. In the 1960s, the feminist movement was successful in convincing legislators that men and women should be equal before the law. In the 1970s, such equality meant that spousal support was intended to promote self-sufficiency. Women who had been out of the workforce were seen as entitled to receive support sufficient enough to get the training needed to gain employment, but no more. Accordingly, awards were small and for a short duration. In the 1980s and 1990s, it became apparent that this rationale for support was appropriate in some cases but not in others. Thus, both the courts and the relevant statutes began to distinguish between short- and long-term marriages.

In the former, in marriages of 10 or fewer years' duration, women were typically still young and thus eligible for remarriage, and many had continued to work and so suffered no loss of seniority associated with marriage. In such cases, when both spouses' incomes were comparable, spousal support might be waived altogether. In cases where the spouses' incomes were unequal or in which one parent stayed home with the children, a limited award was seen as warranted but based on the notion of compensation as opposed to self-sufficiency. That is, the mother's contribution was seen as just as important as father's, although different in kind. For that contribution and for her concomitant loss of employment seniority, she deserved to be compensated on divorce.

The situation was quite different for women in long-term marriages, those lasting more than 10 years and often 20, 30, or even 40 years. For such middle-aged or elderly women, remarriage would be difficult. Similarly, many had never worked, were virtually unemployable, and had completely sacrificed income and seniority for the sake of the family, especially the children. In such cases, compensatory spousal support was necessary for life, although the size of the award was tied to husband's actual income and so might be rather modest.

In contemporary cases, then, spousal support turns primarily on *three* dimensions:

- the duration of the marriage;
- the nature of each spouse's contribution, both financial and otherwise; and
- the current financial situation of each spouse, as an expression of his or her respective need and ability to pay.

Duration

Technically, duration is the interval between the date of marriage and the date of separation, that is, the date when one partner left the matrimonial home and set up residence elsewhere. In practice, these requirements can be problematic. Couples who cohabit will have no marriage date, although they can point to the date when they began living together. Similarly, an increasing proportion of legally married couples will have lived together for a time prior to marriage. In both cases, couples may have felt "married" long before they meet the legal requirement of having been so. The same applies to the date of separation. Although the date when one partner changed residences is the legal requirement, some couples may use other, psychologically significant dates— for example, when she took off her marriage ring or he tore up his picture of her. Another level of complexity arises when couples claim to have "separated" although they continued to live together in the matrimonial home. This sometimes arises when fathers are told by their lawyer to remain in the home lest they be seen by the court as having abandoned the children. Alternately, the husband may refuse to move, for example, because "I built this house with my own two hands." Whatever the reason(s) given, the couple will be seen as separated so long as they do not act like husband and wife—that is, they live apart (typically on different floors of the home), have no sexual contact, and no longer assist each other (as regards meals, laundry, etc.). Although such behavior may meet the technical requirements for separation, it leaves arbitrary the date of separation, which must be negotiated in mediation.

Finally, using the logic of compensation, the duration of marriage is relevant to the duration of spousal support but by itself does not establish per se whether such an arrangement is warranted.

Contribution

The contribution of each spouse, both to the marriage and to the children (if any), will become apparent as part of the marital history during intake/assessment. This should include an employment history for both spouses, with specific reference to their proportional contribution to the family's changing income. Although much variation is possible, more so today than ever before, two typical arrangements are as follows:

- In one arrangement, both parents worked—the husband continuously, the wife intermittently—in response to childbearing and child rearing. Moreover, as a function of their different skill sets and accumulating seniority, the husband will consistently have earned between 60% and 80% of the family's income. In this arrangement, the husband, wife, or both may report having managed the family's finances. On divorce, the wife can at least fall back on ongoing employment, although her income from it will be inadequate to reestablish a lifestyle anything like the one both spouses enjoyed while they were together.

- In the second arrangement, on consent, the husband was the sole breadwinner, and the wife stayed home to care for the children and so has no work history. In this arrangement, it is overwhelmingly the husband who has managed the family's finances. On divorce, the wife will be completely dependent on husband and/or her relatives for financial support. Failing that, she will have no alternative but to rely on social assistance.

In both typical arrangements, the wife would be entitled to some spousal support, with the size and duration of such support greater in the second than in the first scenario. In the first scenario in particular, it is easy to imagine variations in which support might be waived altogether. Both spouses, for example, may report comparable income, such that each contributed about 50% of the family's income. Alternatively, with the wife working as a lawyer and husband as a teacher, she may earn more than he does and so pay him spousal support.

Current Status

Finally, in deciding exactly how much money, if any, will change hands, it is important to establish each spouse's current income and expenses. This may already have been done with the aid of their respective lawyers. Alternately, this may be done in mediation, either using forms available through the local family court or with forms created by the mediator using any of a number of available spreadsheet software programs. If this process is to be done through mediation, it should be done in session. Doing so serves several objectives:

- meets the requirements of full disclosure;
- continues the process of building trust between the spouses;
- establishes the level of comparable income;

- determines each spouse's disposable income, that is, the monies available *after* they have paid their monthly expenses; and
- describes their monthly financial needs, especially if either are subject to monthly arrears.

Whether these forms are completed with the help of a lawyer or a mediator, they must be sworn before their respective lawyers to be legally valid.

With these data in place, it is then possible for the spouses to decide whether spousal support is warranted and, if so, how much and for how long, that is, for a specified duration or for life. Furthermore, should support be warranted, they also have the option of making periodic (usually monthly) payments or paying the full amount as a lump sum.

Taxation

As noted above, in both the United States and Canada, alimony is deductible by the payer and a taxable benefit to the recipient. This can be problematic if, for some reason, the recipient requires at least a specific amount every month. Given that such payments are taxable, a *gross-up* may be required. That is, the monthly amount may need to be increased such that the recipient receives a specified amount in after-tax dollars.

Furthermore, in both countries, alimony is taxable if it is paid periodically, typically monthly. However, in Canada, if it is paid in lump sum, it is exempt from tax because it is treated as transfer of property between spouses pursuant to divorce. The same applies in the United States if the payments are characterized as a "buyout" of certain assets as opposed to alimony. Additional tax provisions apply in the United States:

- Some states provide for alimony deductions on top of federal deductions.
- If alimony is reduced by more than $15,000 per year during the first 3 years of an award, the IRS has special "recapture" rules, making excess alimony nondeductible.

Property Division

The final element of a mediated financial plan is that of *property division*. This is a complex undertaking, made amenable to family mediation by being broken into a number of small, manageable "steps." In the interests of clarity, the discussion that follows will divide the process into eight steps:

- Step 1: List all assets
- Step 2: Asset valuation
- Step 3: List debts (liabilities)

- Step 4: Assign assets acquired during the marriage
- Step 5: Identify premarital and special assets
- Step 6: Tax consequences
- Step 7: Negotiate final settlement
- Step 8: Divide personal property

Here, available approaches to property division in the United States and Canada are similar in some respects and different in others. Steps 1 to 5 and Step 8, in the process, are virtually identical (or nearly so) in both countries, but there are some differences in the handling of the remaining steps.

Before proceeding, a word is in order concerning the three goals of property division—namely, equity, contextual sensitivity, and lawfulness. Among other things, marriage is an economic contract concerning the division of roles, the accumulation of assets, and the use of those assets through time. In divorce, it is reasonable for both parties to expect to walk away with a fair share of the assets they have both worked so hard to accumulate. But as will become more apparent in Chapter 12, each party's perspective on what is fair very much reflects the quality of the marital relationship. Given that couples in mediation are invariably in dispute, it will come as little surprise that their views of what would constitute a fair division of assets often diverge. Property division, then, is often hotly, even savagely, contested.

Next, the process of property division must be sensitive to the circumstances of the parties, particularly as regards their relative needs and resources. Property division, then, quite properly explores a range of factors, including their accumulated assets, their health (both physical and mental), their employment status, their earning capacity and future prospects, the duration of the marriage, the circumstances of their decision to divorce (including [in the United States] evidence of marital fault), their relative contribution to the marriage (both monetary and nonmonetary), and, of course, the presence of dependent children and the manner in which their care will be shared between the parties. In general, the process of property division should be such that both parties share the gain as well as the pain.

Finally, the process of mediating financial plans necessarily occurs within the "shadow of the law," that is, the laws and conventions of the local jurisdiction. However, without exception, the texts we consulted in preparing this section were written or coauthored by lawyers, with or without mediation training. Implicit in their treatment were settlements constructed in and by the court and thus strictly subject to existing statutes. In contrast, most mediators are not lawyers and as such strive to balance statutory concerns with client self-determination. TFM-based mediators do this in three ways: by exposing clients to a wide range of settlement options, empowering them to make choices that are perceived by both parties as fair and practical in their circumstances, and settling their dispute in ways most likely to promote a cooperative, business-like relationship between them over the long term. Most of these settlements will be consistent with local statutes. Some, however, may abrogate one or more statutory provisions with the aim of achieving a lasting peace between the parties, with both of them having made a sacrifice in the best interests of their children.

In light of these important qualifications, let us walk through the steps in doing property division. Given the purposes of the process, it should be understood by both parties that the disposition of any assets will be pursuant to their mediated financial plan. Accordingly, until that plan is in place, except for monies needed for their day-to-day affairs, neither is free to dispose of *any* existing assets. Indeed, in some states (such as Connecticut), application for divorce is automatically accompanied by a court order freezing all assets.

Step 1: List All Assets

For purposes of mediation, an asset may be simply defined as an item of property that is present at the date of separation and has an objective value in dollars.

With one exception (see below, Step 5), the first step in property division asks the clients to construct a comprehensive inventory of their assets. Some clients, especially those in court-based mediation, may have few, if any, assets and so either skip the asset division process altogether (save for personal property) or use it to allocate existing debts. The same may be true of middle-class couples, especially those who have mismanaged their financial affairs. However, a more typical scenario would be one in which couples with modest means have an inventory that would consist of a handful of assets, typically including the following:

- a matrimonial home,
- one or two cars,
- one or two employment-based pensions, and
- a small amount of cash, typically in a bank account.

More affluent clients, including some middle-class clients who have managed their financial affairs especially well, may generate an inventory containing a much wider array of assets, such as the following:

- investments (stocks, bonds, and "full life" insurance policies that have a cash surrender value),
- a family-owned business or professional practice,
- electronic equipment (computers, stereo systems),
- recreational vehicles (boats, trucks, skidoos, seadoos, ATVs, motorcycles, airplanes),
- employment benefits (stock options, stock ownership plans, bonuses, commissions, and other monies owing),

- fine art (paintings, antiques, jewelry),
- collectibles (stamps, coins, baseball cards),
- farm equipment (tractors, bailers) and livestock,
- other residences (cottage or chalet),
- investment properties (condominium),
- receivables (monies owed but not yet paid, royalties, tax refunds), and
- other (intellectual property, licenses, losses carried forward for tax purposes).

In addition, all clients have "personal property" (in the United States) or "chattel" (in Canada), that is, the furniture, clothing, china, and other goods that make up their household. Unless specific items are unusually valuable, an inventory of such items is compiled but *not* included in the inventory of assets because their combined market value is typically very low. As such, they will be addressed separately (see below, Step 8).

For many couples, creating such an inventory of assets is not problematic. For others, this task will be a major challenge. For example, confusion can arise as to the definition of an asset for purposes of property division. Over the course of a long-term marriage, couples may own a succession of cars and even homes. Conflict may arise over the disposition of one or more assets that *no longer exist at the point of separation*. Similarly, conflict can arise over the value threshold below which a given asset should be omitted and whether "value" includes sentimental value or is restricted to monetary value only. In such disputes, the onus is on the mediator to be crystal clear as to the rules and definitions that apply in their local jurisdiction.

As noted already (see Chapter 6), the one aspect of property division that is especially problematic for the mediator is the charge that a spouse has "hidden" assets. Short of engaging a forensic accountant or other such experts, there is little that a mediator can do because discovery is not part of the mediation process. If the issue cannot be resolved to the couple's satisfaction, mediation should be terminated and the couple referred to their lawyers.

Step 2: Valuing Assets

The next step is to review the inventory of assets and assign a value to each asset as of the date of separation, also known as the date of *valuation*. In some states, replacement value may apply to items both parties want or need. However, in most states and all provinces, fair market value (what a buyer would be willing to pay for the asset in question) is the standard method of valuation. This method of valuation sometimes means that assets that clients perceived as having significant sentimental value may, in fact, be worth considerably *less* in the marketplace. It often takes some time for this unpleasant realization to sink in. Moreover, clients quickly discover another unpleasant fact—namely, that some assets are easy to value, but others are considerably more difficult.

Asset valuation is simple and easy when documents are readily available that can be used for this purpose. Of the assets listed above, the following would be considered easy to value:

- *Matrimonial home.* Real estate agencies maintain extensive computerized records of all house sales over time. In the hopes of selling the clients' home, most agents would be happy to provide a written estimate of the value of the home by comparing it to similar homes in the area that have sold in the 6 months prior to the separation date. To be doubly sure that this estimate is accurate, two or even three agents can be contacted independently for their estimates of the home's market value. Such services are free of charge. For the clients who are still not satisfied, professional engineering firms are available who specialize in home appraisal, for a fee. The same applies to residential and other properties, including condominiums, cottages, chalets, farms, and unimproved land. Although more expense is involved, the same process can be used to value foreign residential properties, such as condominiums in Florida or villas in France or Italy. Note, however, that spouses may only claim *one home* as their matrimonial home, that is, their principal residence at separation; other homes owned concurrently (such as a summer cottage) and/or previously owned matrimonial homes do not qualify.

- *Motor vehicles.* Various "books" exist to value used vehicles of all sorts, including cars, trucks, boats, and planes of any make, model, or year. In addition, newspaper "want ads" can be used for this purpose. The same applies to farm equipment and livestock.

- *Investment vehicles.* Stock markets in New York and Toronto maintain comprehensive records concerning the changing values of all stocks, bonds, and mutual funds. This information is readily available through stock brokers and financial planners as well as in local daily newspapers. The same applies to insurance companies as regards policies with a cash surrender value, such as "whole life" insurance policies. Typically, the company will be happy to provide a written estimate of a policy's cash surrender value as of the separation date. Note that "term insurance" policies, unlike "whole life" policies, have no market value.

- *Electronic equipment.* There is a growing market for used electronic equipment. Accordingly, "books" have been created to value such property at the date of separation. Similarly, "buy and sell" magazines exist for this express purpose, as do sections in most daily newspapers.

- *Fine art, collectibles, and jewelry.* All three assets are subject to appraisal for insurance purposes, such that their valuation is typically not problematic. In the event that such items were never appraised or if an existing appraisal is out of date, a recent reappraisal may be required as of the date of separation.

•   *Employee pension plans.* Known generically as "defined contribution plans," in the United States they come in various guises, including thrift plans, 401Ks (named for the IRS law that created them), employee stock option plans, profit-sharing plans (Keough plans), 457b plans, individual retirement accounts (IRAs, such as the Roth IRA), tax-sheltered annuities, and other plans. With some exceptions (such as the Roth IRA), employee pension plans are those to which the client (the employee) alone contributes regularly, typically by way of payroll deduction. That is, such plans are paid for with pretax dollars, deducted from income *before* taxation. As such, they do not avoid taxation but only defer it to a specified retirement age. Moreover, such plans may or may not be "vested," with vested plans those in which the beneficiary has had sufficient time to earn some sort of return, even if he or she left the firm tomorrow. In any event, efforts to liquidate such plans would immediately make them subject to taxation, often with some sort of penalty, such that this is seldom a viable option. Rather, such plans are important assets whose value is equal to the accrued amount contributed to them plus any earned interest. In this regard, they are very much like savings account in banks, and, like such accounts, their value is readily available by requesting that information in writing from the client's employer or the bank. In the case of bank accounts, the bankbook or statement of account for the date in question will usually suffice.

•   *Government pension plans.* In Canada, all people who work for their income pay into the Canada Pension Plan (CPP), either through payroll deductions (among employees) or through quarterly or year-end tax contributions (among those who are self-employed). In doing so, they accumulate CPP "credits" that determine the monthly amount they will be entitled to receive on retirement. By law, on notice of divorce, these credits are automatically "equalized" between the two spouses (see pamphlet MP90-3/1-3-1997E, Human Resources Development Canada).

In contrast to the assets discussed above, some assets are considerably more difficult to value. Consider the following:

•   *Employment-based pensions.* We have already noted that "defined contribution plans" are rather like bank accounts and thus simple to value. The other type of plan, the "defined benefit plan," is much more difficult. In this type of plan, the employer alone contributes to the plan and, on the employee's retirement, contracts to pay the employee a pension in monthly installments. Determining the present value of these future payments depends on a number of factors, including the age at which the employee retires, how long he or she is likely to live (and thus how many payments he or she can expect to receive), the number of years the employee worked or will work for the employer, and what the employee's highest years' earnings will be. Such complexity requires the involvement of an *actuary* who uses a series of tables to estimate the answers to these and other questions and thus provides a reasonable estimate of the current market value of each spouse's pension. Depending on the state or province, separate calculations may also be required to determine that portion of each spouse's pension that is marital property (see below, Step 4); pension benefits accrued before marriage and after separation are typically regarded as separate property. Furthermore, it should be understood that actuarial estimates depend on the validity of the assumptions used. For example, it is assumed that each spouse will live long enough to retire. Should that not be true, these estimates would be worthless. In some cases, the alternative is a buyout in which, on leaving the firm, the employee waives such future benefits in exchange for payment of a specified amount by the employer.

- *Individual pension plans.* In Canada, an additional variation is noteworthy—namely, the Registered Retirement Savings Plan (RRSP). Such plans are like "defined benefit plans" in two senses: They are deferred, with clients normally drawing on them only on retirement (in this case, at age 69), and they are seen for tax purposes as income and thus attract tax liability only on retirement. For that reason, calculating their value at separation involves discounting their face value by up to 30%. However, they are distinct from employment-based pensions in that they are based on client contributions only (up to 18% of taxable income per year) and are tax deductible in each year of contribution.

- *Receivables.* Including receivables in the list of assets depends on the degree to which they are secure. Monies to be received from an employer or the government in tax rebates are secure and should be included. Personal loans to a relative may be another matter altogether. Although they may have promised to repay the loan, the likelihood that they will ever do so is uncertain. Clients would be well advised to list only secure debts while agreeing informally to split any personal debt repayment that they actually receive.

- *Family-owned business and professional practices.* Valuing a business is complex and best left to professional business evaluators or to chartered accounts. Several different valuation methods are available, each with advantages and disadvantages. *Book value* refers to the value of the equipment and the receivables minus any outstanding debt, but it ignores the firm's profitability as well as various intangibles, such as the firm's reputation in the marketplace. *Profit value* is another approach that estimates value by multiplying the profit by a factor of between 3 and 6. But estimating the profit is a complex matter in itself, and selecting the exact multiplier can be problematic. Similarly, the *receivables value* approach involves taking a base amount plus a factor of between 2.0 and 2.5. However, calculating the base is problematic in its own right, as is the choice of an add-on factor. Finally, the *market value* approach is based strictly on what the firm would have sold for on the date of separation. This approach applies only if one intends to sell. Furthermore, the value would normally be a function of negotiation because sellers tend to bid high, whereas buyers tend to bid low. Further still, the meaning of *high* and *low* will fluctuate with market conditions, such that the timing of the sale is another source of complexity. This necessarily brief discussion makes clear that valuing businesses is a matter typically beyond the competence of most clients and should be left to qualified specialists. The same is true for professional practices. Here, an additional consideration is whether the practice has any market value whatsoever. For example, it is possible to estimate the value of a medical doctor by examining the number of active cases, his or her average annual revenue, and his or her annual profit, that is, his or her actual take-home pay. This same approach might not apply to the income of a mediator, for example, whose practice is exclusively dependent on his or her reputation in the community as the basis for ongoing referrals. In his or her absence, the practice might literally have no market value whatever.

- *Other assets.* Finally, the valuation of other assets, such as licenses and intellectual property, is complex and requires the assistance of experts, such as lawyers and chartered accountants. However, these sorts of assets apply to very few mediation clients and are included here for the sake of completeness.

This discussion of valuation makes two things abundantly clear. First, asset valuation can be a complex, time-consuming, and even expensive undertaking. Second, valuation is seldom a mechanical exercise. Rather, the value of clients' assets reflects both their sentimental attachment to these assets and the extent to which these assets symbolize their marital relationship. As such, valuation can be a simple, straightforward process, or it can trigger and escalate conflict between couples.

Step 3: List All Debts (Liabilities)

The next step in the process of property division involves listing all debts or liabilities. Debts are divided into two classes or categories—namely, those that are *secured* and those that are not. Secured debts are those that are attached to other assets or *collateral*, such as a home or a car. Car loans, bank loans, and mortgages on residential or commercial property are examples of secured liabilities. Thus, the *net value* of such assets (their *equity*) involves the fair market value at separation *minus* any secured debt. For example, a matrimonial home valued at $250,000 and with an outstanding mortgage of $110,000 would have a net value of $140,000. (In the event that the clients elect to sell the home [see below, Step 7], their equity would be reduced by another 10% to 15% to take account of disposition costs, such as the real estate agent's fee, taxes, and lawyers' fees and disbursements.)

Unsecured debt is debt that is not attached to collateral, including personal debt and credit card debt. For example, it would not be uncommon for a client to have several credit cards, each of which has an unpaid balance. In such cases, the principal amount is listed, excluding (in the United States) or including (in Canada) any accrued interest. Moreover, as a function of circumstances, such debt may be regarded as separate or marital property.

With the liabilities in place, it is now possible to determine the client's asset/debt ratio. In most cases, this ratio is positive; that is, assets exceed debts, making it possible to negotiate the division of assets. Unfortunately, in some cases, the ratio is negative; that is, couples must confront the double disaster of divorce plus substantial debt. Here, there is no property to divide; rather, the property division process is used to decide how the debt will be shared between the spouses.

Debt, as much as the division of assets, can be a source of intense conflict. For example, as we will see in Step 4, each spouse is responsible for his or her own debt. But that may not be fair. If Robert used his credit card to purchase his winter coat and a new set of snow tires for his car, then that is clearly *his* debt. But suppose Jane claims that although her purchases were made on her credit card, they consisted mostly of marital or "community" property— namely, clothes for the kids, a new toaster for the kitchen, socks and underwear for her husband, and food for the week; only the new lipstick was for her own personal use. Even granting her claim that this debt should be community debt, it is still unclear how that debt should be shared. If Jane works part-time and only contributes 30% of the family's income, it would be unfair to ask her to pay 50% of this debt. And what of Samantha, who remains at home to care for the children and thus is completely dependent on her husband's income? Because he contributes 100% of the income, perhaps he should be fully responsible for the family's debt? These examples make clear that although listing assets and liabilities may be a simple chore in itself, the decisions that flow from these lists are often complex and conflictual and thus very much appropriate to TFM.

Step 4: Assigning Assets Acquired During the Marriage

With a comprehensive list of assets and debts in place, the client is then asked to *assign* each asset to one of three categories: separate property, marital property to which each spouse has an equal claim, and property that is partly separate and partly marital. The logic used in assigning property is different in the United States and Canada.

United States. Property assignment is determined by the statutory regime. In the United States, two such regimes exist. In 42 states, property assignment is based on the principle of *equitable distribution*, taken from English common law, but in 8 states (California, Idaho, Nevada, New Mexico, Oregon, Texas, Washington, and Wisconsin), the operative principle is that of *community property*, taken from Spanish civil law.

Among states following equitable distribution, all property acquired during or before the marriage is subject to division. Property assignment is primarily based on ownership (who holds title), but a range of other factors can be considered, including each spouse's relative contribution to the marriage (both monetary and nonmonetary); each spouse's earning capacity; the duration of the marriage; each spouse's age, health, and education; and the reason(s) for the breakdown of the relationship, including the issue of marital fault. That said, there are few specific guidelines, such that the courts (and thus the clients) have wide discretion to create a settlement that is fair and reasonable.

A case in point concerns the matrimonial home. The deed to a matrimonial home will describe ownership as either joint tenancy, tenancy in common, or community property. Joint tenancy and community property suggest that the spouses shared ownership equally, on a 50/50 basis. In contrast, tenancy in common may involve wide variation in proportional ownership. For example, if one spouse owned the home before marriage, but marital property was used to pay the mortgage and maintain and improve the house, then both spouses may claim a proportional share of the property. By the same logic, the home may be seen as an entirely separate property. Moreover, states vary in the significance they attach to different factors, such as the name on the title, whether the spouses had a written or verbal understanding regarding ownership, what would have been paid by way of rental, who paid the mortgage, and whether marital or separate property was used to that end. Situational factors may also come into play. Given a home that has failed to appreciate in value, it may be in both their interests to have one spouse's contribution characterized as a "loan" rather than both claiming part ownership. Finally, in the absence of state law or a prior agreement, the exact nature of each spouse's interest in the property is entirely subject to negotiation.

State laws may also cover a variety of special situations. For example, one spouse's gambling debts may be deducted from marital property to compensate the other spouse. Conversely, both the principal on separate property (such as stocks and bonds) as well as its appreciated value may be regarded as separate property. Although professional licenses are not subject to division, they may warrant a trade-off in other property or an increase in alimony to even out each spouse's differential earning capacity.

Turning to states following community property, despite variation between states and several specific exceptions (see below, Step 5), *all* property acquired during the marriage would be seen as marital property and thus subject to equal division; property acquired by either spouse prior to marriage would be seen as separate property. Similarly, all debts would be seen as community debt, even gambling debts, and even if these debts were acquired by one spouse without the other spouse's knowledge or consent. In general, the laws in these states assume that property is marital unless shown otherwise.

Even so, different states recognize a variety of exceptions. For example, spousal education funded with marital property would mean that the other spouse is entitled to claim half of those costs. Loans taken out by one spouse for education purposes are their separate responsibility. There are also some contexts in which situational factors come into play. For example, given a business acquired by one spouse prior to marriage, if the appreciated value of that asset was due to the nature of the business alone, then it would be viewed as separate property. However, if that appreciated value resulted from the combined efforts of both spouses, then it would be regarded as marital property.

Canada. Although there is some variation in property laws across provinces, they are alike in adopting a community property perspective. As in community property states, in Canada, with some specific exceptions (see below, Step 5), all property acquired during the marriage is seen as serving the common good and assigned as marital or community property. This is especially true of the matrimonial home, which is given special status and is *always* seen as community property, irrespective of whose name is on the deed. Although separate property is recognized, it is given special treatment, being listed twice—once in the list of assets and again as "excluded property" that is *subtracted* from the value of community assets. As in the United States, the onus is on the spouse to show that specific assets are separate property.

That said, the assignment process does not ignore individual (rather than separate) ownership of assets. Accordingly, the value of some assets, such as the matrimonial home, will be equally split and assigned to each spouse. The same may be true of other assets, or they may be assigned to one spouse or the other, based on ownership or use. For example, in households that have two cars, the value of the vehicle driven by the wife will be assigned to her, whereas that of the husband will be assigned to him. The same process will be used to assign all marital assets, including employment-based and individual pensions—assets that are usually second in value to their share of the matrimonial home. On some occasions, this process of assignment will show that the value of the husband's and wife's assets will be equal or approximately so. More often, given the husband's generally greater earning capacity, it will show that the value of his accumulated assets is greater—sometimes much greater—than that of his wife's.

Step 5: Identifying Premarital and Special Assets

Identification is an extension of the assignment process, attaching additional information to each asset in order to specify if it is marital, separate, or mixed property. In practice, assignment and what we have called "identification" occur together. We discuss it here as an extra step in the interests of clarity.

Identification, then, asks clients to review their list of assets and debts and further describe them in *three* ways. First, they are asked to specify *when* they acquired the asset or debt in question, either *before* they were married or *during* the course of their marriage; in both the United States and Canada, assets or debts acquired after the date of separation are automatically excluded from property division. Unlike assets acquired during the course of marriage, which are valued as of the date of separation, premarital assets are typically valued as of the date of marriage, that is, closer to the time when they were originally acquired. For clients who are dissolving their first marriage, this is seldom a problem because most couples enter their first marriage with few, if any, assets. However, when such claims do apply, they often create an anomalous situation given that they often refer to one or more assets that *no longer exist*. That being the case, most clients will be satisfied with a rough "guesstimate" of the value of these assets. Claims regarding premarital property are more often the case when one or both spouses have entered and are now dissolving their second or later marriage and may bring with them substantial assets.

Second, clients are asked to specify *how* each asset was acquired, that is, whether it was *given* to them by way of gift or inheritance, resulted from a personal injury lawsuit, or was *purchased* or otherwise acquired by either spouse.

Finally, they are asked how each asset has been *used* during the course of the marriage, that is, whether the asset has been used exclusively for the personal benefit of each spouse or for the common good, thus benefiting the entire family.

The interpretation of the answers to these questions will vary by statutory regime.

United States. For clients who live in states committed to equitable distribution, *all* assets may be subject to division, irrespective of when or how they were acquired. However, in distinguishing between separate and marital property, the initial focus will be on property acquired during the course of the marriage. If circumstances are such as to ensure a reasonable settlement—if there is a positive asset/debt ratio, both spouses have an earning capacity sufficient to their needs, and there are no other special circumstances—then premarital assets may be ignored. If that is not the case, then premarital assets and assets acquired through gift or inheritance may need to be examined as part of the final settlement.

For clients who live in states committed to community property, premarital property and property acquired through gift or inheritance will be seen as separate property and excluded from division on divorce. This includes the proceeds flowing from those assets, either through appreciation (such as interest-bearing stocks and bonds) or rental (such as a commercial property). The same applies to premarital debt.

Finally, irrespective of state commitments, property may be deemed separate if it is so identified by virtue of a domestic contract (prenuptial agreement). Similarly, wherever possible, claims concerning separate property should be backed up by documentary evidence, including deeds, wills, insurance policies, contracts, purchase orders, receipts, and so forth.

Canada. As in community property states, in all provinces in Canada, premarital property and property acquired through gift or inheritance will be seen as separate property. The value of property acquired through gift or inheritance will be excluded from assets, that is, *subtracted* from the total value of each spouse's assets. Similarly, the value of premarital property will be *subtracted* from the total of each spouse's assets.

However, four complications arise in the Canadian context. One concerns the case, noted above, in which proceeds flow from premarital property. Here, such proceeds would be regarded as marital property and included in the owner-spouse's list of assets. The second complication applies in the United States and Canada and concerns *commingling*, that is, the mixing of separate and marital property. In the case of an inheritance, for example, if it remained intact in the name of one spouse, in Canada, only the accrued interest would be seen as marital property. However, suppose the recipient spouse chose to split the principal, with part of it retained in his or her own name and the other part used, for example, to renovate the matrimonial home. In that case, the interest accruing on the principal would be seen as marital property, whereas the monies used for renovation would be converted into marital property because it benefited the common good. The third complication concerns the matrimonial home, which, as noted previously, is always seen as community property. In many cases, the couple's first home is purchased jointly, making its disposition on divorce simple because it is clearly marital property. But suppose one or both spouses owned a home prior to marriage. If each sold the home prior to marriage, then the proceeds would be seen as separate property and could be reclaimed on divorce. However, if one of those homes became the matrimonial home on marriage, then it would become marital property. The first owner would be entitled to reclaim the equity at marriage as premarital property, and the spouses would split the appreciated equity at separation. The fourth and final complication concerns premarital debt that carries forward into the marriage. Whereas premarital assets are *subtracted* from marital assets, premarital debt is *added* to marital assets.

Step 6: Tax Consequences

The process of property division can be complex and thus often subject to multiple solutions, each of which may have different short- and long-term consequences. It is incumbent on the mediator to ensure that clients make informed choices in selecting among these options. This is especially true as regards taxation, which can make the difference between options that are practical or impractical. In both the United States and Canada, taxation will primarily concern income, capital gains, and transfers of assets. Income tax will apply to assets purchased with pretax dollars, such as pensions. Combining taxes and penalties, efforts to liquidate such assets will not be practical, unless spouses are desperate for cash. Capital gains will apply when the selling price of an asset exceeds its purchase price. In some cases, the difference can involve tens or even hundreds of thousands of dollars. Finally, as part of their divorce settlement, one spouse may wish to transfer assets to the other spouse. The application of these taxes varies between the United States and Canada.

United States. Irrespective of the state, in the past, capital gains tax used to apply to the sale of all assets. That is no longer true. For example, although rates vary from state to state, the federal tax on the sale of stocks or bonds currently stands at about 20%. In recent years, applicable tax regulations have been changed to allow some exemptions. Such exemptions are particularly salient as regards the matrimonial home. If a couple has lived at that residence for at least 2 of the past 5 years, and if the home is sold while they are still married, they would be entitled to an exemption on the first $500,000 of capital gains. Were the home to be sold after divorce, the exemption drops to $250,000. Moreover, this exemption can be used an unlimited number of times, so that there is no penalty if a couple chooses to buy or sell a home several years after the divorce.

As to transfer taxes, if the transfer of assets is pursuant to divorce and occurs within 12 months of it, then the transaction would be tax free. Moreover, such an exemption can be applied by court order to transfers that would normally be taxed. For example, a Qualified Domestic Relations Order (QDRO) can allow for the division of pension plans free of transfer taxes. That said, two cautions are in order. First, although transfers between spouses may be exempt from taxation, later transfer of assets to a third party, either by sale or gift, would attract both capital gains and transfer taxes. Second, although transfers of marital property are exempt from taxes, the same usually *cannot* be said for the sale or transfer of separate property, a fact that can be potentially problematic when seeking to trade off separate property against marital property. In such cases, the two assets may have the same face value, but their differential vulnerability to taxes may make any such deals potentially inequitable.

Canada. Although capital gains tax applies to the sale of most assets, irrespective of their status as separate or marital property, the matrimonial home is given special status, being totally exempt from such tax. Similarly, the transfer of assets pursuant to divorce, whether marital or separate property, is exempt from transfer taxes, including monies within either spouse's RRSP.

Step 7: Negotiate Final Settlement

In both the United States and Canada, the final step in the process of property division involves two sets of decisions—namely, the following:

- Negotiating a final settlement
- Deciding how that settlement should be enacted

Both sets of decisions will vary somewhat in the United States and Canada.

United States. Although property division is governed by state law, the final settlement will typically be determined through negotiation among the parties. The central goal of the process is to arrive at an arrangement that is fair and reasonable to both parties, given their respective circumstances. That will often involve a series of trade-offs. For example, a common scenario is one in which there are dependent children who live with a primary parent, typically their mother. In that case, the matrimonial home would usually go to the mother, and the father would get other assets in compensation. The spouses would split various items of marital property, either evenly or unevenly and sometimes in exchange for separate property, with further adjustments often required in states that either do not favor alimony or allow it in a limited way. Other adjustments may reflect various special situations and will need to account for any existing debt, whether separate or marital, while taking account of the short- and long-term consequences of income, capital gains, and transfer taxes. Furthermore, for the settlement to be final, it is crucial that all assets be considered; the omission of any significant assets may force the parties to reopen the settlement in the future.

Having finally decided who gets what, various decisions remain as to *how* the proposed settlement will be enacted. A case in point concerns the matrimonial home. Mercer and Pruett (2001, pp. 108-110) list various pros and cons for selling the home. It would be reasonable to *sell* the home if the spouses

- are unable to afford the mortgage,
- are unable to afford the upkeep,
- have too much money tied up in equity,
- have too many bad memories, and/or
- owe money to others.

Conversely, it would be reasonable to *keep* the home

- to ensure stability for the primary parent and the children,
- if one spouse is unable to refinance the mortgage or buy out the other spouse,
- if one spouse had a sufficient diversity of assets that he or she did not need additional money,
- if one spouse had sufficient resources to pay the mortgage and maintain the upkeep of the house, and/or
- if there were tax advantages in doing so, including the deductibility of mortgage payments and the avoidance of capital gains taxes.

Selling the house means absorbing preparation and disposition costs. It also raises concerns about the timing of the sale, both in terms of the real estate market (and the price they can expect to get for the property) and the needs of the children (sell now or after the children have graduated from high school or college). Keeping the house means sole ownership (i.e., buying out the other spouse and refinancing the mortgage) or joint ownership (e.g., giving the other spouse a share in the equity when the house is sold by means of a "notice of equitable interest" or by giving him or her a mortgage on the property). Other options include taking out a second mortgage or a long-term loan, paying the other spouse rent (while saving to buy out his or her share in the future), deferring a buyout for a specific interval, or having the other spouse agree to make a sacrifice for the sake of the children and accept a buyout for less than his or her fair share of the property.

Canada. Arriving at a final settlement involves a series of between two and three steps. First, the clients need to calculate each spouse's *net family property* (NFP). This is done by adding up each spouse's assets, subtracting each spouse's debts, including each spouse's excluded or separate property, and either subtracting any assets prior to marriage or adding any premarital debt.

Next, these figures are plugged into a standard formula to *equalize* their assets: the larger NFP *minus* the smaller NFP divided by 2.

For example, if the husband's NFP is $540,000 and the wife's NFP is $220,000, then the equalization amount is $320,000 divided by 2, or $160,000. That is, the husband would owe his wife $160,000 by way of property division. Next, either the spouses find this amount acceptable or they negotiate some other figure that they can live with. In a recent case, a husband owed his wife $10,000 in spousal support and an additional $50,000 in equalization. After extended negotiation, they agreed that the husband would pay the wife $45,000 in lump sum, $10,000 in spousal support, and $35,000 in equalization. The wife reasoned that it was worth accepting a lower figure in exchange for lasting peace between them over this issue, thus increasing the likelihood that they would be able to work together cooperatively in parenting.

What remains is negotiating *how* the amount in question is to be paid. For example, in the above example, the $35,000 equalization amount does *not* take into account the wife's share of the equity in the matrimonial home—in that case, another $100,000. Thus, further negotiation will be required. Possibilities include transferring RRSP assets in order for the husband to buy out the wife's share of the home and pay the equalization, taking out a second mortgage on the home, or taking out a long-term loan, and so forth. In other cases, if lump-sum payment is *not* practical, periodic payments may be the only alternative. Under law, such payments may extend no longer than 10 years, with the debt subject to interest (often at or near the prime rate) and with wife holding a lien on the house or some other large asset as security against default.

Step 8: Dividing the Personal Property

With negotiation of a final settlement, the clients have successfully disposed of all assets of value. However, it remains to divide their personal property (in the United States), also known (in Canada) as their "chattel." Although these items of household property have little market value, they may have substantial sentimental and practical value. Accordingly, negotiation around their division may be brief and unemotional or extended and highly conflictual, up to and including impasse.

Following completion of an inventory of personal property, in both the United States and Canada, a handful of standard methods are used to help clients divide said property. These methods may be used alone or in some combination.

The primary method involves making a series of trade-offs. Each spouse is asked to review the inventory and place every item in one of five categories:

1. of interest to me alone,

2. of interest to my spouse alone,

3. of interest to neither spouse and therefore slated for disposal,

4. of interest to both spouses, and

5. of interest to the children alone.

Items in the third category can be given away to charity, sold at a garage sale, or simply placed at the roadside for garbage pickup. On consent, each spouse will take possession of items in the first and second categories, which typically consist of personal clothing and items of sentimental or practical importance, such as pictures and mementos of either spouse's family or the wife's sewing things and the husband's carpentry tools. Disposition of items in the fifth category will depend in part on how they plan to share time with the children. Typically, the children's things go with the children or are split (evenly or unevenly) between the parents on anticipation of the children's needs and preferences. Finally, items in the fourth category are subject to trade-offs. If one spouse gets the refrigerator, the other gets the stove. If one gets the bedroom set, the other gets the dining room set, and so on, until the list of items has been exhausted. Such trade-offs should be mindful of the approximate market value of the items, so they are fair and even-handed.

Should difficulties rise, they will often be related to the sentimental value of the property and, most important, what these items have come to symbolize in their relationship. How the items were acquired (through gift or purchase), with whose money or from whose relative(s), how and by whom the items were used, and who is in charge of the process all bear on the ease or difficulty with which division of personal property is negotiated.

This approach will typically dispose of most property in question. Of any remaining items in dispute, the parties may use a variety of supplementary approaches:

- Write down items of roughly equal value on separate cards, place the cards in a hat, and have each take turns picking items from the hat. Alternately, flip a coin; the winner gets first pick from the list, the loser second choice, and so on.
- Hold an auction, with the item going to the spouse willing to pay the most for it; after all items in contention are auctioned off, any difference in the final balance may be equalized through the division of liquid assets.
- Use the two-pile approach, with one spouse dividing the items in question into two piles. The other spouse gets first pick from one of the piles, the other spouse gets first pick from the other pile, and so on, until all items have been chosen.

Even so, in some cases, so committed are the spouses to the fight between them and their struggle for control that the division of personal property can lead to impasse. Often, the spouses will know that they are acting irrationally but cannot stop themselves from doing so. In addition to the various impasse-breaking methods cited above (see Chapter 6), it can be useful to ask couples in this situation to consider two questions: Will all of this really matter 5 years from now? And how do you want your children to remember this time in their lives, when they look on it 10 years from now? Thus asked to consider the potentially disastrous consequences of their actions, many couples will pull back from the brink and complete the process of dividing their person property. A small proportion of couples will be unable to do so, thus throwing away weeks or even months of patient and successful negotiation in family mediation. Such is a mediator's lot!

_____ **Discussion**

Using mediation to arrive at a financial plan is a complex process. As will now be apparent, it requires that mediators be thoroughly knowledgeable about the statutes and conventions in their local jurisdiction and across a range of issues, some of them quite complex. Mediators should be honest in knowing their strengths and weaknesses; there is no shame in including various experts in the process and/or asking for input from the lawyers on both sides. Conversely, in our view, this knowledge is well within the capacity of any college-educated and competent family mediator, irrespective of his or her disciplinary background.

That said, technical knowledge alone, no matter how extensive or expert, will not guarantee agreement between spouses in conflict. As we have noted repeatedly, the key to constructive resolution will hinge on the character of the relationship between the spouses, the meaning various assets have come to have for each spouse, and the respective circumstances (financial, social, physical) that shape how they approach negotiation around financial issues. It is to these relationships and circumstances that we turn next.

12 Financial Plans

Part 2: Patterns of Conflict

It will now be apparent that doing financial mediation involves at least two sets of knowledge: general knowledge about finances (including mortgages, interest rates, taxation, and the like) and specific knowledge about the three key aspects of finances in divorce (child support, alimony, and property division). It will also be clear that such technical knowledge *in and of itself* is insufficient for competence in the mediation of financial plans. This is so because these technical aspects of financial mediation are superimposed on a complex relational dynamic. Indeed, in our experience, couples in mediation fall into three broad categories: those that are in conflict over children but not about money, those in conflict about money but not about children, and those in conflict about children *and* money. What is missing from the available literature concerning financial mediation is a systematic formulation linking relational dynamics, money, and intervention practices. Below, we make a start toward creating such a formulation.

Before proceeding, several qualifications are in order. First, the relational patterns to be described below derive from our clinical experience and from discussions with colleagues; it would not surprise us if readers, whose comments we eagerly invite, have had other experiences and could identify additional patterns of conflict. Second, given the therapeutic family mediation (TFM) model from which we work, the intervention options described below are typically, though not always, therapeutic in character. Third, in the interests of clarity and simplicity, the patterns described below are all "pure" forms. In practice, couples will occasionally present with a combination of patterns. This varies as a function of marital duration and stage of mediation. Fourth, the patterns described below are more about power and control over resources (the golden rule) then gender per se. Consequently, it would hardly be surprising if couples were to present with the same patterns but in which the genders were reversed. Similarly, we would expect the patterns to hold whether or not couples were legally married. Finally, the case vignettes are all synthetic in character, each one deriving from several similar cases rather than the experience of any one couple. Moreover, each reflects a positive outcome, a deliberate choice intended to suggest that one can work successfully with couples across patterns of conflict. However, it will be apparent that some patterns present more difficulties for the mediator than others.

Part 2: Relational Concerns

In attempting to characterize the link between relational dynamics, money, and intervention practices, we describe five common patterns of interaction among couples seeking to mediate their financial concerns.

Pattern 1: Money as Power

As the title suggests, the underlying basis for conflict in these couples centers on power and control and with it a sense of entitlement. Typically organized along traditional lines, these are families in which husbands have been firmly in control of the family's resources, often as the sole bread-winner. These husbands feel that in mediation, they should determine how these resources will be divided in divorce.

Husbands in these family systems have come to believe that the money belongs to them and are both offended and confused by notions of "community property." This view is likely reflected in a fairly clean division of family roles, with work, finances, and much of the external world (e.g., politics, international affairs) in the husband/father's realm, whereas family and emotional matters, including child care, household management, education, and health care, are in the wife's or mother's realm. In accordance with this arrangement, husbands typically give their wives a regular household "allowance" but otherwise have had control of the remainder. It follows that in divorce, the husband feels that he, and he alone, should decide how the money should be divided and, conversely, that any claims that she might make lack all credibility.

On the surface, the behavior of some wives is often consistent with this view. For example, they may have no knowledge concerning what their husbands earn, whether and how much has been saved, and whether there are any investments. They may also have little or no knowledge of the tax system or the valuation of pensions, investments, or the matrimonial home and, more generally, feel overwhelmed by the entire process of negotiating around financial matters.

Consequently, husbands and wives approach mediation in very different terms. Husbands are often contemptuous of their wives' lack of knowledge about money, deny that they had any role in maintaining their wives' lack of financial knowledge, and are often very angry that state or provincial statutes force them to share assets that they feel belong to them. In contrast, wives often report a long and ultimately futile struggle to achieve a more balanced relationship. Wives approach mediation with a combination of anger, intimidation, and helplessness.

In such cases, intervention options include power balancing, confrontation, education, and role reversal, with storytelling also potentially useful. For example, individual caucusing may be used to give these wives a short introduction to money and the power that goes with it. It is critical to invoke the full disclosure clause in the mediation contract to ensure that both spouses have a clear picture of the assets (money) under discussion. That clear picture will be central in doing reality testing with both spouses to ensure that their respective claims are reasonable under the circumstances and tied to some set of facts available to both parties. The mediator's control over the process will be critical to ensure that both parties have an equal opportunity to say their piece rather than have husbands overwhelm their wives. The mediator may also need to confront husbands' distorted beliefs, for example, that the money *belongs* to them, that wives contributed little of value, that wives' lack of knowledge about money is irremediable, that husbands' contempt of their wives (and contemptuous behavior toward them) is justifiable, or that financial mediation merely involves a good business plan devoid of affect. Similarly, it will be important to confront wives' distorted beliefs, for example, that husbands care *only* about the money, that husbands' control over the family's resources represents a character flaw, that negotiating with them is futile, or that the organization of their roles in the family was a personal choice and thus independent of any larger forces in society.

Furthermore, both parents must become aware that a husband's oppressive control over his wife negatively affected and continues to affect their children. Apart from direct confrontation, one way of addressing these beliefs is through role reversal, with each spouse being asked to speak in the other's voice and then report what that felt like. Wives may also be encouraged to supplement their growing financial knowledge by calling on the advice of experts, including their lawyers and/or accountants. Finally, stories, fables, and metaphors may all be used to highlight the benefits to both spouses and children of more balanced and democratic ways of handling and dividing the money, both now and in the future.

In short, family mediation with Pattern 1 couples will heavily emphasize the mediator's educative role. Giving information and confronting distorted beliefs allow these spouses to negotiate with each other on a roughly equal basis and, in turn, to hear clearly, often for the first time, what the other has to say. Once this begins to happen, the loud intensity of conflict will typically lessen dramatically, and the content of each spouse's contribution will often change significantly, with the husband becoming warmer and more affectively charged and the wife becoming cooler, less angry, and more sensitive to their material circumstances. As in all cases involving financial mediation, spouses will routinely be asked to consult with their lawyers to ensure that any agreement between them is fair and reasonable.

Consider the case of Mark and Dorothy Gentle. Dorothy had been born into a secure, middle-class family. Her father had always been in charge of the family's resources, so she was not surprised when Mark did the same when they married. Mark had come from a working-class family where every dollar counted and where both parents shared in financial decision making. He was both surprised and flattered to find himself in charge of the money when he married. Because they had little money to speak of at the time—Dorothy had married for love and against parental resistance—that control was easy to assume. His later success as an entrepreneur changed everything, leaving him in charge of a comfortable income, mounting debts, and an unwillingness to share either with Dorothy. Instead, he spent lavishly on his wife and his three children. But the time needed to generate that income—time away from his family—eroded his marriage, and his refusal to share control over the money with Dorothy eroded it further. When she had a rather public affair with a younger (and much poorer) man, even marital counseling could not save their relationship; it was all over for both of them.

In mediation, the Gentles were cordial and mutually respectful as they, together, created a parenting plan. But when the discussion turned to money, they transformed into a high-conflict couple, raging at each other through their tears. Their initial conversation was loud, filled with mutual accusations and name-calling, and quite unproductive. Furthermore, with his background in business, Mark was completely contemptuous of the size of Dorothy's claim for property division and alimony. Individual caucusing with Dorothy revealed that she felt overwhelmed and quite unprepared to negotiate the money issues. Subsequent efforts to educate her, control their emotional outbursts, give each a glimpse of what the other was experiencing, and create a level playing field proved lengthy but ultimately successful. Their hard-fought final agreement was not only mutually acceptable but was based on a newfound mutual respect and some new skills around conflict management. Both lawyers confirmed that the deal they reached was a reasonable one.

Pattern 2: Money as Security

The tremendous influx of women into the workplace has created a kind of couple that combines elements of the new with elements of the traditional.

They are a new couple in that both work, contribute to their combined family income, and so share in financial decision making. However, they are often traditional in at least two senses: Wives remain largely responsible for child care, and the organization of the workplace means that they often earn less—sometimes much less—than their husbands. Although their income gives these wives options that their mothers did not enjoy, it still leaves many of them in a position of financial dependence. Among families with children, wives' income may be dedicated to their needs, whereas all other expenses are paid for out of their husbands' income. Divorce, then, can create a dilemma and in some cases may even push these wives and their children into poverty. Among those in long-term marriages, whose children are often grown and no longer living with them, divorce confronts these wives with the bleak prospect of facing retirement alone and with very limited resources. Young or old, for Pattern 2 couples, financial mediation turns on the issue of financial security.

Consequently, among Pattern 2 couples, there is often a hysterical edge to negotiation, as husbands and wives talk at cross-purposes. Husbands tend to use the language of business: fact based, unemotional, and centered on creating a sound business plan. In contrast, wives use the language of hurt feelings. They complain that husbands have not listened to their concerns and still continue not to do so. They insist that mediation must give them what they deserve for years of faithful service. But underneath it all, they speak the language of fear and deep uncertainty.

Efforts to get at these different agendas will often be difficult in joint sessions, as the spouses talk past each other. Instead, individual caucusing can be very helpful, either for an entire session or for parts of joint sessions. In turn, role reversal can be helpful in encouraging spouses to really hear what the other is saying. It is especially important to have husbands hear their wives' fears and address them directly. Public disclosure of family resources is also vital to ensure that both spouses negotiate with real numbers. Under these circumstances, husbands can often be quite generous, with "his" pension used as one basis for trade-offs.

For example, consider the case of Sam and Maria Papas. Sam and Maria met in their last year in high school. They were attracted to each other because both were of Greek extraction, had had virtually no dating experience, and thought the other "nice." They continued to date until both graduated from university, when they married. However, within a few months of their marriage, both realized that they were dramatically incompatible in a variety of ways. Divorce was not an option, however, as both were devout Eastern Orthodox Christians. Through tacit agreement, they simply carried on. Thirty years later, when their last child left for university, they finally decided to get divorced.

Throughout their time together, Sam had been continuously employed in the computer industry. In contrast, Maria, although qualified in education, stayed home with the children until they entered primary school.

Consequently, although Sam was well prepared financially for retirement, Maria was not. Moreover, their efforts to negotiate around money issues were blocked by a very destructive conflict style in which issues were seldom, if ever, resolved. Role reversal was useful in giving each some insight into the other's concerns and fears, and explicit training in conflict and communication skills allowed them to negotiate issues to resolution for the first time. So successful was this that Sam and Maria briefly toyed with the idea of reconciliation. In the end, both decided to carry on with their divorce. In addition, once Sam realized that he could keep his pension and trade-off for other assets, he made Maria a fair financial offer that she accepted, after conferring with her lawyer. They also agreed to put aside some money to ensure that their youngest child would complete university.

Pattern 3: Money as Painkiller/Revenge

Just as marriages vary in how they begin, so they vary in how they end. Three common routes to divorce include (a) the unilateral or mutual loss of interest; (b) the buildup of frustration and misunderstanding, leading to chronic conflict; and (c) the buildup of frustration and anger, culminating in some sort of traumatic event, such as a violent episode or, more typically, infidelity. For the last two variations, money can be one path to redemption by acting as a painkiller and/or as the basis on which one spouse seeks to get revenge on the other.

In this pattern, the "injured" spouse will typically make exaggerated claims for property division, based on his or her pain rather than any real numbers. In some cases, one party may manipulate the numbers to his or her own ends. For example, in a recent instance in Edmonton, Alberta, a husband abandoned his wife of 27 years for a woman 14 years his junior. In revenge, his wife spent or liquidated more than half a million dollars in assets so that she might claim a large alimony award. In other cases in which we have been involved, property may be damaged or sold, spouses may become obsessed with money matters, or apartments or houses may be broken into. In short, Pattern 3 situations can bring out the worst in people and can engage them in behavior that is absolutely out of keeping with their normal conduct.

As the typical injured party, wives' emotional tone varies between unbridled rage, intense pain, great bitterness, and, underneath it all, deep sadness. By contrast, husbands' emotional tone varies between contempt, anger, guilt, and confusion. Both may attempt to recruit the children to their side and in front of them may paint the other parent in the blackest possible terms. In turn, in the vice of a loyalty bind, the children may show various signs of distress and/or alienation. The spouses may be unaware of their children's distress or may lay blame squarely on the shoulders of the other parent, thus denying their own role in this process.

Under these chaotic conditions, families fall into two groups. Those who are committed to "winning" in litigation will be uninterested in mediation and may stonewall any such suggestions by judges, lawyers, or the other spouse. Such couples would likely make very poor candidates for mediation in any event because these spouses typically advance entrenched and often frankly irrational beliefs about the other spouse and, at this point, are prepared to risk everything they own or can borrow to "win." Those who have at least some awareness of what this process is doing to their children can sometimes be persuaded, either by a lawyer and/or a parent, to try mediation.

In mediation, such couples present as emotionally unstable, impulsive, and very difficult to control. They are often more interested in expressing their feelings than engaging in productive negotiation, and the underlying trauma may or may not be mentioned explicitly. However, in individual sessions, they do recognize that what is happening between them has been harmful to their children and often turn to the mediator to help them stop their emotional outbursts when they themselves cannot; temporarily, they may need external controls when their internal controls have been overwhelmed by their feelings.

Being effective with such couples involves three steps. The first step involves a heavy-handed, even authoritarian, emphasis on the rules of conduct in mediation. This is coupled with the repeated emphasis on the best interests of the children as the key motive for staying in mediation. (Other sorts of appeals—to common sense, the cost of litigation, and the destructive ways in which couples have chosen to remain engaged with each other—will be futile.) In effect, such couples cannot interact productively unless the mediator establishes external limits and controls. With such controls in place, Step 2 involves addressing the sources of their respective anger. Here, techniques emphasize moving between joint and individual sessions, role reversal, and the public airing of family secrets. In some cases, the construction of a forgiveness ritual in which pain, guilt, and forgiveness play central roles can be helpful. In some cases, direct involvement of the children can also be helpful, in effect giving the mediator permission to say for them what they themselves cannot say to their parents. In some cases, distancing strategies can be useful in diminishing the pain. In combination, these efforts reduce the level of rage and give these spouses the opportunity to hear each other. These efforts do not eliminate the pain, but they do make it possible for these spouses to work past it for the sake of their children. Finally, Step 3, which can overlap Step 2, involves addressing the substantive issues that brought them to mediation in the first place. This is often a slow process but, given tight control and dogged determination on the part of the mediator, can move these couples ahead to the point where a full agreement is possible.

In this regard, consider the case of Adam and Maria Quinn. The Quinns came from very different backgrounds. Maria came from a large, volatile, but loving Italian family. She was not at all put off by loud conflict and was herself prone to loud angry outbursts. But these outbursts were short-lived and followed by displays of affection. In contrast, Adam was the only child of a rigidly controlled British family in which open displays of feelings were forbidden. Thus, opposites attracted, for their initial relationship was intense and passionate. Over time, however, these differences took their toll, with Adam preferring to escape the conflict rather than confront it. He had his first brief "fling," as he put it, after 8 years of marriage. Over the next 10 years, six more flings occurred, all brief and kept secret from Maria. It was a fling that turned serious that finally led to their separation.

In mediation, initial efforts at negotiation proved futile. Maria's anger would quickly boil over into furious attacks on Adam. Adam responded by alternating between becoming cold and distant or guilty and apologetic. In either case, productive negotiation was impossible. To get the couple on track, rigid rules of respectful conduct were laid down and scrupulously enforced. Although outwardly they displayed dwindling resistance, inwardly we suspect that they were relieved. The intensity of their feelings was such that self-control was impossible. Moving between joint and individual sessions, as well as using role reversal and communication exercises, allowed them the opportunity to talk out their feelings and gain some understanding that both were going through a very difficult time. Maria focused on her sense of betrayal, failure, and loss, and Adam had some opportunity to express his guilt, anger, and bitterness. Both were reluctantly able to acknowledge that Maria's tendency to attack and Adam's tendency to withdraw were poor ways of handling conflict. This allowed Maria to accept Adam's apology, although it did not diminish either one's pain. The couple could then go on to negotiate their substantive issues, though maintaining this focus proved difficult. It was repeatedly necessary to insist that they contain their feelings and that they be reminded of the consequences to their children if they failed in mediation. In the end, they did agree on all issues in dispute, with the "memorandum" sent on to their respective lawyers for detailed review.

Pattern 4: Money as Compensation

In long-term relationships, both partners have worked to create their joint success, and each expects to be rewarded for his or her individual contribution. Property division is thus an exercise in assigning compensation. However, spouses often find themselves in conflict because they do not value their respective contribution in similar terms.

Husbands, for example, may acknowledge that their wives have been good housekeepers and good mothers. However, husbands also complain that their wives have failed to recognize or appreciate just how hard they have worked ("slaved") over the years, often in a job they did not particularly enjoy, to make their wives' good life possible. Accordingly, husbands may enter mediation believing that they deserve a greater share than their wives of their accumulated assets, especially husbands' pensions.

Wives, for example, may acknowledge that their husbands have been good and reliable providers. However, wives also complain that their husbands have participated little in parenting and may have paid little attention to them as spouses, their sexual and romantic lives having long ago become mechanical and unsatisfying. Accordingly, wives may enter mediation with the view that their marriage has been a poor bargain, such that they deserve a greater share of the assets.

Invariably, these arguments reflect the longstanding conflict that has culminated in their divorce, and their negotiation style, typified by lack of closure, reflects their dysfunctional marital relationship. Left alone, such relations could turn mediation into a long process of petty disputes, with no detail unworthy of lengthy debate. Past and present hurts get conflated, arguments lack focus, and closure proves elusive. Among such couples, the mediator is hard-pressed to keep such spouses on topic while avoiding their constant bickering.

Intervention techniques among Pattern 4 couples rely heavily on reframing their conflict in terms of protecting the children and abandoning their failed marriages so they can move on. It is useful to address ongoing attachment issues by both spouses, with bickering used to prolong their relationship rather than end it. It is important to have the spouses publicly acknowledge to each other that their relationship is over and that each has let the other down in various ways. Mutual forgiveness is framed as the beginning of a new life, however frightening that new life may be. In a similar vein, it can be helpful to have such couples recognize what fine children they have and thus what a fine job they may have done as parents. This leads to a focus on the future and how family mediation of their financial issues can assist them in beginning to design such a future. Finally, these couples will benefit enormously from improvement in their basic communication skills, either in terms of explicit training or given the mediator as a role model.

Consider the case of Karl and Matti Gunther. Of German origin, Karl was an expert tool and die maker, a job he did well but which he had never particularly enjoyed. Matti, also of German origin, had preferred to stay home to raise their three children. However, the time had hung heavy on her after her youngest child started school. Even so, while the children were around to absorb their time and energy, both spouses reported a moderately satisfying relationship marked by little overt conflict and much routine bickering. It was only after the last child left home for university that their relationship had become markedly dissatisfying, especially for Matti. Matti in particular had not "really loved" Karl in some time. Eventually, she decided that there was little point in continuing and had asked Karl to leave the home. Karl responded with anger and confusion but did leave. They had lived apart for 9 months when they entered mediation.

With this couple, family mediation of their financial issues appeared simple and straightforward. Although Karl had worked for 25 years for the same firm and brought in an adequate wage, the cost of raising three children was such that their accumulated assets were modest and the division of their assets simple at law. But initial efforts to negotiate the division of these assets proved unproductive. Both presented as the aggrieved spouse and as such demanded an unequal share of what little assets they had. Karl's pension proved particularly contentious. But even more important than any specific grievance was the constant bickering that characterized their approach to negotiation. Resolution of the substantive issue turned on the public acknowledgment that their relationship was over and that both had contributed in different ways to its demise. It was especially helpful for Karl to admit that he was unprepared for the future and might benefit from referral to an accountant and/or a financial planner. Having gotten past the sense of mutual blame, it was then possible to turn to the substantive issues. Their negotiation was facilitated by repeated modeling of clear communication, which allowed the spouses to compromise around specific proposals. In the end, the spouses left mediation feeling they had a reasonable deal, and with the recommendation that they would each benefit from brief separation counseling. Review by their respective lawyers confirmed that the deal they had struck was a reasonable one.

Pattern 5: Money as Closure

As noted above, some marriages end in anger and conflict, whereas others close in silence and chronic fatigue. The latter characterizes Pattern 5 couples. There are no fireworks here, only depressed resignation. Couples present with low energy and a series of vague concerns, mostly centered on anxious uncertainty about the future. Thus, their primary concern is to bring matters to a close as soon as possible, but they are unclear as to the technical matters involved in doing so. Token conflict can occur around assets of sentimental value, but otherwise such couples are in general agreement about asset valuation and division. Assured of equity in asset division, money is often not an important issue for such couples.

In this context, the mediator has three things to offer such couples. First, a clear and structured process for addressing all substantive issues is crucial. Having someone who knows what he or she is doing and can walk them through the process greatly assists such couples and dramatically reduces their anxiety. It often raises a series of financial issues neither would have thought of if left to their own devices. Second, good technical knowledge is important, so that spouses will have the information on which to make informed choices. With couples having many assets, the involvement of their respective lawyers and/or accountants can be very important. And third, more than anything, such couples need a great deal of emotional support. Given their sadness, spouses may not have the energy to make the decisions they need to make, or they may act impulsively, without thinking through the consequences of one or another choice. They may retreat from decision making in confusion or uncertainty and may have difficulty staying focused. Support supplies the energy they need to continue, provides them with a context in which to explore their sense of mutual failure, and gives them the hope of full and final closure, so that they can each move on with their lives. Although Pattern 5 couples tend to have been involved in long-term relationships, this pattern can occur among couples married for any duration.

Consider the case of David and Astrid Samosa. Both had married late in recognition of their educational and professional objectives—he as an economist, she as a financial planner. Both soon discovered, however, that their real commitment was to their respective careers and not to each other. Five years into their marriage, childless but affluent, they decided to end their marriage by mutual consent. Although both were very well informed about finances, they had little knowledge about asset division in divorce. That uncertainty, coupled with their depression and anxiety, led them to mediation. Mediation with this couple was centered more on support than on negotiation. In fact, once the various components of financial mediation were explained to them, consensus based on equity was relatively easy to achieve. Indeed, more time was spent exploring their feelings and helping them achieve a sense of closure on their relationship than discussing money. With the completion of their agreement, separation counseling was recommended to help them understand why their marriage had failed and to move on with their respective lives.

Discussion

Mediators with a mental health background are often very reluctant to undertake family mediation involving financial matters. In large part, this reflects their professional socialization in which money is typically seen as a taboo topic. They therefore respond with apprehension and withdrawal to the technical complexities of this form of family mediation. Such fears are mostly based on misinformation. The majority of divorcing couples present with modest assets and uncomplicated financial situations. Similarly, the basic principles underlying property division, child support, and alimony are less difficult than they fear and easily within the grasp of anyone with the education and the skills requisite to family mediation practice. Moreover, it is important to emphasize that practitioners need not be alone in this area of practice. Allied professionals, including lawyers, accountants, financial planners, and real estate evaluators, are always available to assist. For the novice, comediation with an experienced comprehensive family mediator or a mediation-trained lawyer is another option.

Perhaps most important, as we have tried to show throughout this chapter, family mediation of financial issues is as much concerned with relational dynamics as it is about money per se. Different patterns of spousal conflict reflect the various routes that couples have taken in coming to divorce and the different meanings that money has come to acquire for them. In this context, nonlawyer family mediators, especially those with knowledge of both family processes and clinical intervention techniques, may be particularly well equipped to provide mediation services with respect to financial matters.

In that sense, the range of patterns of spousal conflict around money is intended to support three conclusions. The first is a call for cross-disciplinary collaboration among mediators from different disciplines. Lawyers and mental health practitioners in mediation have much to learn from each other. Second, mediators from a mental health background have a great deal to offer couples undergoing divorce. This is no less true when it concerns money than when it does children, for in both cases we suggest the key blockages to agreement are more likely to be relational than technical. To avoid mediating financial matters because they are "technically complex" thus does both clients and mediators a disservice. Finally, our description of these various patterns is intended to help practitioners determine what to look for in an initial assessment and the techniques to use to maximize the likelihood of reaching agreement by addressing the critical underlying issues.

References

Betcher, W., & Macauley, R. (1990). *The seven basic quarrels of marriage: Recognize, defuse, negotiate, and resolve your conflicts.* New York: Villard.

Bush, K. H. B., & Folger, J. P. (1996). *The promise of mediation: Responding to conflict through empowerment and recognition.* San Francisco: Jossey-Bass.

Carter, B., & Peters, J. K. (1996). *Love, honor and negotiate: Making your marriage work.* New York: Pocket Books.

Emery, R. E. (1994). *Renegotiating family relationships: Divorce, child custody, and mediation.* New York: Guilford.

Erickson, S. K., & Erickson, M. S. M. (1988). *Family mediation casebook: Theory and process.* New York: Brunner/Mazel.

Fisher, R., Ury, W., & Patton, B. (1991). *Getting to yes: Negotiating agreement without giving in* (2nd ed.). Boston: Houghton Mifflin.

Folberg, J., & Taylor, A. (1984). *Mediation: A comprehensive guide to resolving conflicts without litigation.* San Francisco: Jossey-Bass.

Friedman, J. T. (1999). *The divorce handbook* (Rev. ed.). New York: Random House.

Gigy, L., & Kelly, J. (1992). Reasons for divorce: Perspectives of divorcing men and women. *Journal of Divorce & Remarriage, 18*(1/2), 169-187.

Gottman, J. M., & Silver, N. (1999). *The seven principles for making marriage work*. New York: Crown.

Haynes, J. M. (1981). *Divorce mediation: A practical guide for therapists and counselors*. New York: Springer.

Haynes, J. M., & Haynes, G. L. (1989). *Mediating divorce: Casebook of strategies for successful family negotiation*. San Francisco: Jossey-Bass.

Irving, H. H., & Benjamin, M. (1987). *Family mediation: Theory and practice of dispute resolution*. Toronto: Carswell.

Irving, H. H., & Benjamin, M. (1995). *Family mediation: Contemporary issues*. Thousand Oaks, CA: Sage.

James, P. (1997). *The divorce mediation handbook: Everything you need to know*. San Francisco: Jossey-Bass.

Johnson, L. A., & Benesek, T. (Eds.). (1997). *Divorce strategy: Tactics for a civil financial divorce*. New York: Broken Heart Publications.

Karpel, M. A. (1986). Questions, obstacles, contributions. In M. A. Karpel (Ed.), *Family resources: The hidden partner in family therapy* (pp. 3-61). New York: Guilford.

Kronby, M. C. (2001). *Canadian family law* (8th ed.). Toronto: Stoddard.

Landau, B., Wolfson, L., Landau, N., Bartoletti, M., & Mesbur, R. (2000). *Family mediation handbook* (3rd ed.). Toronto: Butterworths.

McKay, M., Rogers, P., Blades, J., & Gosse, R. (1999). *The divorce book: A practical and compassionate guide*. Oakland, CA: New Harbinger.

Mercer, D., & Pruett, M. K. (2001). *Your divorce advisor: A lawyer and a psychologist guide you through the legal and emotional landscape of divorce*. New York: Fireside.

Millman, M. (1991). *Warm heart and cold cash: The intimate dynamics of families and money*. New York: Free Press.

Moore, C. W. (1986). *The mediation process: Practical strategies for resolving conflict*. San Francisco: Jossey-Bass.

Patterson, J. M. (1989). A family stress model: The family adjustment and adaptation response. In C. N. Ramsey, Jr. (Ed.), *Family systems in medicine* (pp. 95-118). New York: Guilford.

Sitarz, D. (1999). *Divorce laws of the United States*. St. Peters, MO: Nova.

Wallerstein, J. S., Lewis, J. M., & Blakeslee, S. (2000). *The unexpected legacy of divorce: A 25 year landmark study*. New York: Hyperion.

Walters, M., Carter, B., Papp, P., & Silverstein, O. (1988). *The invisible web*. New York: Guilford.

Woodhouse, V., & Fetherling, D. (2000). *Divorce and money: How to make the best financial decisions during divorce* (5th ed.). New York: Nolo.

PART 4

SPECIAL ISSUES

13 TFM and Cultural Diversity

To have a clear view of a topic as complex as culture or ethnicity, we need to see it from two different perspectives at the same time, that is, from the "inside" and from the "outside." From the "inside" or subjectively, culture is generally understood as a set of values, beliefs, attitudes, and behaviors (including language) shared by a particular group of people that makes them separate and distinctive from all others (Alba, 1985; Duryea, 1992; Hofstede, 1980; Yinger, 1985). In this sense, diversity or difference is a mantle the group wears happily, often proudly. At the same time, such diversity may be imposed from without, by "outsiders" enacting a stereotype, and in so doing structurally advantaging or, more often, disadvantaging a group by denying them, for example, income, jobs, or housing (Anderson, 1991). In this sense, diversity or difference can be a stigma and a burden that can shape, direct, and limit the life course of group members (Katz, 1985; Tator, 1996).

The intersection of the subjective and the objective yields a very large number of possible groups. In the United States, for example, using race or skin color as a criterion attribute, five cultural groups are typically recognized: Blacks, Whites, Hispanics, Asians, and Native Americans (Benjamin, 1996; Irving & Benjamin, 1995). Using national origin instead, more than 160 groups would be recognized. Related groups would emerge using religion, language or dialect, food preference, marriage customs, shared history, and so on. Whatever the criterion in use, the same conclusion is inescapable—namely, that our social world is highly diverse and becoming ever more so.

The difficulty with such use of criterion attributes is that the group definitions that emerge rely too heavily on seeing them only from the "outside," that is, as homogeneous and monolithic. A more balanced approach, although acknowledging the diversity *across* groups, would also recognize the diversity *within* them (Ponterotto & Casas, 1991). This is true in at least two senses. First, seen from within, group members invariably recognize further and finer subdivisions or subgroups and may be offended when outsiders lump them in with the larger group. Benjamin (1996), for example, in distinguishing between 7 distinctive Asian subgroups—others recognize as many as 32 subgroups (see Dana, 1993)—observed that

> if native speakers from each group were placed in a room together, they would not only be unable to communicate, having different written and spoken languages, they would not even be able to share a meal, since the H'mong prefer sticky rice, the Japanese short-grained rice and the Chinese long-grained rice. (pp. 71-72)

Second, although outsiders may assume group membership by virtue of the presence of some criterion attribute, subjective identification within the group varies widely (Benjamin, 1996; Johnson, 1990; Saari, 1993). Rather, members vary on a continuum. At one end are those that identify closely with the group or subgroup and espouse traditional values, attitudes, and beliefs. At the midpoint are those who are functionally bicultural, enacting one set of values when with other group members, another set of values when with outsiders, and equally comfortable in relating to and interacting with both. At the other end of the continuum are those that identify loosely with the group and espouse modern values, attitudes, and beliefs indistinguishable from those in the larger community. Among the latter, there will also be those who frankly reject membership in the group and may go to some length to blend in with the larger community.

Finally, it will now be clear that whatever their identification(s), the impact of culture is simply pervasive and inescapable. In the words of McGoldrick (1988),

> [Culture] plays a major role in determining what we eat, how we work, how we relate, how we celebrate holidays and rituals, and how we feel about life, death, and illness. We see the world through our own cultural filters and we often persist in our established views in spite of evidence to the contrary. (p. 69)

Given the profound impact of culture, the desirability of what Katz (1985) has called "culturally competent programs" or what Barsky, Este, and Collins (1996) have called simply "cultural competence" is apparent. This has certainly been the case in counseling (Cross, Bazron, Dennis, & Isaacs, 1989; Green, 1995; Pendersen, 1991; see McMahon & Allen-Meares, 1992) and other service disciplines (Devore & Scheslinger, 1996; Falicov, 1996; McGoldrick, Pearce, & Giordano, 1982; Sue, Ivey, & Pederson, 1996; Wehrly, 1995). With rare exceptions (Becker & Slaton, 1987; Cloke, 1987; Irving & Benjamin, 1995; LeBaron, 1997; LeResche, 1992; Meierding, 1992; Taylor & Sanchez, 1991; Wong, 1995), this has *not* been true of family mediation. Rather, major teaching texts continue to ignore this dimension of practice (Boulle & Kelly, 1998; Emery, 1994; James, 1997; Landau, Wolfson, Landau, Bartoletti, & Mesbur, 2000; Saposnek, 1998), perhaps because cultural material tends to call in question mediation's fundamental beliefs and assumptions (Gunning, 1995).

Although the exceptions cited above help move the field in what we believe is the right direction, what is absent is an integrated framework that could be used to train mediators in effective cross-cultural practice. Here, older approaches are not useful because they invariably advance a deficit model of minority groups—some frankly racist—that we now dismiss as blaming the victim (Casas, 1985; Sue, Arrendondo, & McDavis, 1992; Trickett, Watts, & Birman, 1994).

Tsang and George (1998) review more recent efforts, suggesting that they fall into two broad categories. In their "pure" form, "cultural literacy" models (such as Benjamin, 1996, or Roberts, 1990) tend to do the following:

- treat the practitioner as an expert,
- assume that he or she has superior knowledge,
- regard culture as a homogeneous system,
- necessarily regard the client as a member of a cultural group,
- advance culture-specific clinical techniques, and
- require of the practitioner no self-examination.

In contrast, in their "pure" form, phenomenological models (such as Dyche & Zayas, 1995) tend to do the following:

- treat the practitioner as learner;
- assume that he or she will approach clients from a position of deliberate naivete and curiosity;
- assume that as a function of life experience, clients have internalized not one but many cultures;
- necessarily regard the client as a unique individual;
- advance process-oriented clinical techniques; and
- require of the practitioner thoughtful and continuous critical self-examination.

Seeing these two approaches as the ends of a single continuum is highly problematic. In practice, no practitioner we have ever met enacts either of these models in their "pure" form. Rather, they use knowledge and experience when they can and otherwise rely on process-oriented techniques. "Pure" models, then, are a fiction; they represent "straw man" positions that are useful only in the following:

- acknowledging that culturally competent practice requires more than merely knowledge and tolerance for diversity (Kavanaugh & Kennedy, 1992) and
- highlighting the need for a more integrated framework.

Tsang and George's (1998) framework emphasized four components: attitude, knowledge, skills, and research. The attitudes of the competent practitioner include a concern for social justice and equality, the importance of difference and being open to such differences, a readiness to learn from clients, and the willingness to be self-critical and self-reflective. The knowledge base includes specific cultural content, recognition of the systemic context of culture, the salience of the internalized or self-identified culture, and the dynamics of cross-cultural communication. Skills should include the ability to manage one's emotional responses, the recognition that service occurs within a specific institutional context, the use of communication and relationship skills, and the use of specific change strategies. Finally, competent practitioners should include a feedback loop between process-oriented and change strategies and outcome effectiveness data.

In a related vein, Barsky et al. (1996) emphasize three components: values, skills, and knowledge. Values include tolerating difference, valuing diversity, respecting the inherent dignity of all cultures, acknowledging heterogeneity within cultures, having cultural relativism (no one view is correct), and being self-aware of one's own biases and stereotypical perspectives. Skills include nonjudgmental perspectives, attending behavior aimed at establishing a connection with the clients, and basic communication skills. As to knowledge, they go beyond content knowledge to list core dimensions, such as group self-definition, the meaning and importance of family, and barriers to seeking and receiving service (such as language).

Both efforts at integration have much in common and significantly advance our understanding of what it should mean to be a culturally competent practitioner. However, in light of our previous work (Benjamin & Irving, 1992), there is an aspect of both models that is glaring by its absence—namely, a feminist component recognizing the unique and distinctive experience of women (Bauer Maglin & Perry, 1996; Frankenberg, 1993; Goldberger, Tarule, Clinchy, & Belenky, 1996; Hare-Mustin & Maracek, 1990; Lieblich & Josselson, 1994; Reid, 1993; Rosen & Kuehlwein, 1996). The social structures that may oppress cultural minorities, such as those associated with race, do so differently for men and women and suggest the need for gender-based differences in clinical practice (Greene, 1994).

Taken together, these various components of an integrated approach inform a therapeutic family mediation (TFM) perspective on cross-cultural family mediation, including the following:

- the *values* of tolerance, respect, and relativism;
- the *attitudes* of openness, learning readiness, and critical self-reflection;

- the *skills* associated with affective self-management, communication and relationship, and specific change strategies;
- the *culture-specific* knowledge of family patterns, approaches to conflict (see Duryea & Grundison, 1993), and perspectives on institutions and organizations (Benjamin, 1996), including family mediation;
- the perspective on *gender*, with special reference to the social and familial structures that disadvantage women; and
- the orientation to *research* that supports the notion of advancing the objectives of mediation in general and TFM in particular through process and outcome testing procedures.

Given the attributes of the TFM model, the inclusion of this integrated approach to culture requires only modest adaptation. The model recognizes that each family enters mediation with a unique microculture. Accordingly, the model is already heavily process oriented, designed to fit the service to meet the needs of clients. Similarly, it already emphasizes respect for individual variation, the development of communication and relationship skills, and the use of various change strategies. Adaptation to cross-cultural service delivery centers on two areas: recognition of the value and dignity associated with cultural diversity and culture-specific knowledge. To the other areas in which practitioners should remain up-to-date (see Chapter 2, this volume), we would now add contemporary information concerning culture, especially as regards Blacks, Asians, Hispanics, and aboriginal groups, as well as the more prominent European (White) nationalities, such as the English, French, Germans, and Italians.

That said, three important qualifications are in order: It is impossible to maintain contemporary information about *all* possible cultural groupings, least of all because that information simply does not exist; the information that is available may not be relevant, with many families displaying little, if any, cultural identification, despite their racial, national, or other attributes; and just as psychoanalytic practitioners sometimes see "a cigar as just a cigar," so much marital interaction may merely be interaction, devoid of any cultural content.

Case Illustration: Latino Families

To illustrate this approach to culturally competent practice in mediation, the balance of this chapter will focus on a specific cultural group, namely, Latino families.[1] In general, such families tend to display a constellation of sociodemographic attributes, including the following: Spanish as a mother tongue; immediate or ultimate origin in Mexico, Cuba, Puerto Rico, Central or South America, or Spain; faith in Roman Catholicism; and a preference for families larger than the population norm. We focus on such families because in the United States, they are the second largest (in 1990: 22.4 million) and fastest

growing minority group (Ruiz, 1995). Other reasons for our interest include
the relative abundance of research material delineating family attributes in
the clinical (Green, 1995) and cross-cultural literatures (Essandoh, 1996;
Patterson, 1996) and the scanty coverage of such families in the mediation
literature (Duryea & Grundison, 1993; Taylor & Sanchez, 1991).

Thus, we will selectively examine each of these literatures in turn with
the primary intent of constructing a contemporary portrait of Latino family
systems, with special attention throughout to the changing role of women.
That portrait will then serve as the basis for drawing a series of inferences in
an effort to characterize culturally sensitive mediation practice with Latino
couples undergoing divorce. In turn, our reliance on data drawn from clinical literatures suggests that these inferences will likely generalize best to
those mediation models toward the therapeutic end of the spectrum (Kruk,
1997; Schwebel, Gately, Renner, & Milburn, 1994; Wong, 1995), particularly the TFM model (Irving & Benjamin, 1995) and Bush and Folger's
(1994) transformational approach.

In general, for us to address the issue of cultural diversity involves a form
of meta-mediation in which mediators and clients need to negotiate a shared
understanding. This implies the importance for mediators of becoming
aware of their own cultural values and biases, striving for greater sensitivity
and understanding of clients' worldviews, and acquiring greater expertise in
the choice and application of culturally appropriate intervention techniques
and strategies.

Latino Families: Generic Attributes

The clinical and intercultural literatures are complementary in helping us
construct a contemporary portrait of Latino family systems. Although these
literatures are complex and overlapping, in general the clinical literature
addresses *internal* family dynamics, whereas the intercultural literature
addresses relations *between* Latinos and the White or Anglo majority.

Internal Family Dynamics

The portrait of Latino family systems that emerges from the clinical
literature involves four components concerned, respectively, with values,
conduct, commonality, and how these compare with majority family norms.

Values. In anthropological terms, Latinos may be described as having an allo-
centric culture, that is, one that emphasizes the interests of the group and relations between group members as taking precedence over individual concerns
or internal psychological states (Albert, 1996). This generalized interpersonal
orientation helps explain the centrality of at least eight culture values.

The most salient of these values is that of *familism*, which places the multigenerational, informal extended family at the core of the culture (Devore & Scheslinger, 1996). This idea of family thus extends vertically to include grandparents, aunts, uncles, and cousins (to the fourth generation) and laterally to include godparents (*compadre, comadres*) as well as close family friends (*cuatismo*). Thus, *la familia* refers to the kin network as opposed to *la casa*, which denotes the immediate or nuclear family (Falicov, 1996).

Within *la casa*, spouses have culturally distinctive roles and responsibilities. *Machismo* means that the husband, as the head of the household, has primary responsibility to protect and preserve the family's well-being, including its income and its honor in the community (Guttman, 1996; Mayo, 1997; Mirande, 1997; Ybarra, 1995). *Marianismo/hembrismo* means that the wife and mother have primary responsibility for caregiving and household management, including flexibility, self-sacrifice, and perseverance in the face of troubles (Comas-Diaz, 1989; Davenport & Yurich, 1991; Miralles, 1989), typically seen as inevitable (*aguantarse*).

In its dealings with extended family and friends, *familismo* is associated with *compadrazgo*, which emphasizes the salience of interdependence and mutual obligation (Taylor & Sanchez, 1991), and with *personalism,* in which personal relationships take priority over standardized rules, procedures, or schedules (Weaver & Wodersksi, 1996). Mutual obligation is especially important when resources are low, allowing all to benefit when only some have resources to contribute. In times of crisis, for example, Latino family boundaries are sufficiently permeable to support child lending and taking in relatives for varying durations (Garcia-Preto, 1996). As for personal relations, this represents a view of time that sees it in terms of an extended present, thus rendering it flexible and in the service of social relations rather than vocational or other pursuits (Harris & Moran, 1991).

These values make for extended family systems that are extraordinarily close and cohesive (Dana, 1993), with related values that serve to promote harmony and good will while avoiding or at least controlling interpersonal conflict. For example, while *simpatia* has no exact English equivalent, it positively connotes individuals seen by others as likeable, sensitive, and easygoing (Marin & Triandis, 1985). *Dignidad* denotes the essential worthiness of others (Albert, 1996), and *respeto* emphasizes the importance of mutual respect and public honor (Falicov, 1996). Finally, *controlarse* refers to control of sexual and aggressive impulses (Sewell, 1989). As Hall (1976) explains, Latinos are caught in a dilemma, sensitive to insult or criticism that might offend their pride or honor yet prohibited from direct confrontation. Accordingly, interpersonal conflict is likely to be handled indirectly (*indirectas*), either through avoidance or the involvement of a *compadre* or a priest acting as an intermediary or go-between (Dana, 1993).

Conduct. This constellation of values serves to promote social relations marked by closeness, harmony, cooperation, and sensitivity. Some of this is explicit, with social interaction characteristically friendly, spontaneous, and emotional (Duryea & Grundison, 1993). Extended kin often live in close residential proximity (Falicov, 1996). Social contact, which is frequent, typically involves hugging (*abraza*), public kissing, and other forms of physical contact (Axtell, 1985). Emotions are close to the surface and easily expressed in tears, rage, or laughter, with much effort made to create a warm and accepting atmosphere (*ambiente*) in which nearly everything is highly personalized. As Keefe (1984) explains, "For [Latinos], it is important to see relatives regularly face-to-face, to embrace, to touch, and to simply be with one another, sharing the minor joys and sorrows of daily life" (p. 68).

Despite such lavish affective displays, from the perspective of an outsider, social relations among Latinos are deceptive, appearing simple and straightforward when, in fact, they are subtle and complex. Indeed, Latino culture is generally characterized as "high context" (Hall, 1976). This is intended in three senses: the centrality of close social relations, the reliance on control over external social contexts, and the pervasive use of elaborate and indirect forms of expression, especially nonverbal cues. This way of organizing social relations has two consequences. One consequence is that in handling conflict, Latinos are characterized by a short series of rapidly escalating steps (Hall, 1976). Should the efforts of a go-between fail, confrontations can be bitter and prolonged, with violence a real possibility. The second consequence is that Latinos make a clear distinction between insiders and outsiders. Although the boundaries within the extended family are fluid and permeable, those between the extended system and outsiders are rigid and relatively impermeable (Duryea & Grundison, 1993). Marital difficulties, for example, if they are discussed overtly at all (given *indirectas*), would only be discussed with extended kin as opposed to strangers, including therapists.

Commonality. The above portrait will be meaningful in relation to many Latino families. However, recent research suggests that Latino family systems are far more heterogeneous than was once thought (Baca Zinn, 1995; Del Castillo, 1994; Mayo, 1997; Mirande, 1997). Such efforts suggest a distinction between the ways in which, for example, Latino couples present themselves to the world, the *social fiction*, and the ways they actually operate on a daily basis, the *social reality*. The fiction is that husbands, in accord with machismo, are powerful, authoritarian, and distant, whereas wives, in accord with *hembrismo*, are passive, compliant, and submissive. The reality is that Latino couples distribute across a continuum of spousal relations, from husband dominant to egalitarian to wife dominant (Hondagneu-Sotelo, 1994; Hurtado, 1995; Ybarra, 1995). Thus, although the above generic portrait is a good place to begin, only detailed assessment will locate a given couple on spousal and other continua related, for example, to parenting, conflict management, financial management, relations with extended kin, religious beliefs and practices, and relations with employers and work mates.

Majority Family Norms: Enmeshment

Recent research has taken a critical look at not only Latino family dynamics but also the way in which such dynamics have been viewed by "outsider" researchers. That critical review supports three conclusions:

1. Outside researchers have tended to view Latino families through the lens of majority family norms and values.

2. The result has been the emergence of a cultural deficit model.

3. On the basis of that model, outside researchers have tended to blame Latino family values for stifling individual initiatives and aspirations and have portrayed the Latino family as primitive, deficient, and repressive (Zambrana, 1995).

A case in point concerns the notion of family enmeshment. Developed by Minuchin (1974), the notion refers to family systems characterized by diffuse intergenerational boundaries, poor individual differentiation, and parental intrusion and overinvolvement in the lives of their children. Given the deficit model noted above, it is hardly surprising that the close, cohesive relations that typify Latino families would be characterized as enmeshed (Inclan, 1990). Operating from the "inside," however, recent studies have tended to de-pathologize Latino families, with their authors arguing that in applying enmeshment to Latino families, majority authors have tended to conflate two separate processes: closeness, which promotes secure attachment and mutual cohesion, and intrusive overinvolvement, which promotes dysfunctional adaptive strategies and processes (Falicov, 1996; Garcia-Preto, 1996; Koss-Chioino, 1995). Green and Werner (1996) speculate that the majority tendency to equate closeness with enmeshment may be due to "androcentric European/American, middle-class ethnocentric models of mental health, which place comparatively lower value on closeness and caregiving (and higher value on individuals' separateness and self-sufficiency) in family relations" (p. 130).

Dealings With the Outside World

The portrait of Latino family systems that emerges from the cross-cultural literature involves three components concerned, respectively, with discrimination, acculturation, and underutilization.

Discrimination. The opportunities available to Latino families are severely constrained by limited employment opportunities, the result of which is that nearly half of all Latino families report income that is either below, at, or just above the poverty line (Benjamin, 1996). By referring to the family attributes described above, the temptation is to blame Latinos for their status. In contrast, available data suggest that poverty among Latinos is primarily related to key structural and systemic barriers to employment. Structural barriers refer to the fact that the majority of Latinos have both limited formal education and English-language proficiency (Portes & Truelove, 1987). This is especially true among recent immigrants (Duryea & Grundison, 1993; Pedraza, 1991). Systemic barriers refer to widespread racism and discrimination (Chavez, 1990; Turner, Fix, & Struyk, 1991). In combination, these various barriers ensure that Latinos display high rates of unemployment and underemployment, with those who do find work often confined to jobs characterized by low wages, low prestige, and high turnover (Rodriguez & Melendez, 1992).

In relation to Latino family values such as machismo, poverty and unemployment among males, especially if this involves a dramatic change from their status in the home country, are associated with shame, which in turn promotes marital conflict, desertion, separation, and divorce (Duryea & Grundison, 1993). The divorce rate among Latinos in the United States is roughly on a par with Whites (Cox, 1993). However, unlike Whites, whose divorce rate has been relatively stable (Cox, 1993), there is some evidence that the comparable rate among Latinos may be rising (Del Castillo, 1994).

Acculturation. For some time, it was widely assumed that there was a direct relationship between acculturation—that is, learning to speak English and adopting the values of the dominant culture—and mental health (Turner, 1991). Authors adopting a more critical stance have decried such a view as simplistic (Cortes, 1994; Hardwood, 1994; Rogler, Cortes, & Malgady, 1991), even characterizing this traditional approach as a form of "psychological imperialism" (Strier, 1996). This alternate perspective is consistent with recent research that, among other things, indicates the following:

- Cultural identification is positively related to mental health.

- Compared to first- and second-generation Latinos, their third-generation counterparts display higher rather than lower levels of maladjustment.

- Similarly, there is a direct relationship between Latinos' mental health problems and efforts at Americanization.

- The most successful Latinos are those who have become bicultural, that is, who have become sufficiently skilled in dealing with *both* Latinos and Anglos that they feel at home in both cultures (Domino, 1992; Falicov, 1996; Green, 1995; Gushue & Sciarra, 1995; Padilla, 1994; Weaver & Wodersksi, 1996).

Based on evidence of intergenerational conflict (Delgado-Gaitan, 1994) and a shift in authority among Latino families in which wives work outside the home (Duryea & Grundison, 1993), we may speculate that difficulties around immigration, transition, and acculturation may, in addition to male shame, constitute primary sources of marital conflict.

Underutilization. Finally, in comparison to Whites, Latinos have traditionally been portrayed as less likely to use and more likely to terminate mental health services (Solomon, 1988). Although various explanations have been proposed, most tend to pathologize Latino family attributes, suggesting, for example, that values such as machismo equate help seeking with evidence of weakness, thus prohibiting the use of needed services (Padilla & de Snyder, 1985). As with the cultural reconstruction of enmeshment, recent and more critical reviews of the notion of underutilization have shifted the focus from client attributes to service effectiveness and responsiveness. Such efforts reveal that Latino cultural and economic attributes play a minor role. Rather, underutilization is primarily related to barriers to service use, some institutional (such as the lack of culturally appropriate counseling services or Spanish-speaking therapists), others structural (such as the lack of local services, the absence of ancillary services associated with transportation and child care, or services that are only available during business hours) (Woodward, Dwinell, & Arons, 1992). Indeed, there is growing evidence that culturally responsive and accessible agencies do increase service use and client satisfaction while decreasing premature termination (Malgady & Rodriguez, 1994).

Culturally Sensitive Mediation Practice

This portrait of Latino families supports at least 15 implications for practice, listed below in no particular order of importance. Seen collectively, these inferences represent the initial stage of creating professional standards of culturally sensitive mediation practice with Latino families.

That said, two qualifications are in order. First, as will shortly be apparent, the inferences in question are generic in character, having equal application to marital and family therapy as well as therapeutic styles of family mediation, such as TFM. However, it must be stressed that therapy and mediation have very different goals. Whereas therapy is concerned with long-term reorganization of family systems, mediation is concerned with removing blockages to productive negotiation and clarifying the nature of postdivorce spousal relations. Thus, the purpose in whose service these inferences are used distinguishes between these two approaches. Second, these inferences apply to Latino family systems. The extent to which they generalize to other ethnic minority groups is an empirical question. Indeed, in extending these standards of practice to other groups, most notably

Blacks and Asians, analyses such as ours regarding Latinos would be extremely important (see Hairston, 1999).

1.   *Need for detailed assessment.* Latino families distribute on a continuum regarding group identification. Some families will identify passionately with their Latino origin. Others will repudiate that origin, but most will fall somewhere between these extremes. Although the above portrait is a beginning, only detailed assessment will indicate where on the continuum a given family should be placed. At present, there are at least a dozen instruments useful for that purpose, including Congress's (1994) "culturagram" and Irving and Benjamin's (1995, p. 356) "ethnic group client protocol" (see Ivey, Ivey, & Simek-Morgan, 1997). Alternatively, given the notion of *personalismo,* the practitioner may prefer to rely on eliciting client-centered personal narratives.

2.   *Personal involvement.* Among Latino families, rapport is likely to involve more than merely developing trust. It will mean moving from the status of "outsider" to that of "insider" with whom private family matters may be freely discussed (Falicov, 1996). To that end, practitioners will need to develop a personal relationship with key family members. Such personal involvement will place demands on the self that are not usually experienced in dealing with White clients, including issues of self-disclosure, the boundary between professional and personal, and established notions of professional expertise having to do, for example, with public touching and the display of affect.

3.   *Time to commitment.* Given discriminatory treatment by White institutions, Boyd-Franklin (1989) observed that Blacks may take much longer than Whites to join with the therapist and risk being labeled "resistant" as a consequence. A similar institutional history coupled with norms of privacy predicts that Latino families may be similarly slow to warm to a non-Latino mediator. Accordingly, practitioners are well advised to cultivate patience with Latino client couples.

4.   *Respect hierarchy.* In keeping with machismo, Latino families are organized hierarchically, with husbands at the head. As we have seen, this arrangement may be real or represent a social fiction. Accordingly, part of the assessment process will need to include explicit inquiry into the organization of the marital relationship, especially as regards any recent changes to it. With such information in place, the practitioner is advised to respect the existing hierarchy in terms, for example, of the order in which spouses' responses are elicited. However, this is one area on which the difference between therapy and mediation is glaring. Whereas therapists may see a power imbalance as unproblematic if it is accepted by both spouses, mediators cannot allow such imbalances to stand for fear that the terms of any agreement may be similarly biased (Kelly, 1995).

5.   *Use indirect methods.* Efforts at power balancing and other interventions, however, may involve a variety of methods. Among Latino families, the notion of *indirectas* recommends that the practitioner avoid confrontational techniques and prefer those that are more subtle and indirect, such as allusion, proverbs, folk tales, storytelling, humor, metaphor, and reframing (Zuniga, 1992).

6.   *Social reframing.* Latino families, particularly those new to the country, do not exist in a vacuum but rather against the backdrop of social, cultural, economic, and political processes over which they have little control. Through the lens of *familism,* such processes can indirectly promote marital and intergenerational conflict. Through the use of social reframing, which acknowledges these larger processes, mediators can normalize feelings of guilt and inadequacy, recast feelings of blame and betrayal into shared responsibility, and help establish a climate of mutual understanding and collaboration.

7.   *Involvement of extended kin.* In part, the choice of technique depends on who is present in any given session. Normally (i.e., with White client couples), only the spouses themselves would be present for most sessions. Occasionally, children and, still more rarely, new partners may also be included. Among Latinos, with their extended notion of family, the inclusion of extended kin and extrasystemic *compadres* may be both more typical and more useful. This may be especially important in an effort to maintain family unity despite divorce, restore harmony, and promote relationship and community healing (Gold, 1993).

8.   *Home-based versus clinic-based service.* To the extent that each client couple is different from all others, mediation necessarily requires flexibility on the part of practitioners. However, dealing with Latino clients moves the issue of flexibility to a new level because it is integral to the culture itself. This manifests in several different ways. One area where flexibility may be required concerns the site of service delivery. Traditionally, service occurs at the mediator's office. This may be appropriate for many Latino client couples. However, in keeping with *personalismo* and *ambiente,* many Latino clients may prefer service in their own home. For the mediator, this choice of sites may be problematic. Assuming that the spouses have separated, the home of each spouse may be seen by the other as territory that is anything but neutral. The alternative may be for the mediator to create an alliance with a local community multiservice agency. Such an alliance would provide the mediator with periodic access to a neutral service site as well as wider credibility with the Latino community (Castro, Coe, Gutierres, & Saenz, 1996; Vega & Murphy, 1990). In the end, the choice of site will depend on the individual preferences of the Latino couples being served.

9.   *Warm and accepting atmosphere.* One reason favoring home-based service concerns the importance for Latino clients of creating a warm and accepting atmosphere in keeping with *ambiente.* That atmosphere may be crucial in relieving tension and anxiety and increasing the likelihood of productive exchange, that is, exchanges that are open, frank, and trusting. Although possible, this is less likely to materialize in agency sites, which are invariably more formal and less familiar than their home-based counterparts.

10.   *Time as an extended present.* As noted above, Latinos tend to view time as an extended present, thus rendering it much more elastic and less constraining than in the majority culture. For the practitioner, this may mean that sessions frequently do not begin at a fixed time or last a fixed duration. Rather, meeting times will vary as a function of various social contingencies, and session duration will be determined by the quality of interaction among the participants and progress on substantive issues in conflict. Such temporal flexibility argues against home-based service, wherein the mediator travels to the client, and in favor of agency-based service, wherein the client travels to the mediator. In the latter circumstance, the mediator can be productively engaged in other tasks until the clients arrive.

11.   *Language: Spanish or English.* Most (90%) native-born Latinos speak English, and the same is true of 35% to 65% of first-generation immigrants (Portes & Truelove, 1987). Consequently, among the former, mediation may typically be conducted in English. Conversely, among most of the latter, it will almost certainly need to be conducted in Spanish. In both cases, the ideal would be a cadre of native-born Latinos trained in mediation because they would be both bilingual and intimately familiar with cultural nuances. Such a cadre may be in the making, as an increasing number of Latinos complete their university education (Benjamin, 1996). At present, however, Latino professionals are in chronic undersupply, partly because foreign professional credentials are typically not recognized in the United States and Canada. The alternative is for English-speaking mediators to pair with bicultural Latino members of the community, the latter acting as translators and cultural guides to the former. Although such an arrangement increases the likelihood of misunderstanding, it affords the Spanish-speaking Latino community access to mediation as opposed to the adversary system.

12.   *The role of nonverbal cues.* The high-context character of the Latino culture means that much of the message in interpersonal communication will be encoded nonverbally. For the mediator accustomed to the low-context character of the Anglo culture, wherein most content is contained in verbal exchange, the sudden transition to the Latino culture will be unmanageably difficult. For example, mediators should be aware that silence, a guarded posture, and the avoidance of eye contact, especially on

initial contact, are in keeping with the Latino nonverbal communication style that is used in the presence of an authority figure and imply neither resistance nor lack of cooperation. The preferred route to such cultural competence would involve either formal training or a form of cultural apprenticeship. Our impression is that most mediation training programs still give only passing attention to cultural diversity. Indeed, one of the implicit purposes of this chapter is to begin to reverse this trend. The only alternative is the sort of apprenticeship noted above, in which a non-Latino mediator is paired with a community member. Of course, the point is that only culturally competent mediators should provide service, however that competence is acquired. What is *not* acceptable but all too often the case is that Latino clients are expected to conform to the implicit cultural requirements of their non-Latino mediators.

13. *Transition difficulties.* Although Latino immigrants likely anticipate that coming to North America will not be easy, few are emotionally prepared for it to be as difficult as it often is. Maternal employment, school-based norms of parenting, cross-generational conflict, under- or unemployment, and major status loss can tear such families apart. Accordingly, it will be crucial that initial assessment efforts thoroughly explore these and related transition issues. On one hand, such issues may well shape the course of mediation. On the other hand, such issues may suggest that divorce may be only one of several alternatives and that issues that couples perceive as intractable may in fact have available solutions.

14. *Public education.* In addition to low income, many Latino spouses have little formal education. Consequently, there is no reason to expect that in divorce, such families would have any reason to be aware of the mediation alternative. To get the word out will require considerable public education. To ensure that that message is tailored to the needs of the Latino community and is received as credible and trustworthy, mediators need to forge alliances with community leaders and with community-based service agencies.

15. *Family life following divorce.* Finally, the centrality of the extended family in Latino culture is such that divorce is likely to be viewed as a process that is threatening in the extreme, potentially disrupting the flow of relations and the exchange of resources. In this context, we suggest that mediation as opposed to litigation displays a much better fit with the needs of the community. Rather than promote conflict and enmity, mediation encourages cooperation and trust. In addition, it can and should make postdivorce relations—among the spouses, the extended kin, and the larger community—a topic of explicit concern. This is especially true of the TFM model, in which practitioners have a relational focus and are comfortable with the expression of feelings.

Discussion

Quality in mediation service means that all practitioners meet at least minimum standards of competence and that all client couples, regardless of their ethnic origin, receive service appropriate to their needs. At present, attention to cultural diversity issues remains scanty, both in the mediation literature and the curricula of most mediation training programs. This implies that at least some visible minority clients are probably receiving substandard service. This state of affairs is clearly inconsistent with professionalism in mediation. The portrait of Latino families presented above, together with the inferences derived from it, suggests that we can do better—much better. Minority clients deserve no less. The incorporation of an integrated cross-cultural framework into the TFM model is a step in that direction. More generally, such a framework highlights the profound significance of including cultural diversity as a central part of competent family mediation practice. In our view, such inclusion is critical to the future development of the field, and its treatment here should be understood as a call to the profession.

Note

1. This section of the chapter is taken, in part, from the following recent publication: Irving, H. H., Benjamin, M., & San Pedro, J. (1999). Family mediation and cultural diversity: Working with Latino families. *Mediation Quarterly, 16*(4), 325-339.

References

Alba, R. D. (1985). *Italian-Americans: Into the twilight of ethnicity*. Englewood Cliffs, NJ: Prentice Hall.

Albert, R. D. (1996). A framework and model for understanding Latin American and Latino/Hispanic cultural patterns. In D. Landris & R. S. Bhagat (Eds.), *Handbook of intercultural training* (2nd ed., pp. 327-348). Thousand Oaks, CA: Sage.

Anderson, K. J. (1991). *Vancouver's Chinatown: Racial discourse in Canada, 1985-1990*. Kingston, Ontario: McGill-Queens University Press.

Axtell, R. E. (1985). *Do's and taboos around the world: A guide to international behavior*. New York: John Wiley.

Baca Zinn, M. (1995). Social science theorizing for Latino families in the age of diversity. In R. E. Zambrana (Ed.), *Understanding Latino families: Scholarship, policy and practice* (pp. 177-189). Thousand Oaks, CA: Sage.

Barsky, A., Este, D., & Collins, D. (1996). Cultural competence in family mediation. *Mediation Quarterly, 13*(3), 167-178.

Bauer Maglin, N., & Perry, D. (Eds.). (1996). *Good girls/bad girls: Women, sex, violence and power in the 1990s.* New Brunswick, NJ: Rutgers University Press.

Becker, T., & Slaton, C. D. (1987). Cross-cultural mediation training. *Mediation Quarterly, 17*(6), 55-67.

Benjamin, M. (1996). *Cultural diversity, educational equity and the transformation of higher education: Group profiles as a guide to policy and programming.* Westport, CT: Praeger.

Benjamin, M., & Irving, H. H. (1992). Towards a feminist-informed model of therapeutic family mediation. *Mediation Quarterly, 10*(2), 129-153.

Boulle, L., & Kelly, K. J. (1998). *Mediation: Principles, process, practice* (Canadian ed.). Toronto: Butterworths.

Boyd-Franklin, N. (1989). *Black families in therapy: A multisystem approach.* New York: Guilford.

Bush, R. A. B., & Folger, J. P. (1994). *The promise of mediation: Responding to conflict through empowerment and recognition.* San Francisco: Jossey-Bass.

Casas, M. J. (1985). A reflection on the status of racial/ethnic minority research. *Counseling Psychologist, 13*(4), 581-598.

Castro, F. G., Coe, K., Gutierres, S., & Saenz, D. (1996). Designing health promotion programs for Latinos. In P. M. Kato & T. Mann (Eds.), *Handbook of diversity issues in health psychology* (pp. 319-346). New York: Plenum.

Chavez, L. R. (Ed.). (1990). Immigrants in U.S. cities [Special issue]. *Urban Anthropology, 19*(1/2).

Cloke, K. (1987). Politics and values in mediation: The Chinese experience. *Mediation Quarterly, 17*(7), 69-82.

Comas-Diaz, L. (1989). Culturally relevant issues and treatment implications for Hispanics. In D. R. Koslow & E. P. Salett (Eds.), *Cross cultures in mental health* (pp. 76-98). Washington, DC: SIETAR International.

Congress, E. P. (1994). The use of culturagrams to assess and empower culturally diverse families. *Families in Society, 75*(9), 531-540.

Cortes, D. E. (1994). Acculturation and its relevance to mental health. In R. G. Malgady & O. Rodriguez (Eds.), *Theoretical and conceptual issues in Hispanic mental health* (pp. 53-68). Malabar, FL: Krieger.

Cox, F. D. (1993). *Human intimacy: Marriage, the family and its meaning* (6th ed.). St. Paul, MN: West.

Cross, T. L., Bazron, B. J., Dennis, K. W., & Isaacs, M. R. (1989). *Toward a culturally competent system of care: A monograph on effective services for minority children who are severely emotionally disturbed.* Washington, DC: Georgetown University Child Development Center, CASSP Technical Assistance Center.

Dana, R. H. (1993). *Multicultural assessment perspectives for professional psychology.* Boston: Allyn & Bacon.

Davenport, D. S., & Yurich, J. M. (1991). Multicultural gender issues. *Journal of Counseling and Development, 70*(1), 64-71.

Del Castillo, A. R. (1994). Gender and its discontinuities in male/female domestic relations: Mexicans in cross cultural context. In D. R. Maciel & I. D. Ortiz (Eds.), *Chicanos/Chicanas at the crossroads: Social, economic and political change* (pp. 205-230). Tucson: University of Arizona Press.

Delgado-Gaitan, C. (1994). Socializing young children in Mexican-American families. In P. M. Greenfield & R. R. Cocking (Eds.), *Cross-cultural roots of minority child development* (pp. 56-74). Hillsdale, NJ: Lawrence Erlbaum.

Devore, W., & Scheslinger, E. G. (1996). *Ethnic-sensitive social work practice* (4th ed.). Boston: Allyn & Bacon.

Domino, G. (1992). Acculturation of Hispanics. In S. B. Knause, P. Rosenfeld, & A. Culbertson (Eds.), *Hispanics in the workplace* (pp. 56-74). Newbury Park, CA: Sage.

Duryea, M. L. (1992). *Conflict and culture: A literature review and bibliography.* Victoria, British Columbia: Institute for Dispute Resolution, University of Victoria.

Duryea, M. L., & Grundison, J. B. (1993). *Conflict and culture: Research in five communities in Vancouver, British Columbia.* Victoria, British Columbia: University of Victoria Institute for Dispute Resolution.

Dyche, L., & Zayas, L. H. (1995). The value of curiosity and naivete for the cross-cultural therapist. *Family Process, 34,* 389-399.

Emery, R. E. (1994). *Renegotiating family relationships: Divorce, child custody, and mediation.* New York: Guilford.

Essandoh, P. K. (1996). Multicultural counseling as the "Fourth Force": A call to arms. *Counseling Psychologist, 24*(1), 126-137.

Falicov, C. J. (1996). Mexican families. In M. McGoldrick, J. Giordano, & J. K. Pearce (Eds.), *Ethnicity and family therapy* (2nd ed., pp. 169-182). New York: Guilford.

Frankenberg, R. (1993). *White women, race matters: The social construction of Whiteness.* Minneapolis: University of Minnesota Press.

Garcia-Preto, N. (1996). Latino families. In M. McGoldrick, J. Giordano, & J. K. Pearce (Eds.), *Ethnicity and family therapy* (2nd ed., pp. 141-154). New York: Guilford.

Gold, L. (1993). Influencing unconscious influences: The healing dimension of mediation. *Mediation Quarterly, 11*(1), 55-66.

Goldberger, N., Tarule, J., Clinchy, B., & Belenky, M. (Eds.). (1996). *Knowledge, difference, and power: Women's ways of knowing.* New York: Basic Books.

Green, J. W. (1995). *Cultural awareness in the human services: A multi-ethnic approach* (2nd ed.). Boston: Allyn & Bacon.

Green, R. J., & Werner, P. D. (1996). Intrusiveness and closeness-caregiving: Rethinking the concept of family "enmeshment." *Family Process, 35*(2), 115-136.

Greene, B. (1994). Diversity and difference: Race and feminist psychotherapy. In M. P. Mirkin (Ed.), *Women in context: Toward a feminist reconstruction of psychotherapy* (pp. 333-351). New York: Guilford.

Gunning, I. R. (1995). Diversity issues in mediation: Controlling negative cultural myths. *Journal of Dispute Resolution, 1*(1), 55-93.

Gushue, G. V., & Sciarra, D. T. (1995). Culture and families: A multidimensional approach. In J. G. Ponterotto, J. M. Casas, L. A. Suzuki, & C. M. Alexander (Eds.), *Handbook of multicultural counseling* (pp. 586-606). Thousand Oaks, CA: Sage.

Guttman, M. C. (1996). *The meaning of macho.* Berkeley: University of California Press.

Hairston, C. D. (1999). African Americans in mediation literature: A neglected population. *Mediation Quarterly, 16*(4), 357-375.

Hall, E. T. (1976). *Beyond culture.* New York: Anchor.

Hardwood, A. (1994). Acculturation in a postmodern world: Implications for mental health research. In R. G. Malgady & O. Rodriguez (Eds.), *Theoretical and conceptual issues in Hispanic mental health* (pp. 4-17). Malabar, FL: Krieger.

Hare-Mustin, R. T., & Maracek, J. (Eds.). (1990). *Making a difference: Psychology and the construction of gender.* New Haven, CT: Yale University Press.

Harris, P. R., & Moran, R. T. (1991). *Managing cultural differences: High-performance strategies for a new world of business* (3rd ed.). Houston, TX: Gulf.

Hofstede, G. (1980). *Cultures consequences: International differences in work-related values.* Beverly Hills, CA: Sage.

Hondagneu-Sotelo, P. (1994). *Gendered transitions: Mexican experiences of immigration.* Berkeley: University of California Press.

Hurtado, A. (1995). Variations, combinations, and evolutions: Latino families in the United States. In R. E. Zambrana (Ed.), *Understanding Latino families: Scholarship, policy and practice* (pp. 40-61). Thousand Oaks, CA: Sage.

Inclan, J. (1990). Understanding Hispanic families: A curriculum outline. *Journal of Strategic and Systemic Therapies, 9*(2), 64-82.

Irving, H. H., & Benjamin, M. (1995). *Family mediation: Contemporary issues.* Thousand Oaks, CA: Sage.

Ivey, A. E., Ivey, M. B., & Simek-Morgan, L. (1997). *Counseling and psychotherapy: A multicultural perspective* (4th ed.). Boston: Allyn & Bacon.

James, P. (1997). *The divorce mediation handbook: Everything you need to know.* San Francisco: Jossey-Bass.

Johnson, S. D. (1990). Toward clarifying culture, race, and ethnicity in the context of multicultural counseling. *Journal of Multicultural Counseling and Development, 18,* 41-50.

Katz, J. (1985). The sociopolitical nature of counseling. *Counseling Psychologist, 13,* 615-624.

Kavanaugh, K. H., & Kennedy, P. H. (1992). *Promoting cultural diversity.* Thousand Oaks, CA: Sage.

Keefe, S. E. (1984). Real and ideal extended familism among Mexican-Americans and Anglo-Americans: On the meaning of "close" family ties. *Human Organization, 43,* 65-70.

Kelly, J. (1995). Power imbalance in divorce and interpersonal mediation: Assessment and intervention. *Mediation Quarterly, 13*(2), 85-98.

Koss-Chioino, J. D. (1995). Traditional and folk approaches among ethnic minority families. In J. F. Aponte, R. Y. Rivers, & J. Wohl (Eds.), *Psychosocial interventions and cultural diversity* (pp. 145-163). Boston: Allyn & Bacon.

Kruk, E. (1997). Parenting disputes in divorce: Facilitating the development of parenting plans through parent education and therapeutic family mediation. In E. Kruk (Ed.), *Mediation and conflict resolution in social work and the human services* (pp. 55-79). Chicago: Nelson-Hall.

Landau, B., Wolfson, L., Landau, N., Bartoletti, M., & Mesbur, R. (2000). *Family mediation handbook* (3rd ed.). Toronto: Butterworths.

LeBaron, M. (1997). Mediation, conflict resolution, and multicultural reality: Culturally competent practice. In E. Kruk (Ed.), *Mediation and conflict resolution in social work and the human services* (pp. 315-335). Chicago: Nelson-Hall.

LeResche, D. (1992). Comparison of the American mediation process with a Korean-American harmony restoration process. *Mediation Quarterly, 9*(4), 323-339.

Lieblich, A., & Josselson, R. (Eds.). (1994). *Exploring identity and gender: The narrative study of lives* (Vol. 2). Thousand Oaks, CA: Sage.

Malgady, R. G., & Rodriguez, O. (Eds.). (1994). *Theoretical and conceptual issues in Hispanic mental health.* Malabar, FL: Krieger.

Marin, G., & Triandis, H. C. (1985). Allocentrism as an important characteristic of the behavior of Latin Americans and Hispanics. In R. Diaz-Guerrero (Ed.), *Cross-cultural and national studies in social psychology* (Vol. 2, pp. 212-228). Amsterdam: North-Holland.

Mayo, Y. (1997). Machismo, fatherhood and the Latino family: Understanding the concept. *Journal of Multicultural Social Work, 5*(1/2), 49-62.

McGoldrick, M. (1988). Ethnicity and the family life cycle. In B. Carter & M. McGoldrick (Eds.), *The changing family life cycle: A framework for family therapy* (2nd ed., pp. 69-90). New York: Gardner.

McGoldrick, M., Pearce, J. K., & Giordano, J. (Eds.). (1982). *Ethnicity and family therapy.* New York: Guilford.

McMahon, A., & Allen-Meares, P. (1992). Is social work racist? A content analysis of recent literature. *Social Work, 37*(6), 533-539.

Meierding, N. R. (1992). The impact of cultural and religious diversity in the divorce mediation process. *Mediation Quarterly, 9*(4), 297-305.

Minuchin, S. (1974). *Families and family therapy.* Cambridge, MA: Harvard University Press.

Miralles, M. A. (1989). *A matter of life and death: Health-seeking behavior of Guatemalan refugees in South Florida.* New York: AMS.

Mirande, A. (1997). *Hombres y Machos: Masculinity and Latino culture.* Boulder, CO: Westview.

Padilla, A. M. (1994). Bicultural development: A theoretical and empirical examination. In R. G. Malgady & O. Rodriguez (Eds.), *Theoretical and conceptual issues in Hispanic mental health* (pp. 19-52). Malabar, FL: Krieger.

Padilla, A. M., & de Snyder, N. S. (1985). Counseling Hispanics: Strategies for effective intervention. In P. Pedersen (Ed.), *Handbook of cross-cultural counseling and therapy* (pp. 157-164). Westport, CT: Greenwood.

Patterson, C. H. (1996). Multicultural counseling: From diversity to universality. *Journal of Counseling and Development, 74*(3), 227-237.

Pedraza, S. (1991). Women and migration: The social consequences of gender. *Annual Review of Sociology, 17,* 303-325.

Pendersen, P. B. (1991). Multiculturalism as a generic approach to counseling. *Journal of Counseling & Development, 70*(1), 6-19.

Ponterotto, J. G., & Casas, M. (1991). *Handbook of racial/ethnic minority counseling research.* Springfield, IL: Charles C Thomas.

Portes, A., & Truelove, C. (1987). Making sense of diversity: Recent research on Hispanic minorities in the United States. *Annual Review of Sociology, 13,* 359-385.

Reid, P. (1993). Poor women in psychological research: Shut up and shut out. *Psychology of Women Quarterly, 17*(2), 133-150.

Roberts, R. (1990). *Developing culturally competent programs for families of children with special needs* (2nd ed.). Washington, DC: Georgetown University Child Development Center.

Rodriguez, C. E., & Melendez, E. (1992). Puerto Rican poverty and labor markets: An introduction. *Hispanic Journal of Behavioral Science, 14*(1), 4-15.

Rogler, L. H., Cortes, D. E., & Malgady, R. G. (1991). Acculturation and mental health status among Hispanics: Convergence and new directions for research. *American Psychologist, 46*(6), 585-597.

Rosen, H., & Kuehlwein, K. (Eds.). (1996). *Constructing realities: Meaning making perspectives for psychotherapists.* San Francisco: Jossey-Bass.

Ruiz, P. (1995). Assessing, diagnosing and treating culturally diverse individuals: A Hispanic perspective. *Psychiatric Quarterly, 66*(4), 329-341.

Saari, C. (1993). Identity complexity as an indicator of health. *Clinical Social Work Journal, 21*(1), 11-24.

Saposnek, D. (1998). *Mediating child custody disputes* (Rev. ed.). San Francisco: Jossey-Bass.

Schwebel, A. I., Gately, D. W., Renner, M. A., & Milburn, T. W. (1994). Divorce mediation: Four models and their assumptions about change in parties' positions. *Mediation Quarterly, 11*(3), 211-227.

Sewell, D. (1989). *Knowing people: A Mexican-American community's concept of a person.* New York: AMS.

Solomon, P. (1988). Racial factors in mental health service utilization. *Psychosocial Rehabilitation Journal, 11*(1), 3-12.

Strier, D. R. (1996). Coping strategies of immigrant parents: Directions for family therapy. *Family Process, 35*(3), 363-376.

Sue, D. W., Arrendondo, P., & McDavis, R. J. (1992). Multicultural counseling competencies and standards: A call to the profession. *Journal of Multicultural Counseling and Development, 20*(1), 64-88.

Sue, D. W., Ivey, A., & Pederson, P. (1996). *A theory of multicultural counseling and therapy.* Pacific Grove, CA: Brooks/Cole.

Tator, C. (1996). Anti-racism and the human service delivery system. In C. James (Ed.), *Perspectives on racism and the human service sector: A case for change* (pp. 152-170). Toronto: University of Toronto Press.

Taylor, A., & Sanchez, E. A. (1991). Out of the white box: Adapting mediation to the needs of Hispanic and other minorities within American society. *Family and Conciliation Courts Review, 29*(2), 114-128.

Trickett, E. J., Watts, R. J., & Birman, D. (1994). Toward an overarching framework for diversity. In E. J. Trickett, R. J. Watts, & D. Birman (Eds.), *Human diversity: Perspectives on people in context* (pp. 1-24). San Francisco: Jossey-Bass.

Tsang, A. Ka Tat, & George, U. (1998). Toward an integrated framework for cross-cultural social work practice. *Canadian Social Work Review, 15*(1), 73-93.

Turner, J. E. (1991). Migrants and their therapists: A trans-context approach. *Family Process, 30*(4), 407-419.

Turner, M., Fix, M., & Struyk, R. (1991). *Opportunities denied, opportunities diminished: Racial discrimination in hiring.* Washington, DC: Urban Institute Press.

Vega, W. A., & Murphy, J. W. (1990). *Culture and the restructuring of community mental health.* New York: Greenwood.

Weaver, H. N., & Wodersksi, J. S. (1996). Social work practice with Latinos. In D. F. Harrison, B. A. Thyer, & J. S. Wodersksi (Eds.), *Cultural diversity and social work practice* (2nd ed., pp. 52-86). Springfield, IL: Charles C Thomas.

Wehrly, B. (1995). *Pathways to multicultural counseling competence: A developmental journey.* Pacific Grove, CA: Brooks/Cole.

Wong, R. R. (1995). Divorce mediation among Asian Americans: Bargaining in the shadow of diversity. *Family & Conciliation Courts Review, 33*(1), 110-128.

Woodward, A. M., Dwinell, A. D., & Arons, B. S. (1992). Barriers to mental health care for Hispanic Americans: A literature review and discussion. *Journal of Mental Health Administration, 19*(3), 224-235.

Ybarra, L. (1995). Marital decision-making and the role of machismo in the Chicano family. In A. Sedillo Lopez (Ed.), *Latina issues: Fragments of historia* (pp. 252-268). New York: Garland.

Yinger, M. (1985). Ethnicity. *Annual Review of Sociology, 11,* 151-180.

Zambrana, R. E. (Ed.). (1995). *Understanding Latino families: Scholarship, policy and practice.* Thousand Oaks, CA: Sage.

Zuniga, M. E. (1992). Using metaphors in therapy: Dichos and Latino clients. *Social Work, 37*(1), 55-60.

14 Research in Family Mediation

A Decade Review, 1990-1999

I n this chapter, we provide a decade review of research in family mediation. Such reviews are not normally included in practice texts such as this. It is included here because we have always believed that there is a great deal of overlap between the goals of practice and those of research. Specifically, research in family mediation is intended to serve a variety of functions:

- to provide guidance to practitioners;
- to serve as a reality check;
- to respond to issues, especially criticism;
- to assess existing practice models and provide the basis for the construction of new models;
- to support the credibility of family mediation;
- to ensure continuing funding of mediation service agencies;
- to inform consumers of mediation services; and
- to inform policymakers and politicians in the area of family law and public policy.

How well or poorly it has fulfilled these functions is unclear; to our knowledge, such uses of research have themselves never been the subject of research. What *is* clear is that, over time, especially in the decade just past, the volume and diversity of such research have increased significantly. For the busy practitioner, keeping up-to-date in the field is no mean feat. For many, that task has been allocated to a handful of reviewers (Benjamin & Irving, 1992, 1995; Clement & Schwebel, 1993; Irving & Benjamin, 1995; Kelly, 1996; Kelly & Gigy, 1989; Pearson & Thoennes, 1989; see Stamato, 1992).

The present chapter builds on this impressive body of work in an effort to (a) identify trends and (b) discover gaps in coverage. Toward the latter, we will begin by constructing a research framework against which to compare existing research work. Toward the former, using our newly minted framework, we will explore a representative sample of studies during the period in question, with apologies to any whose work we may inadvertently have overlooked. We will close by discussing the implications of this large data set for future research, policy, and practice.

Family Mediation: A Research Framework

On the face of it, identifying gaps in coverage sounds simple and straightforward. On sober second thought, it is no simple task, for a comprehensive framework against which to compare existing work does not now exist in the literature. To advance this task, then, we needed to create such a framework. Specifically, family mediation as a service activity can be divided into at least five components—namely, the following:

- Person
- Setting
- Process
- Outcome(s)
- General

That is, family mediation necessarily involves the direct and indirect interaction among several persons in a given setting who engage in a particular process intended to produce one or more outcomes. At the same time, one may seek to characterize family mediation in more general terms, including cross-national and international descriptions and comparisons. Unpacking these individual components suggests both the range and complexity of the research undertaking in this area.

Person

Family mediation involves a cast of characters whose attributes, both individual and social, cannot but affect what happens in mediation. For example, clients may be described individually in terms of a range of attributes that are thought to have a bearing on their conduct in mediation. Such attributes include the following:

- *Sociodemographic:* gender, age, marital status, income, education, religious affiliation, cultural identification
- *Psychological:* personality, learning disability, mental health status, cognitive competence, postdivorce adjustment, feelings about self (esteem, assertiveness) and other (hostility, attachment), stress

- *Social:* social network, support, isolation, involvement, skills
- *Marital:* history, conflict, cooperation, issues in dispute, current arrangements, violence and domination, abuse of alcohol and/or drugs
- *Parental:* parenting competence, parental involvement, visiting arrangements (real and preferred), custodial arrangements (real and preferred), violence
- *Other:* employment history, residential movement, current living arrangements, welfare status, prison/probation record

Related attributes apply to the children, including their involvement in mediation (see McIntosh, 2000).

The other key participant, the mediator, can also be described along a series of dimensions:

- Disciplinary background, including mental health, law, or other
- Formal education
- Mediation training
- Practice status, typically private or public
- Practice involvement, typically full- or part-time, and either paid or volunteer
- Years of experience
- Adherence to one or more models of practice
- Values and beliefs
- Sociodemographic attributes, especially gender and age

Finally, given that divorce is a legal procedure, legal actors such as lawyers and judges often act as gatekeepers by deciding who gets referred to mediation and who does not. Accordingly, their experience of and their attitudes toward mediation are important pieces of information.

Setting

All mediation occurs in a setting having particular characteristics that cannot help but shape the process transacted there. Here, a key distinction is between public and private practice. The former refers to mediators who provide service through the courts and who are funded through public means. The latter refers to practitioners who usually charge a fee for service and operate either alone or through an agency. In both cases, mediators can be expected to vary by caseload, hours of service, number of total sessions, model of practice, intervention strategies, and so on. More generally, the presence of a fee may be expected to act as a selection mechanism, with more affluent clients likely to seek private service and less affluent clients likely to seek public service.

Setting is also likely to have an additional reference to the larger legal regime. Across states, provinces, and countries (see Bowen, 1999), great variation can be expected in family law statutes, court resources, policies and procedures, the availability and type of mediation services, the type and variety of social service agencies, and the range and types of facilities for mediation training. Consequently, the experience of mediation by all key participants—clients, mediators, lawyers, and judges—is likely to vary systematically and to have concomitant effects on both process and outcome.

Finally, the interaction between person and setting raises additional issues for both practitioners and researchers. From a clinical perspective, there is growing consensus as to the core competencies required for effective mediation practice. There is no such consensus regarding the core competencies required of clients to ensure their meaningful participation and the reasonable expectation of a positive outcome. *Readiness* is one perspective on this issue and implies an absolutist stand, that is, some set of criteria that are independent of context and refer solely to some necessary collection of client attributes. In contrast, *screening* is a more relative notion that typically refers to the fit between client and service attributes. For example, whereas a private service, with ample time available, may welcome a particularly complex case, it may be "screened out" by a public service with very strict time limits. Such screening is an agency prerogative, whereas self-screening is a choice of clients. Thus, some clients may be blocked from accessing a service they want, whereas other clients may be offered the service but refuse, preferring a litigated solution instead.

Among researchers, related notions include *assignment* and *comparability*. Assignment refers to the basis on which clients join one group or another. Ideally, random assignment is preferred. This serves to control for self-selection while diminishing the importance of person attributes. Any client changes may thus more cleanly be interpreted as a result of service intervention. In practice, such "clean" interpretations are scarce because researchers may be forced to accept convenience samples, based on agency policies and procedures. The result is naturally occurring groups whose comparability may be suspect because the people are different, the settings are different, and the services are different.

Process

Characterizing service delivery in mediation involves an additional set of variables that attach to the clients, the mediator, their interaction, or the involvement of other participants. As a reflection of their attributes and relationships, client conduct may vary across a range of dimensions, including prosocial/antisocial, positive/negative affect, coherent/incoherent, past/future orientation, cooperative/uncooperative, compliant/noncompliant, and so on.

Similarly, their relations with their former spouse may be characterized in terms of conflict, mood, cooperation, empathy, insight, and so on.

Turning to the mediators, they routinely have at their disposal a wide range of possible interventions and strategies. What interventions they actually select will be responsive to both proximate and distal considerations. Proximal consideration refers to the conduct of the clients and their interaction, together with the practitioners' objectives in any given session and in the case as a whole. The practitioners' preferred practice model or models will also be relevant. Distal considerations refer to the constraints imposed by the statutory regime and agency policies and procedures, both of which may limit some of the mediator's strategic choices while favoring or encouraging other choices. For example, simple interventions will be preferred when time limits are tight, whereas more complex interventions will be an option when time limits are more forgiving. Such choices may also reflect the mediator's training and experience, with the conduct of novice practitioners rather different from that of their more seasoned counterparts.

These choices may be further constrained by the practitioner's decision as to who to include or exclude from the session. In theory, flexibility is the hallmark of mediation. In practice, clinical and pragmatic considerations may limit choices. Possible additional participants include new romantic partners, children, grandparents, friends, professionals, and consultants. Inclusion of any of these others may change the shape of the process and may or may not affect the outcomes. Again, in theory, process and outcome are discrete and separate. In practice, these distinctions blur and overlap. Session, case, and long-term outcome operate on different time lines and may combine in different ways, with the outcomes of several sessions necessary to achieve given case outcomes.

Finally, it remains unclear who is the best person or persons to assess process: the client, the mediator, or a third-party researcher. There are pros and cons associated with each choice. Only the clients know what it feels like to go through the process, such that they are uniquely positioned to describe it. But they also ignore or may be unaware of the mediator's real intentions and may be further handicapped by retrospective memory loss and distortion. Such limits on memory affect the mediators as much as the clients, but only the former can speak to their clinical objectives and the interventions used in their pursuit. As to the researcher, he or she has the advantage of objective recording methods (if available) and some emotional distance from the action. But the days are long past when researchers were regarded as dispassionate and objective observers. Rather, all analyses are now understood as necessarily selective, pursuant to a host of considerations, including data collection method(s), theoretical preferences, research objectives, grant limitations, and setting and technical constraints. Analysis is also subject to a variety of practical considerations, with observation methods, for example, highly demanding of time, money, and expertise. Such demands mean that most researchers will prefer approaches that are less expensive, including self-report measures or the use of role-plays, simulations, and lifelike case vignettes.

Outcome(s)

The primary objective of all family mediation services is agreement between the parties or disputants, either full and complete or at least partial. In turn, partial outcomes include clarification of issues, better understanding of issues, reductions in conflict and antisocial conduct, and the increments in cooperation and empathy. Related outcomes refer to the content of agreements, both as to their level of detail as well as their content, including the amount of time each parent spends with the children, the way decisions are to be made about them, future communications between the parents, the degree to which property division is equitable, the amount of child support, the amount of alimony, the planned response to parental relocation (mobility), efforts to secure the children's financial future, and the manner in which future impasses are to be dealt with.

Secondary or long-term outcomes can only be assessed on follow-up, typically 6, 12, or 18 months after mediation has ended. Psychological outcomes focus on adult and/or child adjustment and can include levels of anger, anxiety and depression, stress management, cognitive performance, and, in the case of the children, school performance and evidence of regression. Interpersonal outcomes refer to levels of parental cooperation and conflict, including violence and harassment. Such outcomes also include parent-child relations, both as to quality and closeness as well as in terms of compliance with the agreement, including time sharing, child support payments, alimony, and informal or litigated changes to same. Other possible changes include friendship networks, relations with new intimates, extended family, cultural identity, and life satisfaction (quality of life).

From a research perspective, outcome measures are problematic in terms of comparability. Consider the four designs common in this area of inquiry—one descriptive, the other three comparative. Descriptive studies involve delivery of a relatively standard intervention to a diverse array of clients and then assessing outcome(s). Such studies control for setting and process but are vulnerable to variation due to self-selection. This leaves uncertain if *agreement* actually means the same thing in every case. As to comparative designs, mediation may be compared to litigation, private mediation may be compared to its public counterpart, and different client groups (e.g., violent vs. nonviolent marriages) may be compared within the same mediation service. Within-service comparisons are the least problematic because they control for setting and process. What is unclear is the extent to which the two client groups are comparable save for the key attribute (such as violence) on which they differ. Comparisons across services are still more problematic because outcome measures are confounded by variation in person, setting, and process. Most problematic are comparisons across discipline, such as studies comparing mediation with lawyer negotiation. Such research is confounded on multiple grounds. For example, each lawyer's formal commitment is to secure an agreement between the parties that serves the best interests of his or her adult client, whether or not the process promotes conflict between the parties and independent of any unintended psychological consequences of the process, positive or negative. Such is not the case with the mediator, especially one working from a therapeutic model (such as therapeutic family mediation [TFM]) in which the process is intended to have psychological and interpersonal consequences in addition to securing an agreement. Furthermore, interaction between setting (public, private) and model (structural, problem solving, therapeutic) means that even the process can vary widely. Reference to "mediation" is thus misleading because although all family lawyers are at least trained to operate in one way (whether or not they actually do so in practice), mediation training ensures the opposite, that different mediators may operate in many different ways. From this description, it is quite unclear whether the outcome(s) in each process are comparable.

General

Finally, each mediator and each agency operate in the larger context of family mediation as a technology or as a movement. Here, concerns include the number, distribution, and training of mediators nationwide, along with the similar distribution of training facilities. Also relevant are the identity and membership of professional organizations for mediation, whether they operate within a state or province or constitute national associations; the rules and procedures they promulgate; and the extent to which members adhere to such guidelines.

In a sense, the evolution of family mediation as a field of professional practice can be said to have paralleled research practice. Maturation of the field has seen a shift in focus. Concerns about efficacy in the 1980s (Irving & Benjamin, 1995) determined whether the fledgling movement would live or die. In contrast, the current proliferation of organizations, mediators, agencies, and training facilities speaks to a technology that has entered the mainstream of family law and practice. One would thus expect a shift in emphasis, from outcome (Does it work?) to process (What works? With which clients? Under what circumstances? With what short- and long-term consequences?). It remains to be seen whether such a shift has actually occurred.

More generally, this research framework makes clear that the family mediation enterprise is complex and obviously beyond the purview of any single study, no matter how ambitious. Conversely, the extent to which such complexity has been adequately addressed by the corpus of work in the 1990s, and thus whether there are gaps in the literature, are questions to which we will return later in this chapter. It is the substantive trends in that literature to which we turn next.

Substantive Trends

As seen in Table 14.1, our review of the literature has been organized in keeping with the five areas of inquiry noted above. In the interests of clarity and simplicity, each study has been cited only once and located in the area that, in our judgment, comes closest to its primary focus. In most cases, such placement was obvious and straightforward. In some cases, it was arbitrary because complex studies yielded results pertinent to more than one area of inquiry. In each area, our concern will be to identify key trends rather than review specific studies, with all such trends listed for review in Appendix 14.1. In addition, in a handful of cases, we will note relevant studies in areas of mediation other than family mediation.

Person (P)

There are six P trends apparent in this body of work; discussion of three additional P trends will be deferred to later sections.

P1: Awareness of family mediation among judicial actors (judges, lawyers) is high.

Among judicial actors, such as judges and lawyers, the majority are aware of family mediation; that is, most are aware of the availability of such services and the content of such service. Indeed, a minority of lawyers report having received training in mediation. Unfortunately, such still does not appear to be true of the general population. In a study of single-parent groups in three states, Hauser (1993) found that awareness was poor, and there was considerable confusion over content and much skepticism because the service was not connected to the legal system. Such evidence constitutes a challenge in marketing family mediation service.

P2: Attitudes toward family mediation among judicial actors are generally positive.

In general, among those judicial actors who are aware of family mediation, attitudes toward family mediation are positive, especially as regards reducing the time to settlement and efforts to facilitate client negotiation.

(Text continued on page 355)

Table 14.1 Family Mediation Research Studies (1990–1999) by Area of Inquiry

Author(s)	Date	Place	Number	Results
Area of inquiry: Person (*n* = 9)				
Bohmer and Ray[a]	1996	NY, GA	?	FM > 50/50 split property versus lawyer, judge 60/40 > H
Cavanagh	1997	IL	18	Lawyers aware FM but seldom refer
Harrell	1995	FL	150	Lawyer attend FM, protect and control client; not trust FM
Lee, Beauregard, and Huntsley[b]	1998a	ON	161	Lawyer as gatekeeper to FM: positive attitude; gender 0
Koopman, Hunt, Favretto, Coltri, and Britten	1991	US	248	Judge > lawyer positive toward FM; female > male
Medley and Schellenberg	1994b	IN	187	Judge positive attitude toward FM
Medley and Schellenberg	1994a	IN	226	Lawyer weak positive attitude toward FM; > experience, < positive; female > male
Neilson	1994	UK	D	FM female, 50+ years, secondary occupation, p-t, SW ed, limited FM ed
Tan[c]	1991	US	133	Instrument assesses client FM readiness on six dimensions
Areas of inquiry: Setting (*n* = 3)				
Goettler, Herrman, and Grace	1999	GA	339	Private FM > public FM or government agency: male, education, income, career, age
Kelly[d]	1993	CA	248	Private FM versus lawyer negotiation: FM > client talk, < conflict, > AG, sat
Kelly and Duryea	1992	CA	184	Private versus court FM: positive attitude FM, women > men see FM skillful, men/women equally influential, women > sat

(Continued)

349

Table 14.1 (Continued)

Author(s)	Date	Place	Number	Results
Areas of inquiry: Process (n = 15)				
Cobb[e]	1994a	??	1	Case study, divorce: first narrative told tends to colonize subsequent narrative(s)
Dingwall, Greatbatch, and Ruggerone[f]	1998	UK	30	FM-client interaction depends on professional identity, not gender; FM control shape AG
Donohue, Drake, and Roberto[g]	1994	IL	22	Lawyer/FM > AG > attend client relational needs
Fuller, Kimsey, and McKinney	1992	VA	24	Role-play: different perception of FM fairness depends on who tells story first; see FM < controlling
Guerra and Elliott	1996	TX	?	Instrument to assess FM cognitive roles; > rigid client, > FM multiple roles
Kandel	1998	CA	3	Case study; FM strict neutrality impractical and unethical
Kimsey, Fuller, Bell, and McKinney	1994	VA	118	Role-play: use integration, compensation strategies; > client sees FM competent
Kruk	1998b	BC	10	Case simulation using real FM: 90% AG-driven approach; ignore client relational needs
Kruk	1998a	CAN	250	National survey: 56% female, 64% private, 77% comprehensive, AG 68%; combine structured negotiation 92% with therapeutic model 65%; various strategies
Lansky, Swift, Manley, Elmore, and Gerety	1996	US	324	National survey of AFM members: 77% see child but rarely; mental > lawyer; public = private
Littlejohn, Shailor, and Pearce	1994	MA	1	Case study divorce: greater differences in moral, conflict, and justice realities, < AG

350

Author(s)	Date	Place	Number	Results
Newmark, Harrell, and Salem	1995	OR, MN	422	Public FM: FV versus non-FV: non-FV > empowerment, decision making, < risk of harm, conflict; stress need for screening
Rudd	1996	US	87	Client > prosocial, compliance-gaining strategies, > sat FM
Tracy and Spradkin	1994	US	1	Conversational analysis role-play using four experienced FM: similar moves establish authority, different moves using bargaining versus nonbargaining (therapeutic) style
Welsh and Lewis	1998	MN	30	Cambodian client: negotiation, withdrawal OK; prefer FM stature in community, evaluative intervention
Areas of inquiry: Outcome (n = 28)				
Arbuthnot and Kramer	1998	US	253	National survey of AFM members: FM > L cooperation, communication skills, AG; 65% support mandatory FM
Burrell, Narus, Bogdanoff, and Allen	1994	IL	584	FM < client stress (self-esteem), > AG; FM as a child advocate
Camplair and Stolberg	1990	?	76	Public FM: 69% AG, < hostility, > time with child, > overall family functioning
Chandler	1990	HI	216	FM FV versus non-FV: AG 50% both groups; FV > complex, < income, ed, age
Coltri and Hubt	1998	?	178	FM on telephone: average duration 75 minutes, AG 56%
Davies and Ralph[h]	1998	AUS	292	FM FV versus non-FV: AG 71%, high sat (84%) both groups, gender 0
Duryea	1992	CA	209	Public FM versus L: 76% FM AG avg. 3 hours, strong prefer FM, women > men sat (express views, focus important issues)
D'Errico and Elwork	1991	NJ	94	Public FM vs. L: FM > sat but > conflict; FM AG require > cooperation, so > opportunity for conflict

(Continued)

Table 14.1 (Continued)

Author(s)	Date	Place	Number	Results
Depner, Cannata, and Simon	1992	CA	1,699	Public FM: serious problems, including FV; AG 46%, high sat process, outcome
Depner, Cannata, and Ricci	1995	CA	1,388	Public FM: 50% moderate conflict, AG 55%, shared parenting 15%
Ellis and Stuckless	1992	ON	73	FM FV versus non-FV: AG 73%, high sat; pre-FM frightened, hassled predictor post-FM abusive behavior; importance of screening and prevention in FM
Ellis and Stuckless[i]	1996	ON	363	FV, non-FV equally likely achieve desired outcomes, see self as powerful as spouse; assess violence and power separately since vary inversely; only use violence if unable achieve outcomes by non-FV means
Emery[j]	1994	NC	71	Random assignment to public FM or L: AG 77% versus 28%; 65% relitigation; FM > sat, especially H; H > time child; no difference psychological outcomes
Irving and Benjamin	1992	ON	72	Private FM: client severe stress, average 13 hours of service, FM supportive strategies, AG 76%, high sat
Jones and Bodtker[k]	1999	PA	230	Public FM versus L: FM AG 61%, relitigation 18%, > sat (but moderate 59%); outcome & sat highly correlated (AG > sat)
Kressel, Frontera, Forlenza, Butler, and Fish	1994	NJ	32	Public FM: problem solving versus settlement oriented > AG, durable, positive process, client sat
Magana and Taylor	1993	CA	100	Co-FM FV cases: AG 51% first session, > protective outcome with high-risk cases
Marcus, Marcus, Stilwell, and Doherty	1999	CT	400	Private FM, L: few differences financial agreement; FM women retain > assets, > years, alimony, > child support amount, < postjudgment modifications

Author(s)	Date	Place	Number	Results
Mathis and Yingling	1991	TX	72	Public FM: average 4 hours, AG 73%; no relation consensus regarding divorce and outcome
Mathis and Yingling[1]	1998	US	?	Instrument classifies FM families as competent, discordant, disoriented, or chaotic; > competent, > AG
Meierding	1993	CA	94	Private FM: follow-up among AG client: very positive perception FM; 11% relitigation
Pearson	1991	CA	302	Public FM, private FM, L: AG 59%-80%; few differences by setting; FM < expensive, > sat; private FM > financial support for women and children
Pearson	1997	CA	D	Public FM FV cases: average < extreme, < 5% excluded, focus ability to negotiate, often no AG; FM training in FV needed
Raisner	1997	IL	441	Public FM: no difference AG rate married versus never married (66% vs. 59%); no difference among never married if FV or non-FV (64% vs. 62%)
Slater, Shaw, and Duquesnel	1992	CA	557	Public FM, L: no difference AG rate (41% vs. 38%); FM > sat (even among non-AG)
Sullivan, Schwebel, and Lind	1997	OH	387	Public FM: 63% sat, 52% made progress in FM; rules and fees undermine sat; sat & fees related to progress
Tjersland	1999	NOR	38	FM: sat couples 6 elements: allowed to speak, readiness to confirm relations, rewrite marital history; FM ask questions about special situations, solutions based on parental competence, help parents put decisions on paper
Whiting	1994	US	106	Family versus nonfamily cases: family > multiple issues and ongoing relationships > AG

(Continued)

Table 14.1 (Continued)

Author(s)	Date	Place	Number	Results
Areas of inquiry: General (n = 2)				
McKinney, Kimsey, and Fuller	1996	US	146	National survey: FM firmly established in United States; most agencies small, p-t, volunteers, nonprofit, caseload 200 to 1,900, majority report AG > 50%
Ricci et al.	1992	CA	75	In 1991, 65,494 cases, a 32% increase from 1988: typical case from one to two 90-minute sessions

Total number = 57

NOTE: Place = state(s), province, country; FM = family mediation; L = litigation; H = husband; W = wife; AG = agreement; ? = not stated; D = diverse sample; ed = training; sat = satisfaction; FV = family violence.

a. See Bohmer and Ray (1993).
b. See Lee, Beauregard, and Huntsley (1998b).
c. See Dennis (1991).
d. See Kelly (1991a, 1991b) and Thoennes, Salem, and Pearson (1995).
e. See Cobb (1991, 1994a, 1994b, 1997), Cobb and Rifkin (1991a, 1991b), and Rifkin, Millen, and Cobb (1991).
f. See Dingwall and Greatbatch (1991) and Greatbatch and Dingwall (1989, 1994, 1997).
g. See Donohue (1991).
h. See Davies, Ralph, Hawton, and Craig (1995).
i. See Ellis and Wright (1998).
j. See Emery, Matthews, and Kitzman (1994); Emery, Matthews, and Wyer (1991); Emery (1995); Dillon and Emery (1996); and Kitzman and Emery (1993).
k. See Jones and Bodtker (1998).
l. See Mathis and Yingling (1990, 1992).

P3: Attitudes toward family mediation among judicial actors vary by position (judges, lawyers), experience, and gender.

That said, judicial opinions are hardly unqualified, and they do vary. For example, judges appear more positive than lawyers in their views of mediation. Indeed, in some samples, the attitudes of many lawyers were decidedly tepid, with reservations based on concerns about mediator qualifications, limited effectiveness, and (especially among civil as opposed to family law lawyers) a sense that many cases would be inappropriate for mediation. In addition, these reservations were more typical of lawyers who were highly experienced and male; more positive views were typical of lawyers called to the bar more recently and female. Indeed, the key reason some lawyers insisted on attending mediation sessions was to protect their clients' rights—protection that mediators could not, in their view, be relied on to provide.

P4: Attitudes and referral practices among judicial actors are linked.

Not surprisingly, judicial attitudes toward mediation and subsequent referral practices were linked. Lawyers and judges who were aware of and positively inclined toward family mediation were much more likely than those with negative views to refer clients to mediation. It is unclear from these data whether this trend holds for lawyer/mediators because they may be inclined to provide service themselves. It is also unclear whether judicial actors who do refer display a preference for public as opposed to private mediation.

P5: The definition of fairness varies by discipline.

Disciplinary training and socialization are powerful influences on student perceptions. They are intentional and presumably carry forward to influence the conduct of professionals long after graduation. Such reasoning suggests that actors with judicial or mental health backgrounds may perceive family law issues in divorce quite differently. This was evident among P studies that found that the perception of what constituted a fair settlement varied systemically. Whereas judges and lawyers equated "fair" settlements as those that came close to what a court would have ordered, mediators interpreted fairness more in keeping with their own sense of equity, rooted in their background in mental health. In the work of Bohmer and Ray (1993, 1996), for example, such differences were hardly idle and directly affected both process and outcome. For example, whereas lawyers felt most comfortable addressing financial issues first, mediators typically began with parenting issues. Similarly, whereas settlements arrived at through the aid of judicial actors gave 65% of the property to husbands, those arrived at through mediation were more likely to split the property on a 50/50 basis.

P6: Such definitions establish the practical limits within which most, if not all, mediated agreements are likely to fall.

Discussions and research about outcomes in mediation focus almost exclusively on those processes in mediation through which such outcomes are achieved. P studies suggest that outcomes are also shaped by a negotiated consensus among professionals in the family law area, including judges, lawyers, and mediators. Studies in this area leave unclear how such negotiations are conducted but imply that such understandings are loose and informal. Even so, such understandings appear to carry considerable weight in establishing the limits of what constitute fair settlements and are enacted subtly through the enormous influence of judges, lawyers, and mediators. As will become apparent in later sections, such influence constitutes a direct challenge to conventional notions of client self-determination and mediator impartiality. Here, it will suffice to note the indirect influence of the mediators' community of peers and colleagues on their mediation practice.

Setting (S)

The degree to which our distinction between person and setting is arbitrary is evident in studies in this section because they suggest two trends in each area. Further evidence in support of these trends will become apparent in later sections.

P7: Interest in and sensitivity to psychological and interpersonal issues among clients vary by disciplinary background and are more likely among mediators per se than lawyers.

Further evidence of the power of disciplinary socialization is provided by S studies, especially the impact of background in shaping the way practitioners interact with clients. Such differences became apparent when mediators and lawyers were compared. In assuming control of a given case, lawyers preferred to have communication between the parties flow through them, thus deliberately blocking direct communication between the parties. They also focused on facts relevant to statutory matters and avoided discussion of clients' feelings and their past relations with the other party. In contrast, mediators encouraged talk between the parties, only deferring it to mediation, and were much more willing to explore clients' feeling and relationships. This differential preference for psychological and interpersonal issues resulted in a process that clients experienced very differently, with direct implications for short- and long-term outcomes.

P8: Degree of family dysfunction among clients prior to entering mediation is a good predictor of mediation outcome: The higher the degree of premediation dysfunction, the lower the probability of one or more positive outcomes.

Notions of readiness and screening, discussed above, suggest that although family mediation may be an appropriate choice for many couples going through divorce, this will *not* be true for at least some of them. In comparing the experience of clients in mediation and lawyer negotiation, Kelly (1993) reached the same conclusion, arguing that mediation will likely be either ineffective or inappropriate for as many as 30% of divorcing couples who are highly dysfunctional, including those involved in family violence, substance abuse, and child abuse and/or who show evidence of psychiatric disorder. As we will see in later sections, this conclusion remains controversial, with some in the field taking a much more qualified stand on the issue (see Van Slyck, Stern, & Newland, 1992).

S1: There are few gender differences in the way clients see family mediators, irrespective of whether service is provided in a private or a public setting.

There is much evidence that men and women see the world in different ways and so respond to conflict and negotiation differently (Stamato, 1992). In light of this evidence, it would be reasonable to assume that gender differences should extend to mediation. In fact, there is growing evidence that any such differences among clients are suppressed in mediation. The work of Kelly and Duryea (1992) is a case in point, although only one of a series of studies to examine this issue (see below). In essence, their findings indicated few differences in the ways in which men and women experience mediation, whether their contact was in a public or a private setting. In general, all clients experienced mediation as a very positive experience, though demanding and even emotionally draining. Indeed, such positive views were as likely among clients who completed the process as among those who dropped out prematurely. Women were especially appreciative of mediators who helped them express their views, focus on important issues, stand up to their spouses, and put aside their anger.

S2: The rights of men and women are as likely to be protected in mediation as in lawyer negotiation; charges that women's rights may be compromised in family mediation appear to be unfounded.

The feminist critique of mediation has had a profound impact on the field (Benjamin & Irving, 1992), prompting much research in response. Kelly and Duryea (1992) presented the first of a series of such studies. Both in private and public mediation, men and women reported that they each felt equally free to influence the mediation process. Indeed, women more than men felt able to express their views and stand up to their spouses. The only exception concerned financial issues, which many of the women who dropped out found confusing or too complex, thus ceding an advantage in knowledge to their husbands. On one hand, this evidence suggested that women dropped out of mediation for appropriate reasons. On the other hand, these data raise questions about the appropriate roles of the mediator. Previously, we have argued that two of these are the roles of educator and the purveyor of information. Given that the enactment of such roles necessarily takes time away from negotiation, what may be available to clients in private mediation, with 15 service hours to spare, may not be available in public mediation, with access to only 8 hours or (often) fewer service hours.

Process (Pc)

Process studies are complex and demanding. Accordingly, we noted their scarcity in a previous review (Irving & Benjamin, 1995) and are pleased to note a substantial increase in their number in recent years. Such studies support five trends.

Pc1: The organization of family mediation tends to suppress gender differences in client conduct.

The relative absence of gender differences among P studies is elaborated by Pc studies, which suggest that the organization of family mediation tends to suppress gender differences in client conduct. This was especially evident in the work of Dingwall and Greatbatch (1991), whose findings highlight what we have called mediator procedural control. Among other things, this often means that clients talk to the mediator, not to each other, and learn quickly to wait their turn on the mediator's signal. Consequently, conversation tends to be ordered on the basis of substantive issues and situational constraints rather than gender. Similarly, spousal differences are more apt to reflect their divergent bargaining positions than their gender. For example, women defend the status quo based on experiential knowledge of the children, and men push for change based on abstract knowledge of the children.

P9: Evidence of gender-based differences in practice style among male and female mediators remain equivocal.

In a related vein, evidence of gender-based differences in the conduct of family mediators remains equivocal. For example, Wall and Dewhurst (1991), in a study of mediation in small claims court, found that female mediators were more inclined to frame issues in terms of clarity, whereas male mediators were more inclined to do so in terms of control. Consequently, clients were more likely to perceive women mediators as both fairer and more competent. Similarly, Maxwell (1992), in a study of mediation in criminal misdemeanor cases, found that male and female practitioners were equally effective in gaining an initial agreement, but females were more effective in gaining a final binding agreement.

Supportive evidence from Pc studies was indirect. Kruk (1998b), for example, in a national Canadian survey, found that female mediators were more likely to have a mental health background, to prefer a therapeutic practice model, and, as a result, to be more interventionist. Male mediators were more likely to have a legal background, to prefer a structured negotiation model, and, as a result, to be less interventionist. Such results led Kruk to conclude that mediators with mental health and legal backgrounds "appear . . . to be practicing family mediation in markedly different ways" (p. 209). By inference, such differences included gender differences. In contrast, the work of Dingwall and Greatbatch (1991) in the United Kingdom and Kandel (1998) in the United States found no such differences, with mediator conduct shaped more by their professional role than by their gender.

Pc2: Evidence of model-related differences in practice style among family mediators remains equivocal.

There is little evidence among Pc studies that family mediators rely on one practice model or another, and what evidence is available is mixed. For example, both Kruk (1998b) in Pc studies and Neilson (1994) in P studies found a general divide between proponents of therapeutic as opposed to structural models. However, Kruk also found that many mediators rely on two or more models and simultaneously supported notions of neutrality and intervention. Neither study, nor any other evidence examined in this review, has explored the link between professed practice model and actual conduct. Indeed, if anything, available data suggest that many mediators tend to be eclectic and entirely pragmatic in their effort to help clients solve problems. In both Donohue, Drake, and Roberto's (1994) experimental study and Kruk's simulated study, mediators focused on facts and issues and either ignored or blocked discussion of feelings and relationships. Similarly, Rudd (1996) found that clients who used compliance-gaining strategies were more satisfied with the mediation process compared with those who were argumentative or verbally aggressive. Put differently, these data suggest that mediators were more supportive of cooperative clients than their uncooperative counterparts. This interpretation is consistent with Guerra and Elliott (1996), who found that mediators had to work harder with clients whose initial position was rigid as opposed to those who were flexible.

Pc3: Family mediators routinely use their authority to shape both process and outcome(s).

Several Pc studies—including Dingwall and Greatbatch (1991); Fuller, Kimsey, and McKinney (1992); Kandel (1998); Kimsey, Fuller, Bell, and McKinney (1994); and Newmark, Harrell, and Salem (1995)—speak to a contradiction in mediation practice. Formal guidelines consistently emphasize mediator neutrality and client self-determination. Conversely, there is pervasive evidence that mediators are enormously influential in shaping the process in such a way as to help clients achieve what Kandel (1998) calls "sensible workable resolutions to disputes" (p. 312). This is true whether it involves selecting who tells their story first, empowering clients in violent families, employing one intervention strategy or another, or training clients to comply with the turn-taking rules the mediator imposes. In using what Kandel calls their "situated substantive expertise," mediators believe they are acting responsibility and ethically, both in persuading clients to accept what is workable under their circumstances and in preserving the interests of parties who not at the table, especially the children.

Clearly, having power opens up the possibility of its misuse. Restraining or limiting such power would be futile, for such a move would fail to "recognize the inevitability of substantive intervention" (Kandel, 1998, p. 312). Rather, the solution lies in informing clients of its presence, so they are not misled by the mediator's talk about neutrality (Dingwall & Greatbatch, 1991), and making its responsible use part and parcel of mediator training and professional development.

Pc4: The inclusion of children has a positive effect on the mediation process.

Most mediators have had some experience of including the children in the mediation process, typically with positive consequences. Limited research confirms this clinical judgment. Lansky, Swift, Manley, Elmore, and Gerety (1996) found that 77% of the U.S. mediators in their sample saw the children from time to time. Their inclusion was typically at a parent's request and/or in an effort to change the process by avoiding impasse, reality testing, and/or influencing the balance of power. In a more recent study, MacIntosh (2000) reported similar results using an Australian sample. Child inclusion changed parental behavior, defused conflict and blaming, and provided a direct benefit to the children by giving them a chance to speak and be heard. However, Lansky et al. add several reasons for excluding children, including avoiding loyalty conflicts and further intrusion, putting the children under pressure, and/or giving the children too much power.

Pc5: The impact of culture on the mediation process remains problematic as a research topic.

In a previous chapter (see Chapter 13), we noted that culture has only now begun to receive attention as a topic worthy of sustained clinical attention in mediation. Regrettably, this is not yet the case in research. We uncovered no Pc studies of culture in family mediation. One P study, by Goldstein (1998), noted already, found no differences in the way Asian and European American mediators responded to a conflict scale. Culture, like gender, may be overwhelmed by the demands of the professional role. In a related study of mediation in neighbor justice, Welsh and Lewis (1998) interviewed a group of Cambodians in Minneapolis to discover how they managed conflict about family and nonfamily issues. They found the following: Both discussion and withdrawal were acceptable responses, there was a clear preference for mediators who had more stature in the community than their clients, and informants preferred intervention efforts that were clearly evaluative as opposed to merely facilitative. These data would suggest that cultural variation should be associated with substantive variations in the mediation process. However, it is also clear that these data alone are insufficient as a basis for informing the field as to needed changes. Rather, much more work of this sort needs to be done and with awareness as to the availability of an enormous body of ethnocultural research that we have reviewed elsewhere (Benjamin, 1996).

Outcome

Of the four areas of inquiry, studies of outcome were the most voluminous and supported several trends.

O1: Family mediation is an effective technology based on a range of primary outcomes, including (a) agreement rate, (b) time to agreement, (c) relative cost, (d) relitigation rate, and (e) agreement durability.

There is virtual consensus across a range of studies that more than half of all cases seen in family mediation end in full or partial agreement; most studies reviewed for this chapter reported agreement rates between 60% and 80%. Although the agreement rate varied little by setting, time to agreement was clearly setting related; mediation in private settings required three to four times as many service hours as their public counterparts. Indeed, Coltri and Hubt (1998) reported a 56% agreement rate after a single 75-minute session held on the telephone. Similarly, there was good evidence that mediation was less costly than litigation, although this was obviously less true of private as opposed to public mediation. With few exceptions (see Emery, 1994), the relitigation rate was typically low, that is, less than 20%, with most revisions to mediated agreements made informally between the parties themselves. That is, on 6-, 12-, 18-, or 24-month follow-up, the majority of mediated agreements had shown good durability.

O2: Family mediation is an effective technology based on a range of secondary outcomes, including (a) client satisfaction, (b) perceived fairness, (c) client sense of empowerment, (d) financial support, (e) parent-child relations, and (f) parental cooperation.

There is growing consensus that family mediation routinely yields secondary outcomes that are either better than or on a par with litigation. With few exceptions (see Jones & Bodtker, 1998), to the extent that mediation allowed clients to have their say and address important issues, clients were consistently more satisfied than their counterparts in litigation. In part, this was likely because they consistently reported that mediation provided a process that was perceived to be fairer than litigation and in which they were more likely to feel empowered. Financial concerns typically turn on how well or poorly women fair in negotiation. In this regard, compared to their counterparts in litigation, women were either on a par (in public mediation) or did somewhat better (in private mediation). As for parent-child relations, the focus now shifts to men. Here, maternal sole custody was equally likely in mediation or litigation. However, mediated agreements tended to accord fathers more time with their children. The mediation process was also more likely to be associated with reduced parental conflict and hostility. Finally, several of these outcomes were linked to agreement status. That is, mediation clients who reached agreement were more likely than those that did not to be satisfied with the process, regard it as fair and empowering, and would recommend mediation to others. That said, Wallerstein, Lewis, and Blakeslee (2000) reported, following Dillon and Emery (1996), that "long-term studies show no significant differences in the child's adjustment at home or in school whether the parents use lawyers or mediators to settle their differences" (p. 207).

O3: Family mediation is effective with divorce cases involving family violence.

Of the O studies in Table 14.1, seven explored the effectiveness of family mediation in cases involving family violence—specifically, spousal abuse (see Maxwell, 1999). Despite variation in design (some were descriptive, others comparative), three findings were reported consistently. First, about half of all violence cases involved in family mediation ended in agreement, with similar results in comparable cases in which violence was not an issue. Second, clients in violence cases were very satisfied with both the process and the outcome of mediation and at a level comparable to nonviolent cases. Third, on average, cases involving violence were characterized by moderate spousal conflict in which abuse had stopped 6 to 12 months prior to entering mediation and in which screening demonstrated that both spouses were able to negotiate.

Two additional findings are noteworthy. First, violence cases could be more complex than their nonviolent counterparts, involving both the use of special techniques (such as comediation, shuttle mediation, and/or the addition of a support person) as well as more "protective" outcomes (such as supervised access). Second, although mediation was associated with the significant reduction in postmediation abuse and "hassles," it offered no guarantee that such behavior would stop altogether. Ellis and his colleagues (Ellis & Stuckless, 1996; Ellis & Wight, 1998), for example, found that "being frightened" and premediation hassles and abuse were moderate to strong predictors of postmediation abuse. Unfortunately, such follow-up efforts have not been widely used in this literature, nor have follow-up outcomes been compared in cases subject to mediation as opposed to litigation.

These findings suggest the need for both improved screening techniques and for specialized mediation training. They also speak to the feminist critique of mediation, which argues that cases involving violence are simply not appropriate for family mediation and ought to be dealt with exclusively through the court. The findings reviewed above indicate not only that mediation can be both appropriate and empowering for women and men in violence cases but that such services exist, in part, to meet client demand.

O4: Several variables show promise as correlates of outcome in family mediation.

Various studies have sought to identify potential correlates of outcome in mediation. Some efforts have shown positive results, others not. Among the latter, there was no relationship with either marital status or spousal consensus and mediation outcome. Among the former, divorce education programs appeared to enhance mediation outcomes by helping parents focus on the needs of their children and improving parental communication and cooperation. Similarly, there was an inverse relationship between parental stressors and mediation outcome; as stress declined, the likelihood of agreement increased. The same was true of adaptability as a general measure of family function, in keeping with P8, and conflict over multiple as opposed to single issues also increased the likelihood of "win-win" outcomes in mediation.

Most recently, in an Australian study, Bickerdike and Littlefield (2000) tested several hypotheses concerning the link between antecedent conditions and family mediation outcomes. Their findings showed that high levels of premediation anger and "attachment disparity" were linked to outcome via conflict and problem-solving behavior. That is, the higher the levels of anger and attachment disparity, the higher the level of conflict; the lower the level of productive problem solving, the lower the level of outcome agreement. They also found that the more contentious the couple, the more mediators were inclined to use "strong" interventions. Although mediators might use enactment to change behavior, when both partners were very angry, this process proved very difficult to control.

O5: Mediators who use a therapeutic style produce better outcomes than those who rely on structured negotiation.

There is some confusion in the literature concerning the notions of a practice model as opposed to a practice style. Kressel, Frontera, Forlenza, Butler, and Fish (1994) define mediator style as "a cohesive set of strategies that characterize the conduct of a case" (p. 67). To our mind, this differs little from how one would define adherence to a given practice model and points to the need for research exploring the relative effectiveness of different models with various client groups or attributes. Unfortunately, such studies are rare, with Kressel et al. a happy exception. Based on intensive study of a small group of court-based mediation cases, the authors distinguished between mediators who adopted a "settlement-oriented" as opposed to a "problem-solving" practice style.

Settlement-oriented mediators focused on facts and issues in an effort to reach agreement and remained strictly neutral. Problem-solving mediators focused on values and relationships as well as facts and issues to understand the basis for the conflict and were willing to depart from strict neutrality, especially in highly dysfunctional families.

These two "styles" of mediation were linked to previous studies. For example, these are reminiscent of Kressel and Pruitt's (1989) account of "task-oriented" versus "person-oriented" styles and consistent with our previous distinction between "structured negotiation" and "therapeutic mediation." Such distinctions are also directly relevant to the work of Dingwall and Greatbatch (1991) and Kruk (1998a, 1998b) and indirectly related to the work of Donohue et al. (1994) and Emery (1994, 1995). Related distinctions crop up in studies of community mediation by Honoroff, Matz, and O'Connor (1990) and Pruitt, Peirce, McGillicuddy, Welton, and Castriano (1993).

Kressel et al. (1994) found that, compared to settlement-oriented mediators, problem-solving mediators "produced a more focussed, structured, and vigorous approach" (p. 75) that yielded more frequent agreements, more durable agreements, and more positive attitudes toward the mediation experience among clients.

Although impressive, the generalizability of these results is limited because the results represent a single study with a small sample. However, taken together with the other, related studies noted earlier, these findings suggest that mediators who operate using a therapeutic style or approach may be more likely to produce quality agreements than their counterparts who rely on a structured negotiation style or approach.

O6: The common element in predicting mediation outcome success may be the quality of the mediator-client relationship, especially the degree of emotional engagement.

Differential outcomes based on mediator style beg the questions of why this should be so. The same applies to similar outcomes in public and private mediation despite marked differences in client attributes and mediation processes. Is there some common practice element that might help explain these findings? A promising candidate is the family therapy notion of *emotional engagement* (Johnson, 1996). In the context of family mediation, the notion suggests two linked processes—namely, a collaborative problem-solving effort associated with strong positive feelings. The more of both, the more likely settlement through agreement, which promotes further collaboration and positive feelings supportive of future compliance and informal change.

This speculative formulation derives from at least two bodies of work. As regards the central role of affect, the work of Gottman and his colleagues (Gottman, 1994a, 1994b; Gottman, Coan, Carrere, & Swenson, 1998) has repeatedly demonstrated "the compelling role of emotion in marital distress and the need to explicitly address emotion in marital therapy" (Johnson, 1996, p. 3). Furthermore, among marital and family therapists, "there is now clearer recognition that the regulation of emotion and emotional expression and responsiveness are defining features of close relationships and constitute what systems theorists call 'leading elements' in the couple system" (Johnson & Lebow, 2000, p. 32). There is every reason to believe that this is as true of couples in family mediation as in marital therapy and suggests that effectiveness in both areas of practice involve the ways in which such feelings are addressed, with processes associated with positive feelings key to change processes (Greenberg & Safran, 1987; Johnson & Greenberg, 1994).

In a related vein, recent reviews of research in marital therapy (Dunn & Schwebel, 1995; Jacobson & Addis, 1993) have shown that one of the keys to success is the level of engagement and collaboration. Based on a recent review, Nichols and Schwartz (1998), for example, concluded that "results from several studies suggest that a perceived sense of engagement, cooperation, and collaboration increases over time in treatment and predicts couples' evaluation of the depth and value of a session, posttreatment marital satisfaction, and therapist-rated outcome" (p. 519). Again, there is every reason that related processes should be true of family mediation.

If so, these findings cast outcome data in family mediation research in a new light. Client perceptions of fairness and empowerment and procedural equality, which ensures that both have their say, can now be seen as contributing to a sense of engagement. Similarly, client process satisfaction can now be seen not as merely ancillary to a fair process but as creating the positive affect that leads to settlement. In turn, satisfaction with outcomes creates the basis not only for future compliance but also for reduced conflict and increased cooperation.

That said, it seems clear that emotional engagement cannot operate in isolation but likely interacts with other factors, including mediator background (P7), degree of family dysfunction (P8), mediator-controlled clinical processes that suppress gender differences (Pc1), and sensitivity to issues of diversity and culture (Pc5). Although positive outcomes can and do occur independent of mediator background, those with a mental health background are more likely than their legally trained counterparts to attend to affect, values, and relationships and thus promote both engagement and positive affect. Such attention will be increasingly crucial as family dysfunction increases, at least to some point beyond which a mediated solution is not viable. Within some range of amenability, then, processes that focus on relationships and issues and suppress gender bias are more likely to enhance engagement, as is clear evidence of mediator cultural competence.

General

The few studies in this general or miscellaneous category support a single trend:

G1: Demand for family mediation services is rising.

From a statistical perspective, court-based mediation services have an advantage over their private counterparts, for only the former are obliged to keep records and make them available in the public domain. Accordingly, we know that in California, demand for mediation services in the family courts has risen substantially, from nearly 50,000 cases in 1988 to more than 65,000 in 1991. More recent data would likely confirm that upward trend, and we suspect the same would be true in other jurisdictions across North America. Family mediation, it seems, has come of age, entering the mainstream and having become an established form of alternate dispute resolution across the continent and elsewhere in the developed world (Bowen, 1999).

That said, there is also evidence from P (Neilson, 1994), S (Goettler, Herrman, & Grace, 1999), Pc (Kruk, 1998b), and G (McKinney, Kimsey, & Fuller, 1996) studies that

- the majority of mediators are women,
- the majority view mediation as a secondary occupation that they do on a part-time basis, and
- like other female social service workers in the "pink" ghetto, many earn a modest income.

These findings are disquieting. One would hope that this portrait would slowly change with the gradual professionalization of family mediation.

Gaps in the Literature

Through time, the central research question in mediation has changed. As little as 10 years ago, that central question concerned outcome effectiveness—that is, "Does family mediation *work*?" As the above review confirms, contemporary researchers are beginning to focus far more on process—that is, "*How* does family mediation work?" We suggest that in the future, the central question needs to become increasingly specific—that is, "What intervention(s), in what setting or set of circumstances and with what type or group of clients, is most likely to have what consequences over the short and long term?"

Comparing the research framework set out at the beginning of this chapter with the research trends explored above helps identify gaps in the literature that prevent us from answering this research question. Such gaps cross the four primary areas of inquiry.

As regards *person*, our knowledge of the role of family dysfunction in the process and outcome(s) of mediation remains general and fairly primitive. For example, mediation comparisons between violent as opposed to nonviolent families fail to exploit Johnston and Campbell's (1993) fivefold typology of violent families. Similarly, the gradual emergence of standardized instruments specific to mediation, such as those of Tan (1991) and Mathis and Yingling (1998), hold the promise of increased specificity in the ways future researchers may characterize mediation clients. There have been some efforts to assess premediation child adjustment, but such efforts remain rare when they ought to be commonplace. Finally, it may be fruitful to borrow from instruments widely used by custody and access assessors to evaluate parenting competence. More generally, baseline measures in current use are too often limited to sociodemographic attributes. Increased specificity will require more in-depth description.

As regards *setting*, there are several areas in which greater specificity would be helpful. Of special importance are issues of selection and screening mechanisms and procedures. These appear critical to the mediation enterprise but are seldom described in any detail and, more important, have not been used in a planful way as part of the research process. Although we have learned a great deal over the past decade about public mediation, the same cannot be said about private mediation, especially the extent of practice variation among this subpopulation of mediators. There is also very little information available about the congruence or lack of the same between mediation training and mediation practice. Finally, the role of the legal regime has been noted by several researchers but not examined in any detail as the extent to which it constrains some practices while facilitating others.

As regards *process*, the fact that such studies constituted the single largest category of inquiry is an important development and signals trends that need to be pursued. Although much has been written about different models of practices, no specific model has been the focus of inquiry. Instead, limited inquiry has focused on the much broader category of practice style. At this point, it is unclear whether *model* or *style* will prove the more useful way of characterizing mediation practice. Furthermore, the microanalytic observational studies that characterize much of the family therapy research literature (Nichols & Schwartz, 1998) are so far absent in mediation research, although some progress has been made in the evaluation of audiotapes of public mediation sessions. Of particular interest are limited findings regarding the use of mediator authority, a line of inquiry that deserves much more attention. Although several studies note varying degrees of mediator experience, the distinction between "novice" and "seasoned" practitioners has never been examined systematically. Finally, research efforts have concentrated on three-party sessions involving the couple and the practitioners. The effect of enlarging the number of participants on the process has yet to be examined, either as regards family members, others, or comediators. Indeed, the lack of a single study on the comparative effectiveness of comediation and sole practice is noteworthy.

Finally, as regards *outcome*, the need for greater specificity is apparent. Most outcome studies are descriptive rather than analytic and relate a black box model of intervention with a series of desirable outcomes. The use of multivariate methods, such as found in the work of Ellis and Stuckless (1996), continue to be uncommon. Although the work of Kressel et al. (1994) in opening the black box holds promise, it too remains rare, leaving unclear what exactly is meant by *mediation* per se or by the equally unclear reference to public or private mediation. Issues concerning methods of addressing impasses and the practitioner's success or lack of it in resolving such difficulties have received no attention, and only very limited attention has been given to the bases for client dropout. Finally, we have speculated concerning the salience of emotional engagement to both process and outcome. It remains to be seen if this notion will prove fruitful.

Implications

It remains to assess the salience of the trends identified above for policy and practice.

Policy

As regards policy, at least four implications derive from our review. The first and most obvious of these implications concerns the ongoing need for further research. Such an implication is almost de rigueur in a chapter on research. Although these may have been true in the past, when the survival of the technology was at stake, the need is even more urgent now that family mediation has entered the mainstream. Ironically, this coincides with the increasing importance of court diversion, as the increasing population and the rate of divorce have ensured that family court dockets remain as full as ever. Looking toward the future, mediation research holds out the promise of increasing efficiency and effectiveness. Thus, significant dividends are likely to flow from research concerning divergent models of mediation and how these are actually enacted in process.

In a related vein, we call attention to research indicating that parental involvement in education programs increases their readiness to participate in mediation and increases the likelihood of agreement. Such data speak to the need for future efforts at *integration*. By this we refer to the synergistic effects of different programs that fit together to effect desirable outcomes. Education and mediation programs are one example. Other, related programs may operate similarly. Parenting programs offer another example. These are programs designed to enhance parenting skills and competencies. Presumably, as these skills are strengthened or improved, parents are less apt to engage in the destructive practices that can be so problematic in mediation. It is easy to imagine still other programs as helpful in this way, including programs concerned with family law, divorce therapy, supervised access, behavior management, group therapy, and the like.

In terms of increasing efficiencies and effectiveness in mediation, no area is more deserving of attention than *screening*. Screening instruments and procedures should have three objectives: to *screen out* couples who have severe problems that render them unable to participate meaningfully in mediation, to *screen in* couples who are able to participate but are reluctant to enter mediation because they are unaware of its availability or benefits, and, of increasing importance, to *stream* couples so as to achieve the best possible fit between their needs and the attributes of available services. At present, screening procedures have made some attempt to meet the first two objectives, whereas the third is outside their purview. Data reviewed above suggest that the design of mediation programs must increasingly move away from a one-size-fits-all approach. Rather, the greater specificity we recommended above in research must have a counterpart in service delivery. Indeed, Dingwall and Greatbatch (1991) note that some clients were "annoyed" at the therapeutic pretensions of some mediators, and so they should be if they merely wished to negotiate an arrangement for Christmas holiday. In one sense, the diversity among mediators is well suited to address this issue. In another, such diversity speaks more to disarray than systematic variation. Sorting out this situation and beginning to create a systematic link between client type(s) and mediation model(s) will require substantial policy support.

Finally, the benefits of mediation are of little use to those who have never heard of them or, worse, have a distorted and mistaken understanding of mediation's utility. Changing that understanding suggests that *promotion* is a final area requiring policy support. Such efforts are likely to pay off on more than one front. The immediate benefits are likely to accrue to separated and divorcing couples (both legal and common law) and especially to their children from mediated arrangements that reduce conflict and ensure the children's ongoing relations with both parents. But as we have noted elsewhere (Irving & Benjamin, 1995), mediation has now gone much beyond divorce to include civil matters, landlord-tenant disputes, child welfare cases, community disputes, and even disputes in small claims court. Thus, mediation not only benefits various particular populations of disputants but also offers an alternative perspective on the resolution of conflict per se. Such efforts will not diminish the need for legal proceedings because mediation is not a panacea. But it does offer a "rational alternative" (Irving, 1980) that should be widely recognized.

Practice

Finally, the above review advances at least three implications for practice. First and foremost, these data speak to the central importance of *relationship* in resolving family disputes. Although substantive in form, disputes are almost invariably rooted in relationship processes that predate the separation while continuing to fuel the conflict. Although mediation can help couples *solve* their various disputes, these issues are not properly *resolved* until and unless they have addressed those underlying relationship issues on which they are truly rooted. This logic underpins the therapeutic family mediation approach, and it is one that will remain controversial for some time to come. For the most part, in the absence of data, the debate has been purely rhetorical. Recent data provide further impetus for this approach, though it is hardly conclusive. For the moment, then, the best we can do is to support an active or dynamic mediation process that includes specific attention to relationship issues.

In a related vein, the salience of data concerning mediator power and authority can hardly be overstated. Such authority inheres in all human service delivery roles, whether in medicine, law, psychotherapy, or family mediation. To have confidence in the advice they get or the treatment they agree to receive, clients demand that providers have skills and knowledge much greater than their own. To have access to that knowledge, clients voluntarily lend their authority to the practitioner and implicitly agree to follow their instructions, even to the extent of becoming hyperaware of even the tiniest indication of the practitioner's preferences and intentions. In a previous chapter (Chapter 9), we addressed the risks that accompany such authority. Here, we wish to emphasize the need for a shift in the way notions of "neutrality" and "client self-determination" are promulgated to the public and taught to mediation students. Both need to change to explicitly acknowledge the mediator's authority, and mediators themselves need to become increasingly self-reflexive in its routine use.

Finally, it has become a cliche to note that we live in a world of increasing diversity. For most mediators, especially those who operate in the public domain, this involves a daily parade of clients from widely divergent ethnic and cultural groups. Such experience necessarily raises concerns about cultural competence, which has begun to be addressed in the clinical literature but is still largely absent from research. Not only does the latter need to change, but such concerns also need to take center stage in passing on our skills to students and in providing quality service to clients, irrespective of their origin.

Appendix 14.1

List of Trends by Area of Inquiry

Person (P)

P1: Awareness of family mediation among judicial actors (judges, lawyer) is high.

P2: Attitudes toward family mediation among judicial actors are generally positive.

P3: Attitudes toward family mediation among judicial actors vary by position (judges, lawyers), experience, and gender.

P4: Attitudes and referral practices among judicial actors are linked.

P5: The definition of fairness varies by discipline.

P6: Such definitions establish the practical limits within which most, if not all, mediated agreements are likely to fall.

P7: Interest in and sensitivity to psychological and interpersonal issues among clients vary by disciplinary background and are more likely among mediators per se than lawyers.

P8: Degree of family dysfunction among clients prior to entering mediation is a good predictor of mediation outcome: The higher the degree of premediation dysfunction, the lower the probability of one or more positive outcomes.

P9: Evidence of gender-based differences in practice style among male and female mediators remains equivocal.

Setting (S)

S1: There are few gender differences in the way clients see family mediators, irrespective of whether service is provided in a private or a public setting.

S2: The rights of men and women are as likely to be protected in mediation as in lawyer negotiation; charges that women's rights may be compromised in family mediation appear to be unfounded.

Process (Pc)

Pc1: The organization of family mediation tends to suppress gender differences in client conduct.

Pc2: Evidence of model-related differences in practice style among family mediators remains equivocal.

Pc3: Family mediators routinely use their authority to shape the process and outcome.

Pc4: The inclusion of children has a positive effect on the mediation process.

Pc5: The impact of culture on the mediation process remains problematic as a research topic.

Outcome (O)

O1: Family mediation is an effective technology on a range of dimensions, including (a) agreement rate, (b) time to agreement, (c) relative cost, (d) relitigation rate, and (e) agreement durability.

O2: Family mediation is an effective technology based on a range of secondary outcomes, including (a) client satisfaction, (b) perceived fairness, (c) client sense of empowerment, (d) financial support, (e) parent-child relations, and (f) parental cooperation.

O3: Family mediation is effective with divorce cases involving family violence.

O4: Several variables show promise as correlates of outcome in family mediation.

O5: Mediators who use a therapeutic style produce better outcomes than those who rely on structured negotiation.

O6: The common element in predicting mediation outcome success may be the quality of the mediator-client relationship, especially the degree of emotional engagement.

General (G)

G1: Demand for family mediation services is rising.

Total trends: $n = 23$.

References

Arbuthnot, J., & Kramer, K. (1998). Effects of divorce education on mediation process and outcome. *Mediation Quarterly, 15*(3), 199-213.

Benjamin, M. (1996). *Cultural diversity, educational equity and the transformation of higher education: Group profiles as a guide to policy and programming.* Westport, CT: Praeger.

Benjamin, M., & Irving, H. H. (1992). Towards a feminist-informed model of therapeutic family mediation. *Mediation Quarterly, 10*(2), 129-153.

Benjamin, M., & Irving, H. H. (1995). Research in family mediation: Review and implications. *Mediation Quarterly, 13*(1), 53-82.

Bickerdike, A. J., & Littlefield, L. (2000). Divorce adjustment and mediation: Theoretically grounded process research. *Mediation Quarterly, 18*(2), 181-201.

Bohmer, C., & Ray, M. L. (1993). Regression to the mean: What happens when lawyers are divorce mediators. *Mediation Quarterly, 11*(2), 109-122.

Bohmer, C., & Ray, M. L. (1996). Notions of equity and fairness in the context of divorce: The role of mediation. *Mediation Quarterly, 14*(1), 37-52.

Bowen, D. (1999). *Mediation as a form of outside intervention: An exploration of the mechanisms associated with the family mediation process.* Unpublished doctoral dissertation, Department of Sociology, Macquarie University, Sydney, Australia.

Burrell, N. A., Narus, L., Bogdanoff, K., & Allen, M. (1994). Evaluating parental stressors of divorcing couples referred to mediation and effects on mediation outcomes. *Mediation Quarterly, 11*(4), 339-352.

Camplair, C. W., & Stolberg, A. L. (1990). Benefits of court sponsored divorce mediation: A study of outcomes and influences on success. *Mediation Quarterly, 7*(3), 199-213.

Cavanagh, T. D. (1997). A quantitative analysis of the use and avoidance of mediation by the Cook County, Illinois, legal community. *Mediation Quarterly, 14*(4), 353-364.

Chandler, D. B. (1990). Violence, fear, and communication: The variable impact of domestic violence on mediation. *Mediation Quarterly, 7*(4), 331-346.

Clement, J. A., & Schwebel, A. I. (1993). A research agenda for divorce mediation: The creation of second order knowledge to inform public policy. *Ohio State Journal of Dispute Resolution, 9*(1), 95-113.

Cobb, S. (1991). Einsteinian practice and Newtonian discourse: Ethical crisis in mediation. *Negotiation Journal, 7*(1), 87-102.

Cobb, S. (1994a). A narrative perspective on mediation: Toward the materialization of the "storytelling" metaphor. In J. P. Folger & T. S. Jones (Eds.), *New directions in mediation: Communication research and perspectives* (pp. 48-63). Thousand Oaks, CA: Sage.

Cobb, S. (1994b). Theories of responsibility: The social construction of intentions in mediation. *Discourse Processes, 18*(2), 165-186.

Cobb, S. (1997). The domestication of violence in mediation. *Law & Society Review, 31*, 397-440.

Cobb, S., & Rifkin, J. (1991a). Neutrality as a discursive practice: The construction and transformation of narratives in community mediation. In A. Sarat & S. Silbey (Eds.), *Studies in law, politics and society* (Vol. 2, pp. 221-238). Greenwich, CT: JAI.

Cobb, S., & Rifkin, J. (1991b). Practice and paradox: Deconstructing neutrality in mediation. *Law & Social Inquiry, 16*(1), 201-227.

Coltri, L. S., & Hubt, E. J. (1998). A model for telephone mediation. *Family & Conciliation Courts Review, 36*(2), 179-194.

Davies, B., & Ralph, S. (1998). Client and counsellor perceptions of the process and outcomes of family court counselling in cases involving domestic violence. *Family & Conciliation Courts Review, 36*(2), 227-245.

Davies, B., Ralph, S., Hawton, M., & Craig, L. (1995). A study of client satisfaction with family court counseling in cases involving domestic violence. *Family & Conciliation Courts Review, 33*(3), 324-341.

Dennis, D. M. (1991). DMAI: A practitioner's response. *Family & Conciliation Courts Review, 29*(1), 41-44.

Depner, C. E., Cannata, K., & Ricci, I. (1995). Report 4: Mediation agreements on child custody and visitation: 1991 California Family Court Services snapshot study. *Family & Conciliation Courts Review, 33*(1), 87-109.

Depner, C. E., Cannata, K., & Simon, M. B. (1992). Building a uniform statistical reporting system: A snapshot of California family court services. *Family & Conciliation Courts Review, 30*(2), 185-206.

D'Errico, M. G., & Elwork, A. (1991). Are self-determined divorce and child custody agreements really better? *Family & Conciliation Courts Review, 29*(2), 104-113.

Dillon, P. A., & Emery, R. E. (1996). Divorce mediation and resolution of child-custody disputes: Long-term effects. *American Journal of Orthopsychiatry, 66*(1), 131-140.

Dingwall, R., & Greatbatch, D. (1991). Behind closed doors: A preliminary report on mediator/client interaction in England. *Family & Conciliation Courts Review, 29*(3), 291-303.

Dingwall, R., Greatbatch, D., & Ruggerone, L. (1998). Gender and interaction in divorce mediation. *Mediation Quarterly, 15*(4), 277-285.

Donohue, W. A. (1991). *Communication, marital disputes, and divorce mediation.* Hillsdale, NJ: Lawrence Erlbaum.

Donohue, W. A., Drake, L., & Roberto, A. J. (1994). Mediator issue intervention strategies: A replication and some conclusions. *Mediation Quarterly, 11*(3), 261-274.

Dunn, R. L., & Schwebel, A. I. (1995). Meta-analytic review of marital therapy outcomes research. *Journal of Family Psychology, 9*(1), 58-68.

Duryea, M. (1992). Mandatory court mediation: Demographic summary and consumer evaluation of one court service: Executive summary. *Family & Conciliation Courts Review, 30*(2), 260-267.

Ellis, D., & Stuckless, N. (1992). Preseparation abuse, marital conflict, and postseparation abuse. *Mediation Quarterly, 9*(3), 205-225.

Ellis, D., & Stuckless, N. (1996). *Mediating and negotiating marital disputes.* Thousand Oaks, CA: Sage.

Ellis, D., & Wight, L. (1998). Theorizing power in divorce negotiations: Implications for practice. *Mediation Quarterly, 15*(3), 227-244.

Emery, R. E. (1994). Research on custody mediation. In R. E. Emery (Ed.), *Renegotiating family relationships: Divorce, child custody, and mediation* (pp. 175-193). New York: Guilford.

Emery, R. E. (1995). Divorce mediation: Negotiating agreements and renegotiating relationships. *Family Relations, 44,* 377-383.

Emery, R. E., Matthews, S. G., & Kitzman, K. M. (1994). Child custody mediation and litigation: Parents' satisfaction and functioning one year after settlement. *Journal of Consulting & Clinical Psychology, 62*(1), 124-129.

Emery, R. E., Matthews, S. G., & Wyer, M. M. (1991). Child custody mediation and litigation: Further evidence of the differing views of mothers and fathers. *Journal of Clinical and Consulting Psychology, 59,* 410-418.

Fuller, R. M., Kimsey, W. D., & McKinney, B. C. (1992). Mediator neutrality and storytelling order. *Mediation Quarterly, 10*(2), 187-192.

Goettler, D. E., Herrman, M. S., & Grace, J. (1999). Background characteristics and incentives of mediators in Georgia: Exploring differences in public, private, and government agency mediators. *Mediation Quarterly, 16*(3), 221-233.

Goldstein, S. B. (1998). Responses of Asian American and European American mediators to a conflict communication scale. *Mediation Quarterly, 15*(3), 181-186.

Gottman, J. (1994a). An agenda for marital therapy. In S. M. Johnson & L. S. Greenberg (Eds.), *The heart of the matter: Perspectives on emotion in marital therapy* (pp. 256-296). New York: Brunner/Mazel.

Gottman, J. (1994b). *What predicts divorce?* Hillsdale, NJ: Lawrence Erlbaum.

Gottman, J., Coan, J., Carrere, S., & Swenson, C. (1998). Predicting marital happiness and stability from newlywed interactions. *Journal of Marriage & Family, 60*(1), 5-22.

Greatbatch, D., & Dingwall, R. (1989). Selective facilitation: Some preliminary observations on a strategy used by divorce mediators. *Law & Society Review, 23,* 613-641.

Greatbatch, D., & Dingwall, R. (1994). The interactive construction of interventions by divorce mediators. In J. P. Folger & T. S. Jones (Eds.), *New directions in mediation: Communication research and perspectives* (pp. 84-109). Thousand Oaks, CA: Sage.

Greatbatch, D., & Dingwall, R. (1997). Argumentative talk in divorce mediation. *American Sociological Review, 62*(2), 151-170.

Greenberg, L. S., & Safran, J. D. (1987). *Emotion in psychotherapy: Affect and cognition in the process of change.* New York: Guilford.

Guerra, N. S., & Elliott, G. M. (1996). Cognitive roles in the mediation process: Development of the Mediation Inventory for Cognitive Roles Assessment. *Mediation Quarterly, 14*(2), 135-146.

Harrell, S. W. (1995). Why attorneys attend mediation sessions. *Mediation Quarterly, 17*(4), 369-377.

Hauser, J. (1993). An analysis and feasibility study of divorce mediation and a program for its marketing. *Mediation Quarterly, 11*(2), 171-184.

Honoroff, B., Matz, D., & O'Connor, D. (1990). Putting mediation skills to the test. *Negotiation Journal, 6*(1), 37-46.

Irving, H. H. (1980). *Divorce mediation: The rational alternative.* Toronto: Personal Library Publishers.

Irving, H. H., & Benjamin, M. (1992). An evaluation of process and outcome in a private family mediation service. *Mediation Quarterly, 10*(1), 35-55.

Irving, H. H., & Benjamin, M. (1995). Research in family mediation: An integrative review. In H. H. Irving & M. Benjamin (Eds.), *Family mediation: Contemporary issues* (pp. 407-434). Thousand Oaks, CA: Sage.

Jacobson, N. S., & Addis, M. E. (1993). Research on couples and couples therapy: What do we know? Where are we going? *Journal of Consulting & Clinical Psychology, 61*(1), 85-93.

Johnson, S. (1996). *The practice of emotionally focused marital therapy: Creating connection.* New York: Brunner/Mazel.

Johnson, S., & Greenberg, L. S. (Eds.). (1994). *The heart of the matter: Perspectives on emotion in marital therapy.* New York: Brunner/Mazel.

Johnson, S., & Lebow, J. (2000). The "coming of age" of couple therapy: A decade review. *Journal of Marital & Family Therapy, 26*(1), 23-38.

Johnston, J., & Campbell, L. E. G. (1993). A clinical typology of interpersonal violence in disputed child custody divorces. *American Journal of Orthopsychiatry, 63,* 190-199.

Jones, T. S., & Bodtker, A. (1998). Satisfaction with custody mediation: Results from the York County mediation program. *Mediation Quarterly, 16*(2), 185-200.

Jones, T. S., & Bodtker, A. (1999). Agreement, maintenance, satisfaction and relitigation in mediated and non-mediated custody cases: A research note. *Journal of Divorce & Remarriage, 32*(1/2), 17-30.

Kandel, R. F. (1998). Situated substantive expertise: An ethnographic illustration and a proposed standard of practice for mediators. *Mediation Quarterly, 15*(4), 303-317.

Kelly, J. (1991a). Is mediation less expensive? Comparison of mediated and adversarial divorce costs. *Mediation Quarterly, 8*(1), 15-26.

Kelly, J. (1991b). Parent communication after divorce: Comparison of mediated and adversarial divorce processes. *Behavioral Sciences & Law, 9,* 387-398.

Kelly, J. (1993). Developing and implementing post-divorce parenting plans: Does the forum make a difference? In C. E. Depner & J. H. Bray (Eds.),

Non-residential parenting: New vistas in family living (pp. 136-155). Newbury Park, CA: Sage.

Kelly, J. B. (1996). A decade of divorce mediation research: Some answers and questions. *Family & Conciliation Courts Review, 34*(3), 373-385.

Kelly, J. B., & Duryea, M. (1992). Women's and men's views of mediation in voluntary and mandatory mediation settings. *Family & Conciliation Courts Review, 30*(1), 34-49.

Kelly, J. B., & Gigy, L. L. (1989). Divorce mediation: Characteristics of clients and outcomes. In K. Kressel, D. G. Pruitt, & Associates (Eds.), *Mediation research: The process & effectiveness of third-party intervention.* San Francisco: Jossey-Bass.

Kimsey, W. D., Fuller, R. M., Bell, A. J., & McKinney, B. C. (1994). The impact of mediator strategic choices: An experimental study. *Mediation Quarterly, 12*(1), 89-97.

Kitzman, K. M., & Emery, R. E. (1993). Procedural justice and parents: Satisfaction in a field study of child custody dispute resolution. *Law & Human Behavior, 17*(5), 553-567.

Koopman, E. J., Hunt, E. J., Favretto, F. G., Coltri, L. S., & Britten, T. (1991). Professional perspectives on court-connected child custody mediation. *Family & Conciliation Courts Review, 29,* 304-317.

Kressel, K., Frontera, E. A., Forlenza, S., Butler, F., & Fish, F. (1994). The settlement-orientation vs. the problem-solving style in custody mediation. *Journal of Social Issues, 50*(1), 67-84.

Kressel, K., & Pruitt, D. G. (Eds.). (1989). *Mediation research: The process and effectiveness of third-party intervention.* San Francisco: Jossey-Bass.

Kruk, E. (1998a). Deconstructing family mediation practice via the simulated client technique: The case of unresolved marital attachment. *Mediation Quarterly, 15*(4), 321-332.

Kruk, E. (1998b). Practice issues, strategies, and models: The current state of the art of family mediation. *Family & Conciliation Courts Review, 36*(2), 195-215.

Lansky, D. T., Swift, L. H., Manley, E. E., Elmore, A., & Gerety, C. (1996). The role of children in mediation. *Mediation Quarterly, 14*(2), 147-154.

Lee, C. M., Beauregard, C. P. M., & Huntsley, J. (1998a). Attorneys' opinion regarding child custody mediation and assessment services: The influence of gender, years of experience, and mediation practice. *Family & Conciliation Courts Review, 36*(2), 216-226.

Lee, C. M., Beauregard, C. P. M., & Huntsley, J. (1998b). Lawyers' opinions regarding child custody mediation and assessment services. *Professional Psychology: Research and Practice, 29*(2), 115-120.

Littlejohn, S. W., Shailor, J., & Pearce, W. B. (1994). The deep structure of reality in mediation. In J. P. Folger & T. S. Jones (Eds.), *New directions in mediation: Communication research and perspectives* (pp. 67-83). Thousand Oaks, CA: Sage.

Magana, H. A., & Taylor, A. (1993). Child custody mediation and spouse abuse: A descriptive study of a protocol. *Family & Conciliation Courts Review, 31*(1), 50-64.

Marcus, M. G., Marcus, W., Stilwell, N. A., & Doherty, N. (1999). To mediate or not to mediate: Financial outcomes in mediated versus adversarial divorces. *Mediation Quarterly, 17*(2), 143-152.

Mathis, R. D., & Yingling, L. C. (1990). Family functioning level and divorce mediation outcome. *Mediation Quarterly, 8*(1), 3-14.

Mathis, R. D., & Yingling, L. C. (1991). Spousal consensus on the divorce decision and mediation outcome. *Family & Conciliation Courts Review, 29*(1), 56-62.

Mathis, R. D., & Yingling, L. C. (1992). Analysis of pre and posttest gender differences in family satisfaction of divorce mediation couples. *Journal of Divorce & Remarriage, 17*(3/4), 75-85.

Mathis, R. D., & Yingling, L. C. (1998). Family modes: A measure of family interaction and organization. *Family & Conciliation Courts Review, 36*(2), 246-257.

Maxwell, D. (1992). Gender differences in mediation style and their impact on mediation effectiveness. *Mediation Quarterly, 9*(4), 353-364.

Maxwell, J. P. (1999). The use of performance art and Q methodologies in increasing mediator recognition of trauma and domestic violence. *Mediation Quarterly, 16*(3), 269-285.

McIntosh, J. (2000). Child-inclusive divorce mediation: Report on a qualitative study. *Mediation Quarterly, 18*(1), 55-69.

McKinney, B. C., Kimsey, W. D., & Fuller, R. M. (1996). A nationwide survey of mediation centers. *Mediation Quarterly, 14*(2), 155-166.

Medley, M. L., & Schellenberg, J. A. (1994a). Attitudes of attorneys toward mediation. *Mediation Quarterly, 12*(2), 185-198.

Medley, M. L., & Schellenberg, J. A. (1994b). Attitudes of Indiana judges toward mediation. *Mediation Quarterly, 11*(4), 329-337.

Meierding, N. R. (1993). Does mediation work? Survey of long-term satisfaction and durability rates for privately mediated agreements. *Mediation Quarterly, 11*(2), 157-170.

Neilson, L. C. (1994). Mediators' and lawyers' perceptions of education and training in family mediation. *Mediation Quarterly, 12*(2), 165-184.

Newmark, L., Harrell, A., & Salem, P. (1995). Domestic violence and empowerment in custody and visitation cases: An empirical study on the impact of domestic abuse. *Family & Conciliation Courts Review, 33*(1), 30-62.

Nichols, M. P., & Schwartz, R. C. (1998). *Family therapy: Concepts and methods* (4th ed.). Boston: Allyn & Bacon.

Pearson, J. (1991). The equity of mediated divorce agreements. *Mediation Quarterly, 9*(2), 179-197.

Pearson, J. (1997). Mediating when domestic violence is a factor: Policies and practices in court-based divorce mediation programs. *Mediation Quarterly, 14*(4), 319-335.

Pearson, J., & Thoennes, N. (1989). Divorce mediation: Reflections on a decade of research. In K. Kressel & D. G. Pruitt (Eds.), *Mediation research: The process and effectiveness of third-party intervention* (pp. 9-30). San Francisco: Jossey-Bass.

Pruitt, D. G., Peirce, R. S., McGillicuddy, N., Welton, G. L., & Castriano, L. M. (1993). Long-term success in mediation. *Law and Human Behavior, 17,* 313-330.

Raisner, J. K. (1997). Family mediation and never-married parents. *Family & Conciliation Courts Review, 35*(1), 90-101.

Ricci, I., Depner, C. E., Cannata, K. V. (1992). Profile: Child custody mediation services in California superior courts. *Family & Conciliation Courts Review, 30* (2), 229-242.

Rifkin, J., Millen, J., & Cobb, S. (1991). Toward a new discourse for mediation: A critique of neutrality. *Mediation Quarterly, 9*(2), 151-164.

Rudd, J. E. (1996). Communication effects on divorce mediation: How participants' argumentativeness, verbal aggression, and compliance-gaining strategy choices mediate outcome satisfaction. *Mediation Quarterly, 14*(1), 65-78.

Slater, A., Shaw, J. A., & Duquesnel, J. (1992). Client satisfaction survey: A consumer evaluation of mediation and investigation services: Executive summary. *Family & Conciliation Courts Review, 30*(2), 252-259.

Stamato, L. (1992). Voice, place, and process: Research in gender, negotiation and conflict resolution. *Mediation Quarterly, 9*(4), 375-386.

Sullivan, B. F., Schwebel, A. I., & Lind, J. S. (1997). Parties' evaluations of their relationship with their mediators and accomplishments in a court-connected mediation program. *Family & Conciliation Courts Review, 35*(4), 405-417.

Tan, N. T. (1991). Implications of the Divorce Mediation Assessment Instrument for mediation practice. *Family & Conciliation Courts Review, 29*(1), 26-40.

Thoennes, N., Salem, P., & Pearson, J. (1995). Mediation and domestic violence: Current polices and practices. *Family & Conciliation Courts Review, 33*(4), 6-29.

Tjersland, O. A. (1999). Evaluation of mediation and parental cooperation based on observations and interviews with the clients of a mediation project. *Mediation Quarterly, 16*(4), 407-423.

Tracy, K., & Spradkin, A. (1994). "Talking like a mediator": Conversational moves of experienced divorce mediators. In J. P. Folger & T. S. Jones (Eds.), *New directions in mediation: Communication research and perspectives* (pp. 110-132). Thousand Oaks, CA: Sage.

Van Slyck, M. R., Stern, M., & Newland, L. M. (1992). Parent-child mediation: An empirical assessment. *Mediation Quarterly, 10*(1), 75-88.

Wall, V. D., Jr., & Dewhurst, M. L. (1991). Mediator gender: Communication differences in resolved and unresolved mediation. *Mediation Quarterly, 9*(1), 63-85.

Wallerstein, J. S., Lewis, J. M., & Blakeslee, S. (2000). *The unexpected legacy of divorce: A 25 year landmark study.* New York: Hyperion.

Welsh, N. A., & Lewis, D. (1998). Adaptations to the civil mediation model: Suggestions from research into the approaches to conflict resolution used in the twin cities' Cambodian community. *Mediation Quarterly, 15*(4), 345-356.

Whiting, R. A. (1994). Family disputes, nonfamily disputes, and mediation success. *Mediation Quarterly, 11*(3), 247-260.

PART 5

FINAL WORD

15

Final Word

Family mediation has come of age. Once a minor technology, it has now entered the mainstream and exploded. It is now a major source of court diversion and conflict resolution in divorce. Service is now available across North America in communities both big and small. It has also spread internationally and is available throughout Europe, Australia and New Zealand, South Africa, and parts of Asia.

Subsequent proliferation has seen mediation services spring up in a ever-widening array of locations, including the civil courts, landlord and tenant associations, classrooms and school yards, community and environmental settings, prisons, child welfare agencies, and so on.

Rising demand for service has had predictable consequences. Mediation associations now exist in most states and provinces, and national organizations have sprung into existence. In turn, they have promulgated standards of practice and begun an inexorable professional push toward some form of accreditation. Professional journals have similarly opened an ongoing dialogue and attracted students from various disciplines in a widening network of training facilities—some private, others in institutional settings. For the first time, it is now possible to get a university degree in mediation.

These various developments speak to the gradual maturation of a professional practice area, with predictable phases and processes. This has meant concomitant shifts in the dominant discourse. Early pioneers were naturally preoccupied with extolling the virtues of this new approach and thus tended to focus as much on efficiency and effectiveness as on process. Later, there emerged an inevitable division of practice models and the increasing emphasis on process.

Current debates, of which this volume is an exemplar, involve increasing elaboration and specification of various practice models, with the immediate aim of training new waves of practitioners and the ultimate aim of creating and testing a coherent theoretical model of family mediation.

The emergence of one or more such models is still some years in the future. For now, we are content in this volume to present the most complete version of the therapeutic family mediation practice model extant. In overview, this presentation has highlighted eight central themes that operate as the model's skeleton over which are draped various levels of practice advice and detail.

First and foremost, the model emphasizes the central role of relationship in shaping what transpires in mediation. Relationship refers to the organized ways partners relate to each other in what they feel, how they communicate, how they behave, and how they attribute meaning to all of the above. It is in these patterns of relating that their conflict resides and is enacted. It is these patterns that constitute the "problems" that couples bring into mediation. And it is necessarily out of these patterns that some solution will be found or not, as couples and mediators struggle together to achieve meaningful and lasting resolution. In short, it is relationship that is at the very core of mediation, and it is relationship with which practitioners routinely grapple, whether or not they chose to acknowledge it as such.

Next, these patterns do not spring up *de novo* in mediation. Rather, they have been years, even decades, in the making. They were the basis of the divorce, and they necessarily carry over into mediation. Understanding the origin of these patterns in the couple's premediation relationship is one of the tasks of the assessment phase of mediation because these patterns will be potent predictors of outcome. Common sense, practice experience, and most recently empirical research indicate that the more dysfunctional the couple's premediation history, especially the recent past, the more likely they will be unable to reach agreement in mediation.

Although this is generally true, the strength of the association between dysfunction and outcome will be contingent on the mediation practice model in use. Therapeutic family mediation (TFM) applies a practice principle—namely, that the more dysfunctional the couple's conduct in mediation, the stronger and more intensive the interventions the mediator is willing to enact. This involves both procedural and therapeutic interventions in keeping with the short-term objectives of family mediation. Indeed, in accepting into mediation couples who on assessment demonstrate high levels of dysfunction, we suggest that the TFM model can be effective with an extremely wide range of clients. Note well, however, that the reverse also applies—namely, that the more functional the couple's conduct in mediation, the weaker and less intensive are the interventions the mediator is required to enact; they are typically limited to ordinary support and facilitation. Thus, although *therapeutic* family mediation comes by its name honestly, it should not be confused with any form of *therapy* per se.

Concomitantly, TFM explicitly acknowledges the mediator's authority. We hold that, just as in medicine, law, or family therapy, authority inheres in the role of the family mediator. It is *not* something the mediator takes away from the client. Rather, it is something that the clients voluntarily relinquish. Having repeatedly tried and failed to resolve their differences on their own and being unwilling (for the moment) to seek a litigated solution, clients invest the mediator with the authority sufficient to control the process and thus dampen the dysfunctional conduct that has rendered their own informal efforts futile. This is true of all couples in mediation but is especially evident in high-conflict couples who have lost any semblance of self-control and who cannot function in the absence of some source of external constraint. On one hand, the combination of intervention and authority means that the likelihood of achieving a workable solution is many times greater in mediation than would otherwise be the case had the couple been left to their own devices. This is true of all couples in mediation but is more dramatically evident in couples toward the dysfunctional end of the continuum. On the other hand, such authority necessarily places mediation couples at some degree of risk for the abuse of power. This is true but no more or less so in mediation than in any of the service disciplines in which authority inheres in the role. In all these disciplines, including family mediation, the best anyone can do is ensure that training programs produce competent practitioners and that clients have some avenue of recourse should they feel that they have been treated unfairly.

Acknowledging the mediator's authority in TFM serves to underscore the importance of two of the five roles ascribed to the practitioner in this model—namely, those of *therapist* and *advocate*. Of these two roles, that of advocate is undoubtedly the more controversial. This role holds that mediators should be as impartial as they can be *under the circumstances*. However, they have an ethical responsibility to protect and preserve the interests of third parties not at the table, especially those of the children. With couples in the functional range, the advocacy role is simply not required because their proposed solutions are well in keeping with the best interests of their children. But as couples become increasingly dysfunctional, failure to intervene may often yield agreements that are unconscionable and thus violate the mediator's ethical commitments. Here, we judge advocacy as necessary for responsible clinical conduct. Moreover, such conduct remains in keeping with the principle of client self-determination and empowerment, for even advocated solutions cannot go forward without client consent and are often subject to further negotiation. In this sense, the mediator's authority is necessarily offset by the reciprocal character of the mediator-client relationship. All processes in mediation and all outcomes are necessarily *socially constructed*, a product of a process of negotiation both between the mediator and the clients and between the clients themselves. The process of social construction is more apparent in the final three roles of the TFM practitioner—namely, *facilitator*, *educator*, and *information provider*. It is important to remember that most clients have only been divorced once, and they have much to learn at the same time, often when they are emotionally least prepared to absorb new information. Mediation, then, may be the ideal place to teach clients what they need to know—most immediately that the emotional turmoil they are experiencing is entirely normal and will slowly pass, just as their lives will eventually return to an even keel. Providing information is a variation on the teaching role and may involve instructing clients on local statutes, connecting them with community resources, and the like. Facilitating negotiation between partners involves much more than maintaining procedural fairness and may include teaching clients conflict management skills, negotiating techniques, methods of clear communication, and creativity in discovering options that are viable under their circumstances. In all of this, there is necessarily a give-and-take that involves the negotiation or construction of a particular frame of understanding, which makes resolution possible, and that rests with neither client nor mediator alone but is a shared creation. Finally, taken together, these various roles of the TFM mediator are grounded on a normative model of practical family relations in divorce. This model is implicit and derives from different components that comprise the larger TFM practice model itself.

A key element of that larger model concerns the notion of cultural competence. The increasingly diverse character of the North American population makes it imperative that we move away from normative models of either family or child development based on what has (in many states) increasingly become the White minority. In part, this has implications for mediation training, which provides substantive information of normative patterns in key minority groups, such as Asians, Blacks, and Hispanics. However, because it is impossible for any mediator to be as fully informed about the patterns that typify *all* ethnic groups, part of that training must also encompass a generic sensitivity and openness to and acceptance of couples whose values, attitudes, and conduct may be different from that of the mediator. Further still, because such sensitivity to others must necessarily be relative, training in cultural competence would not be complete without including a concern for practitioner self-reflexivity, that is, awareness of one's own cherished values and attitudes and typical behaviors. Only with such well-rounded training can one ensure a culturally competent TFM practitioner who can adapt the model to the varying cultural requirements of different client couples. Interestingly, such sensitivity also means the avoidance of stereotypes, so the need for variation on cultural grounds must be established empirically and not simply or automatically in response to the client's minority status. Indeed, with third- and fourth-generation minority clients, it would not be uncommon to discover little or no difference and thus no need for practice variation.

Another key facet of the TFM model involves explicit reference to theory or, rather, to a collection of theories. These theories fall into two broad categories: substantive and practice or clinical. The various substantive models to which we attribute significance help characterize key premediation processes in client families undergoing divorce. For example, research has shown that attachment processes are not restricted to child socialization but apply as well in relations between adults. Indeed, in previous work, we speculated that discrepancies in attachment in divorce would be reflected in differential readiness to participate in mediation and thus were predictive of mediation outcome. As noted in the previous chapter, recent research has confirmed this notion. Similarly, we have long subscribed to the feminist notion that men and women experience marriage differently and that such differences reflect the differential power of men and women in the larger society. Our commitment to this notion continues to be strong, such that TFM remains a feminist-informed model whose practitioners are trained to be sensitive to power and other differentials (such as knowledge) based primarily on gender. As to the practice model, our generic commitment to a systems theory frame has meant that we have generally drawn on family and marital therapy models for both ideas and clinical or practice techniques. In particular, strategic-, narrative-, and solution-oriented approaches have been especially important in informing TFM practice regimens. These are especially attractive because all are designed around powerful, short-term interventions suitable for use in family mediation, and all assume a shared process that yields socially constructed clinical outcomes. Although we have not attempted to integrate these various models into a coherent theory of mediation, being content to focus on TFM instead, exploiting the theoretical potential of TFM's abstract underpinning is part of our future agenda.

Finally, if "relationship" has the status of a meta-theme of the TFM practice model, then another must surely be the notion of "fit." This argues that practice models must eschew all dogmas, beginning, proceeding, and ending, as always, with "where the client is." This client-centered approach means fitting the model to client needs and thus constantly monitoring client processes in relation to clinical goals and objectives. The result is that there is, literally, no standardized TFM procedure but rather a set of clinical understandings that are flexibly applied based on client feedback. TFM practitioners must be prepared to do whatever is situationally required to achieve short- and long-term objectives. With clients within the functional range, this is often a straightforward process, with limited movement between pre-mediation and negotiation phases. As client dysfunction increases, the TFM model becomes increasingly demanding of mediator flexibility and creativity, with frequent movements between phases.

These various themes speak to the complexity of the model and thus the demands it places on students and clients alike. That said, the satisfaction for both in working from this perspective may be less obvious. For clients, a typical scenario is one in which interaction between them has become onerous because it quickly and routinely breaks down into argument. Repeated experience over time makes such interaction aversive, with each blaming this state of affairs on the other. To avoid the frustration and emotional exhaustion associated with such relations, parents stop talking and begin parenting in parallel, which serves to bring the children into the conflict. Moreover, many parents view these arrangements as impossible to change, having become hopeless in their effort to interact with the other parent.

In this context, clients tend to experience TFM as both liberating and empowering. The application of procedural rules reopens the possibility of productive dialogue. The application of parenting guidelines disposes of various sources of conflict, and provides a safe place to address various grievances further reduces the level of frustration. In as little as one or two joint sessions, the sense of hopelessness lifts, and with it, the level of conflict begins to diminish. Continued support from the mediator, coupled with signs of progress concerning their substantive disputes, paves the way for tentative optimism and the sense that a means out of their informal impasse is possible.

Such progress varies by the level of family dysfunction. Dysfunctional families will not only take longer to respond as above but also involve a more varied clinical course. That course may involve individual caucusing in an effort to work through problems. With these families, a more rigid application of procedural rules is unavoidable, and more time may need to be spent in realigning patterns of conduct and in teaching basic communication skills. However, in most cases, such effort pays off as clients begin to engage in dialogue, begin rebuilding basic trust, and achieve small substantive victories on the way to a full agreement.

Turning to practitioners, students new to TFM typically find the shift from the passive style used in therapy to the more active style used in TFM challenging. Once this is mastered, however, student mediators find this approach liberating. Instead of following standard procedures, they are rewarded for innovation, creativity, and sensitivity to client needs. They discover that the clinical skills they brought with them from other disciplines remain entirely apt in TFM. Novice practitioners, unaccustomed to the intensity of marital interaction among divorcing couples, may become infected by their hopelessness. Only when clients respond to the interventions within TFM do they begin to appreciate the gratification for the practitioner in doing family mediation.

Finally, what of the future of TFM itself? We have already alluded to the possibility of using the theoretical underpinning of the model to construct a coherent theory of family mediation. Although such an effort would be ambitious, it is an area in which family mediation is currently bereft. Next, TFM, like all other practice models in the area, has never been subject to sustained research scrutiny. It is one thing to make various clinical claims and display rich case history material. It is quite another to put such claims to the test of rigorous research. We look forward to mounting such an effort. Finally, as proponents of TFM, we are committed to clinical innovation and thus of finding new or better ways of using TFM to assist clients. This includes experimenting with various questioning techniques, adapting new narrative approaches from the marital and family therapy fields, and exploring the use of different forms of comediation. In this effort, we invite the participation of clients as we ask them to evaluate their experience with us. And having now completed this new text on TFM, we invite reader feedback, as we all strive to serve clients better.

Name Index

Subject Index

About the Authors

Howard H. Irving is a professor at the University of Toronto, Faculty of Social Work, and cross-appointed to the Faculty of Law. He has served as co-director of the university's Joint Law and Social Work Program. Dr. Irving has been a practicing family mediator for more than 25 years. In the past few years, he has developed an international reputation, giving courses and speeches in the United States, Canada, Israel, Hong Kong, and Beijing.

Michael Benjamin is a family sociologist, with specialized training in family mediation and family and marital therapy. He has been involved in family mediation for the past 20 years as a theorist, researcher, trainer, teacher, author, and practitioner, both privately and through the family court. Dr. Benjamin practices as a marital and family therapist, a custody and access assessor, and as a research consultant.